WAR ON TWO FRONTS

Shiloh to Gettysburg

EYEWITNESS HISTORY OF THE CIVIL WAR

WAR ON TWO FRONTS

Shiloh to Gettysburg

Edited by John Cannan

COMBINED BOOKS
Pennsylvania

This revised paperback edition, published by Combined Books, Inc., 1994, was originally published in hardback as two books in 1990 by Gallery Books, *War in the West* and *War in the East*. Combined Books, Inc., prepared and developed the original editions. For information, address:

Combined Books, Inc.
151 E. 10th Avenue
Conshohocken, PA 19428

Library of Congress Cataloging-in-Publication Data
War on two fronts : Shiloh to Gettysburg / [edited by] John Cannan.
p. cm.
Includes bibliographical references.
ISBN 0-938289-42-X : $16.95
1. United States—History—Civil War, 1861-1865—Campaigns.
I. Cannan, John, 1967-
E470.W35 1994   94-34292
973.7'3—dc20   CIP

Combined Books Edition   1   2   3   4   5

This revised paperback edition first published in the United States of America in 1994 by Combined Books, Inc., and distributed in North America by Stackpole Books, Inc., 5067 Ritter Road, Mechanicsburg, PA 17055 and internationally by Greenhill Books, Lionel Leventhal Ltd., 1 Russell Gardens, London NW11 9 NN.

Printed in the United States of America.

CONTENTS

Preface to the Series

Well over a century after its conclusion, the Civil War still remains the gravest crisis in the history of the Republic since the attainment of independence. It was a vast complex struggle which touched the lives of far more Americans than any other war in which the nation has fought. A conflict of momentous import, it still retains an immediate and continuing impact on the life of the nation. The story of the Civil War has been told on numerous occasions and in numerous ways. The literature is enormous, ranging from erudite scholarly tomes to dry official reports, from informative popular histories to vicious partisan tracts. All these have their value. Yet none can ever be entirely satisfactory. After all these years there exists no better way of looking at the Civil War than to see it through the eyes of those who lived through it, the thousands upon thousands for whom the war was a daily reality.

The Civil War was probably the first war in history in which most of the troops could read and write. As a result, there exists an enormous number of firsthand accounts. The range of materials is equally large, from private letters to multi-volume memoirs. These cover everything from the minutia of daily life to serious historical treatments, from amusing anecdotes to vituperative personal attacks. Nothing surpasses such original documents for developing an understanding of the events as they were perceived by the people who lived through them, for the flavor of the times, the emotions of the struggle, the force of the issues, the impact of the events. Such materials have been drawn upon several times already for the creation of a number of anthologies of firsthand accounts of the war, or of particular aspects of it. Yet the amount of material available is so vast, the stories to be told so numerous, that there still remains much material which has not received wide circulation. It was an awareness of this fact which led to the creation of the present series, **Eyewitness History of the Civil War**.

Each volume in **Eyewitness History of the Civil War** covers a distinct aspect of the war as seen by the people who lived through it, as expressed in their personal letters, private diaries, historical accounts, and even in their songs. The typical volume contains approximately forty items selected from among many thousands. These items deal with events ranging from small, otherwise forgotten, incidents to great historical battles. In almost every case, the events depicted were personally witnessed by the authors. In a few instances accounts by contemporary authors who did not witness the events have been included, especially when the writer was someone of particularly interesting identity or possessed unusual perspective on the events.

In preparing **Eyewitness History of the Civil War**, the editor has made no effort to attempt a "balanced" presentation. As a consequence, many events are treated from only a Northern point of view, while others have a Southern slant, and still others are seen from two or three different perspectives. The purpose of the work is neither to achieve historical accuracy nor political balance, but to see events as they were experienced and understood by some of the people who lived through them. There will thus be redundancies, contradictions, and errors, not to mention outright falsehoods.

All of the selections appear almost exactly as they did on their original publication, save for the occasional eliding of extraneous materials. Where necessary, the editor has created titles for selections which lacked such. For the most part, he has avoided the inclusion of explanatory notes, confining himself to the insertion of occasional comments in brackets. Where explanatory notes appear in the original, they have been included only when they seemed of particular importance. In addition, the editor has refrained from modernizing the many little differences in spelling, capitalization, grammar, usage and syntax, which have developed since the Civil War. Needless to say, there has been no attempt to impose a uniformity of style. Thus, in **Eyewitness History of the Civil War** the participants speak for themselves in their own voices.

Chapter I

FORT HENRY AND FORT DONELSON

After the disaster at First Bull Run, the advocates of the Union were heartened over the first great victories of Federal armies in the West. There Ulysses S. Grant, in a campaign lasting from 2 to 16 February 1862, boldly captured a Confederate force of some 12,000 men at Forts Henry and Donelson guarding the Tennessee and Cumberland Rivers respectively. The victory effectively opened the waterways for a Federal invasion of the Volunteer State, pierced the Tennessee-Kentucky line and forced the Confederate forces under Albert Sidney Johnston to fall back from Kentucky and most of Tennessee.

HENRY WALKE

Gunboats on the Tennessee

In campaigning against Forts Henry and Donelson, Grant decided to employ a fleet of shallow-draft ironclad gunboats under the command of Flag Officer Andrew Foote. A bombardment from Foote's fleet, overpowering Federal numbers, and the weakness of the Confederate position at Fort Henry forced the garrison's commander Brigadier General Lloyd Tilghman to surrender on 6 February, but not before he had sent most of his troops to reinforce Fort Donelson. The skipper of the Union gunboat Carondelet, *Commander Henry Walke, described the naval action against Fort Henry in* Battles and Leaders of the Civil War.*

During the winter of 1861-62, an expedition was planned by Flag-Officer Foote and Generals Grant and McClernand against Fort Henry, situated on the eastern bank of the Tennessee River, a short distance south of the line between Kentucky and Tennessee. In January the iron-clads were brought down to Cairo, and great efforts were made to prepare them for immediate service, but only four of the iron-clads could be made ready as soon as required.

On the morning of the 2d of February the flag officer left Cairo with the four armored vessels above named, and the wooden gun-boats *Tyler, Lexington,* and *Conestoga,* and in the evening reached the Tennessee River. On the 4th the fleet anchored six miles below Fort Henry. The next day while reconnoitering, the *Essex* received a shot which passed through the pantry and the officers' quarters, addressed them, and offered a prayer.

Heavy rains had been falling, and the river had risen rapidly to an unusual height; the swift current brought down an immense quantity of heavy driftwood, lumber, fences, and large trees, and it required all the steam-power of the *Carondelet,* with both anchors down, and the most strenuous exertions of the officers and crew working day and night, to prevent the boat from being dragged downstream. This adversity appeared to dampen the ardor of our crew, but when the next morning they saw a large number of white objects, which through the fog looked like polar bears, coming down the stream, and ascertained that they were the enemy's torpedoes forced from their moorings by the powerful current, they took heart, regarding the freshet as providential and as a presage of victory. The overflowing river, which opposed our progress, swept away in broad daylight this hidden peril; for if the torpedoes had not been disturbed, or had broken loose at night while we were shoving the drift-wood from our bows, some of them would surely have exploded near or under our vessels.

The 6th dawned mild and cheering, with a light breeze, sufficient to clear away the smoke. At 10:20 the flag-officer made the signal to prepare for battle, and at 10:50 came the order to get under way and steam up to Panther Island, about two miles below Fort Henry. At 11:35, having passed the foot of the island, we formed in line and approached the fort four abreast,—the *Essex* on the right, then the *Cincinnati, Carondelet,* and *St. Louis.* For want of room the last two were interlocked, and remained so during the fight.

As we slowly passed up this narrow stream, not a sound could be heard nor a moving object seen in the dense woods which overhung the dark and swollen river. The gun-crews of the *Carondelet* stood silent at their posts, impressed with the serious and important character of the service before them. About noon the fort and the Confederate flag came suddenly into view, the barracks, the new earth-works, and the great guns well manned. The captains of our guns were men-of-war's men, good shots, and had their men well drilled.

The flag-steamer, the *Cincinnati,* fired the first shot as the signal for the others to begin. At once the fort was ablaze with the flame of her eleven heavy guns. The wild whistle of their rifle-shells was heard on every side of us. On the *Carondelet* not a word was spoken more than at ordinary drill, except when Matthew Arthur, captain of the starboard bow-gun, asked permission to fire at one or two of the enemy's retreating vessels, as he could not at that time bring his gun to bear on the fort. He fired one shot, which passed through the upper cabin of a hospital-boat, whose flag was not seen, but injured no one. The *Carondelet* was struck in about thirty places by the enemy's heavy shot and shell. Eight struck within two feet of the bow-ports, leading to the boilers, around which barricades had been built—a precaution which I always took before going into action, and which on several occasions prevented an explosion. The *Carondelet* fired 107 shell and solid shot; none of her officers or crew was killed or wounded.

The firing from the armored vessels was rapid and well sustained from the beginning of the attack, and seemingly accurate, as we could occasionally see the earth thrown in great heaps over the enemy's guns. Nor was the fire of the Confederates to be despised; their heavy shot broke and scattered our iron-plating as if it had been putty and often passed completely through the casemates. But our old men-of-war's men, captains of the guns, proud to show their worth in battle, infused life and courage into their young comrades. When these experienced gunners saw a shot coming toward a port, they had the coolness and discretion to order their men to bow down, to save their heads.

After nearly an hour's hard fighting, the captain of the *Essex*, going below, and complimenting the First Division for their splendid execution, asked them if they did not want to rest and give three cheers, which were given with a will.

The *Essex* had fired seventy shots from her two 9-inch guns. A powder boy, Job Phillips, fourteen years of age, coolly marked down upon the casemate every shot his gun had fired, and his account was confirmed by the gunner in the magazine. Her loss in killed, wounded, and missing was thirty-two.

The *St. Louis* was struck seven times. She fired one hundred and seven shots during the action. No one on board the vessel was killed or wounded.

Flag-Officer Foote during the action was in the pilot-house of the *Cincinnati*, which received thirty-two shots. Her chimneys, after-cabin, and boats were completely riddled. Two of her guns were disabled. The only fatal shot she received passed through the starboard front, killing one man and wounding several others. I happened to be looking at the flag-steamer when one of the enemy's heavy shot struck her. It had the effect, apparently of a thunder-bolt, ripping her side-timbers and scattering the splinters over the vessel. She did not slacken her speed, but moved on as though nothing unexpected had happened.

From the number of times the gun-boats were struck, it would appear that the Confederate artillery practice, at first, at least, was as good, if not better, than ours. This, however, was what might have been expected, as the Confederate gunners had the advantage of practicing on the ranges the gun-boats would probably occupy as they approached the fort. The officers of the gun-boats, on the contrary, with guns of different caliber and unknown range, and without practice, could not point their guns with as much accuracy. To counterbalance this advantage of the enemy, the gun-boats were much better protected by their casemates for distant firing than the fort by its fresh earthworks. The Confederate soldiers fought as valiantly and as skillfully as the Union sailors. Only after a most determined resistance, and after all his heavy guns had been silenced, did General Tilghman lower his flag. The Confederate loss, as reported, was 5 killed, 11 wounded, and 5 missing. The prisoners, including the general and his staff, numbered 78 in the fort and 16 in a hospital-boat; the remainder of the garrison, a little less than 2600, having escaped to Fort Donelson.

Our gun-boats continued to approach the fort until General Tilghman, with two or three of his staff, came off in a small boat to the *Cincinnati* and surrendered the fort to Flag-Officer Foote, who sent for me, introduced me to General Tilghman, and gave me orders to take command of the fort and hold it until the arrival of General Grant.

General Tilghman was a soldierly-looking man, a little above medium height, with piercing black eyes and a resolute, intelligent expression of countenance. He was dignified and courteous, and won the respect and sympathy of all who became acquainted with him. In his official report of the battle he said that his officers and men fought with the gravest bravery until 1:50 P.M., when seven of his eleven guns were disabled; and, finding it impossible to defend the fort, and wishing to spare the lives of his gallant men, after consultation with his officers he surrendered the fort.

It was reported at the time that, in surrendering to Flag-Officer Foote, the Confederate general said, "I am glad to surrender to so gallant an officer," and that Foote replied, "You do perfectly right, sir, in surrendering, but you should have blown my boat out of the water before I would have surrendered to you." I was with Foote soon after the surrender, and I cannot believe that such a reply was made by him. He was too much of a gentleman to say anything calculated to wound the feelings of an officer who had defended his post with signal courage and fidelity and whose spirits were clouded by the adverse fortunes of war.

When I took possession of the fort the Confederate surgeon was laboring with his coat off to relieve and save the wounded; and although the officers and crews of the gun-boats gave three hearty cheers when the Confederate flag was hauled down, the first inside view of the fort sufficed to suppress every feeling of exultation and to excite our deepest pity. On every side the blood of the dead and wounded was intermingled with the earth and their implements of war. Their largest gun, a 128-pounder, was dismounted and filled with earth by the bursting of one of our shells near its muzzle; the carriage of another was broken to pieces, and two dead men lay near it, almost covered with heaps of earth; a rifled gun had burst, throwing its mangled gunners into the water. But few of the garrison escaped unhurt.

General Grant, with his staff, rode into the fort about 3 o'clock on the same day and relieved me of the command. The general and staff then accompanied me on board the *Carondelet* (anchored near the fort), where he complemented the officers of the flotilla in the highest terms for the gallant manner in which they had captured Fort Henry. He had expected his troops to take part in a land attack, but the heavy rains had made the direct roads to the fort almost impassable.

The wooden gun-boats *Conestoga*, Commander S.L. Phelps, *Tyler*, Lieutenant-Commander William Gwin, and *Lexington*, Lieutenant J.W. Shirk, engaged the enemy at long range in the rear of the iron-clads. After the battle they pursued the enemy's transports up the river, and the *Conestoga* captured the steamer *Eastport*. The news of the capture of Fort Henry was received with great rejoicing all over the North.

H.L. BEDFORD

The Defense of Fort Donelson

Following the swift capitulation of Fort Henry, Grant and Foote believed the use of gunboats against the fortifications at Fort Donelson might lead to the surrender of that position as well. As Grant's troops began sealing off the garrison from escape by land, the naval war vessels attempted to bombard the fort's guns at close range on 14 February. The move met with disappointing failure as two ships were disabled and another heavily damaged. Foote was injured with a wound that would eventually kill him. An instructor of artillery at the fort, H.L. Bedford witnessed the repulse of the Federal flotilla and recounted his experiences in an address which was originally published in the *Southern Society Historical Papers*.

The operations of the army at this place having proved disastrous to the Confederate cause, it has been condemned as a strategic point, and no one seems particularly anxious to acknowledge the responsibility of its selection. It was the general impression at the Fort that its location had been ordered by the Tennessee authorities as being the most eligible point on the Cumberland River, in close proximity to Fort Henry on the Tennessee. The original intention evidently was the obstruction of the Cumberland. The engineer in charge, Lieutenant Dixon, while tracing the outlines of the earthworks, never dreamed that a persistent stand against an invading army would ever be attempted, and I feel warranted in suggesting that General A.S. Johnston regarded it simply as a protection to his rear.

When I received orders in October, 1861, to report there as Instructor of Artillery, Colonel E.W. Munford, aide to General Johnston, informed me that he was instructed by his chief to impress upon me that the Cumberland river cut his rear, and the occupation of Bowling Green was dependent upon the proper guarding of that stream. If, then, Fort

Donelson was intended to prevent the passage of gunboats, its location was an admirable one; it accomplished its mission, and its founder need feel no hesitation in claiming its paternity. Nor does the final result of the operations of the land forces necessarily convict General Johnston of a mistake in the reinforcement of Donelson. At that time he was believed to possess the ability as a general which events soon verified, and his condemnation will have to rest on surer proofs than the charges of flippant writers. To the average mind the whole matter resolves itself into the simple question: Whether General Johnston sufficiently reinforced Fort Donelson to successfully resist the forces that invaded the State of Tennessee under General Grant by way of Fort Henry; and, if so, is he fairly chargeable with the blunders of his generals, in allowing themselves to be cooped in temporary trenches until reinforcements to the enemy could come up the Cumberland? Any close student of the "Operations at Fort Donelson," embraced in series No. 1, Vol. 7, of the "Records of the Rebellion," will probably detect by whom the mistakes were made. It is doubtless there recorded when and where the opportunity of withdrawing the Confederate forces was disregarded; that General Johnston was unfortunate in the selection, or rather the grouping of his lieutenants, on this occasion, is beyond controversy. His army consisted of raw recruits; his generals were ready made for him; their commissions were presumptions of merit; there had been no opportunity for development, and he had no alternative but to accept the patents of ability issued to them by the War Department. The senior general arrived at the eleventh hour, and seems to have been lacking in disposition or in power to hold his second in due subjection. The latter had been on the ground for about a week; he was full of energy and physical activity and possessed rare executive ability. He was restless under restraint, probably prone to insubordination, and it was almost impossible for him to yield his sceptre to a new comer. He gave orders affecting the whole army without any known rebuke or remonstrance from his chief. The performances of these two chieftains afford an apt illustration of a very homely old saying that will readily recur to most of you. This rule of duality of commanders, according to some of the official reports, seems to have obtained in the heavy batteries, but as it was not then known or recognized, it did not create any confusion. When I reported there for duty very little in the way of defence had been accomplished. Two 32-pounder carronades had been mounted on the river, and three 32-pounders were temporarily mounted on the crest of the bluff. The carronades were utterly useless, except against wooden boats at close quarters, while the three guns on the hill, on account of position, could not be made effectual against ironclads. The garrison, in command of Lieutenant-Colonel Randle McGavock, consisted of a part of Colonel Heiman's Tenth Tennessee regiment, the nucleus of Colonel Sugg's Fiftieth Tennessee (then called Stacker's regiment), and Captain Frank Maney's light battery.

As there were no heavy artillerists, Captain Beaumont's company of Fiftieth Tennessee had been detailed for that duty. At the time of my arrival, there was considerable excitement at the Fort. Smoke was seen rising a few miles down the river, the long-roll was being beat, and there was hurrying to and fro; companies were getting under arms and into line with the rapidity of zealots, though wanting in the precision of veterans. The excitement subsided as the smoke disappeared. In a short while the companies were dismissed, and the men resumed their wonted avocations. The local engineer was also in charge of the works at Fort Henry and was, necessarily, often absent. His duties were onerous and manifold; I, therefore, volunteered to remount the three 32-pounders and place them in the permanent battery; and as the completion of the defense was considered of more importance than the drilling of artillery, I was kept constantly on engineering duty until after the investment. General Tilghman arrived about the middle of December, and took command. He manifested a good deal of interest in forwarding the work. The Fiftieth Tennessee regiment (Colonel Suggs) was organized; the Thirtieth Tennessee (Colonel Head), and the Forty-ninth Tennessee (Colonel Bailey), reported, and these, with Maney's light battery, constituted the garrison, Lieutenant-Colonel McGavock having rejoined Colonel Hieman at Fort Henry.

The work for the completion of the defenses and for the comfort of the soldiers, was pushed on as rapidly as the means at hand would permit. There was no lagging, nor lukewarmness, nor shirking of duty. As one of the many evidences of the zeal manifested by the garrison, I would state that whenever a detail for work of any magnitude was made from any of the regiments, a field officer usually accompanied it, in order to secure promptness and concert of action. This, I believe, was the invariable rule with the Forty-ninth Tennessee. At the time of the arrival of reinforcements, the water batteries were not in that state of incompleteness and disorder which the report of a general officer charges, nor was there any gloom or despondency hanging over the garrison. It is true there was some delay in getting the 10-inch Columbiad in working condition, but no one connected with the Fort was responsible for it. The gun was mounted in ample time, but upon being tested it came very nearly being dismounted by the running back of the carriage against the hurters. It was necessary to increase the inclination of the chassis, which was accomplished by obtaining larger rear traverse wheels from the iron works just above Dover. It was still found, even with a reduced charge of powder, that the recoil of the carriage against the counter-hurters was of sufficient force to cut the ropes tied there as bumpers. There was no alternative but to dismount the piece and lower the front half of the traverse circle; by this means the inclination of the chassis was made so steep that the piece was in danger of getting away from the gunners when being run into battery, and of toppling off in front.

Any paper upon the subject of Fort Donelson would be incomplete without the mention of Lieutenant-Colonel Wilton A. Haynes, of the Tennessee artillery. He was, in the nomenclature of the volunteers, a "West Pointer," and was an accomplished artillerist. He came to Fort Donelson about the middle of January and found the "Instructor of Artillery" engaged in engineering duty and nothing being done in familiarizing the companies detailed for artillery service with their pieces. He organized an artillery battalion, and made a requisition on General Polk, at Columbus, for two drill officers, and whatever of proficiency these companies attained as artillerists is due to him. He was physically unable to participate in the engagements and this may account for the failure of recognition in the official reports.

The artillery battalion as organized by Colonel Haynes was fully competent to serve the guns with success, but General Pillow deemed otherwise and proceeded to the mistake of assigning Lieutenant Dixon to the command of the heavy batteries, instead of attaching him to his personal staff, and availing himself of that officer's familiarity as an engineer with the topography of the battleground and of the surrounding country. The assignment was particularly unfortunate, inasmuch as Dixon was killed before the main fight and the batteries were not only deprived of his services for that occasion, but the Confederate army lost an able engineer. It must be remembered, however, that the great fear was of the gunboats. It was apprehended that their recent achievements at Fort Henry would be repeated at Donelson, and it was natural that the commanding general should make every other interest subservient to the efficiency of the heavy batteries. The river defenses consisted of two batteries. The upper one was on the river bank immediately abreast of the earthworks; it was crescent shaped, and contained one 32-pound calibre rifle gun and two 32-pounder carronades. The other battery was some hundred and fifty yards lower down and consisted of eight 32-pounders and one 10-inch Columbiad. This lower battery, although essentially a straight line, ran *en echelon* to the left over the point of a hill that made down obliquely from the earthworks to the river, with the right piece resting on the brink of the river bank, and the Columbiad over in the valley of a stream, emptying into the river, some hundred and fifty yards lower down. The back water in this stream protected the batteries from a direct assault. About nine hundred yards below the lower battery a floating abattis was placed in the river for the purpose of preventing the passage of boats. This was done by anchoring full-length trees by the roots and allowing the tops to float. In ordinary stages of water this might have offered some impediment, but at the time of the attack the river was very high and the boats passed over without the least halt or break in their line of approach.

In all the accounts that I have seen from the Federal side, the armament of the water batteries is overestimated. Flag-Officer Foote reports that there must have been about twenty heavy guns, and General Lew Wallace places it at seventeen. Admiral Walke, while correctly stating the number in the lower battery, is in error in claiming that the upper was about the same in strength.

On the morning of the 12th of February the finishing touches were put to the Columbiad, and the batteries were pronounced ready for gunboats, whereupon Lieutenant Dixon proceeded to the assignment of the guns. Captain R.R. Ross, of the Maury Company Light Artillery, whose company had been ordered to heavy batteries by General Pillow, was placed in command of the rifle gun and the two carronades. Captain Beaumont's company A, Fiftieth Tennessee, and Captain Bidwell's company, Thirtieth Tennessee, worked the 32-pounders, and the Columbiad was turned over to my command, with a detachment of twenty men under Lieutenant Sparkman, from Captain Ross's company to work it. I received private instructions to continue the firing with blank cartridges, in the event the gun should dismount itself in action. The drill officers, Lieutenants McDaniel and Martin, were assigned to the 32-

pounders, while Captains Culbertson and Shaster had special assignments or instructions, the nature of which I never knew.

As the artillerists, who were to serve the rifle and Columbiad, had no experience with heavy guns, most of them probably never having seen a heavy battery until that morning, it was important that they should be instructed in the manual of their pieces. Drilling, therefore, began immediately, but had continued for a short time only when it was most effectually interrupted by the appearance of a gunboat down the river, which subsequently was ascertained to be the *Carondelet*. She fired about a dozen shots with remarkable precision, and retired without any response from the batteries.

On the morning of the 13th drilling was again interrupted by the firing of this boat, and the same thing happened in the afternoon. It really appeared as if the boat was diabolically inspired, and knew the most opportune times to annoy us. Sometime during the day, probably about noon, she delivered her fire with such accuracy that forbearance was no longer endurable, and Lieutenant Dixon ordered the Columbiad and rifle to respond. The first shot from the Columbiad passed immediately over the boat, the second fell short, but the third was distinctly heard to strike. A cheer of course followed, and Lieutenant Dixon, in the enthusiasm of the moment, ordered the 32-pounders to open fire, although the enemy was clearly beyond their range. The *Carondelet*, nothing daunted, continued the action, and soon one of her shells cut away the right cheek of one of Captain Bidwell's guns, and a flying nut passed through Lieutenant Dixon's head, killing him instantly. In this engagement the flange of one of the front traverse wheels of the Columbiad was crushed, and a segment of the front half of the traverse circle was cupped, both of which proved serious embarrassments in the action next day.

On the morning of the 14th, dense volumes of smoke were seen rising from down the river; it was evident that transports were landing troops. Captain Ross became impatient to annoy them, but having no fuse shells to his guns, he came over to the Columbiad and advised the throwing of shells down the river. The commander declined to do so without orders, whereupon Captain Culbertson, who had succeeded Lieutenant Dixon in the command of the batteries, was looked up, but he refused to give the order, upon the ground that it would accomplish no good, and that he did not believe in the useless shedding of blood. Captain Ross, not to be outdone, set himself to the task of procuring the necessary order and returned to the Columbiad about 3 o'clock P.M. with a verbal order from General Floyd to harass the transports. In obedience to this order, we prepared to shell the smoke. A shell was inserted, the gun was given the proper elevation, the lanyard was pulled, and the missile went hissing over the bend of the river, plunged into a bank of smoke, and was lost to view. This was called by an army correspondent, claiming to have been on one of the gunboats, "a shot of defiance." Before the piece could be reloaded, the prow of a gunboat made its appearance around the bend, quickly followed by three others, and arranging themselves in line of battle, steamed up to the attack. When they had arrived within a mile and a half of the batteries, a solid shot having been substituted for a shell, the Columbiad began the engagement with a ricochet shot, the rifle gun a ready second. The gun-boats returned the fire, right centre boat opening, the others following in quick succession. After the third discharge the rifle remained silent on account of becoming accidentally spiked. This had a bad effect on the men at the Columbiad, causing them considerable uneasiness for their comrades at the upper battery. The Columbiad continued the action unsupported until the boats came within the range of the 32-pounders, when the engagement became general, with ten guns of the batteries opposed to the twelve bow guns of the ironclads, supplemented by those of the two wooden boats that remained in the rear throwing curvated shells. As the boats drew nearer, the firing on both sides became faster, until it appeared as if the battle had dwindled into a contest of speed in firing. When they arrived within three hundred yards of the lower battery they came to a stand, and then it was that the bombardment was truly terrific. The roar of cannons was continuous and deafening, and commands, if necessary, had to be given by signs. Pandemonium itself would hardly have been more appalling, but neither chaos nor cowardice obtruded themselves, and I must insist that General Wallace and Admiral Walke are mistaken in their assertions that the gunners were seen running from their guns. It is true there was some passing from the batteries to the Fort, but not by the artillerists in action, and as the passage was over an exposed place, in fact across the field of fire of the gunboats, it is a fair presumption that the transit was made as swiftly as possible. Of one thing I am certain, there was no fleeing from the Columbiad, and ahough her discharges were necessarily very slow I think every one in hearing that day will testify that her boom was almost as regular as the swinging of a pendulum. If these two Federal officers saw her condition when surrendered, they will admit that it was not likely that panic-stricken cannoniers could have carried her safely through such a furious bombardment, especially to have done the execution with which she is accredited. In his contribution to the *Century* of December, 1884, doubtless by the cursory reading of Captain Bidwell's report, General Wallace is lead into the mistake of saying that each gunner selected his boat and stuck to her during the engagement. I am satisfied that the experienced officers who acted as gunners did not observe this rule. The Columbiad was rigidly impartial, and fired on the boats as chance or circumstances dictated, with the exception of the last few shots, which were directed at the *Carondelet*. This boat was hugging the eastern shore, and was a little in advance of the others. She offered her side to the Columbiad, which was on the left and the most advanced gun of the batteries. Several well-directed shots raked the side and tore away her armor, according to the report of Lieutenant Sparkman, who was on the lookout. Just as the other boats began to drift back, the *Carondelet* forged ahead for about a half length, as though she intended making the attempt to pass the battery, and it is presumable that she then received the combined fire of all the guns.

It is claimed that if Hannibal had marched on Rome immediately after the battle of Cannæ, he could have taken the city and by the same retrospective reasoning, it is probable that if Admiral Foote had stood beyond the range of 32-pounders he could have concentrated his fire on two guns. If his boats had fired with the deliberation and accuracy of the *Carondelet* on the previous day he could have dismounted those guns, demolished the 32-pounders at his leisure, and shelled the Fort to his heart's content. But flushed with his victory at Fort Henry, his success there paved the way for his defeat at Donelson, a defeat that might have proved more disastrous could the Columbiad have used a full charge of powder and the rifle gun participated in the fight. After the battle three of the gunboats were seen drifting helplessly down the stream, and a shout of exultation leaped from the lips of every soldier in the fort. It was taken up by the men in the trenches, and for awhile a shout of victory, the sweetest strain to the ears of those who win, reverberated over the hills and hollows around the little village of Dover.

While the cannoniers were yet panting from their exertion, Lieutenant-Colonel Robb, of the Forty-ninth Tennessee, who fell mortally wounded the next day, ever mindful of the comfort of those around him, sent a grateful stimulant along the line of guns. Congratulations were the order of the hour. Generals Floyd and Pillow personally complemented the artillerists. They came to the Columbiad, called for the commander, and after congratulating him upon the performances of that day, promised that if the batteries would continue to keep back the gunboats, the infantry of their command would keep the land forces at a safe distance. That officer, who had been watching the smoke of the transports landing reinforcements, as he stood there before these generals, just thirty-six hours before surrender, receiving their assurances of protection, wondered if they were able to fulfill the promise, or if they were merely indulging an idle habit of braggadocio.

LEW WALLACE

Fort Donelson Surrenders

Though Grant commanded an army of 15,000 troops, he ably managed to besiege Fort Donelson, commanded by three generals: John B. Floyd, Gideon Pillow, and Simon Bolivar Buckner. Brigadier General Lew Wallace, who commanded a division in Grant's army, would be forever remembered not for his military prowess, but for his celebrated work, *Ben Hur*. Evidence of his romantic penmanship can be found in this article taken from *Battles and Leaders of the Civil War* that describes the Federal operations at Fort Donelson.

The village of Dover was—and for that matter yet is—what our English cousins would call the "shire-town" of the county of Stewart, Tennessee. In 1860 it was a village unknown to fame, meager in population, architecturally poor. There was a court house in the place, and a tavern, remembered now as double-storied, unpainted, and with windows of eight-by-ten glass, which, if the panes may be likened to eyes, were both squint and cataractous. Looking through them gave the street outside the appearance of a sedgy slough of yellow backwater. The entertainment furnished man and beast was good of the kind; though at the time mentioned a sleepy traveler, especially if he were of the North, might have been somewhat vexed by the explosions which spiced the good things of a debating society that nightly took possession of the barroom, to discuss the relative fighting qualities of the opposing sections.

If there was a little of the romantic in Dover itself, there was still less of poetic quality in the country round about it. The only beautiful feature was the Cumberland River, which, in placid current from the south, poured its waters, ordinarily white and pure as those of the springs that fed it, past the village on the east. Northward there was a hill, then a small stream, then a bolder hill round the foot of which the river swept to the west, as if courteously bent on helping Hickman's Creek out of its boggy bottom and cheerless ravine. North of the creek all was woods. Taking in the ravine of the creek, a system of hollows, almost wide and deep enough to be called valleys, inclosed the town and two hills, their bluffest ascents being on the townward side. Westward of the hollows there were woods apparently interminable. From Fort Henry, twelve miles north-west, a road entered the village, stopping first to unite itself with another wagon-way, now famous as the Wynn's Ferry road, coming more directly from the west. Still another road, leading off to Charlotte and Nashville, had been cut across the low ground near the river on the south. These three highways were the chief reliances of the people of Dover for communication with the country and as they were more than supplemented by the river and its boatage, the three were left the year round to the guardianship of the winds and rains.

However, when at length the Confederate authorities decided to erect a military post at Dover, the town entered but little into consideration. The real inducement was the second hill on the north—more properly a ridge. As it rose about a hundred feet above the level of the inlet, the reconnoitering engineer, seeking to control the navigation of the river by a fortification, adopted it at sight. And for that purpose the bold bluff was in fact a happy gift of nature, and we shall see presently how it was taken in hand and made terrible.

It is of little moment now who first enunciated the idea of attacking the rebellion by way of the Tennessee River; most likely the conception was simultaneous with many minds. The trend of the river; its navigability for large steamers; its offer of a highway to the rear of the Confederate hosts in Kentucky and the state of Tennessee; its silent suggestion of a secure passage into the heart of the belligerent land, from which the direction of movement could be changed toward the Mississippi, or, left, toward Richmond; its many advantages as a line of supply and of general communication, must have been discerned by every military student who, in the summer of 1861, gave himself to the most cursory examination of the map. It is thought better and more consistent with fact to conclude that its advantages as a strategic line, so actually obtrusive of themselves, were observed about the same time by thoughtful men on both sides of the contest. With every problem of attack there goes a counter problem of defense.

A peculiarity of the most democratic people in the world is their hunger for heroes. The void in that respect had never been so gaping as in 1861. General Scott was then old and passing away and the North caught eagerly at the promise held out by George B. McClellan; while the South, with as much precipitation, pinned its faith and hopes on Albert Sidney Johnston. There is little doubt that up to the surrender of Fort Donelson the latter was considered the foremost soldier of all who chose rebellion for their part. When the shadow of that first great failure fell upon the veteran, President Davis made haste to reassure him of his sympathy and unbroken confidence. In the official correspondence which has survived the Confederacy there is nothing so pathetic, and at the same time so indicative of the manly greatness of Albert Sidney Johnston, as his letter in reply to that of his chief.

When General Johnston assumed command of the Western Department, the war had ceased to be a new idea. Battles had been fought. Preparations for battles to come were far advanced. Already it had been accepted that the North was to attack and the South to defend. The Mississippi River was a central object; if opened from Cairo to Fort Jackson (New Orleans), the Confederacy would be broken into halves, and good strategy required it to be broken. The question was whether the effort would be made directly or by turning its defended positions. Of the national gun-boats afloat above Cairo, some were formidably iron-clad. Altogether the flotilla was strong enough to warrant the theory that a direct descent would be attempted; and to meet the movement the Confederates threw up powerful batteries, notably at Columbus, Island Number Ten, Memphis, and Vicksburg. So fully were they possessed of that theory that they measurably neglected the possibilities of invasion by way of the Cumberland and Tennessee rivers. Not until General Johnston established his headquarters at Nashville was serious attention given to the defense of those streams. A report to his chief of engineers of November 21st, 1861, establishes that at that date a second battery on the Cumberland at Dover had been completed; that a work on the ridge had been laid out, and two guns mounted; and that the encampment was then surrounded by an abatis of felled timber. Later, Brigadier-General Lloyd Tilghman was sent to Fort Donelson as commandant, and on January 25th he reports the batteries prepared, the entire field-works built with a trace of 2900 feet, and rifle-pits to guard the approaches were begun. The same officer speaks further of reënforcements housed in four hundred log cabins, and adds that while this was being done at Fort Donelson, Forts Henry and Heiman, over on the Tennessee, were being thoroughly strengthened. January 30th, Fort Donelson was formally inspected by Lieutenant-Colonel Gilmer, chief engineer of the Western Department, and the final touches were ordered to be given it. It is to be presumed that General Johnston was satisfied with the defenses thus provided for the Cumberland River. From observing General Buell at Louisville, and the stir and movement of multiplying columns under General U.S. Grant in the region of Cairo, he suddenly awoke determined to fight for Nashville at Donelson. To this conclusion he came as late as the beginning of February; and thereupon the brightest of the Southern leaders proceeded to make a capital mistake. The Confederate estimate of the Union force at that time in Kentucky alone was 119 regiments. The force at Cairo, St. Louis, and the towns near the mouth of the Cumberland River was judged to be about as great. It was also known that we had unlimited means of transportation for troops, making concentration a work of but few hours. Still General Johnston persisted in fighting for Nashville, and for that purpose divided his thirty thousand men. Fourteen thousand he kept in observation of Buell at Louisville. Sixteen thousand he gave to defend Fort Donelson. The latter detachment he himself called "the best part of his army." It is difficult to think of a great master of strategy making an error so perilous.

Having taken the resolution to defend Nashville at Donelson, he intrusted the operation to three chiefs of brigade—John B. Floyd, Gideon J. Pillow and Simon B. Buckner. Of these, the first was ranking officer, and he was at the time under indictment by a grand jury at Washington for malversation as Secretary of War under President Buchanan, and for complicity in an embezzlement of public funds. As will be seen, there came a crisis when the recollection of the circumstance exerted an unhappy influence over his judgment. The second officer had a genuine military record; but it is said of him that he was of a jealous nature, insubordinate, and quarrelsome. His bold attempt to supersede General Scott in Mexico was green in the memories of living men. To give pertinency to the remark, there is reason to believe that a personal misunderstanding between him and General Buckner, older than the rebellion, was yet unsettled when the two met at Donelson. All in all, therefore, there is little doubt that the junior of the three commanders was the fittest for the enterprise intrusted to them. He was their equal in courage; while in devotion to the cause and to his profession of arms, in tactical knowledge, in military bearing, in the faculty of getting the most service out of his inferiors, and inspiring them with confidence in his ability—as a soldier in all the higher meanings of the word,—he was greatly their superior.

The 6th of February, 1862, dawned darkly after a thunderstorm. Pacing the parapets of the work on the hill above the inlet formed by the junction of Hickman's Creek and the Cumberland River, a sentinel, in the serviceable butternut jeans uniform of the Confederate army of the West, might that day have surveyed Fort Donelson almost ready for battle. In fact, very little was afterward done to it. There were the two water-batteries sunk in the northern face of the bluff, about thirty feet above the river; in the lower battery 9 32-pounder guns and 1 10-inch Columbiad, and in the upper another Columbiad, bored and rifled as a 32-pounder, and 2 32-pounder carronades. These guns lay between the embrasures, in snug revetment of sand in coffee-sacks, flanked right and left with stout traverses. The satisfaction of the sentry could have been no wise diminished at seeing the backwater lying deep in the creek; a more perfect ditch against assault could not have been constructed. The fort itself was of good profile, and admirably adapted to the ridge it crowned. Around it, on the landward side, ran the rifle-pits, a continuous but irregular line of logs, covered with yellow clay. From Hickman's Creek they extended far around to the little run just outside the town on the south. If the sentry thought the pits looked shallow, he was solaced to see that they followed the coping of the ascents, seventy or eighty feet in height, up which a foe must charge, and that, where they were weakest, they were strengthened by trees felled outwardly in front of them, so that the interlacing limbs and branches seemed impassable by men under fire. At points inside the outworks, on the inner slopes of the hills, defended thus from view of an enemy as well as from his shot, lay the huts and log-houses of the garrison. Here and there groups of later comers, shivering in their wet blankets, were visible in a bivouac so cheerless that not even morning fires could relieve it. A little music would have helped their sinking spirits, but there was none. Even the picturesque effect of gay uniforms was wanting. In fine, the Confederate sentinel on the ramparts that morning, taking in the whole scene, knew the jolly rollicking picnic days of the war were over.

To make clearer why the 6th of February is selected to present the first view of the fort, about noon that day the whole garrison was drawn from their quarters by the sound of heavy guns, faintly heard from the direction of Fort Henry, a token by which every man of them knew that a battle was on. The occurrence was in fact expected, for two days before a horseman had ridden to General Tilghman with word that at 4:30 o'clock in the morning rocket signals had been exchanged with the picket at Bailey's Landing, announcing the approach of gun-boats. A second courier came, and then a third; the latter, in great haste, requesting the general's presence at Fort Henry. There was quick mounting at headquarters, and, before the camp could be taken into confidence, the general and his guard were out of sight. Occasional guns were heard the day following. Donelson gave itself up to excitement and conjecture. At noon of the 6th, as stated, there was continuous and heavy cannonading at Fort Henry and greater excitement at Fort Donelson. The polemicists in Dover became uneasy and prepared to get away. In the evening fugitives arrived in groups, and told how the gun-boats ran straight upon the fort and took it. The polemicists hastened their departure from town. At exactly midnight the gallant Colonel Heiman marched into Fort Donelson with two brigades of infantry rescued from the ruins of Forts Henry and Heiman. The officers and men by whom they were received then knew that their turn was at hand; and at daybreak, with one mind and firm of purpose, they set about the final preparation.

Brigadier-General Pillow reached Fort Donelson on the 9th; Brigadier-General Buckner came in the night of the 11th; and Brigadier-General Floyd on the 13th. The latter, by virtue of his rank, took command.

The morning of the 13th—calm, spring-like, the very opposite of that of the 6th—found in Fort Donelson a garrison of 28 regiments of infantry: 13 from Tennessee, 2 from Kentucky, 6 from Mississippi, 1 from Texas, 2 from Alabama, 4 from Virginia. There were also present 2 independent battalions, 1 regiment of cavalry and artillerymen for 6 light batteries, and 17 heavy guns, making a total of quite 18,000 effectives.

General Buckner's division—6 regiments and 2 batteries—constituted the right wing, and was posted to cover the land approaches to the water-batteries. A left wing was organized into six brigades, commanded respectively by Colonels Heiman, Davidson, Drake, Wharton, McCausland, and Baldwin, and posted from right to left in the order named. Four batteries were distributed amongst the left wing. General Bushrod R. Johnson, an able officer, served the general commanding as chief-of-staff. Dover was converted into a depot of supplies and ordnance stores. These dispositions made, Fort Donelson was ready for battle.

It may be doubted if General Grant called a council of war. The nearest approach to it was a convocation held on the *New Uncle Sam*, a steamboat that was afterward transformed into the gun-boat *Blackhawk*. The morning of the 11th of February a staff-officer visited each commandant of division and brigade with the simple verbal message: "General Grant sends his compliments, and requests to see you this afternoon on his boat." Minutes of the proceedings were not kept; there was no adjournment; each person retired when he got ready knowing that the march would take place next day probably in the forenoon.

There were in attendance on the occasion some officers of great subsequent notability. Of these Ulysses S. Grant was first. The world knows him now; then his fame was all before him. A singularity of the volunteer service in that day was that nobody took account of even a first-rate record of the Mexican War. The battle of Belmont, though indecisive, was a much better reference. A story was abroad that Grant had been the last man to take boat at the end of that affair, and the addendum that he had lingered in face of the enemy until he was hauled aboard with the last gangplank, did him great good. From the first his silence was remarkable. He knew how to keep his temper. In battle, as in camp, he went about quietly speaking in a conversational tone; yet he appeared to see everything that went on, and was always intent on business. He had a faithful assistant adjutant-general, and appreciated him; he preferred, however, his own eyes, word, and hand. His aides were little more than messengers. In dress he was plain, even negligent; in partial amendment of that his horse was always a good one and well kept. At the council—calling it such by grace—he smoked, but never said a word. In all probability he was framing the orders of march which were issued that night. Charles F. Smith, of the regular army, was also present. He was a person of superb physique, very tall, perfectly proportioned, straight, square-shouldered, ruddy-faced, with eyes of perfect blue, and long snowwhite moustaches. He seemed to know the army regulations by heart, and caught a tactical mistake, whether of command or execution, by a kind of mental *coup d'œil*. He was naturally kind, genial, communicative, and never failed to answer when information was sought of him; at the same time he believed in "hours of service" regularly published by the adjutants as a rabbi believes in the Ten Tables, and to call a court-martial on a "bummer" was in his eyes a sinful waste of stationery. On the occasion of a review General Smith had the bearing of a marshal of France. He could ride along a line of volunteers in the regulation uniform of a brigadier-general, plume, chapeau, epaulets and all, without exciting laughter—something nobody else could do in the beginning of the war. He was at first accused of disloyalty and when told of it, his eyes flashed wickedly; then he laughed, and said, "Oh, never mind! They'll take it back after our first battle." And they did. At the time of the meeting on the *New Uncle Sam* he was a brigadier-general, and commanded the division which in the land operations against Fort Henry had marched up the left bank of the river against Fort Heiman.

Another officer worthy of mention was John A. McClernand, also a brigadier. By profession a lawyer, he was in his first of military service. Brave, industrious, methodical, and of unquestioned cleverness, he was rapidly acquiring the art of war.

There was still another in attendance on the *New Uncle Sam* not to be passed—a young man who had followed General Grant from Illinois, and was seeing his first of military service. No soldier in the least familiar with headquarters on the Tennessee can ever forget the slender figure, large black eyes, hectic cheeks, and sincere, earnest manner of John A. Rawlins, then assistant adjutant-general, afterward major-general and secretary of war. He had two special devotions—to the cause and to his chief. He lived to see the first triumphant and the latter first in peace as well as in war. Probably no officer of the Union was mourned by so many armies.

Fort Henry, it will be remembered, was taken by Flag-Officer Foote on the 6th of February. The time up to the 12th was given to reconnoitering the country in the direction of Fort Donelson. Two roads were discovered: one of twelve miles direct, the other almost parallel with the first, but, on account of a slight divergence, two miles longer.

By 8 o'clock in the morning, the First Division, General McClernand commanding, and the Second, under General Smith were in full march. The infantry of this command consisted of twenty-five regiments in all, or three less than those of the Confederates. Against their six field-batteries General Grant had seven. In cavalry alone he was materially stronger. The rule in attacking fortifications is five to one; to save the Union commander from a charge of rashness, however, he had also at control a fighting quality ordinarily at home on the sea rather than the land. After receiving the surrender of Fort Henry, Flag-Officer Foote had hastened to Cairo to make preparation for the reduction of Fort Donelson. With six of his boats, he passed into the Cumberland River; and on the 12th, while the two divisions of the army were marching across to Donelson, he was hurrying, as fast as steam could drive him and his following, to a second trial of iron batteries afloat against earth batteries ashore. The *Carondelet*, Commander Walke, having preceded him, had been in position below the fort since the 12th. By sundown of the 12th, McClernand and Smith reached the point designated for them in orders.

On the morning of the 13th of February General Grant, with about twenty thousand men, was before Fort Donelson. We have had a view of the army in the works ready for battle; a like view of that outside and about to go into position of attack and assault is not so easily to be given. At dawn the latter host rose up from the bare ground, and, snatching bread and coffee as best they could, fell into lines that stretched away over hills, down hollows, and through thickets, making it impossible for even colonels to see their regiments from flank to flank.

Pausing to give a thought to the situation, it is proper to remind the reader that he is about to witness an event of more than mere historical interest; he is about to see the men of the North and North-west and of the South and South-west enter for the first time into a strife of arms; on one side the best blood of Tennessee, Kentucky, Alabama, Mississippi, and Texas, aided materially by fighting representatives from Virginia; on the other, the best blood of Illinois, Ohio, Indiana, Iowa, Missouri, and Nebraska.

We have now before us a spectacle seldom witnessed in the annals of scientific war—an army behind field-works erected in a chosen position waiting quietly while another army very little superior in numbers proceeds at leisure to place it in a state of siege. Such was the operation General Grant had before him at daybreak of the 13th of February. Let us see how it was accomplished and how it was resisted.

In a clearing about two miles from Dover there was a log-house, at the time occupied by a Mrs. Crisp. As the road to Dover ran close by, it was made the headquarters of the commanding general. All through the night of the 12th, the coming and going was incessant. Smith was ordered to find a position in front of the enemy's right wing, which would place him face to face with Buckner. McClernand's order was to establish himself on the enemy's left, where he would be opposed to Pillow.

A little before Birge's sharp-shooters were astir. Theirs was a peculiar service. Each was a preferred marksman, and carried a long-range Henry rifle, with sights delicately arranged as for target practice. In action each was perfectly independent. They never manœuvered as a corps. When the time came they were asked, "Canteens full?" "Biscuits for all day?" Then their only order, "All right; hunt your holes, boys." Thereupon they dispersed, and, like Indians, sought cover to please themselves behind rocks and stumps, or in hollows. Sometimes they dug holes; sometimes they climbed into trees. Once in a good location, they remained there the day. At night they would crawl out and report in camp. This morning, as I have said, the sharp-shooters dispersed early to find places within easy range of the breastworks.

The movement by Smith and McClernand was begun about the same time. A thick wood fairly screened the former. The latter had to cross an open valley under fire of two batteries, one on Buckner's left, the other on a high point jutting from the line of outworks held by Colonel Heiman of Pillow's command. Graves commanded the first, Maney the second; both were of Tennessee. As always in situations where the advancing party is ignorant of the ground and of the designs of the enemy, resort was had to skirmishers, who are to the main body what antenna are to insects. Theirs it is to unmask the foe. Unlike sharp-shooters, they act in bodies. Behind the skirmishers, the batteries started out to find positions, and through the brush and woods, down the hollows, up the hills the guns and caissons were hauled. Nowadays it must be a very steep bluff in face of which the good artillerist will stop or turn back. At Donelson, however, the proceeding was generally slow and toilsome. The officer had to find a vantage-ground first; then with axes a road to it was hewn out; after which, in many instances, the men, with the prolongs over their shoulders, helped the horses along. In the gray of the dawn the sharp-shooters were deep in their deadly game; as the sun came up, one battery after another opened fire, and was instantly and gallantly answered; and all the time behind the hidden sharpshooters, and behind the skirmishers, who occasionally stopped to take a hand in the fray, the regiments marched, route-step, colors flying, after their colonels.

About 11 o'clock Commander Walke, of the *Carondelet*, engaged the water-batteries. The air was then full of the stunning music of battle, though as yet not a volley of musketry had been heard. Smith, nearest the enemy at starting, was first in place; and there, leaving the fight to his sharp-shooters and skirmishers and to his batteries, he reported to the chief in the loghouse, and, like an old soldier, calmly waited orders.

McClernand, following a good road, pushed on rapidly to the high grounds on the right. The appearance of his column in the valley covered by the two Confederate batteries provoked a furious shelling from them. On the double-quick his men passed through it; and when, in the wood beyond, they resumed the route-step and saw that nobody was hurt, they fell to laughing at themselves. The real baptism of fire was yet in store for them.

When McClernand arrived at his appointed place and extended his brigades, it was discovered that the Confederate outworks offered a front too great for him to envelop. To attempt to rest his right opposite their extreme left would necessitate a dangerous attenuation of his line and leave him without reserves. Over on their left, moreover, ran the road already mentioned as passing from Dover on the south to Charlotte and Nashville, which it was of the highest importance to close hermetically so that there would be no communication left General Floyd except by the river. If the road to Charlotte were left to the enemy they might march out at their pleasure.

The insufficiency of his force was thus made apparent to General Grant, and whether a discovery of the moment or not, he set about its correction. He knew a reënforcement was coming up the river under convoy of Foote; besides which a brigade, composed of the 8th Missouri and the 11th Indiana infantry and Battery A, Illinois, had been left behind at Forts Henry and Heiman under myself. A courier was dispatched to me with an order to bring my command to Donelson. I ferried my troops across the Tennessee in the night, and reported with them at headquarters before noon the next day. The brigade was transferred to General Smith; at the same time an order was put into my hand assigning me to command the Third Division, which was conducted to a position between Smith and McClernand, enabling the latter to extend his line well to the left and cover the road to Charlotte.

Thus on the 14th of February the Confederates were completely invested, except that the river above Dover remained to them. The supineness of General Floyd all this while is to this day incomprehensible. A vigorous attack on the morning of the 13th might have thrown Grant back upon Fort Henry. Such an achievement would have more than offset Foote's conquest. The morale to be gained would have alone justified the attempt. But with McClernand's strong division on the right, my own in the center, and C.F. Smith's on the left, the opportunity

37

was gone. On the side of General Grant, the possession of the river was all that was wanting; with that Grant could force the fighting, or wait the certain approach of the grimmest enemy of the besieged—starvation.

It is now—morning of the 14th—easy to see and understand with something more than approximate exactness the oppositions of the two forces. Smith is on the left of the Union army opposite Buckner. My division, in the center, confronts Colonels Heiman, Drake, and Davidson, each with a brigade. McClernand, now well over on the right, keeps the road to Charlotte and Nashville against the major part of Pillow's left wing. The infantry on both sides are in cover behind the crests of the hills or in thick woods, listening to the ragged fusillade which the sharpshooters and skirmishers maintain against each other almost without intermission. There is little pause in the exchange of shells and round shot. The careful chiefs have required their men to lie down. In brief, it looks as if each party were inviting the other to begin.

These circumstances, the sharpshooting and cannonading, ugly as they may seem to one who thinks of them under comfortable surroundings, did in fact serve a good purpose the day in question in helping the men to forget their sufferings of the night before. It must be remembered that the weather had changed during the preceding afternoon: from suggestions of spring it turned to intensified winter. From lending a gentle hand in bringing Foote and his iron-clads up the river, the wind whisked suddenly around to the north and struck both armies with a storm of mixed rain, snow and sleet. All night the tempest blew mercilessly upon the unsheltered, fireless soldier, making sleep impossible. Inside the works, nobody had overcoats; while thousands of those outside had marched from Fort Henry as to a summer fete, leaving coats, blankets, and knapsacks behind them in the camp. More than one stout fellow has since admitted, with a laugh, that nothing was so helpful to him that horrible night as the thought that the wind, which seemed about to turn his blood into icicles, was serving the enemy the same way; they, too, had to stand out and take the blast. Let us now go back to the preceding day and bring up an incident of McClernand's swing into position.

About the center of the Confederate outworks there was a V-shaped hill, marked sharply by a ravine on its right and another on its left. This Colonel Heiman occupied with his brigade of five regiments—all of Tennessee but one. The front presented was about 2500 feet. In the angle of the V on the summit of the hill, Captain Maney's battery, also of Tennessee, had been planted. Without protection of any kind, it nevertheless completely swept a large field to the left, across which an assaulting force would have to come in order to get at Heimarr or at Drake, next on the south.

Maney, on the point of the hill, had been active throughout the preceding afternoon, and had succeeded in drawing the fire of some of McClernand's guns. The duel lasted until night. Next morning it was renewed with increased sharpness, Maney being assisted on his right by Graves's battery of Buckner's division, and by some pieces of Drake's on his left.

McClernand's advance was necessarily slow and trying. This was not merely a logical result of unacquaintance with the country and the dispositions of the enemy; he was also under an order from General Grant to avoid everything calculated to bring on a general engagement. In Maney's well-served guns he undoubtedly found serious annoyance, if not a positive obstruction. Concentrating guns of his own upon the industrious Confederate, he at length fancied him silenced and the enemy's infantry on the right thrown into confusion—circumstances from which he hastily deduced a favorable chance to deliver an assault. For that purpose he reënforced his Third Brigade, which was nearest the offending battery and gave the necessary orders.

Up to this time, it will be observed, there had not been any fighting involving infantry in line. This was now to be changed. Old soldiers, rich with experience, would have regarded the work proposed with gravity; they would have shrewdly cast up an account of the chances of success, not to speak of the chances of coming out alive; they would have measured the distance to be passed, every foot of it, under the guns of three batteries, Maney's in the center, Graves's on their left and Drake's on their right—a direct line of fire doubly crossed. Nor would they have omitted the reception awaiting them from the rifle-pits. They were to descend a hill entangled for two hundred yards with underbrush, climb an opposite ascent partly shorn of timber; make way through an abatis of treetops; then, supposing all that successfully accomplished, they would be at last in face of an enemy whom it was possible to reënforce with all the reserves of the garrison—with the whole garrison, if need be. A veteran would have surveyed the three regiments selected for the honorable duty with many misgivings. Not so the men themselves. They were not old soldiers. Recruited but recently from farms and shops, they accepted the assignment heartily and with youthful confidence in their prowess. It may be doubted if a man in the ranks gave a thought to the questions, whether the attack was to be supported while making, or followed up if successful, or whether it was part of a general adavnce. Probably the most they knew was that the immediate objective before them was the capture of the battery on the hill.

The line when formed stood thus from the right: the 49th Illinois, then the 17th, and then the 48th, Colonel Haynie. At the last moment, a question of seniority arose between Colonels Morrison and Haynie. The latter was of opinion that he was the ranking officer. Morrison replied that he would conduct the brigade to the point from which the attack was to be made, after which Haynie might take the command, if he so desired.

Down the hill the three regiments went, crashing and tearing through the undergrowth. Heiman, on the lookout, saw them advancing. Before they cleared the woods, Maney opened with shells. At the foot of the descent, in the valley, Graves joined his fire to Maney's. There Morrison reported to Haynie, who neither accepted nor refused the command. Pointing to the hill, he merely said, "Let us take it together." Morrison turned away and rejoined his own regiment. Here was confusion in the beginning, or worse, an assault begun without a head. Nevertheless, the whole line went forward. On a part of the hillside the trees were yet standing. The open space fell to Morrison and his 49th, and paying the penalty of the exposure, he outstripped his associates. The men fell rapidly; yet the living rushed on and up, firing as they went. The battery was the common target. Maney's gunners, in relief against the sky, were shot down in quick succession. His first lieutenant (Burns) was one of the first to suffer. His second lieutenant (Massie) was mortally wounded. Maney himself was hit; still he staid, and his guns continued their punishment; and still the farmer lads and shop boys of Illinois clung to their purpose. With marvelous audacity they pushed through the abatis and reached a point within forty yards of the rifle-pits. It actually looked as if the prize were theirs. The yell of victory was rising in their throats. Suddenly the long line of yellow breastworks before them, covering Heiman's five regiments, crackled and turned into flame. The forlorn hope stopped—staggered—braced up again—shot blindly through the smoke at the smoke of the new enemy, secure in his shelter. Thus for fifteen minutes the Illinoisans stood fighting. The time is given on the testimony of the opposing leader himself. Morrison was knocked out of his saddle by a musket-ball, and disabled; then the men went down the hill. At its foot they rallied around their flags and renewed the assault. Pushed down again, again they rallied, and a third time climbed to the enemy. This time the battery set fire to the dry leaves on the ground, and the heat and smoke became stifling. It was not possible for brave men to endure more. Slowly, sullenly, frequently pausing to return a shot, they went back for the last time; and in going their ears and souls were riven with the shrieks of their wounded comrades, whom the flames crept down upon and smothered and charred where they lay.

Considered as a mere exhibition of courage, this assault, long maintained against odds,—twice repulsed, twice renewed—has been seldom excelled. One hundred and forty-nine men of the 17th and 49th were killed and wounded. Haynie reported 1 killed and 8 wounded.

There are few things connected with the operations against Fort Donelson so relieved of uncertainty as this: that when General Grant at Fort Henry became fixed in the resolution to undertake the movement, his primary object was the capture of the force to which the post was intrusted. To effect their complete environment, he relied upon Flag-Officer Foote and his gun-boats, whose astonishing success at Fort Henry justified the extreme of confidence.

Foote arrived on the 14th, and made haste to enter upon his work. The *Carondelet* (Commander Walke) had been in position since the 12th. Behind a low output of the shore, for two days, she maintained a fire from her rifled guns, happily of greater range than the best of those of the enemy.

At 9 o'clock on the 14th, Captain Culbertson, looking from the parapet of the upper battery, beheld the river below the first bend full of transports landing troops under cover of a fresh arrival of gun-boats. The disembarkation concluded, Foote was free. He waited until noon. The captains in the batteries mistook his deliberation for timidity. The impinging of their shot on his iron armor was heard distinctly in the fort a mile and a half away. The captains began to doubt if he would come at all. But at 3 o'clock the boats took position under fire: the *Louisville* on the right, the *St. Louis* next, then the *Pittsburgh*, then the *Carondelet*, all iron-clad.

Five hundred yards from the batteries, and yet Foote was not content!

In the Crimean war the allied French and English fleets, of much mightier ships, undertook to engage the Russian short batteries, but little stronger than those at Donelson. The French on that occasion stood off 1800 yards. Lord Lyons fought his *Agamennon* at a distance of 800 yards. Foote forged ahead within 400 yards of his enemy, and was still going on. His boat had been hit between wind and water; so with the *Pittsburgh* and *Carondelet*. About the guns the floors were slippery with blood, and both surgeons and carpenters were never so busy. Still the four boats kept on, and there was great cheering; for not only did the fire from the shore slacken; the lookouts reported the enemy running. It seemed that fortune would smile once more upon the fleet, and cover the honors of Fort Henry afresh at Fort Donelson. Unhappily, when about 350 yards off the hill a solid shot plunged through the pilot-house of the flagship, and carried away the wheel. Near the same time the tiller-ropes of the *Louisville* were disabled. Both vessels became unmanageable and began floating down the current. The eddies turned them round like logs. The *Pittsburgh* and *Carondelet* closed in and covered them with their hulls.

Seeing this turn in the fight, the captains of the batteries rallied their men, who cheered in their turn, and renewed the contest with increased will and energy. A ball got lodged in their best rifle. A corporal and some of his men took a log fitting the bore, leaped out on the parapet, and rammed the missile home. "Now boys," said a gunner on Bidwell's battery, "see me take a chimney!" The flag of the boat and the chimney fell with the shot.

When the vessels were out of range, the victors looked about them. The fine form of their embrasures was gone; heaps of earth had been cast over their platforms. In a space of twenty-four feet they had picked up as many shot and shells. The air had been full of flying missiles. For an hour and a half the brave fellows had been rained upon; yet their losses had been trifling in numbers. Each gunner had selected a ship and followed her faithfully throughout the action, now and then uniting fire on the *Carondelet*. The Confederates had behaved with astonishing valor. Their victory sent a thrill of joy through the army. The assault on the outworks, the day before, had been a failure. With the repulse of the gun-boats the Confederates scored success number two, and the communication by the river remained open to Nashville. The winds that blew sleet and snow over Donelson that night were not so unendurable as they might have been.

The night of the 14th of February fell cold and dark, and under the pitiless sky the armies remained in position so near to each other that neither dared light fires. Overpowered with watching, fatigue, and the lassitude of spirits which always follows a strain upon the faculties of men like that which is the concomitant of battle, thousands on both sides lay down in the ditches and behind logs and whatever else would in the least shelter them from the cutting wind, and tried to sleep. Very few closed their eyes. Even the horses, after their manner, betrayed the suffering they were enduring.

That morning General Floyd had called a council of his chiefs of brigades and division. He expressed the opinion that the post was untenable, except with fifty thousand troops. He called attention to the heavy reënforcements of the Federals, and suggested an immediate attack upon their right wing to reopen land communication with Nashville, by way of Charlotte. The proposal was agreed to unanimously. General Buckner proceeded to make dispositions to cover the retreat, in the event the sortie should be successful. Shortly after noon, when the movement should have begun, the order was countermanded at the instance of Pillow. Then came the battle with the gun-boats.

In the night the council was recalled, with general and regimental officers in attendance. The situation was again debated, and the same conclusion reached. Accordingly to the plan resolved upon, Pillow was to move at dawn with his whole division, and attack the right of the besiegers. General Buckner was to be relieved by troops in the forts, and with his command to support Pillow by assailing the right of the enemy's center. If he succeeded, he was to take post outside the intrenchments on the Wynne's Ferry road to cover the retreat. He was then to act as rear-guard. Thus early, leaders in Donelson were aware of the mistake into which they were plunged. Their resolution was wise and heroic. Let us see how they executed it.

Preparations for the attack occupied the night. The troops for the most part were taken out of the riflepits and massed over on the left to the number of ten thousand or more. The ground was covered with ice and snow; yet the greatest silence was observed. It seems incomprehensible that columns mixed of all arms, infantry, cavalry, and artillery, could have engaged in simultaneous movement, and not have been heard by some listener outside. One would think the jolting and rumble of the heavy gun-carriages would have told the story. But the character of the night must be remembered. The pickets of the Federals were struggling for life against the blast, and probably did not keep good watch.

Oglesby's brigade held McClernand's extreme right. Here and there the musicians were beginning to make the woods ring with reveille, and the numbed soldiers of the line were rising from their icy beds and shaking the snow from their frozen garments. As yet, however, not a company had "fallen in." Suddenly the pickets fired, and with the alarm on their lips rushed back upon their comrades. The woods on the instant became alive.

The regiments formed, officers mounted and took their places; words of command rose loud and eager. By the time Pillow's advance opened fire on Oglesby's right, the point first struck, the latter was fairly formed to receive it. A rapid exchange of volleys ensued. The distance intervening between the works on one side and the bivouac on the other was so short that the action began before Pillow could effect a deployment. His brigades came up in a kind of echelon, left in front, and passed "by regiments left into line," one by one, however; the regiments quickly took their places, and advanced without halting. Oglesby's Illinoisians were now fully awake. They held their ground, returning in full measure the fire that they received. The Confederate Forrest rode around as if to get in their rear, and it was then give and take, infantry against infantry. The semi-echelon movement of the Confederates enabled them, after an interval, to strike W.H.L. Wallace's brigade, on Oglesby's left. Soon Wallace was engaged along his whole front, now prolonged by the addition to his command of Morrison's regiments. The first charge against him was repulsed; whereupon he advanced to the top of the rising ground behind which he had sheltered his troops in the night. A fresh assault followed, but, aided by a battery across the valley to his left, he repulsed the enemy a second time. His men were steadfast, and clung to the brow of the hill as if it were theirs by holy right. An hour passed, and yet another hour, without cessation of the fire. Meantime the woods rang with a monstrous clangor of musketry as if a million men were beating empty barrels with iron hammers.

Buckner flung a portion of his division on McClernand's left, and supported the attack with his artillery. The enfilading fell chiefly on W.H.L. Wallace. McClernand, watchful and full of resources, sent batteries to meet Buckner's batteries. To that duty Taylor rushed with his Company B; and McAllister pushed his three 24-pounders into position and exhausted his ammunition in the duel. The roar never slackened. Men fell by the score, reddening the snow with their blood. The smoke, in pallid white clouds, clung to the underbrush and tree-tops as if to screen the combatants from each other. Close to the ground the flame of musketry and cannon tinted everything a lurid red. Limbs dropped from the trees on the heads below and the thickets were shorn as by an army of cradlers. The division was under peremptory orders to hold its position to the last extremity and Colonel Wallace was equal to the emergency.

It was now 10 o'clock, and over on the right Oglesby was beginning to fare badly. The pressure on his front grew stronger. The "rebel yell," afterward a familiar battlecry on many fields, told of ground being gained against him. To add to his doubts, officers were riding to him with a sickening story that their commands were getting out of ammunition, and asking where they could go to a supply. All he could say was to take what was in the boxes of the dead and wounded. At last he realized that the end was come. His right companies began to give way and as they retreated, holding up their empty cartridge-boxes, the enemy were emboldened, and swept more fiercely around his flank, until finally they appeared in his rear. He then gave the order to retire the division.

W.H.L. Wallace from his position looked off to his right and saw but one regiment of Oglesby's in place, maintaining the fight, and that was John A. Logan's 31st Illinois. Through the smoke he could see Logan riding in a gallop behind his line; through the roar in his front and the rising yell in his rear, he could hear Logan's voice in fierce entreaty to his "boys." Near the 31st stood W.H.L. Wallace's regiment, the 11th Illinois, under Lieutenant-Colonel Ransom. The gaps in the ranks of the two were closed up always toward the colors. The ground at their feet was strewn with their dead and wounded; at length the common misfortune overtook Logan. To keep men without cartridges under fire sweeping them front and flank would be cruel, if not impossible; and seeing it, he too gave the order to retire, and followed his decimated companies to the rear. The 11th then became the right of the brigade, and had to go in turn. Nevertheless, Ransom changed front to rear coolly, as if on parade, and joined in the general retirement. Forrest charged them and threw them into a brief conclusion. The greater portion clung to their colors, and made good their retreat. By 11 o'clock Pillow held the road to Charlotte and the whole of the position occupied at dawn by the First

Division, and with it the dead and all the wounded who could not get away.

Pillow's part of the programme, arranged in the council of the night before, was accomplished. The country was once more open to Floyd. Why did he not avail himself of the dearly bought opportunity and march his army out?

Without pausing to consider whether the Confederate general could now have escaped with his troops, it must be evident that he should have made the effort. Pillow had discharged his duty well. With the disappearance of W.H.L. Wallace's brigade, it only remained for the victor to deploy his regiments into column and march into the country. The road was his. Buckner was in position to protect Colonel Head's withdrawal from the trenches opposite General Smith on the right; that done, he was also in position to cover the retreat. Buckner had also faithfully performed his task.

On the Union side the situation at this critical time was favorable to the proposed retirement. My division in the center was weakened by the dispatch of one of my brigades to the assistance of General McClernand; in addition to which my orders were to hold my position. As a point of still greater importance, General Grant had gone on board the *St. Louis* at the request of Flag-Officer Foote, and he was there in consultation with that officer, presumably uninformed of the disaster which had befallen his right. It would take a certain time for him to return to the field and dispose his forces for pursuit. It may be said with strong assurance, consequently, that Floyd could have put his men fairly *en route* for Charlotte before the Federal commander could have interposed an obstruction to the movement. The real difficulty was in the hero of the morning, who now made haste to blight his laurels. General Pillow's vanity whistled itself into ludicrous exultation. Imagining General Grant's whole army defeated and fleeing in rout for Fort Henry and the transports on the river, he deported himself accordingly. He began by ignoring Floyd. He rode to Buckner and accused him of shameful conduct. He sent an aide to the nearest telegraph station with a dispatch to Albert Sidney Johnston, then in command of the Department, asseverating, "on the honor of a soldier," that the day was theirs. Nor did he stop at that. The victory, to be available, required that the enemy should be followed with energy. Such was a habit of Napoleon. Without deigning even to consult his chief, he ordered Buckner to move out and attack the Federals. There was a gorge, up which a road ran toward our central position, or rather what had been our central position. Pointing to the gorge and the road, he told Buckner that was his way and bade him attack in force. There was nothing to do but obey; and when Buckner had begun the movement, the wise programme decided upon the evening before was wiped from the slate.

When Buckner reluctantly took the gorge road marked out for him by Pillow, the whole Confederate army, save the detachments on the works, was virtually in pursuit of McClernand, retiring by the Wynn's Ferry road—falling back, in fact, upon my position. My division was now to feel the weight of Pillow's hand; if they should fail, the fortunes of the day would depend upon the veteran Smith.

When General McClernand perceived the peril threatening him in the morning, he sent an officer to me with a request for assistance. This request I referred to General Grant, who was at the time in consultation with Foote. Upon the turning of Oglesby's flank, McClernand repeated his request, with such a representation of the situation that, assuming the responsibility, I ordered Colonel Cruft to report with his brigade to McClernand. Cruft set out promptly. Unfortunately a guide misdirected him, so that he became involved in the retreat, and was prevented from accomplishing his object.

I was in the rear of my single remaining brigade, in conversation with Captain Rawlins, of Grant's staff, when a great shouting was heard behind me on the Wynn's Ferry road, whereupon I sent an orderly to ascertain the cause. The man reported the road and woods full of soldiers apparently in rout. An officer then rode by at full speed, shouting, "All's lost! Save yourselves!" A hurried consultation was had with Rawlins, at the end of which the brigade was put in motion toward the enemy's works, on the very road by which Buckner was pursuing under Pillow's mischievous order. It happened also that Colonel W.H.L. Wallace had dropped into the same road with such of his command as staid by their colors. He came up riding and at a walk, his leg over the horn of his saddle. He was perfectly cool, and looked like a farmer from a hard day's plowing. "Good-morning," I said. "Good-morning," was the reply. "Are they pursuing you?" "Yes," "How far are they behind?" That instant the head of my command appeared on the road. The colonel calculated, then answered: "You will have about time to form line of battle right here." "Thank you. Good-day." "Good-day."

At that point the road began to dip into the gorge; on the right and left there were woods, and in front a dense thicket. An order was dispatched to bring Battery A forward at full speed. Colonel John A. Thayer, commanding the brigade, formed it on the doublequick into line; the 1st Nebraska and the 58th Illinois on the right, and the 58th Ohio, with a detached company on the left. The battery came up on the run and swung across the road, which had been left open for it. Hardly had it unlimbered, before the enemy appeared, and firing began. For ten minutes or thereabouts the scenes of the morning were reënacted. The Confederates struggled hard to perfect their deployments. The woods rang with musketry and artillery. The brush on the slope of the hill was mowed away with bullets. A great cloud arose and shut out the woods and the narrow valley below. Colonel Thayer and his regiments behaved with great gallantry and the assailants fell back in confusion and returned to the intrenchments. W.H.L. Wallace and Oglesby reformed their commands behind Thayer, supplied them with ammunition, and stood at rest waiting for orders. There was then a lull in the battle. Even the cannonading ceased, and everybody was asking, What next?

Just then General Grant rode up to where General McClernand and I were in conversation. He was almost unattended. In his hand there were some papers, which looked like telegrams. Wholly unexcited, he saluted and received the salutations of his subordinates. Proceeding at once to business, he directed them to retire their commands to the heights out of cannon range, and throw up works. Reënforcements were en route, he said, and it was advisable to await their coming. He was then informed of the mishap to the First Division, and that the road to Charlotte was open to the enemy.

In every great man's career there is a crisis exactly similar to that which now overtook General Grant, and it cannot be better described than as a crucial test of his nature. A mediocre person would have accepted the news as an argument for persistence in his resolution to enter upon a siege. Had General Grant done so, it is very probable his history would have been then and there concluded. His admirers and detractors are alike invited to study him at this precise juncture. It cannot be doubted that he saw with painful distinctness the effect of the disaster to his right wing. His face flushed slightly. With a sudden grip he crushed the papers in his hand. But in an instant these signs of disappointment or hesitation—as the reader pleases—cleared away. In his ordinary quiet voice he said, addressing himself to both officers, "Gentlemen, the position on the right must be retaken." With that he turned and galloped off.

Seeing in the road a provisional brigade, under Colonel Morgan L. Smith, consisting of the 11th Indiana and the 8th Missouri Infantry, going, by order of General C.F. Smith, to the aid of the First Division, I suggested that if General McClernand would order Colonel Smith to report to me, I would attempt to recover the lost ground; and the order having been given, I reconnoitered the hill, determined upon a place of assault, and arranged my order of attack. I chose Colonel Smith's regiments to lead, and for that purpose conducted them to the crest of a hill opposite a steep bluff covered by the enemy. The two regiments had been formerly of my brigade. I knew they had been admirably drilled in the Zouave tactics, and my confidence in Smith and in George F. McGinnis, colonel of the 11th, was implicit. I was sure they would take their men to the top of the bluff. Colonel Cruft was put in line to support them on the right. Colonel Ross, with his regiments, the 175th and 49th, and the 46th, 57th, and 58th Illinois, were put as support on the left. Thayer's brigade was held in reserve. These dispositions filled the time till about 2 o'clock in the afternoon, when heavy cannonading, mixed with a long roll of musketry, broke out over on the left, whither it will be necessary to transfer the reader.

The veteran in command on the Union left had contented himself with allowing Buckner no rest, keeping up a continual sharp-shooting. Early in the morning of the 14th he made a demonstration of assault with three of his regiments, and though he purposely withdrew them, he kept the menace standing, to the great discomfort of his *vis-à-vis*. With the patience of an old soldier, he waited the pleasure of the general commanding, knowing that when the time came he would be called upon. During the battle of the gunboats he rode through his command and grimly joked with them. He who never permitted the slightest familiarity from a subordinate, could yet indulge in fatherly pleasantries with the ranks when he thought circumstances justified them. He never for a moment doubted the courage of volunteers; they were not regulars—that was all. If properly led, he believed they would storm the gates of his Satanic Majesty. Their hour of trial was now come.

From his brief and characteristic conference with McClernand and myself, General Grant rode to General C.F. Smith. What took place between them is not known, further than that he ordered an assault upon the outworks as a diversion in aid of the assault about to be delivered on the right. General Smith personally directed his chiefs of brigade to get their regiments ready. Colonel John Cook by his order increased the number of his skirmishers already engaged with the enemy.

Taking Lauman's brigade, General Smith began the advance. They were under fire instantly. The guns in the fort joined in with the infantry who were at the time in the rifle-pits, the great body of the Confederate right wing being with General Buckner. The defense was greatly favored by the ground, which subjected the assailants to a double fire from the beginning of the abatis. The men have said that "it looked too thick for a rabbit to get through." General Smith, on his horse, took position in the front and center of the line. Occasionally he turned in the saddle to see how the alignment was kept. For the most part, he held his face steadily toward the enemy. He was, of course, a conspicuous object for the sharp-shooters in the rifle-pits. The air around him twittered with minie-bullets. Erect as if on review, he rode on, timing the gait of his horse with the movement of his colors. A soldier said: "I was nearly scared to death, but I saw the old man's white moustache over his shoulder, and went on."

On to the abatis the regiments moved without hesitation, leaving a trail of dead and wounded behind. There the fire seemed to get trebly hot, and there some of the men halted, whereupon, seeing the hesitation, General Smith put his cap on the point of his sword, held it aloft, and called out, "No flinching now my lads!—Here—this is the way! Come on!" He picked a path through the jagged limbs of the trees, holding his cap all the time in sight; and the effect was magical. The men swarmed in after him, and got through in the best order they could—not all of them, alas! On the other side of the obstruction they took the semblance of re-formation and charged in after their chief, who found himself then between the two fires. Up the ascent he rode; up they followed. At the last moment the keepers of the rifle-pits clambered out and fled. The four regiments engaged in the feat—the 25th Indiana, and the 2d, 7th, and 14th Iowa—planted their colors on the breastwork. Later in the day, Buckner came back with his division; but all his efforts to dislodge Smith were vain.

We left my division about to attempt the recapture of the hill, which had been the scene of the combat between Pillow and McClernand. If only on account of the results which followed that assault, in connection with the heroic performance of General C.F. Smith, it is necessary to return to it.

Riding to my old regiments,—the 8th Missouri and the 11th Indiana,—I asked them if they were ready. They demanded the word of me. Waiting a moment for Morgan L. Smith to light a cigar, I called out, "Forward it is, then!" They were directly in front of the ascent to be climbed. Without stopping for his supports, Colonel Smith led them down into a broad hollow and catching sight of the advance, Cruft and Ross also moved forward. As the two regiments began the climb, the 8th Missouri slightly in the lead, a line of fire ran along the brow of the height. The flank companies cheered while deploying as skirmishers. Their Zouave practice proved of excellent service to them. Now on the ground, creeping when the fire was hottest, running when it slackened, they gained ground with astonishing rapidity and at the same time maintained a fire that was like a sparkling of the earth. For the most part the bullets aimed at them passed over their heads and took effect in the ranks behind them. Colonel Smith's cigar was shot off close to his lips. He took another and called for a match. A soldier ran and gave him one. "Thank you. Take your place now. We are almost up," he said, and, smoking, spurred his horse forward. A few yards from the crest of the height the regiments began loading and firing as they advanced. The defenders gave way. On the top there was a brief struggle, which was ended by Cruft and Ross with their supports.

The whole line then moved forward simultaneously, and never stopped until the Confederates were within the works. There had been no occasion to call on the reserves. The road to Charlotte was again effectually shut, and the battle-field of the morning, with the dead and wounded lying where they had fallen, was in possession of the Third Division, which stood halted within easy musket-range of the rifle-pits. It was then about half-past 3 o'clock in the afternoon. I was reconnoitering the works of the enemy preliminary to charging them, when Colonel Webster, of General Grant's staff, came to me and repeated the order to fall back out of cannon range and throw up breastworks. "The general does not know that we have the hill," I said. Webster replied: "I give you the order as he gave it to me." "Very well," said I, "give him my compliments, and say that I have received the order." Webster smiled and rode away. The ground was not vacated, though the assault was deferred. In assuming the responsibility I had no doubt of my ability to satisfy General Grant of the correctness of my course; and it was subsequently approved.

When night fell, the command bivouacked without fire or supper. Fatigue parties were told off to look after the wounded; and in the relief given there was no distinction made between friend and foe. The labor extended through the whole night, and the surgeons never rested. By sunset the conditions of the morning were all restored. The Union commander was free to order a general assault next day or resort to a formal siege.

A great discouragement fell upon the brave men inside the works that night. Besides suffering from wounds and bruises and the dreadful weather, they were aware that though they had done their best they were held in a close grip by a superior enemy. A council of general and field officers was held at headquarters, which resulted in a unanimous resolution that if the position in front of General Pillow had not been reoccupied by the Federals in strength, the army should effect its retreat. A reconnoissance was ordered to make the test. Colonel Forrest conducted it. He reported that the ground was not only reoccupied, but that the enemy were extended yet farther around the Confederate left. The council then held a final session.

General Simon B. Buckner, as the junior officer present, gave his opinion first; he thought he could not successfully resist the assault which would be made by daylight by a vastly superior force. But he further remarked, that as he understood the principal object of the defense of Donelson was to cover the movement of General Albert Sidney Johnston's army from Bowling Green to Nashville, if that movement was not completed he was of opinion that the defense should be continued at the risk of the destruction of the entire force. General Floyd replied that General Johnston's army had already reached Nashville, whereupon General Buckner said that "it would be wrong to subject the army to a virtual massacre, when no good could result from the sacrifice, and that the general officers owed it to their men, when further resistance was unvailing, to obtain the best terms of capitulation possible for them."

Both Generals Floyd and Pillow acquiesced in the opinion. Ordinarily the council would have ended at this point, and the commanding general would have addressed himself to the duty of obtaining terms. He would have called for pen, ink, and paper, and prepared a note for dispatch to the commanding general of the opposite force. But there were circumstances outside the mere military situation which at this juncture pressed themselves into consideration. As this was the first surrender of armed men banded together for war upon the general government, what would the Federal authorities do with the prisoners? This question was of application to all the gentlemen in the council. It was lost to view, however, when General Floyd announced his purpose to leave with two steamers which were to be down at daylight, and to take with him as many of his division as the steamers could carry away.

General Pillow then remarked that there were no two persons in the Confederacy whom the Yankees would rather capture than himself and General Floyd (who had been Buchanan's Secretary of War, and was under indictment at Washington). As to the propriety of his accompanying General Floyd, the latter said, coolly, that the question was one for every man to decide for himself. Buckner was of the same view and added that as for himself he regarded it as his duty to stay with his men and share their fate, whatever it might be. Pillow persisted in leaving. Floyd then directed General Buckner to consider himself in command. Immediately after the council was concluded, General Floyd prepared for his departure. His first move was to have his brigade drawn up. The peculiarity of the step was that, with the exception of one, the 20th Mississippi regiment, his regiments were all Virginians. A short time before daylight the two steamboats arrived. Without loss of time the general hastened to the river, embarked with his Virginians, and at an early hour cast loose from the shore, and in good time, and safely, he reached Nashville. He never satisfactorily explained upon what principle he appropriated all the transportation on hand to the use of his particular command.

Colonel Forrest was present at the council, and when the final resolution was taken, he promptly announced that he neither could nor would surrender his command. The bold trooper had no qualms upon the subject. He assembled his men, all as hardy as himself, and after reporting once more at headquarters, he moved out and plunged into a slough formed by backwater from the river. An icy crust covered its surface, the wind blew fiercely and the darkness was unrelieved by a star. There was fearful floundering as the command followed him. At length he struck dry land, and was safe. He was next heard of at Nashville.

General Buckner, who throughout the affair bore himself with dignity, ordered the troops back to their positions and opened communications with General Grant, whose laconic demand of "unconditional surren-der," in his reply to General Buckner's overtures, became at once a watchword of the war.

The Third Division was astir very early on the 16th of February. The regiments began to form and close up the intervals between them, the intention being to charge the breastworks south of Dover about break-fast-time. In the midst of the preparation a bugle was heard and a white flag was seen coming from the town toward the pickets. I sent my adjutant general to meet the flag halfway and inquire its purpose. Answer was returned that General Buckner had capitulated during the night, and was now sending information of the fact to the commander of the troops in this quarter, that there might be no further bloodshed. The division was ordered to advance and take possession of the works and of all public property and prisoners. Leaving that agreeable duty to the brigade commanders, I joined the officer bearing the flag, and with my staff rode across the trench and into the town, till we came to the door of the old tavern already described, where I dismounted. The tavern was the headquarters of General Buckner, to whom I sent my name; and being an acquaintance, I was at once admitted.

I found General Buckner with his staff at breakfast. He met me with politeness and dignity. Turning to the officers at the table, he remarked: "General Wallace, it is not necessary to introduce you to these gentlemen; you are acquainted with them all." They arose, came forward one by one, and gave their hands in salutation. I was then invited to breakfast, which consisted of corn bread and coffee, the best the gallant host had in his kitchen. We sat at the table about an hour and a half, when General Grant arrived and took temporary possession of the tavern as his headquarters. Later in the morning the army marched in and completed the possession.

Chapter II

PEA RIDGE

While certainly not ranking among the better known battles of the Civil War, Pea Ridge was one of the greatest fights west of the Mississippi River. The action took place on 7-8 March 1862 between a Federal army of 11,000 under Brigadier General Samuel R. Curtis and Confederate forces numbering some 16,000 troops commanded by Major-General Earl Van Dorn. After this bitter struggle in Northern Arkansas, Van Dorn's army was forced to retreat and surrender Missouri forever to the Union.

DABNEY H. MAURY

Bloody Arkansas

Dabney Herndon Maury, who hailed from Virginia, attained the rank of colonel and served as chief of staff to Earl Van Dorn during the Pea Ridge Campaign. After the war, he was noted for founding the Southern Historical Society. This abridged selection on his close relationship with Van Dorn and the battle of Pea Ridge, or Elk Horn Tavern, was originally published in the *Southern Society Historical Papers* under the title "Recollections of Earl Van Dorn."

General Earl Van Dorn was, in the opinion of the writer, the most remarkable man the State of Mississippi has ever known. My acquaintance with him began in Monterey in the fall of 1846. He was aide-de-camp then to General Persifor F. Smith, and was one of the most attractive young fellows in the army. He used to ride a beautiful bay Andalusian horse, and as he came galloping along the lines, with his yellow hair waving in the wind and his bright face lighted with kindliness and courage, we all loved to see him. His figure was lithe and graceful; his stature did not exceed five feet six inches; but his clear blue eyes, his firm-set mouth, with white, strong teeth, his well-cut nose, with expanding nostrils, gave assurance of a man whom men could trust and follow. No young officer came out of the Mexican war with a reputation more enviable than his. After the close of that war he resumed his duties and position in the infantry regiment of which he was a lieutenant.

In 1854 the Second Cavalry was organized, and Van Dorn was promoted to be the major of the regiment. He conducted several of the most important and successful expeditions against the Comanches we have ever made, and in one of them was shot through the body, the point of the arrow just protruding through the skin. No surgeon was at hand. Van Dorn, reflecting that to withdraw the arrow would leave the barbed head in his body, thrust it on through, and left the surgeon little to do.

When the States resumed their State sovereignty he took a bold and efficient part in securing to Texas, where he was serving, all of the war material within her borders. Early in the war he was ordered to join the army under General Joe Johnston at Manassas; whence soon after, in February 1861, he was ordered to take command of the Trans-Mississippi Department.

I was associated with him in this command as chief of his staff and saw him daily for many months. He had conceived the bold project of capturing St. Louis and transferring the war into Illinois, and was actively engaged in preparing for this enterprise when he was summoned by General Price to Boston mountain, where the forces of Price and McCulloch lay in great need of a common superior—for these two generals could not cooperate because of questions of rank. Therefore, Van Dorn promptly responded to Price's summons, and in a few hours was in the saddle and on his way to Van Buren. I went with him, and one aide-de-camp, an orderly and my servant man Jem made up our party. Van Dorn rode a fine thoroughbred black mare he had brought from Virginia. I was mounted on a sorrel I had bought in Pocahontas a few hours before we set out. Except my sorrel mare, Van Dorn's black mare was the hardest trotter in the world, and as we trotted fifty-five miles every day for five or six days, we had a very unusual opportunity of learning all that a hard trotter can do to a man in a long day's march. Had it not been that we slept every night in a feather bed that soothed our sore bones and served as a poultice to our galled saddle pieces, we would have been permanently disabled for cavalry service forever.

My boy Jem alone enjoyed that trip. He rode in the ambulance all day and slept *ad libitum* day and night; and except when he got a ducking by the upsetting of a canoe in Black river, he was as happy as ever he had been since the last herring season on the Potomac. The battle of Elkhorn disturbed Jem's equilibrium even more than the upsetting of the canoe. The excitement of imminent danger, which was never a pleasing emotion to Jem, was kept up at Elkhorn much longer than in Black river, and I could not find him for three days—not, indeed, until we accidentally met on the route of our retreat, when I must say he showed great delight at "meeting up" with me again, and took to himself no little credit for the skill with which he had conducted the movements of that ambulance for the past three days. It had contained all of our clothing and blankets and camp supplies, of no little value to hungry and wearied warriors. The blankets and clothing were all right, but we found nothing whatever for the inner man. Jem was cheerful and cordial and comfortable, but we never could ascertain where he had the ambulance from the time the first shot was fired, until the moment we encountered him in full retreat, and with the last sound of the battle died out in the distance behind him.

Van Dorn had planned the battle of Elkhorn well; he had moved so rapidly from Boston mountain with the forces of Price and McCulloch combined that he caught the enemy unprepared, and with his division so far separated that but for the inevitable indiscipline of troops so hastily thrown together he would have destroyed the whole Federal army. By the loss of thirty minutes in reaching Bentonville we lost the cutting off of Siegel [Sigel] with seven thousand men, who were hurrying to join the main body on Sugar creek. But we pushed him hard all that day, and after he had closed upon the main body Van Dorn, leaving a small force to occupy the attention in front, threw his army, by a night march, quite around the Federal army and across their only road by which retreat to Missouri could be effected. He handled his forces well; always attacking, always pressing the enemy back. When he heard of the death in quick succession of the three principal commanders of his right wing—McCulloch, McIntosh and Hebert—and the consequent withdrawal from the attack of that whole wing, he only set his lips a little firmer; his blue eyes blazed brighter, and his nostrils looked wider, as he said: "Then we must press them the harder." And he did, too, and he had everything moving finely by sundown, and all the enemy's line before us in full retreat at a run, and falling back into their wagon trains; when, by misapprehension on the part of the commander with our advanced troops, the pursuit was arrested, our forces withdrawn from the attack to go into bivouac, and the enemy was permitted to quietly reorganize his army and prepare for a combined attack upon us in the morning. During the night we found that most of our batteries and regiments had exhausted their ammunition, and the ordnance train, with all the reserve ammunition, had been sent away, fifteen miles back, on the road along which we had come, and the enemy lay between. There was nothing left for Van Dorn but to get his train on the road to Van Buren and his army off by the same route and to fight enough to secure them. This he did, and marched away unmolested.

Arrived at Van Buren, Van Dorn addressed himself to the completion of the reorganization of his army, thenceforth known as the Army of the

West, and it was there he gave an illustration of true magnanimity—very rarely known in ambitious men—by the offer he made to move with all his forces to reënforce General Sidney Johnston at Corinth. By this he surrendered the great independent command of the Trans-Mississippi Department and all the plans he had formed for the sake of his views of the best interests of their common country, and became a subordinate commander of an army corps instead of the commander-in-chief of an army. He hoped to reach Johnston in time for the battle in Shiloh, and had he done so, would have given a very different result to that critical battle. But Shiloh had been fought and our army, under Beauregard, was occupying the works of Corinth when Van Dorn, with the Army of the West, sixteen thousand effectives, reached that point. We lay near Corinth more than six weeks, and three times offered battle to Halleck, who, with one hundred thousand men, was cautiously advancing as if to attack us. Three times our army (forty thousand strong) marched out of its entrenchments and advanced to meet Halleck and give him battle, but every time he drew back and declined it. In every council Van Dorn's voice was for war. May 30, 1862, Beauregard evacuated his works in a masterly manner, and marched south unmolested to Tupelo, when he halted the army and held it ready for battle. In June Van Dorn was ordered to go to Vicksburg, which was threatened with attack, and was in poor condition for defence. He evinced here great energy and ability. He repulsed the enemy's fleet, put the place in a good condition of defense, occupied Port Hudson, and there erected such works as enabled us for a year longer to control the Mississippi river and its tributaries so as to keep open free intercourse with the trans-Mississippi, whence large supplies for the armies on this side were drawn. He organized an expedition against Baton Rouge during this time, which but for the cholera, which swept off half of the force, and the untimely breaking down of the ram Arkansas' engine when almost within range of that town, would have been a brilliant and complete success.

After this Van Dorn urged General Price, who had been left at Tupelo with the Army of the West when Bragg moved to Chattanooga, to unite all their available forces in Mississippi, carry Corinth by assault, and sweep the enemy out of West Tennessee. This, unfortunately, Price, under his instructions, could not then do. Our combined forces would then have exceeded twenty-five thousand effectives, and there is no doubt as to the results of the movement. Later, after Breckenridge had been detached with six thousand men and Price had lost about four thousand on the Iuka expedition (mainly stragglers), the attempt on Corinth was made. Its works had been greatly strengthened and its garrison greatly increased. Van Dorn attacked with his usual vigor and dash. His left and centre stormed the town, captured all the guns in their front and broke Rosecrans' centre. The division comprising our right wing remained inactive, so that the enemy, believing that our right was merely making a feint, detached Stanley with six thousand fresh men from his left and drove us out of the town.

Never was a general more disappointed than Van Dorn; but no man in all our army was so little shaken in his courage by the result as he was. I think his was the highest courage I have ever known. It rose above every disaster, and he never looked more gallant than when his broken army in utter disorder was streaming through the open woods which then environed Corinth and its formidable defenses. However much depression all of us showed and felt, he alone remained unconquered, and if he could have gotten his forces together would have tried it again. But seeing that was impossible, he brought Lovell's Division, which not having assaulted was unbroken, to cover the rear, and moved back to Chewalla, seven miles west of Corinth, encouraging officers and men to reform their broken organizations as we marched along.

Chapter III

SHILOH

While the Federal disaster of First Bull Run served as a harbinger that the Civil War would not be a brief affair, Shiloh proved what the true cost of modern war would be. Forced out of Missouri, Kentucky, and losing Tennessee, the commander of Confederate forces in the West, Albert Sidney Johnston, concentrated the troops under his command to surprise Grant's isolated command at Pittsburg Landing and Shiloh Church in southwestern Tennessee on 6 April 1862. Grant's army was able to hold the Confederates off until reënforcements arrived, and routed the attackers the next day. At least 13,047 Federals were lost while the Confederates suffered 10,699 casualties, a horrific toll by any standards. Among the Southern dead was one of the most promising Confederate commanders in the Western Theatre, Albert Sidney Johnston.

U.S. GRANT

Shiloh

After the fall of Forts Henry and Donelson, U.S. Grant embarked on what would become a triumphant military career. However, shortly after these victories he was surprised by the Confederate attack on his encampment at Pittsburg Landing. A major defeat here could have led to his removal from command. Another officer caught off guard by the sudden assault was William Tecumseh Sherman, who commanded a division in Grant's Army of the Tennessee. Had events turned differently, both officers probably would have been cashiered and their essential services lost to the Union cause. After the war, Grant authored his reminiscences entitled *Personal Memories of U.S. Grant* from which this selection is taken.

When I reassumed command on the 17th of March I found the army divided, about half being on the east bank of the Tennessee at Savannah, while one division was at Crump's landing on the west bank about four miles higher up, and the remainder at Pittsburg Landing, five miles above Crump's. The enemy was in force at Corinth, the junction of the two most important railroads in the Mississippi valley—one connecting Memphis and the Mississippi River with the East, and the other leading south to all the cotton states. Still another railroad connects Corinth with Jackson, in west Tennessee. If we obtained possession of Corinth the enemy would have no railroad for the transportation of armies or supplies until that running east from Vicksburg was reached. It was the great strategic position at the West between the Tennessee and the Mississippi rivers and between Nashville and Vicksburg.

I at once put all the troops at Savannah in motion for Pittsburg Landing, knowing that the enemy was fortifying at Corinth and collecting an army there under Johnston. It was my expectation to march against that army as soon as Buell, who had been ordered to reënforce me with the Army of the Ohio, should arrive; and the west bank of the river was the place to start from. Pittsburg is only about twenty miles from Corinth, and Hamburg landing, four miles further up the river, is a mile or two nearer. I had not been in command long before I selected Hamburg as the place to put the Army of the Ohio when it arrived. The roads from Pittsburg and Hamburg to Corinth converge some eight miles out. This disposition of the troops would have given additional roads to march over when the advance commenced, within supporting distance of each other.

Before I arrived at Savannah, Sherman, who had joined the Army of the Tennessee and been placed in command of a division, had made an expedition on steamers convoyed by gunboats to the neighborhood of Eastport, thirty miles south, for the purpose of destroying the railroad east of Corinth. The rains had been so heavy for some time before that the lowlands had become impassable swamps. Sherman debarked his troops and started out to accomplish the object of the expedition; but the river was rising so rapidly that the back-water up the small tributaries threatened to cut off the possibility of getting back to the boats, and the expedition had to return without reaching the railroad. The guns had to be hauled by hand through the water to get back to the boats.

On the 17th of March the army on the Tennessee River consisted of five divisions, commanded respectively by Generals C.F. Smith, McClernand, L. Wallace, Hurlbut and Sherman. General W.H.L. Wallace was temporarily in command of Smith's division, General Smith, as I have said, being confined to his bed. Reënforcements were arriving daily and as they came up they were organized, first into brigades, then into a division, and the command given to General Prentiss, who had been ordered to report to me. General Buell was on his way from Nashville with 40,000 veterans. On the 19th of March he was at Columbia, Tennessee, eighty-five miles from Pittsburg. When all reënforcements should have arrived I expected to take the initiative by marching on Corinth, and had no expectation of needing fortifications, though this subject was taken into consideration. McPherson, my only military engineer, was directed to lay out a line to intrench. He did so, but reported that it would have to be made in rear of the line of encampment as it then ran. The new line, while it would be nearer the river, was yet too far away from the Tennessee, or even from the creeks, to be easily supplied with water, and in case of attack these creeks would be in the hands of the enemy. The fact is, I regarded the campaign we were engaged in as an offensive one and had no idea that the enemy would leave strong intrenchments to take the initiative when he knew he would be attacked where he was if he remained. This view, however, did not prevent every precaution being taken and every effort made to keep advised of all movements of the enemy.

Johnston's cavalry meanwhile had been well out towards our front, and occasional encounters occurred between it and our outposts. On the 1st of April this cavalry became bold and approached our lines, showing that an advance of some kind was contemplated. On the 2d Johnston left Corinth in force to attack my army. On the 4th his cavalry dashed down and captured a small picket guard of six or seven men, stationed some five miles out from Pittsburg on the Corinth road. Colonel Buckland sent relief to the guard at once and soon followed in person with an entire regiment, and General Sherman followed Buckland taking the remainder of a brigade. The pursuit was kept up for some three miles beyond the point where the picket guard had been captured, and after nightfall Sherman returned to camp and reported to me by letter what had occurred.

At this time a large body of the enemy was hovering to the west of us, along the line of the Mobile and Ohio railroad. My apprehension was much greater for the safety of Crump's landing than it was for Pittsburg. I had no apprehension that the enemy could really capture either place. But I feared it was possible that he might make a rapid dash upon Crump's and destroy our transports and stores, most of which were kept at that point, and then retreat before Wallace could be reënforced. Lew. Wallace's position I regarded as so well chosen that he was not removed.

At this time I generally spent the day at Pittsburg and returned to Savannah in the evening. I was intending to remove my headquarters to Pittsburg, but Buell was expected daily and would come in at Savannah. I remained at this point, therefore, a few days longer than I otherwise should have done, in order to meet him on his arrival. The skirmishing in our front, however, had been so continuous from about the 3d of April that I did not leave Pittsburg each night until an hour when I felt there would be no further danger before the morning.

On Friday the 4th, the day of Buckland's advance, I was very much injured by my horse falling with me, and on me, while I was trying to get to the front where firing had been heard. The night was one of impenetrable darkness, with rain pouring down in torrents; nothing was visible to the eye except as revealed by the frequent flashes of lightning. Under these circumstances I had to trust to the horse, without guidance, to keep the road. I had not gone far, however, when I met General W.H.L. Wallace and Colonel (afterwards General) McPherson coming from the direction of the front. They said all was quiet so far as the enemy was concerned. On the way back to the boat my horse's feet slipped from under him, and he fell with my leg under his body. The extreme softness of the ground, from the excessive rains of the few preceding days, no doubt saved me from a severe injury and protracted lameness. As it was, my ankle was very much injured, so much so that my boot had to be cut off. For two or three days after I was unable to walk except with crutches.

On the 5th General Nelson, with a division of Buell's army, arrived at Savannah and I ordered him to move up the east bank of the river, to be in a position where he could be ferried over to Crump's landing or Pittsburg as occasion required. I had learned that General Buell himself would be at Savannah the next day, and desired to meet me on his arrival. Affairs at Pittsburg Landing had been such for several days that I did not want to be away during the day. I determined, therefore, to take a very early breakfast and ride out to meet Buell, and thus save time. He had arrived on the evening of the 5th, but had not advised me of the fact and I was not aware of it until some time after. While I was at breakfast, however, heavy firing was heard in the direction of Pittsburg Landing, and I hastened there, sending a hurried note to Buell informing him of the reason why I could not meet him at Savannah. On the way up the river I directed the dispatch-boat to run in close to Crump's landing, so that I could communicate with General Lew. Wallace. I found him waiting on a boat apparently expecting to see me, and I directed him to get his troops in line ready to execute any orders he might receive. He replied that his troops were already under arms and prepared to move.

Up to that time I had felt by no means certain that Crump's landing might not be the point of attack. On reaching the front, however, about eight A.M., I found that the attack on Pittsburg was unmistakable, and that nothing more than a small guard, to protect our transports and stores, was needed at Crump's. Captain Baxter, a quartermaster on my staff, was accordingly directed to go back and order General Wallace to march immediately to Pittsburg by the road nearest the river. Captain Baxter made a memorandum of this order. About one P.M., not hearing from Wallace and being much in need of reënforcements, I sent two more of my staff, Colonel McPherson and Captain Rowley to bring him up with his division. They reported finding him marching towards Purdy, Bethel, or some point west from the river, and farther from Pittsburg by several miles than when he started. The road from his first position to Pittsburg Landing was direct and near the river. Between the two points a bridge had been built across Snake Creek by our troops, at which Wallace's command had assisted, expressly to enable the troops at the two places to support each other in case of need. Wallace did not arrive in time to take part in the first day's fight. General Wallace has since claimed that the order delivered to him by Captain Baxter was simply to join the right of the army and that the road over which he marched would have taken him to the road from Pittsburg to Purdy where it crosses Owl Creek on the right of Sherman; but this is not where I had ordered him nor where I wanted him to go.

I never could see and do not now see why any order was necessary further than to direct him to come to Pittsburg Landing, without specifying by what route. His was one of three veteran divisions that had been in battle, and its absence was severely felt. Later in the war General Wallace would not have made the mistake that he committed on the 6th of April, 1862. I presume his idea was that by taking the route he did he would be able to come around on the flank or rear of the enemy, and thus perform an act of heroism that would redound to the credit of his command, as well as to the benefit of his country.

Some two or three miles from Pittsburg Landing was a log meeting-house called Shiloh. It stood on the ridge which divides the waters of Snake and Lick creeks, the former emptying into the Tennessee just north of Pittsburg Landing, and the latter south. This point was the key to our position and was held by Sherman. His division was at that time wholly raw, no part of it ever having been in an engagement; but I thought this deficiency was more than made up by the superiority of the commander. McClernand was on Sherman's left, with troops that had been engaged at forts Henry and Donelson and were therefore veterans so far as western troops had become such at that stage of the war. Next to McClernand came Prentiss with a raw division, and on the extreme left, Stuart with one brigade of Sherman's division. Hurlbut was in rear of Prentiss, massed, and in reserve at the time of the onset. The division of General C.F. Smith was on the right, also in reserve. General Smith was still sick in bed at Savannah, but within hearing of our guns. His services would no doubt have been of inestimable value had his health permitted his presence. The command of his division devolved upon Brigadier-General W.H.L. Wallace, a most estimable and able officer; a veteran too, for he had served a year in the Mexican war and had been with his command at Henry and Donelson. Wallace was mortally wounded in the first day's engagement, and with the change of commanders thus necessarily effected in the heat of battle the efficiency of his division was much weakened.

The position of our troops made a continuous line from Lick Creek on the left to Owl Creek, a branch of Snake Creek, on the right, facing nearly south and possibly a little west. The water in all these streams was very high at the time and contributed to protect our flanks. The enemy was compelled, therefore, to attack directly in front. This he did with great vigor, inflicting heavy losses on the National side, but suffering much heavier on his own.

The Confederate assaults were made with such a disregard of losses on their own side that our line of tents soon fell into their hands. The ground on which the battle was fought was undulating, heavily timbered with scattered clearings, the woods giving some protection to the troops on both sides. There was also considerable underbrush. A number of attempts were made by the enemy to turn our right flank, where Sherman was posted, but every effort was repulsed with heavy loss. But the front attack was kept up so vigorously that, to prevent the success of these attempts to get on our flanks, the National troops were compelled, several times, to take positions to the rear nearer Pittsburg Landing. When the firing ceased at night the National line was all of a mile in rear of the position it had occupied in the morning.

In one of the backward moves, on the 6th, the division commanded by General Prentiss did not fall back with the others. This left his flanks exposed and enabled the enemy to capture him with about 2,200 of his officers and men. General Badeau gives four o'clock of the 6th as about the time this capture took place. He may be right as to the time, but my recollection is that the hour was later. General Prentiss himself gave the hour as half-past five. I was with him, as I was with each of the division commanders that day, several times, and my recollection is that the last time I was with him was about half-past four, when his division was standing up firmly and the general was as cool as if expecting victory.

But no matter whether it was four or later, the story that he and his command were surprised and captured in their camps is without any foundation whatever. If it had been true as currently reported at the time and yet believed by thousands of people, that Prentiss and his division had been captured in their beds, there would not have been an all-day struggle, with the loss of thousands killed and wounded on the Confederate side.

With the single exception of a few minutes after the capture of Prentiss, a continuous and unbroken line was maintained all day from Snake Creek or its tributaries on the right to Lick Creek or the Tennessee on the left above Pittsburg. There was no hour during the day when there was not heavy firing and generally hard fighting at some point on the line, but seldom at all points at the same time. It was a case of Southern dash against Northern pluck and endurance. Three of the five divisions engaged on Sunday were entirely raw and many of the men had only received their arms on the way from their States to the field. Many of them had arrived but a day or two before and were hardly able to load their muskets according to the manual. Their officers were equally ignorant of their duties. Under these circumstances it is not astonishing that many of the regiments broke at the first fire. In two cases, as I now remember, colonels led their regiments from the field on first hearing the whistle of the enemy's bullets. In these cases the colonels were constitutional cowards, unfit for any military position; but not so the officers and men led out of danger by them. Better troops never went upon a battle-field than many of these, officers and men, afterwards proved themselves to be, who fled panic-stricken at the first whistle of bullets and shell at Shiloh.

During the whole of Sunday I was continuously engaged in passing from one part of the field to another, giving directions to division commanders. In thus moving along the line, however, I never deemed it important to stay long with Sherman. Although his troops were then under fire for the first time, their commander, by his constant presence with them, inspired a confidence in officers and men that enabled them to render services on that bloody battle-field worthy of the best of veterans. McClernand was next to Sherman, and the hardest fighting was in front of these two divisions. McClernand told me on that day, the 6th, that he profited much by having so able a commander supporting him. A casualty to Sherman that would have taken him from the field that day would have been a sad one for the troops engaged at Shiloh. And how near we came to this! On the 6th Sherman was shot twice, once in the hand, once in the shoulder, the ball cutting his coat and making a slight wound, and a third ball passed through his hat. In addition to this he had several horses shot during the day.

The nature of this battle was such that cavalry could not be used in front; I therefore formed ours into a line in rear, to stop stragglers—of whom there were many. When there would be enough of them to make a show, and after they had recovered from their fright, they would be sent to reënforce some part of the line which needed support, without regard to their companies, regiments or brigades.

On one occasion during the day I rode back as far as the river and met General Buell, who had just arrived; I do not remember the hour, but at that time there probably were as many as four or five thousand stragglers lying under cover of the river bluff, panic-stricken, most of whom would have been shot where they lay without resistance, before they would have taken muskets and marched to the front to protect themselves. This meeting between General Buell and myself was on the dispatch-boat used to run between the landing and Savannah. It was brief, and related specially to his getting his troops over the river. As we left the boat together, Buell's attention was attracted by the men lying under cover of the river bank. I saw him berating them and trying to shame them into joining their regiments. He even threatened them with shells from the gunboats near by. But it was all to no effect. Most of these men afterward proved themselves as gallant as any of those who saved the battle from which they had deserted. I have no doubt that this sight impressed General Buell with the idea that a line of retreat would be a good thing just then. If he had come in by the front instead of through the stragglers in the rear, he would have thought and felt differently. Could he have come through the Confederate rear, he would have witnessed there a scene similar to that at our own. The distant rear of an army engaged in battle is not the best place from which to judge correctly what is going on in front. Later in the war, while occupying the country between the Tennessee and the Mississippi, I learned that the panic in the Confederate lines had not differed much from that within our own. Some of the country people estimated the stragglers from Johnston's army as high as 20,000. Of course this was an exaggeration.

The situation at the close of Sunday was as follows: along the top of the bluff just south of the log house which stood at Pittsburg Landing, Colonel J.D. Webster, of my staff, had arranged twenty or more pieces of artillery facing south or up the river. This line of artillery was on the crest of a hill overlooking a deep ravine opening into the Tennessee. Hurlbut with his division intact was on the right of this artillery, extending west and possibly a little north. McClernand came next in the general line, looking more to the west. His division was complete in its organization and ready for any duty. Sherman came next, his right extending to Snake Creek. His command, like the other two, was complete in its organization and ready like its chief, for any service it might be called upon to render. All three divisions were, as a matter of course, more or less shattered and depleted in numbers from the terrible battle of the day. The division of W.H.L. Wallace, as much from the disorder arising from changes of division and brigade commanders, under heavy fire, as from any other cause, had lost its organization and did not occupy a place in the line as a division. Prentiss' command was gone as a division, many of its members having been killed, wounded or captured; but it had rendered valiant services before its final dispersal, and had contributed a good share to the defense of Shiloh.

The right of my line rested near the bank of Snake Creek, a short distance above the bridge which had been built by the troops for the purpose of connecting Crump's landing and Pittsburg Landing. Sherman had posted some troops in a log-house and out-buildings which over-looked both the bridge over which Wallace was expected and the creek above that point. In this last position Sherman was frequently attacked before night, but held the point until he voluntarily abandoned it to advance in order to make room for Lew. Wallace, who came up after dark.

There was, as I have said, a deep ravine in front of our left. The Tennessee River was very high and there was water to a considerable depth in the ravine. Here the enemy made a last desperate effort to turn our flank, but was repelled. The gunboats *Tyler* and *Lexington*, Gwin and Shirk commanding, with the artillery under Webster, aided the army and effectually checked their further progress. Before any of Buell's troops had reached the west bank of the Tennessee, firing had almost entirely ceased; anything like an attempt on the part of the enemy to advance had absolutely ceased. There was some artillery firing from an unseen enemy, some of his shells passing beyond us; but I do not remember that there was the whistle of a single musket-ball heard. As his troops arrived in the dusk General Buell marched several of his regiments part way down the face of the hill where they fired briskly for some minutes, but I do not think a single man engaged in this firing received an injury. The attack had spent its force.

General Lew. Wallace, with 5,000 effective men, arrived after firing had ceased for the day and was placed on the right. Thus night came, Wallace came, and the advance of Nelson's division came; but none—unless night—in time to be of material service to the gallant men who saved Shiloh on that first day against large odds. Buell's loss on the 6th of April was two men killed and one wounded, all members of the 36th Indiana infantry. The Army of the Tennessee lost on that day at least 7,000 men. The presence of two or three regiments of Buell's army on the west bank before firing ceased had not the slightest effect in preventing the capture of Pittsburg Landing.

So confident was I before firing had ceased on the 6th that the next day would bring victory to our arms if we could only take the initiative, that I visited every commander in person before any reënforcements had reached the field. I directed them to throw out heavy lines of skirmishers in the morning as soon as they could see, and push them forward until they found the enemy following with their entire divisions in supporting distance, and to engage the enemy as soon as found. To Sherman I told the story of the assault at Fort Donelson, and said that the same tactics would win at Shiloh. Victory was assured when Wallace arrived, even if there had been no other support. I was glad, however, to see the reënforcements of Buell and credit them with doing all there was for them to do. During the night of the 6th the remainder of Nelson's division, Buell's army, crossed the river and were ready to advance in the morning, forming the left wing. Two other divisions, Crittenden's and McCook's, came up the river from Savannah in the transports and were on the west bank early on the 7th. Buell commanded them in person. My command was thus nearly doubled in numbers and efficiency.

During the night rain fell in torrents and our troops were exposed to the storm without shelter. I made my headquarters under a tree a few hundred yards back from the river bank. My ankle was so much swollen from the fall of my horse the Friday night preceding, and the bruise was so painful, that I could get no rest. The drenching rain would have precluded the possibility of sleep without this additional cause. Some time after midnight, growing restive under the storm and the continuous pain, I moved back to the log-house under the bank. This had been taken as a hospital, and all night wounded men were being brought in, their wounds dressed, a leg or an arm amputated as the case might require, and everything being done to save life or alleviate suffering. The sight was more unendurable than encountering the enemy's fire, and I returned to my tree in the rain.

The advance on the morning of the 7th developed the enemy in the camps occupied by our troops before the battle began, more than a mile back from the most advanced position of the Confederates on the day before. It is known now that they had not yet learned of the arrival of Buell's command. Possibly they fell back so far to get shelter of our tents during the rain, and also to get away from the shells that were dropped upon them by the gunboats every fifteen minutes during the night.

The position of the Union troops on the morning of the 7th was as follows: General Lew. Wallace on the right; Sherman on his left; then McClernand and then Hurlbut. Nelson, of Buell's army, was on our extreme left, next to the river. Crittenden was next in line after Nelson and on his right; McCook followed and formed the extreme right of Buell's command. My old command thus formed the right wing, while the troops directly under Buell constituted the left wing of the army. These relative positions were retained during the entire day, or until the enemy was driven from the field.

In a very short time the battle became general all along the line. This day everything was favorable to the Union side. The enemy was driven back all day, as we had been the day before, until finally he beat a precipitate retreat. The last point held by him was near the road leading from the landing to Corinth, on the left of Sherman and right of McClernand. About three o'clock being near that point and seeing that the enemy was giving way everywhere else, I gathered up a couple of regiments, or parts of regiments, from troops near by, formed them in line of battle and marched them forward, going in front myself to prevent premature or long-range firing. At this point there was a clearing between us and the enemy favorable for charging, although exposed. I knew the enemy were ready to break and only wanted a little encouragement from us to go quickly and join their friends who had started earlier. After marching to within musket-range I stopped and let the troops pass. The command, *Charge*, was given, and was executed with loud cheers and with a run; when the last of the enemy broke.

During this second day of the battle I had been moving from right to left and back, to see for myself the progress made. In the early part of the afternoon, while riding with Colonel McPherson and Major Hawkins, then my chief commissary, we got beyond the left of our troops. We were moving along the northern edge of a clearing, very leisurely, toward the river above the landing. There did not appear to be an enemy to our right, until suddenly a battery with musketry opened upon us from the edge of the woods on the other side of the clearing. The shells and balls whistled about our ears very fast for about a minute. I do not think it took us longer than that to get out of range and out of sight. In the sudden start we made, Major Hawkins lost his hat. He did not stop to pick it up. When we arrived at a perfectly safe position we halted to take an account of damages. McPherson's horse was panting as if ready to drop. On examination it was found that a ball had struck him forward of the flank just back of the saddle, and had gone entirely through. In a few minutes the poor beast dropped dead; he had given no sign of injury until we came to a stop. A ball had struck the metal scabbard of my sword, just below the hilt, and broken it nearly off; before the battle was over it had broken off entirely. There were three of us: one had lost a horse, killed; one a hat and one a sword-scabbard. All were thankful that it was no worse.

After the rain of the night before and the frequent and heavy rains for some days previous, the roads were almost impassable. The enemy carrying his artillery and supply trains over them in his retreat, made them still worse for troops following. I wanted to pursue, but had not the heart to order the men who had fought desperately for two days, lying in the mud and rain whenever not fighting, and I did not feel disposed to positively order Buell, or any part of his command, to pursue. Although the senior in rank at the time I had been so only a few weeks. Buell was and had been for some time past, a department commander, while I commanded only a district. I did not meet Buell in person until too late to get troops ready and pursue with effect; but had I seen him at the moment of the last charge I should have at least requested him to follow.

I rode forward several miles the day after the battle, and found that the enemy had dropped much, if not all, of their provisions, some ammunition and the extra wheels of their caissons, lightening their loads to enable them to get off their guns. About five miles out we found their field hospital abandoned. An immediate pursuit must have resulted in the capture of a considerable number of prisoners and probably some guns.

Shiloh was the severest battle fought at the West during the war, and but few in the East equalled it for hard, determined fighting. I saw an open field, in our possession on the second day, over which the Confederates had made repeated charges the day before, so covered with dead that it would have been possible to walk across the clearing, in any direction, stepping on dead bodies, without a foot touching the ground. On our side National and Confederate troops were mingled together in about equal proportions; but on the remainder of the field nearly all were Confederates. On one part, which had evidently not been ploughed for several years, probably because the land was poor, bushes had grown up, some to the height of eight or ten feet. There was not one of these left standing unpierced by bullets. The smaller ones were all cut down.

Contrary to all my experience up to that time, and to the experience of the army I was then commanding, we were on the defensive. We were without intrenchments or defensive advantages of any sort, and more than half the army engaged the first day was without experience or even drill as soldiers. The officers with them, except the division commanders and possibly two or three of the brigade commanders, were equally inexperienced in war. The result was a Union victory that gave the men who achieved it great confidence in themselves ever after.

The enemy fought bravely, but they had started out to defeat and destroy an army and capture a position. They failed in both, with very heavy loss in killed and wounded, and must have gone back discouraged and convinced that the "Yankee" was not an enemy to be despised.

After the battle I gave verbal instructions to division commanders to let the regiments send out parties to bury their own dead, and to detail parties, under commissioned officers from each division, to bury the Confederate dead in their respective fronts and to report the numbers so buried. The latter part of these instructions was not carried out by all; but they were by those sent from Sherman's division, and by some of the parties sent out by McClernand. The heaviest loss sustained by the enemy was in front of these two divisions.

The criticism has often been made that the Union troops should have been intrenched at Shiloh. Up to that time the pick and spade had been but little resorted to at the West. I had, however, taken this subject under consideration soon after re-assuming command in the field, and, as already stated, my only military engineer reported unfavorably. Besides this, the troops with me, officers and men, needed discipline and drill more than they did experience with the pick, shovel and axe.

LEANDER STILLWELL

Shiloh—A Private's View

The battle of Shiloh or Pittsburg Landing was similar to the eastern battle of First Bull Run in the fact that both armies were primarily composed of rookie soldiers who had yet to experience the realities of brutal warfare or the discipline needed to undertake complex maneuvers in combat. Among the ranks of inexperienced fighting men was Leander Stillwell, who was motivated to join the 61st Illinois Regiment after the events of Firt Bull Run. He later wrote of his experiences in the Federal Army in his book *The Story of a Common Soldier.*

Let the generals and historians, therefore, write of the movements of corps, divisions, and brigades. I have naught to tell but the simple story of what one private soldier saw of one of the bloodiest battles of the war.

The regiment to which I belonged was the 61st Illinois Infantry. It left its camp of instruction (a country town in southern Illinois) about the last of February 1862. We were sent to Benton Barracks, near St. Louis, and remained there drilling (when the weather would permit) until March 25th. We left on that day for the front. It was a cloudy, drizzly, and most gloomy day as we marched through the streets of St. Louis down to the levee, to embark on a transport that was to take us to our destination. The city was enveloped in that pall of coal smoke for which St. Louis is celebrated. It hung heavy and low and set us all to coughing. I think the colonel must have marched us down some by-street. It was narrow and dirty with high buildings on either side. The line officers took the sidewalks, while the regiment, marching by the flank, tramped in silence down the middle of the street, slumping through the nasty slimy mud. There was one thing very noticeable on this march through St. Louis, and that was the utter lack of interest taken in us by the inhabitants. From pictures I had seen in books at home, my idea was that when soldiers departed for war, beautiful ladies stood on balconies and waved snowy-white handkerchiefs at the troops, while the men stood on the sidewalks and corners and swung their hats and cheered.

There may have been regiments so favored, but ours was not one of them. Occasionally a fat, chunky-looking fellow, of a German cast of countenance, with a big pipe in his mouth, would stick his head out of a door or window, look at us a few seconds, and then disappear. No handkerchiefs nor hats were waved, we heard no cheers. My thoughts at the time were that the Union people there had all gone to war, or else the colonel was marching us through a "Secesh" part of town.

We marched to the levee and from there on board the big sidewheel steamer, Empress. The next evening she unfastened her moorings, swung her head out into the river, turned down stream, and we were off for the "seat of war." We arrived at Pittsburg Landing on March 31st. Pittsburg Landing, as its name indicates, was simply a landing place for steamboats. It is on the west bank of the Tennessee river, in a thickly wooded region about twenty miles northeast of Corinth. There was no town there then, nothing but "the log house on the hill" that the survivors of the battle of Shiloh will all remember. The banks of the Tennessee on the Pittsburg Landing side are steep and bluffy, rising about 100 feet above the level of the river. Shiloh church, that gave the battle its name, was a Methodist meeting house. It was a small, hewed log building with a clapboard roof, about two miles out from the landing on the main Corinth road. On our arrival we were assigned to the division of General B.M. Prentiss, and we at once marched out and went into camp. About half a mile from the landing the road forks, the main Corinth road goes to the right, past Shiloh church, the other goes to the left. These two roads come together again some miles out. General Prentiss' division was camped on this left-hand road at right angles to it. Our regiment went into camp almost on the extreme left of Prentiss' line. There was a brigade of Sherman's division under General Stuart still further to the left, about a mile, I think, in camp near a ford of Lick Creek, where the Hamburg and Purdy road crosses the creek; and between the left of Prentiss' and General Stuart's camp there were no troops. I know that, for during the few days intervening between our arrival and the battle I roamed all through those woods on our left, between us and Stuart, hunting for wild onions and "turkey peas."

The camp of our regiment was about two miles from the landing. The tents were pitched in the woods, and there was a little field of about twenty acres in our front. The camp faced nearly west, or possibly southwest.

I shall never forget how glad I was to get off that old steamboat and be on solid ground once more, in camp out in those old woods. My company had made the trip from St. Louis to Pittsburg Landing on the hurricane deck of the steamboat, and our fare on the route had been hardtack and raw fat meat, washed down with river water, as we had no chance to cook anything, and we had not then learned the trick of catching the surplus hot water ejected from the boilers and making coffee with it. But once on solid ground, with plenty of wood to make fires, that bill of fare was changed. I shall never again eat meat that will taste as good as the fried "sowbelly" did then, accompanied by "flapjacks" and plenty of good, strong coffee. We had not yet got settled down to the regular drills, guard duty was light, and things generally seemed to run "kind of loose." And then the climate was delightful. We had just left the bleak, frozen north, where all was cold and cheerless, and we found ourselves in a clime where the air was as soft and warm as it was in Illinois in the latter part of May. The green grass was springing from the ground, the "Johnny-jump-ups" were in blossom, the trees were bursting into leaf, and the woods were full of feathered songsters. There was a redbird that would come every morning about sunup and perch himself in the tall black-oak tree in our company street, and for perhaps an hour he would practice on his impatient, querulous note, that said, as plain as a bird could say, "Boys, boys! get up! get up! get up!" It became a standing remark among the boys that he was a Union redbird and had enlisted in our regiment to sound the reveille.

So the time passed pleasantly away until that eventful Sunday morning, April 6, 1862. According to the Tribune Almanac for that year, the sun rose that morning in Tennessee at 38 minutes past five o'clock. I had no watch, but I have always been of the opinion that the sun was fully an hour and a half high before the fighting began on our part of the line. We had "turned out" about sunup, answered to roll-call, and had cooked and eaten our breakfast. We had then gone to work, preparing for the regular Sunday morning inspection, which would take place at nine o'clock. The boys were scattered around the company streets and in front of the company parade grounds, engaged in polishing and brightening their muskets, and brushing up and cleaning their shoes, jackets, trousers, and clothing generally. It was a most beautiful morning. The sun was shining brightly through the trees, and there was not a cloud in the sky. It really seemed like Sunday in the country at home. During week days there was a continual stream of army wagons going to and from the landing, and the clucking of their wheels, the yells and oaths of the drivers, the cracking of whips, mingled with the braying of mules, the neighing of the horses, the commands of the officers engaged in drilling the men, the incessant hum and buzz of the camps, the blare of bugles, and the roll of drums,—all these made up a prodigious volume of sound that lasted from the coming-up to the going-down of the sun. But this morning was strangely still. The wagons were silent, the mules were peacefully munching their hay, and the army teamsters were giving us a rest. I listened with delight to the plaintive, mournful tones of a turtle-dove in the woods close by while on the dead limb of a tall tree right in the camp a woodpecker was sounding his "long roll" just as I had heard it beaten by his Northern brothers a thousand times on the trees in the Otter Creek bottom at home.

Suddenly away off on the right, in the direction of Shiloh church, came a dull, heavy "Pum!" then another, and still another. Every man sprung to his feet as if struck by an electric shock, and we looked inquiringly into one another's faces. "What is that?" asked every one, but no one answered. Those heavy booms then came thicker and faster, and just a few seconds after we heard that first dull, ominous growl off to the southwest, came a low sullen, continuous roar. There was no mistaking that sound. That was not a squad of pickets emptying their guns on being relieved from duty; it was the continuous roll of thousands of muskets, and told us that a battle was on.

What I have been describing just now occurred during a few seconds only and with the roar of musketry the long roll began to beat in our camp. Then ensued a scene of desperate haste, the like of which I certainly had never seen before, nor ever saw again. I remember that in the midst of this terrible uproar and confusion, while the boys were buckling on their cartridge boxes, and before even the companies had been formed, a mounted staff officer came galloping wildly down the line from the right. He checked and whirled his horse sharply around right in our company street, the iron-bound hoofs of his steed crashing among the tin plates lying in a little pile where my mess had eaten its breakfast that morning. The horse was flecked with foam and its eyes and nostrils were red as blood. The officer cast one hurried glance around him, and exclaimed: "My God! this regiment not in line yet! They have been fighting on the right over an hour!" And wheeling his horse, he disappeared in the direction of the colonel's tent.

I know now that history says the battle began about 4:30 that morning; that it was brought on by a reconnoitering party sent out early that morning by General Prentiss; that General Sherman's division on the right was early advised of the approach of the Rebel army and got ready to meet them in ample time. I have read these things in books and am not disputing them, but am simply telling the story of an enlisted man on the left of Prentiss' line as to what he saw and knew of the condition of things at about seven o'clock that morning.

Well, the companies were formed, we marched out on the regimental parade ground, and the regiment was formed in line. The command was given: "Load at will; load!" We had anticipated this, however, as most of us had instinctively loaded our guns before we had formed company. All this time the roar on the right was getting nearer and louder. Our old colonel rode up close to us, opposite the center of the regimental line, and called out, "Attention, battalion!" We fixed our eyes on him to hear what was coming. It turned out to be the old man's battle harangue.

"Gentlemen," said he, in a voice that every man in the regiment heard, "remember your State, and do your duty today like brave men."

That was all. A year later in the war the old man doubtless would have addressed us as "soldiers," and not as "gentlemen," and he would have omitted his allusion to the "State," which smacked a little of Confederate notions. However, he was a Douglas Democrat, and his mind was probably running on Buena Vista, in the Mexican war, where, it is said, a Western regiment acted badly and threw a cloud over the reputation for courage of the men of that State which required the thunders of the Civil War to disperse. Immediately after the colonel had given us his brief exhortation, the regiment was marched across the little field I have before mentioned, and we took our place in line of battle, the woods in front of us, and the open field in our rear. We "dressed on" the colors, ordered arms, and stood awaiting the attack. By this time the roar on the right had become terrific. The Rebel army was unfolding its front, and the battle was steadily advancing in our direction. We could begin to see the blue rings of smoke curling upward among the trees off to the right, and the pungent smell of burning gun-powder filled the air. As the roar came traveling down the line from the right it reminded me (only it was a million times louder) of the sweep of a thunder-shower in summer-time over the hard ground of a stubble-field.

And there we stood, in the edge of the woods, so still, waiting for the storm to break on us. I know mighty well what I was thinking about then. My mind's eye was fixed on a little log cabin, far away to the north, in the backwoods of western Illinois. I could see my father sitting on the porch, reading the little local newspaper brought from the post-office the evening before. There was my mother getting my little brothers ready for Sunday-school; the old dog lying asleep in the sun; the hens cackling about the barn; all these things and a hundred other tender recollections rushed into my mind. I am not ashamed to say now that I would willingly have given a general quit-claim deed for every jot and title of military glory falling to me, past, present, and to come, if I only could have been miraculously and instantaneously set down in the yard of that peaceful little home, a thousand miles away from the haunts of fighting men.

The time we thus stood, waiting the attack, could not have exceeded five minutes. Suddenly obliquely to our right, there was a long, wavy flash of bright light, then another, and another! It was the sunlight shining on gun barrels and bayonets—and—there they were at last! A long brown line, with muskets at a right shoulder shift, in excellent order, right through the woods they came.

We began firing at once. From one end of the regiment to the other leaped a sheet of red flame, and the roar that went up from the edge of that old field doubtless advised General Prentiss of the fact that the Rebels had at last struck the extreme left of his line. We had fired but two or three rounds when, for some reason,—I never knew what,—we were ordered to fall back across the field, and did so. The whole line, so far as I could see to the right, went back. We halted on the other side of the field, in the edge of the woods, in front of our tents, and again began firing. The Rebels, of course, had moved up and occupied the line we had just abandoned. And here we did our first hard fighting during the day. Our officers said, after the battle was over, that we held this line an hour and ten minutes. How long it was I do not know. I "took no note of time."

We retreated from this position as our officers afterward said, because the troops on our right had given way and we were flanked. Possibly those boys on our right would give the same excuse for their leaving, and probably truly, too. Still, I think we did not fall back a minute too soon. As I rose from the comfortable log from behind which a bunch of us had been firing, I saw men in gray and brown clothes, with trailed muskets, running through the camp on our right, and I saw something else, too, that sent a chill all through me. It was a kind of flag I had never seen before. It was a gaudy sort of thing, with red bars. It flashed over me in a second that that thing was a Rebel flag. It was not more than sixty yards to the right. The smoke around it was low and dense and kept me from seeing the man who was carrying it, but I plainly saw the banner. It was going fast, with a jerky motion, which told me that the bearer was on a doublequick. About that time we left. We observed no kind of order in leaving; the main thing was to get out of there as quick as we could. I ran down our company street, and in passing the big Sibley tent of our mess I thought of my knapsack with all my traps and belongings, including that precious little packet of letters from home. I said to myself, "I will save my knapsack, anyhow;" but one quick backward glance over my left shoulder made me change my mind, and I went on. I never saw my knapsack or any of its contents afterwards.

Our broken forces halted and re-formed about half a mile to the rear of our camp on the summit of a gentle ridge, covered with thick brush. I recognized our regiment by the little gray pony the old colonel rode, and hurried to my place in the ranks. Standing there with our faces once more to the front, I saw a seemingly endless column of men in blue, marching by the flank, who were filing off to the right through the woods, and I heard our old German adjutant, Cramer, say to the colonel, "Dose are de troops of Sheneral Hurlbut. He is forming a new line dere in de bush." I exclaimed to myself from the bottom of my heart, "Bully for General Hurlbut and the new line in the bush! Maybe we'll whip 'em yet." I shall never forget my feelings about this time. I was astonished at our first retreat in the morning across the field back to our camp, but it occurred to me that maybe that was only "strategy" and all done on purpose; but when we had to give up our camp, and actually turn our backs and run half a mile, it seemed to me that we were forever disgraced, and I kept thinking to myself: "What will they say about this at home?"

I was very dry for a drink, and as we were doing nothing just then, I slipped out of ranks and ran down to the little hollow in our rear, in search of water. Finding a little pool, I threw myself on the ground and took a copious draught. As I rose to my feet, I observed an officer about a rod above me also quenching his thirst, holding his horse meanwhile by the bridle. As he rose I saw it was our old adjutant. At no other time would I have dared accost him unless in the line of duty but the situation made me bold. "Adjutant," I said, "What does this mean—our having to run this way? Ain't we whipped?" He blew the water from his moustache, and quickly answered in a careless way: "Oh, no; dat is all ride. We yoost fall back to form on the reserve. Sheneral Buell vas now crossing der river mit 50,000 men, and vill be here pooty quick; and Sheneral Lew Vallace is coming from Crump's Landing mit 15,000 more. Ve vips 'em; ve vips 'em. Go to your gompany." Back I went on the run, with a heart as light as a feather. As I took my place in the ranks beside my chum, Jack Medford, I said to him: "Jack, I've just had a talk with the old adjutant, down at the branch where I've been to get a drink. He says Buell is crossing the river with 75,000 men and a whole world of cannon, and that some other general is coming up from Crump's Landing with 25,000 more men. He says we fell back here on purpose, and that we're going to whip the Secesh, just sure. Ain't that just perfectly bully?" I had improved some on the adjutant's figures, as the news was so glorious I thought a little variance of 25,000 or 30,000 men would make no difference in the end. But as the long hours wore on that day and still Buell and Wallace did not come, my faith in the adjutant's veracity became considerably shaken.

It was at this point that my regiment was detached from Prentiss' division and served with it no more that day. We were sent some distance to the right to support a battery the name of which I never learned. It was occupying the summit of a slope, and was actively engaged when we reached it. We were put in position about twenty rods in the rear of the battery and ordered to lie flat on the ground. The ground sloped gently down in our direction, so that by hugging it close, the rebel shot and shell went over us.

It was here, at about ten o'clock in the morning, that I first saw Grant that day. He was on horseback, of course, accompanied by his staff and was evidently making a personal examination of his lines. He went by us in a gallop, riding between us and the battery at the head of his staff. The battery was then hotly engaged; shot and shell were whizzing overhead, and cutting off the limbs of trees, but Grant rode through the storm with perfect indifference, seemingly paying no more attention to the missiles than if they had been paper wads.

We remained in support of this battery until about 2 o'clock in the afternoon. We were then put in motion by the right flank, filed to the left, crossed the left-hand Corinth road; then we were thrown into the line by the command: "By the left flank, march." We crossed a little ravine and up a slope, and relieved a regiment on the left of Hurlbut's line. This line was desperately engaged, and had been at this point, as we afterwards learned, for fully four hours. I remember as we went up the slope and began firing, about the first thing that met my gaze was what out West we would call a "windrow" of dead men in blue; some doubled up face downward, others with their white faces upturned to the sky, brave boys who had been shot to death in "holding the line." We were then relieved by another regiment. We filled out cartridge boxes again and went back to the support of our battery. The boys laid down and talked in low tones. Many of our comrades alive and well an hour ago, we had left dead on that bloody ridge. And still the battle raged. From right to left, everywhere, it was one never-ending, terrible roar, with no prospect of stopping.

Somewhere between 4 and 5 o'clock, as near as I can tell, everything became ominously quiet. Our battery ceased firing; the gunners leaned against the pieces and talked and laughed. Suddenly a staff officer rode up and said something in a low tone to the commander of the battery, then rode to our colonel and said something to him. The battery horses were at once brought up from a ravine in the rear, and the battery limbered up and moved off through the woods diagonally to the left and rear. We were put in motion by the flank and followed it. Everything kept so still, the loudest noise I heard was the clucking of the wheels of the gun-carriages and caissons as they wound through the woods. We emerged from the woods and entered a little old field. I then saw to our right and front lines of men in blue moving in the same direction we were, and it was evident that we were falling back. All at once, on the right, the left, and from our recent front, came one tremendous roar, and the bullets fell like hail. The lines took the double-quick towards the rear. For awhile the attempt was made to fall back in order, and then everything went to pieces. My heart failed me utterly. I thought the day was lost. A confused mass of men and guns, caissons, army wagons, ambulances, and all the debris of a beaten army surged and crowded along the narrow dirt road to the landing, while that pitiless storm of leaden hail came crashing on us from the rear. It was undoubtedly at this crisis in our affairs that the division of General Prentiss was captured.

I will digress here for a minute to speak of a little incident connected with this disastrous feature of the day that has always impressed me as a pathetic instance of the patriotism and unselfish devotion to the cause that was by no means uncommon among the rank and file of the Union armies.

There was in my company a middle-aged German named Charles Oberdieck. According to the company descriptive book, he was a native of the then kingdom of Hanover, now a province of Prussia. He was a typical German, flaxen-haired, blue-eyed, quiet and taciturn, of limited and meager education, but a model soldier, who accepted without question and obeyed without a murmur the orders of his military superiors. Prior to the war he had made his living by chopping cord-wood in the high, timbered hills over the mouth of the Illinois river, or by working as a common laborer in the country on the farms at $14 a month. He was unmarried, his parents were dead, and he had no other immediate relative surviving, either in his fatherland or in the country of his adoption. He and I enlisted from the same neighborhood. I had known him in civil life at home, and hence he was disposed to be more communicative with me than with the other boys of the company. A day or two after the battle he and I were sitting in the shade of a tree, in camp, talking over the incidents of the fight. "Charley," I said to him, "How did you feel along about four o'clock Sunday afternoon when they broke our lines, we were falling back in disorder, and it looked like the whole business was gone up generally?" He knocked the ashes from his pipe and, turning his face quickly towards me, said: "I yoost tells you how I feels. I no care anydings about Charley; he haf no wife nor children, fadder nor mudder, brudder nor sister; if Charley get killed, it makes no difference; dere vas nobody to cry for him, so I dinks nudding about myselfs; but I tells you, I yoost den feels bad for de Cause!"

Noble, simple-hearted old Charley! It was the imminent danger only to the Cause that made his heart sink in that seemingly fateful hour. When we heard in the malignant and triumphant roar of the Rebel cannon in our rear what might be the deathknell of the last great experiment of civilized men to establish among the nations of the world a united republic, freed from the curse of pampered kings and selfish, grasping aristocrats—it was in that moment, in his simple language, that the peril to the Cause was the supreme and only consideration.

It must have been when we were less than half a mile from the landing on our disorderly retreat before mentioned, that we saw standing in line of battle, at ordered arms, extending from both sides of the road until lost to sight in the woods, a long, well-ordered line of men in blue. What did that mean? and where had they come from? I was walking by the side of Enoch Wallace, the orderly sergeant of my company. He was a man of nerve and courage, and by word and deed had done more that day to hold us green and untried boys in ranks and firmly to our duty than any other man in the company. But even he, in the face of this seemingly appalling state of things, had evidently lost heart. I said to him: "Enoch, what are those men there for?" He answered in a low tone: "I guess they are put there to hold the Rebels in check till the army can get across the river." And doubtless that was the thought of every intelligent soldier in our beaten column. And yet it goes to show how little the common soldier knew of the actual situation. We did not know then that this line was the last line of battle of the "Fighting Fourth Division" under General Hurlbut; that on its right was the division of McClernand, the Fort Donelson boys; that on its right, at right angles to it, and, as it were; the refused wing of the army was glorious old Sherman, hanging on with a bulldog grip to the road across Snake Creek from Crump's Landing by which Lew Wallace was coming with 5,000 men. In other words, we still had an unbroken line confronting the enemy made up of men who were not yet ready by any manner of means, to give up that they were whipped. Nor did we know then that our retreating mass consisted only of some regiments of Hurlbut's division, and some other isolated commands, who had not been duly notified of the recession of Hurlbut and of his falling back to form a new line, and thereby came very near sharing the fate of Prentiss' men and being marched to the rear as prisoners of war. Speaking for myself it was twenty years after the battle before I found these things out, yet they are true, just as much so as the fact that the sun rose yesterday morning. Well, we filed through Hurlbut's line, halted, re-formed, and faced to the front once more. We were put in place a short distance in the rear of Hurlbut, as a support to some heavy guns. It must have been about five o'clock now. Suddenly on the extreme left, and just a little above the landing, came a deafening explosion that fairly shook the ground beneath our feet, followed by others in quick and regular succession. The look of wonder and inquiry that the soldiers' faces wore for a moment disappeared for one of joy and exultation as it flashed across our minds that the gunboats had at last joined hands in the dance, and were pitching big twenty-pound Parrott shells up the ravine in front of Hurlbut, to the terror and discomfiture of our adversaries.

The last place my regiment assumed was close to the road coming up from the landing. As we were lying there I heard the strains of martial music and saw a body of men marching by the flank up the road. I slipped out of ranks and walked out to the side of the road to see what troops they were. Their band was playing "Dixie's Land," and playing it well. The men were marching at a quick step, carrying their guns, cartridge-boxes, haversacks, canteens, and blanket-rolls. I saw that they had not been in the fight, for there was no powder-smoke on their faces. "What regiment is this?" I asked of a young sergeant marching on the flank. Back came the answer in a quick, cheery tone, "The 36th Indiana, the advance guard of Buell's army."

I did not, on hearing this, throw my cap into the air and yell. That would have given those Indiana fellows a chance to chaff and guy me, and possibly make sarcastic remarks, which I did not care to provoke. I gave one big, gasping swallow and stood still, but the blood thumped in the veins of my throat and my heart fairly pounded against my little infantry jacket in the joyous rapture of this glorious intelligence. Soldiers need not be told of the thrill of unspeakable exultation they all have felt at the sight of armed friends in danger's darkest hour. Speaking for myself alone, I can only say in the most heart-felt sincerity that in all my obscure military career, never to me was the sight of reinforcing legions so precious and so welcome as on that Sunday evening when the rays of the descending sun were flashed back from the bayonets of Buell's advance column as it deployed on the bluffs of Pittsburg Landing.

My account of the battle is about done. So far as I saw or heard, very little fighting was done that evening after Buell's advance crossed the river. The sun must have been fully an hour high when anything like regular and continuous firing had entirely ceased.

What the result would have been if Beauregard had massed his troops on our left and forced the fighting late Sunday evening would be a matter of opinion, and a common soldier's opinion would not be considered worth much.

My regiment was held in reserve the next day and was not engaged. I have, therefore, no personal experience of that day to relate. After the battle of Shiloh, it fell to my lot to play my humble part in several other fierce conflicts of arms, but Shiloh was my maiden fight. It was there I first saw a gun fired in anger, heard the whistle of a bullet, or saw a man die a violent death, and my experiences, thoughts, impressions, and sensations on that bloody Sunday will abide with me as long as I live.

WILLIAM G. STEVENSON

Behind Confederate Lines

One of the more interesting accounts of the Civil War belongs to
William G. Stevenson in his *Thirteen Months in the Rebel Army*. A
transplanted Northerner living in Arkansas, Stevenson narrowly escaped being lynched for his Yankee background by enlisting in Jeff
Davis' Invincibles. By the time of Shiloh, this reluctant Johnny Reb had
risen to the rank of lieutenant and aide-de-camp to Brigadier General
John C. Breckenridge. Following the battle, Stevenson was able to effect
an escape into Federal territory where he wrote *Thirteen Months* to
convince the North of the deadly earnest with which the Southerners
were willing to fight for their cause.

General Breckenridge, about the 1st of April, let me know that he would
soon wish me to act on his staff as special *aid-de-camp*, and advised me
to instruct the next officers in command what to do in my absence.

But, before proceeding further, let us return to the one for another,
until each had sped away; and turning to me, he said, "You will act as a
special *aid-de-camp*." This announcement I received with especial grati-
fication, as it would relieve me of all actual fighting against the Old Flag,
and give me an opportunity to see far more of the progress of the battle
which was to ensue than If I were confined to the ranks. The special
danger of the mission to which I was called made no impression upon
me. I can not recall any time when I had a fear of falling, and I had none
then. From that hour until the close of the battle on Monday I was near
General Breckenridge, or conveying dispatches to others from him;
hence my narrative of the scenes of the next three days will be mainly of
what occurred in General Breckenridge's division, and what I saw while
traversing the field of action, which I crossed and recrossed twelve times.

On Friday at eight P.M., we commenced to move toward Shiloh, in
silence, and with great circumspection, the army on different, but

converging roads. We made eight miles, and reached Monterey, a little more than seven miles from Shiloh, at five o'clock on Saturday morning. Here the different divisions formed a junction, and marched forward prepared for action, though not immediately expecting it. We proceeded with extreme caution until within three and a half miles of Grant's pickets, and until our scouts had determined their situation. We could get no nearer without bringing on an engagement; and as General Beauregard had great confidence that the reënforcements would arrive by morning, the afternoon of Saturday was spent in making all necessary disposition of the forces for an early and combined attack on Sunday morning.

While it is no part of my duty in this narrative to criticise military movements, and especially those of the Union forces, I may state that the total absence of cavalry pickets from General Grant's army was a matter of perfect amazement to the Rebel officers. There were absolutely none on Grant's left, where General Breckenridge's division was meeting him, so that we were able to come up within hearing of their drums entirely unperceived.

The Southern generals always kept cavalry pickets out for miles, even when no enemy was supposed to be within a day's march of them. The infantry pickets of Grant's forces were not above three-fourths of a mile from his advance camps, and they were too few to make any resistance. With these facts all made known to our headquarters on Saturday evening, our army was arranged for battle with the certainty of a surprise, and almost the assurance of a victory. Every regiment was carefully and doubly guarded, so that no man might glide away from our ranks and put the Union forces on their guard. This I noted particularly; I was studying plans of escape that night, that I might put the loyal forces on their guard against the fearful avalanche ready to be hurled upon them. I already saw that they would stand no fair chance for victory taken completely at unawares. But the orders were imperative to allow no man to leave the ranks, and to shoot the first who should attempt it on any pretense. Then of the nature of the ground between the opposing forces I knew nothing, except that it was said to be crossed and seamed by swamps, in many places almost impassable by daylight, much more so at night. If, then, I should attempt to desert, I must run the gauntlet of our own double guard, risk the chance of making the three or four miles through woods and swamps in deep darkness, and the more hazardous chance on reaching the Federal lines, of being shot by their pickets. I was therefore compelled to relinquish the hope of escape that night—a sad necessity for if I had succeeded, it might have saved many Union lives.

About eight o'clock P.M. a council of war was held among the principal generals, and the plan of battle arranged. In an open space, with a dim fire in the midst, and a drum on which to write, you could see grouped around their "little Napoleon," as Beauregard was sometimes fondly called, ten or twelve generals, the flickering light playing over their eager faces, while they listened to his plans and made suggestions as to the conduct of the fight. He soon warmed with his subject, and throwing off his cloak to give free play to his arms, he walked about in the group, gesticulating rapidly and jerking out his sentences with a strong French accent. All listened attentively and the dim light just revealing their countenances showed their different emotions of confidence or distrust in his plans. General Sidney Johnson stood apart from the rest, with his tall straight form standing out like a specter against the dim sky, and the illusion was fully sustained by the light-gray military cloak which he folded around him. His face was pale, but wore a determined expression, and at times he drew nearer the center of the ring and said a few words, which were listened to with great attention. It may be he had some foreboding of the fate he was to meet on the morrow for he did not seem to take much part in the discussion. General Breckenridge lay stretched out on a blanket near the fire, and occasionally sat upright and added a few words of counsel. General Bragg spoke frequently and with earnestness. General Polk sat on a camp-stool at the outside of the circle, and held his head between his hands, seeming buried in thought. Others reclined or sat in various positions. What a grand study for a Rembrandt was this, to see these men, who held the lives of many thousands in their power, planning how best to invoke the angel Azrael to hurl his darts with the breaking of morning light.

For two hours the council lasted, and as it broke up, and the generals were ready to return to their respective commands, I heard General Beauregard say,—raising his hand and pointing in the direction of the Federal camps, whose drums we could plainly hear,—"Gentlemen, we sleep in the enemy's camp tomorrow night."

The Confederate generals had minute information of General Grant's position and numbers. This knowledge was obtained through spies and informers, some of whom had lived in that part of the country and knew every foot of the ground.

Yet that was a dreary night to prepare for the dreadful battle of to-morrow. The men were already weary, hungry, and cold. No fires were allowed, except in holes in the ground, over which the soldiers bent with their blankets round their shoulders, striving to catch and concentrate the little heat that struggled up through the bleak April air. Many a poor fellow wrote his last sentence in his notebook that night by the dim light of these smothered fires, and sat and talked in undertones of home, wife, and mother, sister or sweetheart. Promises were made to take care of each other, if wounded, or send word home, if slain; keepsakes were looked at again for the last time, and silent prayers were offered by men unused to look above. What an awful thing is war! Here lay almost within cannon-shot of one another, eighty or ninety thousand men—brothers of the same race and nation, many of them blood relations; thousands of them believing in the same Saviour, and worshiping the same God, their prayers meeting that night at the throne of Heavenly Grace;—yet waiting for the light of the holy Sabbath that they may see how most surely to destroy one another! And yet the masses of these have no ill feeling. It is human butchery, at the bidding of archconspirators. Upon them be all the blood shed! A fearful guilt is theirs!

What sleep the men could get on the cold, damp ground, with little protection or fire, they secured during the early part of Saturday night. On Sunday morning, the 6th of April, we were under arms and ready to move by three o'clock.

General Hardee, one of the bravest men in the Confederate service, led the advance and center, and made the attack. Had I not been called to staff duty, I should have been in the advance with my company. Glad was I that I was not called to fire upon the unsuspecting soldiers of my Northern home. As the day dawned we could hear the musketry, first in dropping shots, then volley after volley, as the battle grew hotter. A little after daylight we passed General Beauregard and staff, who were then over a mile in rear of the troops engaged. He addressed each brigade as it passed, assuring them of a glorious victory, telling them to fight with perfect confidence, as he had 80,000 men available, who should come into action as fast as needed; and wherever reënforcements were wanted, Beauregard would be there. This boast of 80,000 men the officers knew to be false, as he had not a man over 45,000; but as he expected 30,000 under Price and Van Dorn he counted them in, and added 10,000 more to strengthen confidence. But neither he nor any other Confederate general asks any defence for such statements. "Military necessity" will justify any course they choose to take in advancing their cause. After we passed Beauregard, a few minutes of "double quick" brought our division to Grant's advance pickets, who had been surprised and cut down by Hardee's cavalry. This was the first time many of the soldiers had seen men killed in battle, and they stepped carefully around the dead bodies, and seemed to shudder at the sight. General Breckenridge observing it, said quickly, "Never mind this, boys; press on!" Before night, those who remained walked over dead bodies in heaps without a shudder. We soon reached an open field, about eighty rods wide, on the further side of which we could see the camps, and the smoke of battle just beyond. We here made a sharp *détour* to the right, and ascended a broken range of hills, pressing on for nearly a mile. Here we took position just in front of General Albert Sidney Johnson and staff, and awaited orders. General Breckenridge rode up to General Johnson, and after conversing in a low tone for a few minutes, Johnson said, so that many heard it, "I will lead *your* brigade into the fight to-day; for I intend to show these Tennesseans and Kentuckians that I am no coward." Poor general! you were not allowed the privilege. We then advanced in line of battle, and General Statham's brigade was engaged first. "Boys," said Breckenridge, "we must take that battery which is shelling Statham. Will you do it?" A wild shout of "Ay, ay, sir," and "Forward to take that battery" was the word; but before we reached the ground it was withdrawn. We now advanced, cautiously, and soon entered the camp of the Seventy-first Ohio Volunteers. By this time, ten o'clock A.M., the battle seemed to be raging along the whole line.

A part of the original plan of battle was to have a space several hundred yards wide between Breckenridge's left and Hardee's right, and thus invite Grant's men into a trap. They refusing to be entrapped, and keeping their front unbroken, Breckenridge sent me to General Johnson for new instructions. When I had come within about ten rods of Johnson's staff, a shell burst in the air about equi-distant from myself and the staff. The missiles of death seemed to fill the air in every direction, and almost before the fragments had found their resting-place, I reined up my horse and saluted. General Johnson, who was in front of his staff, had turned away his horse and was leaning a little forward, pressing his right knee against the saddle. In a moment, and before the dispatch was delivered, the staff discovered that their leader was wounded, and hastened to his assistance. A piece of the shell, whose fragments had flown so thick around me as I came up, had struck his thigh half way between his hip and knee, and cut a wide path through, severing the femoral artery. Had he been instantly taken from his horse and a tourniquet applied, he might perhaps have been saved. When reproached by Governor Harris, chief of staff and his brother-in-law, for concealing his wound while his life-blood was ebbing away he replied, with true nobility of soul, "My life is nothing to the success of this charge; had I exclaimed I was wounded when the troops were passing, it might have created a panic and defeat." In ten minutes after he was lifted from his horse he ceased to breathe. Thus died one of the bravest generals in the Rebel army. My dispatch was taken by Colonel Wickliffe and handed to Harris, who directed me to take it to General Beauregard. When he had read it, he asked:

"Why did you not take this to General Johnson?"

"I did, sir."

"Did he tell you to bring it to me?"

"General Johnson is dead, sir."

"How do you know?"

"I saw him die ten minutes ago."

"How was he killed?"

I told him. He then dictated two dispatches, one to Governor Harris and one to General Breckenridge, telling them to conceal the death of Johnson, and bidding me not to speak of it to any one. So far as the report of his death was circulated the officers denied it, some affirming that it was Governor Johnson of Kentucky who was killed, others admitting that General A.S. Johnson was slightly wounded. The army knew not of his death till they reached Corinth.

When I returned to General Breckenridge's staff they had advanced half a mile, and were furiously engaged within half-musket range with both small-arms and artillery. About noon General Bowen's brigade—Breckenridge's left—was forced to fall back for ammunition and to reform, their place being supplied by two regiments of Louisiana troops. Here, from two to four P.M., was the hardest fighting in the battle. Breckenridge's own brigade losing nearly one-fourth within two hours. The fire of the Union troops was low and very effective. A battery here did fearful execution among the Rebels with shell, grape, and canister. A wounded gunner belonging to this battery told me the shells were fired with one-second fuses. Our men were ordered to lie down and load, and yet many were killed in this position, so accurate was the fire of the Federal troops. I saw five men killed by the explosion of one shell.

About three o'clock I was sent to the rear with dispatches of the progress of the battle, and asking reinforcements. When about half way to Beauregard's staff, riding at full gallop, my first serious accident occurred, my life being saved by but a hair's breadth. As my horse rose in a long leap, his forefeet in the air and his head about as high as my shoulder, a cannonball struck him above the eye and carried away the upper part of his head. Of course the momentum carried his lifeless body some ten feet ahead, and hurled me some distance further, saber, pistols, and all. I gathered myself up, and to my surprise was not hurt in the least. One second later, the ball would have struck me and spared the horse. Thankful for my life, I threw off my saber and my tight uniform-coat, gave my pistols to a cavalryman near by and started in search of another horse. General Breckenridge had told me in the morning, if my horse was killed to take the first unemployed one I could find. I knew where some of the infantry field-officers had tied their horses in a ravine in the rear, and while seeking them, I met a scene which lives in my memory as if it were but yesterday.

I had just filled my canteen at a spring, and as I turned from it my eye met the uplifted gaze of a Federal officer, I think a colonel of an Illinois regiment, who was lying desperately wounded, shot through the body and both legs, his dead horse lying on one of his shattered limbs. A cannon-ball had passed through his horse and both of his own knees. He looked pleadingly for a drink, but hesitated to ask it of an enemy as he supposed me to be. I came up to him, and said, "You seem to be badly wounded, sir; will you have some water?"

"Oh yes," said he; "but I feared to ask you for it."

"Why?"

"Because I expected no favor of an enemy."

Two other men coming by, I called them to aid in removing the dead horse from his wounded limb. They did so, and then passed on; but I seemed bound to him as by a spell. His manly face and soldierly bearing, when suffering so terribly, charmed me. I changed his position, adjusted his head, arranged his mangled legs in an easy posture, supporting them by leaves stuffed under the blanket on which we had laid him. In the mean time he took out his watch and money, and requested me to hand him his pistols from the saddle-holsters, and urged me to take them, as some one might rob him, and I was the only one who had shown him kindness. I declined, and wrapping them up in a blanket, placed them under his head, telling him the fortunes of war might yet bring his own troops to his side. He seemed overcome, and said, "My friend, why this kindness to an enemy?"

As I gave him another draught of water, I said, *"I am not the enemy I seem,"* and pressing his hand, I walked quickly on.

He could not live long, but I hope his friends found him as they swept back over the ground the next day.

I soon found a splendid horse, and rode to General Beauregard for orders, and reached my own general about four o'clock P.M. I found that the Federal troops had fallen back more than a mile, but were still fiercely contending for the ground. The Rebels were confident of victory, and pressed them at every point. I had scarce time to mark the condition of things however, until I was again dispatched to the commander-in-chief. I had but fairly started, when I was struck on the right side by a piece of a shell almost spent, which yet came near ending my earthly career. My first feeling after the shock was one of giddiness and blindness, then of partial recovery, then of deathly sickness. I succeeded in getting off rather than falling from my horse, near the root of a tree, where I fainted and lay insensible for nearly an hour. At length, I recovered so far as to be able to remount my horse, whose bridle I had somehow held all the time, though unconsciously I had ridden but a few rods when a musketball passed through the neck of this, my second horse, but, to my surprise, he did not fall immediately. A tremor ran through his frame which I felt, convincing me that he was mortally wounded. I dismounted, and stood watching him. He soon sank on his knees, and then slowly lay down on his side. As his lifeblood ebbed away, his eye glazed, and making a last futile effort to rise, he fell back again and died with a groan almost like the last agony of a human being. The pain of my side and my knee, which was never entirely free from pain, grew worse, and I saw that unless I found surgical attendance and rest, I would soon be exhausted. In making my way to the general hospital which was established on the ground where the battle commenced, I met one of Forrest's cavalry wounded in the foot, and very weak from loss of blood. With my handkerchief and a short stick, I made a simple tourniquet, which stopped the bleeding, then I accompanied him to the hospital. After the dressing of my wound, which was an extensive bruise, about five inches in diameter, I took the cavalryman's horse, and started back to my command. When I had reached the camp of the 71st Ohio Volunteers, my strength failed, and after getting something to eat for myself and horse, and a bucket of water to bathe my side during the night, I tied my horse near the door of a tent, and crept in to try to sleep. But the shells from the gunboats, which made night hideous, the groans of the wounded, and the pleadings of the dying, for a time prevented this. Weariness at length overcame me, and sleep followed more refreshing and sound than I hoped for under the circumstances.

The sharp rattle of musketry awakened me early, announcing the opening of the second day's battle. But before I speak of Monday the 7th, I will state why the Confederates ceased to fight at half-past five P.M., on Sabbath evening, when they had another hour of daylight. They had already driven back the Federal forces more than three miles along their whole line, had taken 4000 prisoners, including most of General Prentiss's brigade, had captured about seventy pieces of artillery, according to their statement, had taken an immense baggage-train, with vast quantities of commissary, quartermaster's, and medical stores, and had driven Grant's forces under the shelter of their gunboats. Had the battle ended here, the victory would have been most triumphant for the Rebels. Generals Bragg and Breckenridge urged that the battle should go on, that Grant's force was terribly cut up and demoralized, and another hour would take them all prisoners, or drive them into the river, and that then the transport fleet of more than a hundred boats, would be at the control of the Confederates, who could assume the offensive, and in five days take Louisville. Other officers argued that half of their own troops were disabled or scattered, that it would risk the victory already gained to push the remainder of Grant's forces, which now turned at bay, might make a desperate stand. They estimated their own loss at ten or twelve thousand men, and knew that many thinking the battle was over, had left their commands and were loading themselves with plunder, from the pockets of the dead and the knapsacks lying over the field or found in the Federal camps. Some expressed strong confidence that Price and Van Dorn would arrive during the night, and the victory would be easily completed on the morrow.

While this argument lasted, the men were resting, the hour passed away, and night spread her sable pall over the scene.

The night was spent in removing the wounded, and as much of the captured stores and artillery as possible; but horses and wagons were scarce, and most of the stores and some wounded were left. The Confederates carried off thirty-six pieces of artillery, which were not retaken. Hospitals were established on the road leading to Corinth, and most of the wounded of the first day received every attention possible under the circumstances; though the advance had been made so suddenly that insufficient attention had been given to providing medical stores and surgical instruments. The scattered regiments were gathered, reorganized, and put, as far as possible, in order for battle, and Beauregard ordered a large cavalry force to stretch themselves out in a line a short distance in rear of the army to turn back all stragglers, and gave them instructions to shoot any unwounded man retreating. This was rigidly enforced, and some who attempted to escape were shot. Orders were issued to shoot any one found plundering the dead or wounded. Stragglers were forced into the nearest regiment, and every thing done that could be to insure success.

From the foregoing account it will be seen that the following telegram, sent by Beauregard to Richmond, is not far from literally true:

General S. Cooper, Adjutant-general,—We have this morning attacked the enemy in strong position in front of Pittsburg, and after a severe battle of ten hours, thanks to Almighty God, gained a complete victory, driving the enemy from every position.

The loss on both sides is heavy, including our commander-in-chief, General Albert Sidney Johnson, who fell gallantly leading his troops into the thickest of the fight.

The morning of Monday, April 7th, was dark and gloomy; the men were weary and stiffened by the exertions of the previous day and from the chilling effects of the rain which fell during the night. The dead of both armies lay strewed over the field by hundreds, and many of the desperately wounded were still groaning out their lives in fearful agony. At five A.M. I was in the saddle, though scarcely able to mount, from the pain in knee and side; and in making my way to General Beauregard's staff, my head reeled and my heart grew sick at the scenes through which I passed. I record but one. In crossing a small ravine, my horse hesitated to step over the stream, and I glanced down to detect the cause. The slight rain during the night had washed the leaves out of a narrow channel down the gully some six inches wide, leaving the hard clay exposed. Down this pathway ran sluggishly a band of blood nearly an inch thick, filling the channel. For a minute I looked and reflected, how many human lives are flowing past me, and who shall account for such butchery! Striking my rowels into the horse to escape from the horrible sight, he plunged his foot into the stream of blood, and threw the already thickening mass in ropy folds upon the dead leaves on the bank! The only relief to my feelings was the reflection that I had not shed one drop of that blood.

I took my position on General B.'s staff at six o'clock in the morning, and remained near him most of the day. The Federal forces had already commenced the attack, and the tide of battle soon turned. Grant's reënforcements had come up during the night, but Beauregard's had not, and early in the day it became evident that we were fighting against fearful odds. Beauregard sent forward 3000 of his best troops, held as a reserve during the first day. They did all that so small a number could do, but it was of no avail. Step by step they drove us back, while every foot of ground was yielded only after a determined resistance. The battle raged mainly on our left, General Breckenridge's division doing but little fighting this day, compared with the first day. General Grant seemed determined to outflank our left, and occupy the road behind us, and as the Confederates had not men enough to hold the camps they had taken, and check this flank movement, retreat became necessary. About nine A.M. I rode to General Beauregard for orders; when returning, I heard the report that General Buell had been killed and his body taken toward Corinth. This report that the Federal commander, as many supposed Buell to be, was killed, and his body taken, revived the flagging hopes of the Confederates. Of the fluctuations of the battle from nine A.M. till three P.M. I can say but little as it was mainly confined to our center and left. During this time the Rebel forces had fallen back to the position occupied by Grant's advance Sabbath morning. The loyal troops had regained all the ground lost, and whatever of artillery and stores the Rebels had been unable to convey to the rear, and were now pressing us at every point.

Just before the retreat, occurred one of the most remarkable incidents of the battle; few more wonderful are on record. General Hindman, than whom no more fearless, dashing, or brave man is found in the Rebel service, was leading his men in a fearful struggle for the possession of a favorable position, when a shell from the Federal batteries, striking his horse in the breast and passing into his body, exploded. The horse was blown to fragments, and the rider, with his saddle, lifted some ten feet in the air. His staff did not doubt that their general was killed, and some one cried out, "General Hindman is blown to pieces." Scarcely was the cry uttered, when Hindman sprang to his feet and shouted, "Shut up there, I am worth two dead men yet. Get me another horse." To the amazement of every one, he was but little bruised. His heavy and strong cavalry saddle, and probably the bursting of the shell downward, saved him. In a minute he was on a new horse and rallying his men for another dash. A man of less flexible and steel-like frame would probably have been so jarred and stunned by the shock as to be unable to rise; he, though covered with blood and dust, kept his saddle during the remainder of the day and performed prodigies of valor. But no heroism of officers or men could avail to stay the advance of the Federal troops. At three o'clock P.M. the Confederates decided on a retreat to Corinth; and General Breckenridge, strengthened by three regiments of cavalry—Forrest's, Adams', and the Texas Rangers, raising his effective force to 12,000 men,—received orders to protect the rear. By four P.M. the Confederates were in full retreat. The main body of the army passed silently and swiftly along the road toward Corinth, our division bringing up the rear, determined to make a desperate stand if pursued. At this time the Union forces might have closed in upon our retreating columns and cut off Breckenridge's division, and perhaps captured it. A Federal battery threw some shells, as a feeler, across the road on which we were retreating, between our division and the main body, but no reply was made to them, as this would have betrayed our position. We passed on with little opposition or loss, and by five o'clock had reached a point one and a half miles nearer Corinth than the point of attack Sabbath morning.

Up to this time the pursuit seemed feeble, and the Confederates were surprised that the victorious Federals made no more of their advantage. Nor is it yet understood why the pursuit was not pressed. A rapid and persistent pursuit would have created a complete rout of the now broken, weary and dispirited Rebels. Two hours more of such fighting as Buell's fresh men could have made, would have demoralized and destroyed Beauregard's army. For some reason this was not done, and night closed the battle.

About five o'clock I requested permission to ride on toward Corinth, as I was faint and weary, and from the pain in my side and knee, would not be able to keep the saddle much longer. This was granted, and made a *détour* from the road on which the army was retreating, that I might travel faster and get ahead of the main body. In this ride of twelve miles alongside of the routed army I saw more of human agony and woe than I trust I will ever again be called on to witness. The retreating host wound along a narrow and almost impassable road, extending some seven or eight miles in length. Here was a long line of wagons loaded with wounded, piled in like bags of grain, groaning and cursing, while the mules plunged on in mud and water belly-deep, the water sometimes coming into the wagons. Next came a straggling regiment of infantry pressing on past the train of wagons, then a stretcher borne upon the shoulders of four men, carrying a wounded officer, then soldiers staggering along, with an arm broken and hanging down, or other fearful wounds which were enough to destroy life. And to add to the horrors of the scene, the elements of heaven marshaled their forces,—a fitting accompaniment of the tempest of human desolation and passion which was raging. A cold, drizzling rain commenced about nightfall, and soon came harder and faster, then turned to pitiless blinding hail. This storm raged with unrelenting violence for three hours. I passed long wagon trains filled with wounded and dying soldiers, without even a blanket to shield them from the driving sleet and hail, which fell in stones as large as partridge eggs, until it lay on the ground two inches deep.

Some three hundred men died during that awful retreat, and their bodies were thrown out to make room for others who, although wounded, had struggled on through the storm, hoping to find shelter, rest, and medical care.

By eight o'clock at night I had passed the whole retreating column, and was now in advance, hoping to reach Corinth, still four miles ahead. But my powers of endurance, though remarkable, were exhausted, and I dismounted at a deserted cabin by the wayside, scarce able to drag myself to the doorway. Here a surgeon was tending some wounded men who had been sent off the field at an early hour of the first day. To his question, "Are you wounded?" I replied that my wound was slight, and that I needed refreshment and sleep more than surgical aid. Procuring two hard crackers and a cup of rye coffee, I made a better meal than I had eaten in three days, and then lay down in a vacant room and slept.

When I awoke it was broad daylight, and the room was crowded full of wounded and dying men, so thickly packed that I could hardly stir. I was not in the same place where I had lain down; but of my change of place, and of the dreadful scenes which had occurred during the night, I had not the slightest knowledge.

As I became fully awake and sat up, the surgeon turned to me, and said, "Well, you are alive at last. I thought nothing but an earthquake would wake you. We have moved you about like a log, and you never groaned or showed any signs of life. Men have trampled on you, dying men have groaned all around you, and yet you slept as soundly as a babe in its cradle. Where is your wound?"

How I endured the horrors of that night, rather how I was entirely unconscious of them and slept refreshingly through them, is to me a mystery. But so it was, and it seemed to be the turning-point of my knee-wound, as it has never troubled me so much since.

I now rode on to Corinth, where I changed clothes, had a bath and breakfast, and found a hospital and a surgeon. He decided that I was unfit for duty and must take my place among the invalids. After dressing my wounds he advised rest. I slept again for six hours, and woke in the afternoon almost a well man, as I thought.

Thus ended my courier service, and I then resolved that no earthly power should ever force me into another battle against the Government under which I was born; and I have kept my resolution.

General Beauregard's official dispatch of the second day's battle, given below, was a very neat attempt to cover up defeat. It expresses the general opinion of the people in the South as to the battle of Pittsburg Landing.

To the Secretary of War, Richmond:
We have gained a great and glorious victory. Eight to ten thousand prisoners, and thirty-six pieces of cannon. Buell reënforced Grant, and we retired to our intrenchments at Corinth, which we can hold. Loss heavy on both sides.

WILL S. HAYS

Drummer Boy of Shiloh

This tearful lyric describing the untimely demise of a saintly youth in
the carnage of Shiloh serves as a good example of the romantic writing
of mid-nineteenth century America.

"Look down upon the battlefield,
Oh Thou, Our Heavenly Friend,
Have mercy on our sinful souls."
The soldiers cried, "Amen."
There gathered 'round a little group,
Each brave man knelt and cried.
They listened to the drummer boy
Who prayed before he died.
"Oh, Mother," said the dying boy,
"Look down from heaven on me.
Receive me to thy fond embrace,
Oh, take me home to thee.
I've loved my country as my God,
To serve them both I've tried!"
He smiled, shook hands—death seized the boy,
Who prayed before he died.

Each soldier wept then like a child.
Stout hearts were they and brave.
They wrapped him in his country's flag
And laid him in the grave.
They placed by him the Bible,
a rededicated guide
To those that mourn the drummer boy
Who prayed before he died.

Ye angels 'round the throne of grace,
*   Look down upon the braves,*
Who fought and died on Shiloh's plain,
*   Now slumbering in their graves.*
How many homes made desolate,
*   How many hearts have sighed.*
How many like that drummer boy,
*   Who prayed before he died.*

Chapter IX

KENTUCKY INVADED

Despite the victories at Fort Henry, Fort Donelson, Pea Ridge and Shiloh, the Federals never launched a knockout blow against the demoralized Confederate forces facing them in the West. As the Yankees bided their time, Braxton Bragg and Kirby Smith headed their armies north to gallivant around Kentucky in the late summer of 1862 at about the same time Lee was engaging in his Maryland Campaign in the East. Commanding the Confederate Army of the West, Major General Sterling Price decided to assist his comrades in Kentucky by attempting to invade the Volunteer State, but he was defeated in Mississippi at Iuka on 19 September and Corinth on 3-4 October 1862 by Major General William Rosecrans commanding the Union Army of the Mississippi. Meanwhile, forced to pursue Generals Bragg and Smith, Major General Don Carlos Buell took his Army of the Ohio north to do battle where he engaged the former in the indecisive battle of Perryville, Kentucky, on 8 October 1862. Despite inflicting heavy losses on the Federals, Bragg was forced to abandon his invasion and fall back to Tennessee with Smith.

S.P. BARRON

The Iuka-Corinth Campaign

The battles of both Iuka and Corinth marked two of the few times the Confederacy was on the offensive against the Yankees even though they wielded superior numbers. The Confederates failed to pull out a victory when they most desperately needed one. S.P. Barron, a member of the 3rd Texas Cavalry, related the events of these tragic battles in his book *The Lone Star Defenders.*

In the early days of June our command halted and went into camp near Tupelo, Miss., where it remained for several weeks. Here, as I was physically unfit for service, I voluntarily abandoned my place at General Cabell's headquarters and returned to my own regiment. Obtaining, without difficulty, a thirty days' furlough, I called on Dr. Shaw for medicine, but he informed me that he had nothing but opium, which would do me no good. But he added, "You need a tonic; if you could only get some whisky that would soon set you up." Mounting my horse I went down into Pontotoc County and, finding a goodlooking farmhouse away from the public roads, I engaged board with Mr. Dunn, the proprietor, for myself and horse for thirty days. Mr. Dunn told me of a distillery away down somewhere below the town of Pontotoc, and finding a convalescent in the neighborhood I sent him on my horse to look for it, with the result that he brought me back four canteens of "tonic."

Now Mr. Dunn's family consisted of that clever elderly gentleman, his wife, and a handsome, intelligent daughter, presumably about twenty years of age. I soon realized that I had been very fortunate in the selection of a boarding house and that my lot for the next thirty days had been cast in a pleasant place, for every necessary attention was cheerfully shown me by each member of the family. They had lost a son and brother who had wasted away with consumption, and in my dilapidated and

106

emaciated condition they said I favored him, so they were constantly reminded of a loved one who had gone to his grave in about the same manner I seemed to be going, and they felt almost as if they were ministering to the wants of one of the family. They lived in a comfortable house, and everything I saw indicated a happy well-to-do family. Their table, spread three times a day, was all that could be desired. We had corn bread, fresh milk and butter, fresh eggs, last year's yam potatoes, a plentiful supply of garden vegetables and other good things, everything brought on the table being well prepared. At first I had little or no appetite, but thanks to Miss Dunn's treatment, it soon began to improve. She, using the "tonic," gave me an eggnog just before each meal, and blackberries being plentiful, she gave me blackberries in every form, including pies and cordial, all of which, for one in my condition, was the best possible treatment.

So I improved and gained strength, not rapidly, but steadily and though the thirty days was not as much time as I needed for a complete convalescence, it was all I had asked for. Mr. Dunn manifested a great deal of interest in my welfare; he did not think I could recover my health in the service, and urged me most earnestly to go back to camp, get a discharge, and go to Cooper's Well, a health resort down in Mississippi, and I was almost compelled to promise him I would do so, when in truth I had no such intention. The thirty days having expired, I bade farewell to these good people who had taken in a stranger and so kindly cared for him, and returned to camp, not strong or well by any means, but improved, especially in the matter of an appetite.

Going up to regimental headquarters upon my return to the command I let out my horse for his board, procured a rifle and at once reported to our company commander for duty. The strictest military discipline was maintained by General Louis Hebert in every particular, and one day's duty was very much like the duties of every other day with a variation for Sunday. Of course the same men did not have the same duties to perform every day as guard duty and fatigue duty were regulated by details made from the alphabetical rolls of the companies, but the same round of duties came every day in the week. At reveille we must promptly rise, dress, and hurry out into line for roll call; then breakfast. After breakfast guard-mounting for the ensuing twenty-four hours, these guards walking their posts day and night, two hours on and four hours off. Before noon there were two hours' drill for all men not on guard or some other special duty; then dinner. In the afternoon it was clean up camps, clean guns, dress parade at sundown; then supper, to bed at taps. On Sunday no drill, but, instead, we had to go out for a review, which was worse, as the men had to don all their armor, the officers button up their uniforms to the chin, buckle on their swords, and all march about two miles away through the dust and heat to an old field, march around a circle at least a mile in circumference, and back to camps. All that, including the halting and waiting, usually took up the time until about noon.

With the understanding and agreement that I would be excused from the drill ground when I broke down, and when on guard be allowed to rest when I had walked my post as long as I could, I went on duty as a well man. For quite a while I was compelled to leave the drill ground before the expiration of the two hours, and when I found I could not walk my post through the two hours some one of my comrades usually took my place. It was necessary for me to muster all my courage to do this kind of soldiering, but the exertion demanded of me and the exercise so improved my condition that soon I no longer had to be excused from any part of my duties. We had men in the command afflicted with chronic diarrhea who, yielding to the enervating influence of the disease, would lie down and die, and that was what I determined to avoid if I could.

Among other bugle calls we had "the sick call." Soon after breakfast every morning this, the most doleful of all the calls, was sounded, when the sick would march up and line themselves in front of the surgeon's tent for medical advice and treatment. Our surgeon, Dr. Dan Shaw, was a character worthy of being affectionately remembered by all the members of the Third Texas Cavalry. He was a fine physician, and I had fallen in love with him while he was a private soldier because he so generously exerted his best skill in assisting Dr. McDugald to save my life at Carthage, Mo. He was a plain, unassuming, jolly old fellow, brave, patriotic, and full of good impulses. He was the man who indignantly declined an appointment as surgeon soon after the battle of Oak Hills, preferring to remain a private in "Company B, Greer's Texas regiment," to being surgeon of an Arkansas regiment.

Knowing that he had no medicine except opium, I would go up some mornings, through curiosity, to hear his prescriptions for the various ailments that he had to encounter. He would walk out with an old jackknife in his hand, and conveniently located just behind him could be seen a lump of opium as big as a cannonball. Beginning at the head of the line he would say to the first one: "Well, sir, what is the matter with *you*?" "I don't know, doctor; I've got a pain in my head, or I had a chill last night." "Let me see your tongue. How's your bowels?" He would then turn around and vigorously attack the lump of opium with his knife, and roll out from two to four pills to the man, remarking to each of his waiting patients: "There, take one of these every two hours." Thus he would go, down the line to the end, and in it all there was little variation—none to speak of except in the answers of the individuals, the number of pills, or the manner of taking. And what else could he do? He had told me frankly that he had nothing in his tent that would do me any good, but these men had to have medicine.

For water at Tupelo we dug wells, each company a well, using a sweep to draw it. In this hilly portion of the State good water could be obtained by digging from twenty to twenty-five feet.

From the time of the reorganization at Corinth up to the middle of July Company C had lost a number of men. Some, as McDugald and Dillard, were commissioned officers, and did not reenlist; some were discharged on applications, and others under the conscription law then in force, a law exempting all men under eighteen and over forty-five years of age. Among those discharged I remember the two Ackers, Croft, I.K. Frazer, Tom Hogg, Tom Johnson, W.A. Newton, William Pennington, and R.G. Thompson, all of whom returned to Texas except William Pennington, who remained with us a considerable time, notwithstanding his discharge. In the regimental officers several changes had been made. After the death of Major Barker, Captain Jiles S. Boggess, of Company B, from Henderson, was promoted to major; Colonel R.H. Cumby resigned, and Lieutenant-Colonel Mabry was made colonel. J.S. Boggess, Lieutenant-Colonel and Captain A.B. Stone, of Company A, from Marshall, promoted to major. About the first of August we moved up the railroad to Saltillo, about fifteen miles north of Tupelo, established camps, dug wells, and remained about three weeks. Here the Fortieth (?) or Mississippi regiment joined the brigade. This was a new regiment, just out from home, and it seemed to us, from the amount of luggage they had, that they had brought about all their household goods along. This regiment is remembered for these distinct peculiarities. Aside from the weight and bulk of its baggage they had the tallest man and the largest boy in the army and the colonel used a camel to carry his private baggage. The tall man was rather slender, and looked to be seven feet high; the boy was sixteen or eighteen years old, and weighed more than three hundred pounds.

The brigade now consisted of the Third Texas, Whitfield's Texas Legion, the Third Louisiana, the Fourteenth and Seventeenth Arkansas, and the Fortieth Mississippi. The army here, commanded by General Price, was composed of two divisions commanded by Generals Little and D.H. Maury. Many of the troops that came out of Corinth with General Beauregard had gone with General Bragg into Kentucky. At the end of three weeks we moved farther up the railroad to Baldwin. Here we dug more wells, and it was my fortune to be on the second day's detail that dug our company well. The first detail went down some eight feet, about as deep as they could throw the earth out. The next morning four of us, including C.C. Watkins and myself, the two weakest men, physically, in the company were detailed to continue the digging. We arranged means for drawing the earth out, and began work, two at the time, one to dig and one to draw. At quitting time in the evening we had it down twenty-one feet, and had plenty of water. But we were not to remain long at Baldwin, as preparations for moving on Iuka were soon begun. As commissary supplies were gathered in for the approaching campaign they were stored in the freight department of depot. One R.M. Tevis, of Galveston, was acting as commissary of subsistence, and Charlie Dunn, of Shreveport, was his assistant. They occupied a small room, the station agent's office, in the building during the day. A good many fatigue men were usually about the place during the day to handle the stuff that was brought in.

One day while I was on the platform, a country wagon drove up. Tevis and Dunn seemed to have expected its arrival, as they were soon out looking after the unloading. Among the rest was a barrel, a well-hooped, forty-gallon barrel, and instead of being sent in with the other stores it was hurriedly rolled into the private office of the commissary. This proved to be a barrel of peach brandy. Now peach brandy was "contraband." The character and contents of the barrel were shrewdly guessed by the bystanders as it was hurried into its hiding-place, and its locality after it had been stowed away was clearly observed and mental note made thereof. The depot building was located at the north end of a cut and was elevated fully three feet above the ground, platforms and all. The

Third Texas was camped along on the east side of the cut, say one hundred yards below the depot. The supplies were guarded day and night, the guards walking their beats, around on the platform. The next morning the guards were seen pacing the beats all right enough, but in the bottom of that barrel was an auger hole, and there was an auger hole through the depot floor, but there was not a gill of brandy in the barrel. At dress parade that morning it was unnecessary to call in an expert to determine that the brandy when it leaked out, had come down the railroad cut. The two gentlemen most vitally interested in this occurrence dared not make complaint, but bore their sad bereavement in profound silence, and no one else ever mentioned it.

This brief stay at Baldwin terminated our summer vacation and our study of Hardie's infantry tactics. The constant all-summer drilling and the strict discipline we had been subjected to had rendered our dismounted cavalry the most efficient troops in the army as they were good in either infantry or cavalry service, as was afterwards abundantly proved.

All things being ready, the march to Iuka was begun under General Price, with his two divisions. Up to this time the only infantry marching I had done, beyond drilling and reviews, was the two moves, Tupelo to Sattillo and Sattillo to Baldwin. As we were furnished transportation for cooking utensils only, the men had to carry all their worldly effects themselves and the knapsack must contain all clothing, combs, brushes, writing material and all else the soldier had or wished to carry, in addition to his gun, his cartridge box with forty rounds of ammunition, his cap box, haversack, and canteen. The weather was extremely hot, and the roads dry and fearfully dusty. While I had been on full duty for some time I was very lean, physically weak, and far from being well, and starting out to make a march of several days, loaded down as I was, I had some misgivings as to my ability to make it; but I did not hesitate to try. As the object of the expedition was to move on Iuka and capture the force there before General Grant could reënforce them from Corinth, a few miles west of that place, the troops were moved rapidly as practicable, the trains being left behind to follow on at their leisure. Unfortunately for me, I was on guard duty the last night before reaching our destination, and as we moved on soon after midnight I got no sleep.

Next morning after daylight, being within six or seven miles of Iuka, the Third Texas and Third Louisiana were placed in front, with orders to march at quick time into Iuka. Now literally this means thirty inches at a step and 116 steps per minute; practically it meant for us to get over that piece of road as rapidly as our tired legs could carry us. To keep up with this march was the supreme effort of the expedition on my part. I do not think I could have kept up if Lieutenant Germany had not relieved me of my gun for three or four miles of the distance. We found the town clear of troops, but had come so near surprising them that they had to abandon all their commissary stores, as they did not have time to either remove or destroy them. At the end of the march my strength was exhausted, and my vitality nearly so. The excitement being at an end, I collapsed, as it were, and as soon as we went into camp I fell down on the ground in the shade of a tree where I slept in kind of stupor until nearly midnight.

We remained about a week in and around Iuka, in line of battle nearly all the time, expecting an attack by forces from Corinth; and as it was uncertain by which one of three roads they would come, we were hurried out on first one road and then another. One afternoon we were hurriedly moved out a mile or two on what proved to be a false alarm, and were allowed to return to camps. On returning we found a poor soldier lying in our company camp with a fearful hole in his head, where a buck and ball cartridge had gone through it. A musket was lying near him, and we could only suppose he was behind in starting on the march, and had killed himself accidentally.

On the night of September 18 we marched out about four miles on the Corinth road, leading west, and lay in line of battle until about 4 P.M. the next day, when a courier came in great haste, with the information that the enemy was advancing on the Bay Springs road from the south, with only a company of our cavalry in front of them. We had then to double quick back about three miles in order to get into the road they were on. We found them among the hills about one and a half miles from the town, a strong force of infantry with nine or ten pieces of artillery and occupying a strong position of their own selection. We formed on another hill in plain view of them, a little valley intervening between the two lines. Our fighting force consisted of General Little's division of two brigades, Hebert's, and a brigade of Alabama and Mississippi troops commanded by Colonel John D. Martin, and the Clark battery of four guns, Hebert's brigade in front of their center, with two of Martin's regiments on our right and two on our left. We began a skirmish fire, and kept it up until our battery was in position, when we began a rapid fire with canister shot. We then advanced in double line of battle slowly at first, down the hill on which we had formed, across the little valley and began the ascent of the hill on which the enemy was posted, General W.S. Rosecrans in command. As we ascended the hill we came in range of our own artillery and the guns had to be silenced. The entire Federal artillery fire was soon turned on us, using grape and canister shot, and as their battery was directly in front of the Third Texas, their grape shot and musketry fire soon began to play havoc with our people, four of our men, the two files just to my right, being killed. We charged the battery and with desperate fighting took nine pieces and one caisson. The horses hitched to the caisson tried to run off, but we shot them down and took it, the brave defenders standing nobly to their posts until they were nearly all shot down around their guns, one poor fellow being found lying near his gun, with his ramrod grasped in both hands, as if he were in the act of ramming down a cartridge when he was killed. The infantry fought stubbornly but after we captured their guns we drove them back step by step, about six hundred yards, when darkness put an end to a battle that had lasted a little more than two and a half hours, the lines being within two hundred yards of each other.

I cannot give the number of Federal troops engaged in the battle, but General Rosecrans, in giving his casualties, enumerates eighteen regiments of infantry, three of cavalry, one detached company, and four batteries of artillery. The cavalry was not in the engagement, and I think he had but two batteries engaged. One of these, the Eleventh Ohio Light Battery, lost its guns and fifty-four men. The total Federal loss, reported, was 790, including killed, wounded, and missing. Hebert's brigade, that did the main fighting, was composed of six regiments, reporting 1774 for duty, and lost 63 killed, 305 wounded, and 40 missing; total, 408. Colonel Martin had four regiments (1405 men), and lost 22 killed and 95 wounded; total, 117. We had two batteries with us, the Clark battery and the St. Louis battery, but they only fired a few shots. The Third Texas had 388 men, and lost 22 killed and 74 wounded; total, 96. Company C lost W.P. Bowers, Carter Caldwell, W.P. Crawley and W.T. Harris killed; and J.J. Felps severely wounded. Crawley had a belt of gold around his waist, but only four or five of us knew this, and I presume, of course, it was buried with him. General Maury's division was not engaged. General Henry Little, our division commander, was killed. Lieutenant Odell, of the Third Texas, who was acting regimental commissary, and who was mounted on my horse, was killed, and the horse was also killed. Colonels Mabry and Whitfield, and, I believe, all our other colonels were wounded. The captured artillery was drawn by hand into town that night, where the guns were left next morning, after being spiked, as we had no spare horses to pull them away. Spiking guns means that round steel files were driven hard into the touch-holes, giving the enemy the trouble of drilling these out before the guns can be of any use again.

As General Ord was marching rapidly with a strong force from Corinth to reënforce General Rosecrans, General Price concluded to retreat. Putting the trains in the road some time before daylight, early in the morning the troops marched out southward, leaving our wounded men in Iuka and sending a detail back to bury the dead. As General Hebert's brigade had stood the brunt of the battle the evening before, we were put in front and, to clear the road for the other troops, we had to move at double quick time for six miles. This used me up, and I obtained permission to go as I pleased, which enabled me to outgo the command and to rest occasionally while they were coming up. We made a march of twenty-five miles that day on our way back to Baldwin. But oh, how my feet were blistered! They felt as if I had my shoes filled with hot embers. Late in the afternoon, when I was away ahead of the command I came to Bay Springs. This little village stands on a bluff of a wide, deep creek, and is crossed by a long, high bridge. At this time, when the creek was low, the bridge was at least twenty-five feet above the mud and water below. I climbed down under the bluff, just below the bridge, to a spring, where I slaked my thirst, bathed my burning feet and sat there resting and watching the wagons cross the bridge. Presently a six-mule team, pulling a wagon heavily loaded with ammunition in boxes, was driven onto the bridge, and as it was moving slowly along one of the hind wheels, the right one, ran so close to the edge that the end of the bridge flooring crumbled off and let the wheel down. Gradually this wheel kept sliding until the other hind wheel was off. This let the ammunition go to the bottom of the creek, followed by the wagon bed. Soon off came one fore wheel. This pulled off the other one, then the wagon tongue tripped the offwheel mule and he dangled by the side of the bridge, and soon pulled the saddle mule off and this process gradually went on, until the last mule started, and as he fell off his hamstring caught on the end of the bridge flooring, and for an instant the whole outfit of wagon and six mules hung by the hamstring, then it broke and went down, the wagon and the six mules atop of it. The driver had seen the danger in time to make his escape.

We soon arrived at Baldwin, our starting point. Our wounded left at Iuka fell into the hands of the enemy and were kindly treated and well cared for. The good women of the town and surrounding country came to their rescue nobly and they received every necessary attention.

Captain Dunn, of Company F, was one of our badly wounded men, one of his legs having been broken by a grape shot. Captain Dunn was a unique character. He was a lawyer by profession, a very bright fellow and lived at Athens, Tex. The first I ever knew of him he came to Rusk just before the war, to deliver an address to a Sunday school convention. He was a very small man. In fact, so diminutive in stature that he was almost a dwarf. He was a brave, gallant soldier, a companionable, pleasant associate, and much of a wag. He was a great lover of fun, so much so that he would sacrifice comfort and convenience and risk his reputation in order to perpetrate a joke.

The ladies who came to nurse and care for our wounded soldiers at Iuka were like other women in one particular respect, at least,—they were desirous to know whether the soldiers were married or single, religious or otherwise, and if religious, their church relationship, denominational preferences and so on, and would converse with the boys with a view of learning these particulars. The usual questions were put to Captain Dunn by one of these self-sacrificing attendants. He made no effort to deny that he was married and, with some hesitation, frankly acknowledged that he was a member of the church of the Latter Day Saints, usually called Mormons, which was enough information for one interview. With the exclamation, "Why, *you* a Mormon!" the woman retired. In whispers she soon imparted to all the other ladies who visited the hospital the astounding information that one of the Texas soldiers was a Mormon. They were incredulous, but after being vehemently assured by the interviewer that she had it from his own lips, some believed it was true, while others believed it was a joke or a mistake. To settle the question they appointed a committee of discreet ladies to ascertain the truth of the matter, and the committee promptly waited upon Captain Dunn.

Without loss of time in preliminaries, the spokeswoman of the committee said: "Captain Dunn, we have heard that you are a Mormon and have come to you, as a committee, to learn the truth of the matter. Are you a Mormon?" "Yes, madam," said Captain Dunn. "Have you more than one wife?" "Yes," said Captain Dunn, "I have four wives." "Captain Dunn, don't you think it awful wrong? Don't you think it's monstrous to be a Mormon?" "No, madam," said Dunn, "that's my religion, the religion I was brought up in from childhood. All of my regiment are Mormons. All of them that are married have two or more wives. The colonel has six; some have four, and some five, just as they may feel able to take care of them." A meeting of the ladies was then called, an indignation meeting, and indignation was expressed in unmeasured terms. The very idea! That they had scraped lint, torn their best garments into bandages, had cooked and brought soups and all the delicacies they could prepare to the hospital—done all they could, even to ffering up their prayers, for a detestable Mormon, with four wives! It was unanimously resolved that it could be done no longer. From that good hour, in passing through the hospital ministering to the wants of all the other wounded, they gave Dunn not even as much as a look, to say nothing of smiles, cups of cold water, soups, cakes, pies, and other more substantial comforts.

This neglect of Captain Dunn was eventually noticed by the other soldiers, talked of and regretted by them and its cause inquired into. They earnestly interceded with the ladies in his behalf, and urged them that whatever Captain Dunn's faults might be, he was a brave Confederate soldier, and had been severely wounded in an attempt to defend their homes, that he was suffering greatly from his wounds; that if he was a Mormon he was a human being, and for humanity's sake he deserved some attention and sympathy and should not be allowed to die through neglect. This argument finally prevailed, the resolution was rescinded, and the captain fared well for the rest of the time, even better than he had before the matter came up.

One day one of the ladies asked Captain Dunn how it happened that he got his leg so badly crushed. In the most serious manner he said to her: "Well, madam, I am captain of a company and when we got into the battle the Yankees began shooting cannonballs at us, and to protect my men I got out in front of them and would catch the cannonballs as they came and throw them back at the Yankees; but when the battle grew real hot they came so fast I couldn't catch all of them, and one of them broke my leg."

As soon as our men thought they were able to travel they were paroled and allowed to go free. When Captain Dunn was paroled he went to

Texas for a rest, until he supposed he might be exchanged. On his return, he was traveling through Arkansas when a woman on the train asked him where he was going? He replied, "Madam, I am going to Richmond in the interest of the women of Texas. I am going to make an effort to induce the Confederate congress, in view of the great number of men that are being killed in the war, to pass a law providing that every man, after the war ends, shall have two wives."

When paroling our people their paroles were filled out by a Federal officer and presented to them for their signatures. The majority of the men cared little about the form, but only of the fact that they were to be allowed to go free until they were exchanged. But when they came to Colonel Mabry he read the parole over very carefully. He was described as H.P. Mabry, a colonel in the "so-called Confederate States Army." Mabry shook his head and said, "Sir, can you not leave out that 'so-called'?" He was informed that it could not be done. "Then," said the colonel, "I will not sign it." "In that case," said the officer, "you will have to go to prison." "Well," Mabry replied, "I will go to prison and stay there until I rot before I will sign a parole with that 'so-called Confederate States' in it." Captain Lee, of the Third Texas, was of the same way of thinking, and they both went to prison and remained there until they were exchanged, being sent to some prison in Illinois. Some months after they were exchanged and came back to us we captured some prisoners one day. One of them inquired if the Third Texas was there, and was told that it was. "Then," said he, "take me to Colonel Mabry or Captain Lee, and I'll be all right." This man was a "copperhead" whose acquaintance they had made while in prison. He didn't want to serve in the army against us, but had been drafted in, and was glad of an opportunity of changing his uniform.

At Baldwin about two days was spent in preparation for a march to Ripley, there to join General Van Dorn's command for a move on Corinth. I was on fatigue duty while at Baldwin, and had no time to recuperate after the hard campaign to Iuka and back, having been on guard duty the night before arriving at Ripley. We camped at that town one night and started next morning, September 29, 1862, for Corinth, General Van Dorn in command. On that morning I found myself with a fever, and feeling unequal to a regular march I obtained permission to march at will, and found Lieutenant R.L. Hood and F.M. Dodson in the same condition and having a like permit. We joined our forces and moved up the hot, dusty road about six miles. Being weary, foot-sore, and sick, we turned into the woods, lay down and went to sleep under some oak trees and did not wake until the beef cattle were passing us in the afternoon. This meant that we had slept until the army was ahead of us—cavalry, infantry, artillery, and wagon train. We moved on until night without overtaking our command. Nearing the village of Ruckersville it occurred to me that many years ago this had been the post office of Peter Cotten, my mother's brother. Stopping at a house to make inquiries, learned that Willis Cook, his son-in-law, lived only three-quarters of a mile west of the village. We turned in that direction, and soon found the place without difficulty. My call at the gate was answered by my uncle at the front door. I recognized his voice, although I had not heard it since I was a small boy. Going into the house I made myself known to him and his daughter, Mrs. Crook, and received a cordial welcome, such a welcome as made me and my comrades feel perfectly at home. My good cousin, Tabitha, whose husband, Willis Crook, was in the cavalry service, and in the army then on its way to Corinth, soon had a splendid supper ready for us and in due time offered us a nice bed. We begged out of occupying the beds, however, and with their permission stretched our weary limbs under a shade tree in the yard and enjoyed a good night's sleep.

Next morning one or two of the party had chills, and we rested for the day. We soon learned that a Federal cavalry command had dropped in behind our army and so we were cut off. Had we gone on in the morning we would probably have been captured during the day. Learning how we could find parallel roads leading in the direction we wished to go, late in the evening we started, traveled a few miles and slept in the woods. The next morning we moved on until ten o'clock, and meeting a ten-year-old boy on a pony in a lane, we asked him if he knew where we could get something to eat. He said there was a potato patch right over there in the field. We asked him to whom it belonged, and he answered: "It belongs to my uncle; but he is laying out in the brush to keep out of the army," and told us that his uncle lived up on the hill a short distance ahead of us. We did not go into the potato patch, but went up to the uncle's house. The house was a fairly good one, and in the front were two good-sized rooms with a wide, open hall. As we marched up to the rail fence in front of the house a woman came out into the hall, and we could see that the very looks of us aggravated and annoyed her. By way of getting acquainted with her, Dodson said: "Madam, have you got any water?" In a sharp, cracked voice, she answered: "I reckon I have. If I hain't, I would be in a mighty bad fix!" Having it understood that Dodson was to do the talking, we marched in and helped ourselves to a drink of water each, from a bucket setting on a shelf in the hall. During the next few minutes silence of the most profound sort prevailed. We stood there as if waiting to be invited to sit down and rest, but instead of inviting us to seats she stood scowling on us as if she was wishing us in Davy Jones' locker or some similar place. Hood and myself finally moved a little towards the front of the hall, and the following dialogue took place between Dodson and the woman: Dodson: "Madam, we are soldiers and are tired and hungry. We have been marching hard, and last night we slept in the woods and haven't had anything to eat. Could we get a little something here?" "No, you can't. I don't feed none of your sort. You are just goin' about over the country eatin' up what people's got, and a-doin' no good." "Why, madam, we are fighting for the country" "Yes, you are fightin' to keep the niggers from bein' freed, and they've just as much right to be free as you have." "Oh, no madam; the Bible says they shall be slaves as long as they live." "The Bible don't say no sech a thing." "Oh, yes, it does," said Dodson, gently; "let me have your Bible and I'll show it to you." "I hain't got no Bible." "Madam, where is your husband?" "That's none of your business, sir!" "Is he about the house, madam?" "No, he ain't." "Is he in the army, madam?" "No, he ain't. If you *must* know he's gone off to keep from bein' tuk to Ripley and sold for twenty-five dollars." "Why, madam, is he a nigger?" "No, he ain't a nigger; he'just as white as you air, sir." "Well, madam, I didn't know that they sold white men in Mississippi." "No, you don't know what your own people's a-doin'." During the conversation I kept my eye on the lowest place in the fence. What she said about being sold for twenty-five dollars was in allusion to a reward of that amount offered by the conscript authorities for able-bodied men who were hiding in the brush to keep out of the army.

That night we lodged with a good old Confederate who treated us the best he could. Next morning Dodson bought a pony from him, which we used as a pack-horse to carry our luggage. We then moved much easier. Late in the evening we crossed Hatchie River on the bridge over which the army had passed on its way to Corinth. Here we found Adam's Brigade and Whitfield's Legion guarding the bridge, that it might be used in the event of the army's being compelled to retreat. This bridge was only a short distance south of the Memphis and Charleston Railroad, and a few miles west of Corinth. We took the railroad and followed it nearly all night, turning off to sleep a little while before daylight. Early in the morning we struck across into the main-traveled road, and pushed on in an effort to rejoin our command. About nine or ten o'clock we came to a house, and determined to try for some breakfast, as we were quite hungry. We afterwards learned that a poor old couple occupied the house. Walking up to the front door we asked the old lady if we could get some breakfast, telling her we had been out all night and were hungry and so on, the usual talk. She very readily said yes, if we would wait until she could prepare it. She then invited us to come in and be seated, and said she would have the meal ready in a few minutes.

In a little while she came back and invited us in to breakfast in a little side room used for a kitchen and dining-room. As we started in I was in front, and as we entered the little dining-room and came in sight of the table she began to apologize because she was unable to give us anything more. I glanced at the table and saw a small, thin hoe-cake of corn bread and a few small slices of bacon, "only this and nothing more." I asked her if that was all she had. She answered that it was. Then I said, "Where are you going to get more when that is gone?" She did not know. Not doubting the truth of her statements, I said: "Madam, while we are hungry and do not know when we will get anything to eat, we could not take all you have. While we are just as thankful to you as if you had given us a bountiful breakfast, we are soldiers, and can manage to get something to eat somewhere, and will leave this for you and your husband," and we bade her good-by without sitting down to the table or tasting her scanty offering.

This poor old woman, who must have been sixty or more years old, had said, without a murmur and without hesitation or excuse, that she would prepare us some breakfast, and gone about it as cheerfully as if she had had an abundance, cooking us all the provisions she had, and only regretted she could not do more for us,—this, too, when not knowing where she would get any more for herself.

After leaving this humble abode we soon began to meet troops, ambulances, and so on, and from them we learned that our army was falling back. Instead of going farther we stopped on the road side and waited for our command. Noticing a squad of soldiers out some distance

from the road engaged apparently about something unusual, my curiosity led me out to where they were. To my surprise I found they were
Madison County, Alabama, men, most of whom I knew. They were
burying a poor fellow by the name of Murry, whom I had known for
years, and who lived out near Maysville. They had rolled him up in his
blanket and were letting him down into a shallow grave when I approached, and they told me that some of the boys that I knew were
wounded—in a wagon just across the road. I soon found my old friends,
John M. Hunter and Peter Beasley of Huntsville, Ala., in a common
rough road-wagon. Poor Hunter! he was being hauled over the long,
rough road only that he might die among his friends, which he did in a
few days. Beasley was not dangerously wounded.

We soon after joined our command and marched westward toward
Hatchie bridge. But long before we got there Generals Ord and Hurlbut
had come down from Bolivar, Tenn., with a heavy force of fresh troops,
had driven our guards away and were in undisputed possession of the
crossing. Whitfield's Legion had been on the west side and had been so
closely crowded, with such a heavy fire concentrated on the bridge, that
they had to take to the water to make their escape.

Here was a problem confronting General Van Dorn, a problem which
must be speedily solved, otherwise a dire calamity awaited his whole
army. These two divisions of fresh troops were in front of an army of
tired, hungry worn-out Confederates, with General Grant's victorious
army only a few miles in our rear. What was called the boneyard road
ran some miles south of us and crossed the river on a bridge at Crum's
Mill; but this bridge, as a precautionary measure, had just been burned,
and even now its framework was still aflame. The route we were on led
west from Corinth parallel with, and but a little south of the Memphis
and Charleston Railroad, crossing Hatchie only a short distance south
of Pocahontas. After crossing the river we would turn south on the main
Ripley road, and this road ran parallel with the river, passing not far,
three or four miles perhaps, west of Crum's Mill, so that a force might
move rapidly from Corinth, on the boneyard road, cross at Crum's Mill
and strike us in the flank and possibly capture our trains. Hence the
precaution of burning this bridge. Everything of our army, whether on
wheels, on foot, or on horseback, was now between Ord and Hurlbut in
front and Grant and Rosecrans in the rear, without a crossing on Hatchie.
The trains were parked, with a view as I was told at the time, to burning

them, leaving the troops to get out as they could, and we already had visions of swimming the stream. Personally I was wondering how much of my luggage I could get over with, and whether or not I could make it with a dry gun and cartridge box. General Price, in this dilemma, undertook to get the trains out, and he succeeded notably.

We had a pretty heavy skirmish with the forces at the bridge, with infantry and artillery, but only to divert attention from the trains as they moved out to gain the boneyard road. General Price went to the mill and, pulling down the gable end, cast it on the mill dam, and thus made a temporary bridge over which the trains and artillery were driven. Then that gallant old man, who had just proved himself to be as much at home acting as chief wagon master as when commanding his army corps, sat on his horse at the end of his unique bridge nearly all night, hurrying the wagons and artillery across. On the west bank of the stream he kept a bonfire alight, which threw a flickering glare across the bridge. As each teamster drove on to the east end of the queer bridge, he would slow up his team and peer through the dim light for the proper and safe route. Just as he would slow up one could hear the loud, distinct voice of "Old Pap" shouting: "Drive up there! Drive up! Drive up! Drive up!" And thus it continued until every wheel had rolled across to the west side of the Hatchie.

After we left the vicinity of the bridge and after the skirmishing ceased, there was no time for order in marching, unless it was with the rear guard; no time to wait for the trains to stretch out into the road and to follow it then in twos. We fell into the road pell-mell, and moved in any style we wished to, in among the wagons, or any way just so we moved along and kept out of the way of those behind us. During the afternoon, in the middle of the road, I stumbled upon a small pile of corn meal, half a gallon, maybe, that had sifted out of a commissary wagon, and gathered part of it into my haversack, mixed with a little dirt. I crossed the bridge away along, I suppose, about 11 P.M., after which I stopped and watched General Price's maneuvers and the crossing of the wagons until after midnight.

In the meantime I hunted around and found an old castaway tin cup, dipped up some river water and made up some dough, and then spreading it out on a board, I laid it on General Price's fire until it was partially cooked. Surely it was the most delicious piece of bread I have ever tasted, even to this day.

When a good portion of the Third Texas had come up we moved on into the Ripley road and were sent northward for a mile or two, where we lay in line of battle in ambush, near the road until the trains had all passed.

After daylight we moved on towards Ripley, being again permitted to march at will, as we had marched the night before. Approaching Ruckersville my heart turned again toward my good cousin, Tabitha Crook. Taking little David Allen with me, I made haste to find her home. Arriving there a short time before dinner I said to her, "Cousin, I am powerful hungry." "Oh, yes," she said, "I know you are, Willis came by home last night, nearly starved to death." Soon we were invited into her dining-room and sat down to a dinner fit for a king. Here I met her brother, George Cotten, whom I had never seen before. After dinner Mrs. Crook insisted that we rest awhile, which we did, and presently she brought in our haversacks filled up, pressed down, and running over with the most palatable cooked rations, such as fine, light biscuits, baked sweet potatoes, and such things, and my mess rejoiced that night that I had good kins-people in that particular part of Mississippi, as our camp rations that night were beef without bread.

We then moved on to Holly Springs and rested for some days, after a fatiguing and disastrous campaign, which cost us the loss of many brave soldiers, and lost General Van Dorn his command, as he was superseded by General J.C. Pemberton.

The battle of Corinth was fought October 3 and 4, 1862. I do not know the number of troops engaged, but our loss was heavy. According to General Van Dorn our loss was: Killed, 594; wounded, 2162; missing, 2102. Total, 4858. The enemy reported: Killed 355; wounded, 2841; missing, 319. Total, 3515. But if General Rosecrans stated the truth, our loss was much greater than General Van Dorn gave, as he (General R.) stated that they buried 1423 of our dead, which I think is erroneous. Company C lost our captain, James A. Jones, mortally wounded; John B. Long and L.F. Grisham, captured. As Captain Jones could not be carried off the field, Long remained with him and was taken prisoner, being allowed to remain with Captain Jones until he died. They were sent to Louisville, Ky., and then to Memphis, Tenn., where Captain Jones lingered for three months or more. After his death, Long, aided by some good women of Memphis, made his escape and returned to us.

It was at the battle of Corinth that the gallant William P. Rogers, colonel of the Second Texas Infantry fell in such a manner, and under such circumstances, as to win the admiration of both friend and foe. Even General Rosecrans, in his official report, complemented him very highly. The Federals buried him with military honors. It was at Corinth, too, that Colonel L.S. Ross, with the aid of his superb regiment, the Sixth Texas Cavalry, won his brigadier-general's commission.

The evening before reaching Holly Springs we had what in Texas would be called a wet norther. Crawling in a gin-house I slept on the cotton seed, and when we reached Holly Springs I had flux, with which I suffered very severely for several days, as the surgeon had no medicine that would relieve me in the least. In a few days we moved south to Lumpkin's Mill, where we met our horses and were remounted, the Third, Sixth, Ninth and Whitfield's Legion composing the cavalry brigade, which organization was never changed. The army was soon falling back again, and continued to do so until it reached Grenada, on the south bank of Yalabusha River.

LLOYD BRYNER

A Yankee in Mississippi

The general who was to lead his bluecoats to two successive victories over Price's Confederates was Major-General William S. "Rosey" Rosecrans. His solid fighting ability, while criticized by Grant, won the attention of President Abraham Lincoln who gave Rosecrans the leadership of the Army of the Cumberland on 23 October 1863. Serving in "Old Rosey's" ranks at both Iuka and Corinth was Lloyd Bryner of the 47th Illinois. His account of the battle is taken from his stirring work *Bugle Echoes.*

Upon Col. Bryner's departure, William A. Thrush, who had been made Lieutenant-Colonel after the death of Miles, assumed command of the regiment. The band which, ever since the departure from Peoria, had been a source of pride and pleasure to the regiment, was ordered discharged. The expenses of the government were enormous and all unnecessary impediments were being dispensed with. Bugles, drums and fifes could sound the calls and brass bands were allowed henceforth only to brigade headquarters and fighters and marchers like Mower had no use for them even there.

For almost three weeks the regiment remained at Rienzi, breaking camp August 18th, 1862, and once more starting on a seemingly endless tramp. Eighteen miles this day through a village, they say it is Jacinto; at the end of the day another village on a railroad, which some say is the Memphis and Charleston, and the village Burnsville. The soldier doesn't know until the war is over, when he looks it up on the map, and then knows it is so. Memory of such marches is a horrid nightmare. Stifling dust those August days, parched throats and aching eyes seared by sun and irritated by sand, the smell of sweaty leather from burdening knapsack—weighting cartridge box and haversack—gun barrels that are hot and bayonets whose glint is an irritation, the water in the canteen hot and brackish, though the cloth cover is kept well wet; when a stream is reached, a rush from the ranks, water hastily dipped and dashed in the face, canteen refilled and countless steps again to the camp at night unless, and it often happened, necessity required an all-night march, when the only bivouac fires were God's stars, and the tramp, tramp, tramp, went steadily on, fifty minutes of marching and ten minutes of rest, and so the boys of the "Eagle Brigade" marched for four years and five months.

From Burnsville to Iuka was another eight miles, twelve miles to Bear Creek and another twelve to Cane Creek, Alabama; good camp there and good to remember, plantations large, darkies a-plenty to point out supplies, hens, eggs, sweet potatoes, hams. A soldier's lot is not so bad after all. There are shading pines in Alabama and clear springs, by which to camp at night, and ten miles with the smell of pines and a spring was found at Tuscumbia, near the Tennessee River.

Soldiering is not all heroic. One stops to put shoulder to wheel of mired wagon or gun at times, roads must be cut through woods, enemy's stores are seized and must be loaded upon wagon or railroad trains. It was confiscated cotton at Tuscumbia and the 47th was detailed to do the loading upon cars. Cotton was valuable and the North would welcome it.

September 8th the regiment took the back track towards Corinth again and camped at Cane Creek; twenty-four miles to Bussard's Roost, the "Johnnies" pressing the rear guard and killing one cavalryman. On the 10th they camped at Iuka, reached Burnsville on the 11th and on the 12th were again at the old camp at Clear Creek, which they had left in June. Price captured Iuka almost immediately after the regiment had left there. Other than guerilla operations there had been but little of active operations from June until September.

Determining to crush Price, Grant at once put two columns in motion under Generals E.O.C. Ord and W.S. Rosecrans to accomplish this purpose. Ord was to attack in front while Rosecrans was to attack on flank and in rear. Ord had 5,000 men and additional troops were given him by a division under Gen. Ross. Rosecrans had Generals C.S. Hamilton's and D.S. Stanley's divisions, about 9,000 strong. With Hamilton's division in the advance the "Eagle Brigade" with Stanley's division left Camp Clear Creek on the night of the 18th with three days' cooked rations and 100 rounds of ammunition for each man and marching through a drenching rain only reached San Jacinto, twenty miles south of Iuka, the following evening, having been detained by falling in rear of Ross through fault of the guide. Hamilton had pushed forward, listening for the sound of Ord's guns, and found a line of battle two miles from Iuka on densely wooded heights. The ground was in terrible condition, unknown to the Union troops and with no room for development. Hamilton's skirmishers were driven back and a desperate battle ensued. On the crest of the hill stood the 11th Ohio battery. Hamilton fought three times his own force led by Price in person—the battle became furious. In front, up the road, came the enemy's heavy columns. From the battery upon the hill a deadly fire was poured into the advancing foe. The Confederate musketry concentrating upon the devoted battery soon killed or disabled most of the horses. The wounded animals ran shrieking, mad with pain and fear. On came the line of gray only to be hurled back in disorder. "The Eagle Brigade" came into action on the double quick, the 47th on the left of the 11th Missouri, the 5th Minnesota on the right and the Wisconsin 8th in support. A whole brigade of Texans born down upon the 48th Indiana, which was forced to give about one hundred yards, when it was met and supported by the 4th Minnesota and held its position until relieved by the 47th Illinois. Three times the guns on the crest of the hill were charged by the Confederates, the cannoniers were bayoneted at the guns; seventy-two dying at their posts. In the last desperate attempt two Mississippi brigades were sent to the work. As the first brigade came from the woods, bearing down upon the 11th Missouri and when within one hundred paces a Confederate officer sprang forward and shouted, "Don't fire upon your friends, the 37th Mississippi." He was answered by a withering volley which drove them back in confusion. The Second Confederate brigade followed, darkness had come on, the smoke of battle hung so heavy that objects could scarcely be seen at five paces. On came the brave Mississippians but as vainly beat the waves against the rocks as these Confederate heroes against the Illinois boys of the 11th Missouri. They were received at the point of the bayonet from which they were fired, officers discharged their pistols in the very faces of their foes and the battle closed. The 47th Illinois and 39th Ohio held the front, slightly in front of the advanced regiments, which were withdrawn to replenish their ammunition. It was now night and the battle which had raged for several hours was over. The next morning the enemy was gone. The 47th Illinois lost one killed, five wounded and Major Cromwell captured. After the battle 162 Confederate dead were found, collected for burial, in the rear of their hospital, covered with tarpaulins. The entire Union loss was nearly 800 killed, wounded and missing; the Confederates losing over 1,400, amongst whom were General Little and Colonel Stanton, killed. One thousand six hundred and twenty-nine stand of arms, 13,000 rounds of ammunition and quantities of stores fell into the hands of the Union troops. The usual laudations in general orders followed, of which every regiment in the "Eagle Brigade" received its due share. Iuka was ordered placed upon the colors of the 47th following "Island Ten," "New Madrid" and "Farmington."

Pursuing the enemy, who retreated toward Ripley, there was everywhere found that saddest of sights, the desolated path of a defeated army in flight. The Confederates had been obliged to leave their dead unburied, their wounded to the mercies of the victors. Demoralized and dispirited, discipline had relaxed, and the line of retreat was marked by acts of vandalism. A Confederate soldier wrote: "Corn fields were laid waste, potato patches robbed, barn yards and smoke-houses despoiled, hogs killed and all kinds of outrages, perpetrated in broad daylight and in full view of our officers." It was through such scenes the pursuit was continued to Crippled Deer, thirty miles, where finding it useless to continue further, the brigade returned by way of Jacinto to Rienzi, where it remained a few days watching the movements of Price and Van Dorn, who were concentrating their forces at Ripley, Mississippi, and preparing for advance against Corinth. The combined forces of the Confederates numbered about forty thousand men, while Rosecrans had but about twenty thousand, twelve thousand of whom were strongly entrenched at Corinth and the balance serving upon outpost duty. Late in September, Price and Van Dorn moved forward and encamped on the night of October 2d, within ten miles of Corinth. At 3 o'clock in the morning, Ocotber 1st, 1862, the bugles rang revielle and soon around a thousand fires men were busy preparing rations for a three days' march, which was to commence at daylight. An old campaigner's housekeeping is simple and orderly and sunrise found all in readiness. Assembly sounded, knapsack, haversack and accoutrements adjusted, rifles at a "right shoulder" and the column moved. At ten o'clock the Hatchie River, twelve miles distant, was reached. Here was the crossing of the Ripley and Rienzi Road and here the enemy were to be met and held, should they attempt the crossing. Arms were stacked and the time employed until five o'clock for the most part in digging up and cooking sweet potatoes from a five acre field of Confederate sand. When the halt was made Captain Harmon Andrews of Company "G" was detailed to place pickets and was absent for several hours. Returning late in the afternoon, he reported to General Mower that after placing his pickets he had gone forward several miles, where he saw the Confederate army moving rapidly and in force towards Corinth. After remaining in hiding and watching the enemy until he had counted eighteen batteries, he hurried back to camp and made his report, and at five o'clock imperative orders were issued to march to Kossuth, fifteen miles, that night. The boys knew that battle was impending and cheerfully they marched at "quick step" beneath the sun's sultry rays, in blinding sandy dust and almost without water. Until about nine P.M. all kept well up and then the heat and dust and swift pace began to tell. One by one the boys dropped out, unable to continue further. A rear guard was detailed to keep up the stragglers. With blistered feet and lolling tongues, men threw themselves beneath the trees along the roadside. Less than half the brigade was up when Kossuth was reached at midnight. Some of the companies numbered less than a dozen men. Those who reached their destination threw themselves down in the furrows of an old corn field, too weary to build fires or seek refreshment. Stragglers came up all through the night and early morning.

The morning of the 2d heard eight o'clock breakfast call and saw a change of weather. The sun was veiled by clouds and heat replaced by rain. Mud took the place of dust. There were no tents and through it all was the inimitable, indomitable cheerfulness of the American soldier. You dwellers in palatial homes, who sleep upon high-trade spring mattresses, have no idea how comfortable a bunk of fence rails properly placed upon the ground with swamp grass for a mattress is after such a march upon such a night. The boys had these and slept soundly; many—and one a brave young colonel—for the last time upon this earth. Some of the 47th added fresh pork to their supper menu of hard tack and coffee, having captured a drove of Confederate "razor back" hogs. There was but little sleep that night, for some none at all, for no matter how weary the soldier, guard and picket duty must be done. At one o'clock in the morning, the brigade was aroused; two days' rations hastily prepared—easily enough when you have only to choose between pickled pork raw and pickled pork fried with your "hard tack." The "hard tack" (army bread) was not unlike water wafers and when fresh, good; when mouldy, intolerable; when only wormy, if hungry enough, you are not fastidious. Coffee was issued whole, and ground in a quart cup with the butt end of a bayonet. Brown sugar was supplied and these usually constituted marching rations. Place these rations in a canvas haversack, let it rain all day soaking the haversack through, and at night hunger might possibly prove preferable to supper.

At three o'clock Mower had his men moving and at nine o'clock was within two miles of Corinth, at the outer line of the old Confederate entrenchments. Halting and stacking arms, coffee was prepared and at twelve o'clock the line of march was again resumed and the column moved two miles further toward the left of the already contending Union lines. The Confederates had commenced the attack upon Oliver's Brigade early in the morning and had driven him back. McArthur was sent to his support, but still the Confederate lines came on and pressed the Union line back still further. McKean and Davies had been sent to the aid of Oliver and McArthur, but the Confederates were resolved to capture Corinth with its immense quantities of stores and munitions. In a desperate charge upon the Union lines, two guns were captured. The continuous roll of musketry and the thundering artillery informed the "Eagle Brigade" of the desperate character of the conflict in which they were about to engage. The battle had raged since early dawn and fortune had thus far favored the enemy. Their whole force was now pressing heavily upon the Union center, which was being steadily driven back. The "Union Brigade," under Davies, was being flanked and McKean's position was growing untenable. Mounted orderly after mounted orderly came riding back from McKean with appeals for help. Hurried orders came to immediately advance. Utterly worn from the thirty-four miles' march of the preceding twenty-four hours, the brigade moved forward with alacrity but not sufficiently rapid for the impatient Stanley who constantly urged them to greater speed. To these urgent demands Colonel Thrush replied, "The men are already almost utterly exhausted; to move them faster will render them unfit for action." The calls for help became more and more pressing and frequent. Faster and faster came riding orderlies, excitement grew, aching limps and blistered feet were forgotten; the boys were now on the run; cheer followed cheer as they swung into line.

Passing Fort Robinett, they moved to the right of the "Union Brigade." For fifteen minutes the 47th had been under a scattering fire, but as they took position the fire from the Confederate lines became so fierce it seemed as though a magazine had exploded in their very faces. From both sides the volleys were rapid and terrific. The "Union Brigade" gave way and the left flank of the 47th became exposed. A moment more the regiment would be surrounded and prisoners, but Thrush and Stanley were there. "Fix bayonets," rang out the command from Thrush. "Charge bayonets, forward, charge," and with a rush and a cheer the Confederate line was swept back. God, how the boys fell! Thrush was killed, shot through the heart. A gentle noble soul had gone to God. He fell in the very moment of victory while cheering on his men. The 47th had lost their leader, and Captain John D. McClure took command. Adjutant Rush Chambers, calling to his men to stand fast, ran to the right wing and assumed command there, while Captain Harmon Andrews took charge of the left. Again the battle took a turn and for a while seemed to hang in even scale. The left was still exposed and without support. The men were falling like autumn leaves. Another charge—the enemy again driven back. As they reached their reserves the fight became more stubborn. Brave Captain David DeWolf was dead. Captain Harman Andrews and Lieutenant Edward Tobey wounded—Andrews a prisoner, and McClure alone in command. A portion of the enemy had gained the rear of the line—the 47th was almost without officers, and one-half the men had fallen. The survivors were terribly worn from their severe march and lack of water. A retreat was ordered. Slowly they retired, facing the foe and keeping up a steady fire.

It was now five o'clock and the men had been under a hail of lead for over two hours. The enemy were exultant and threw the whole left wing of their army against this one brigade. An avalanche of gray in ranks of serried steel—on they came. Slowly the old "Eagle Brigade" fell back; steadily pouring their fire into that line of glittering steel—and yet fell back.

Price had said he would rather capture "Old Abe" than a dozen battle flags and that to the Confederate who succeeded would be granted "free pillage" in Corinth. There he was before them and seemingly within their grasp.

There were brave hearts beneath those coats of gray and they beat with exultant hope as on they pressed, firing faster and faster, the flame from the guns almost scorching the faces of the boys in Union blue. The eagle was delirious in the delight of the strange wild storm, his wings were beating and he gave screams of frantic joy. Suddenly he was seen to spring aloft and soar away over the heads of the combatants; a halt of the lines as they paused upon both sides to watch the eagle's flight and then the sharpshooters in gray began to fire at the circling bird as he rose higher and higher with exultant cries. The smoke suddenly cleared and the eagle saw the gleam of the colors below and with magnificent swoop returned to his perch beside the Union flag.

The battle raged again with fury intensified and again the brigade was swept slowly back. They reached the ridge where Thrush had fallen. Stanley called to the men to hold their ground; fiercer the fire and more deadly that the heroic brigade poured into the foe. Not another inch was yielded and the enemy exhausted and defeated retired to the shadow of the woods. One-half of the 47th had fallen, dead or suffering from ghastly wounds.

So closed the day, October 3d, 1862. Night fell; the roar of artillery and sharp crack of musketry replaced by the cries of the wounded, the hoof beats of horses as orderlies rode hither and thither carrying reports and orders for the morrow; rumbling of ambulances bearing wounded to the hospitals; the heavy tramp of marching troops taking position; the measured tread of sentries and, piercing the gloom, an occasional un-canny scream from the woods proclaimed the vulture seeking prey. Around the bivouac fires of the 47th sat the boys—all that was left of them—sad but not dispirited. Their brave young Colonel lay at the Tishomingo Hotel in Corinth, dead. Out under the stars, somewhere upon the field, lay De Wolf and an hundred others. Andrews wounded was a prisoner and ten were missing, captured or dead, who would ever know? And tomorrow, well tomorrow they would fight again.

At one o'clock in the morning, Saturday October 4th, the regiment was aroused and moved, from the support of Fort Robinette to the support of Fort Williams. Sharpshooters were detailed to watch the movements of the enemy and all night long the crack of rifles told of their faithful vigil. The light of the stars had not yet faded when at four o'clock the Confederates opened fire upon the town from a battery of twelve pounder guns posted in the woods to the west of Robinette. Lieutenant Robinette made no reply for twenty minutes; carefully train-ing his guns to meet the expected attack. Dawn was fast approaching.

Companies "E" and "B" of the 47th, under Puterbaugh and Kimnear were upon the skirmish line and opened the fight. Shells were bursting over the heads of the Union troops. One ball passed through the Tishomingo House, killing one of the wounded. Robinette's parrot guns were now speaking; their range was perfect and the enemy were soon obliged to shift their position. Near sunrise all was silent except the occasional angry snarl of a sharpshooter's rifle. Soon after Van Dorn attacked the Union left.

Mower had ridden forward to the skirmish line—no lover more impatient for his mistress than Mower for war's troubles. The 5th Minnesota half-breeds (Hubbard's Indians) with the prudence of the white man and the sagacity of the Indian were ideal skirmishers and a portion of them were upon the skirmish line with the 47th and here was likely to be trouble to Mower's taste. As the enemy advanced the skirmish line was driven back. Mower's horse was shot under him and he was made a prisoner. On came the Confederate lines only to be met by a cross fire from the Union batteries. The fight raged for a half hour when Van Dorn was sent whirling back. A rider, bare-headed, spurring his horse at furious pace, burst from the woods through the line of gray straight for the Union lines. From the wood blazed an hundred rifles. The rider reeled for a moment in his saddle, then righted himself and spurred onward. He had been shot in the neck. As he neared the lines he was recognized; it was Mower. In the confusion of retreat he had seized the horse of a Confederate officer and, springing into the saddle, made for the National lines. Cheer followed cheer along the whole line. The "Eagle Brigade" was wild with joy.

Charge and counter charge followed—feints to conceal the real point of attack while the Confederates were shifting their forces. Orderlies were dashing in every direction; ammunition being distributed; belts tightened and cartridge boxes adjusted; nervous oaths from men unused to utter them—just to show they were not afraid; stern lips from which came no sound; a stillness that spoke aloud; the furies of hell were preparing for wild orgie on that second day at Corinth.

The storm burst at about nine o'clock. After a heavy cannonading, the Confederate forces advanced rapidly in wedge formation and drove straight for Davies. Grape and canister tore terrible lanes through the Confederate ranks, the gaps closed and the magnificent forces of gray swept onward. Seven Union batteries were in action, but the determined men of Arkansas, Texas and Mississippi never faltered. On they came over the fallen timbers. A field battery followed their advancing line to within three hundred yards of Robinette, when a timely shell from Battery Williams killed several of the gunners and horses and the guns were abandoned.

The Confederates captured Fort Powell on Davies' right and fully twenty men reached Rosecrans' headquarters. There was work here for a portion of the "Eagle Brigade," and the 5th Minnesota went to it gallantly. Cheering and cheered they went in with a rush and pressed the enemy back. Fort Powell was retaken by the 56th Illinois, while Hamilton's guns poured, in a steady fire, making fearful havoc in the retreating columns that were compelled to seek cover in the woods.

Meanwhile Lovell made a terrific attack upon Fort Robinette. Within lay prone, Fuller's Ohio Brigade, the 27th Ohio, and Mower's own regiment, the 11th Missouri, in support. Upon the advancing lines the 47th were pouring a deadly enfilading fire with telling effect, the guns of Robinette were double charged and the redoubt was a circle of flame. Magnificently mounted and bearing the Confederate colors aloft, Colonel Rogers of Texas led the line of gray, led them to the very edge of the ditch which he was in the act of leaping when the Ohio Brigade arose and delivered a murderous fire, before which the Confederates recoiled and the heroic Rogers fell; the fighting was magnificent and at the very muzzle of the guns. The line of gray was shattered and trembling, but still undaunted they advanced to the assault.

The 11th Missouri and 27th Ohio poured in a storm of bullets and advanced at a charge. The 47th, beyond the line of the enemy's fire, were pouring lead into the foe as rapidly as they could load and fire. And now the entire line sweeps to the charge and the day is won. It is eighty rods to the woods and forty "grim dogs of war" are let loose to tear at their heels, and hundreds fall. In front of Fort Robinette the Confederate dead lay piled from three to seven deep; for an hundred feet the bodies lay so close it was almost impossible to walk between them. The Confederate loss in killed, wounded and prisoners was over 9,000. The Union loss in the two days' battle and in the pursuit which followed was 2,363, of which number the "Eagle Brigade" lost 644, or more than one-quarter of the entire loss.

STEPHEN C. FOSTER

"My Old Kentucky Home"

Though his songs pre-dated the Civil War, Stephen Foster's melodies such as "Swannee River" and "Old Kentucky Home" were sung by soldiers and civilians of the North and South alike.

The sun shines bright in the old Kentucky home;
'Tis summer, and everyone is gay,
The corn-top's ripe and the meadow's in the bloom,
While the birds make music all the day.
The young folks roll on the little cabin floor,
All merry, all happy and bright;
By-'n-by hard times comes a-knocking at the door:—
Then my old Kentucky home, good-night!

Chorus-
Weep no more, my lady
Oh! weep no more today!
We will sing one song for the old Kentucky home,
For the old Kentucky home, far away.

PATRICK S. GILMORE

"When Johnny Comes Marching Home"

Probably the most famous song from the Civil War is not even associated with that great conflict. Patrick Gilmore's rousing "When Johnny Comes Marching Home" has more often than not been associated with later struggles such as World War One. There is no cause for wonder why this tune was frequently sung by those soldiers mustered out of service.

> When Johnny comes marching home again, Hurrah! Hurrah!
> We'll give him a hearty welcome then, Hurrah! Hurrah!
> The men will cheer, the boys will shout,
>   The ladies they will all turn out.
>
> Chorus—
> And we'll all feel gay
>   When Johnny comes marching home.
> The old church-bell will peal with joy, Hurrah! Hurrah!
> To welcome home our darling boy, Hurrah! Hurrah!
> The village lads and lasses say
>   With roses they will strew the way.

Chapter V

VICKSBURG

By fall of 1862, the Federals controlled most of the Mississippi River save for a comparatively small 150 mile stretch guarded by a garrison at Port Hudson, Louisiana, to the south and the fortified city of Vicksburg, Mississippi, to the north. If the Yankees ever managed to take Vicksburg, the entire range of the Father of Waters would be under Federal control, opening the river to Northern commerce, military movements, and cleaving the Confederacy in two. Beginning in the late October of 1862, U.S. Grant, commanding the Army of the Tennessee, embarked on numerous attempts to storm the Southern citadel of Vicksburg only to meet frustration and failure. Finally, by spring of 1863, Grant had crossed the Mississippi below Vicksburg and inaugurated his brilliant campaign that ended in the successful siege and capture of the city and opened the Mississippi for the Union.

JOSEPH WHEELER

The Perryville Campaign

A native of Augusta, Georgia, Joseph Wheeler rose quickly through
Confederate ranks from lieutenant in the artillery to colonel commanding a cavalry brigade in Bragg's army during the Perryville campaign.
During the later stages of the war, he led mounted operations against
Sherman's lines of supply and communications during the advance on
Atlanta and the successive march to the sea. Following the Civil War,
he returned to military service as Major General of the Volunteers in
the Spanish American War. His account of Bragg's and Smith's ill-fated
invasion of Kentucky is taken from *Battles and Leaders of the Civil War*.

General Bragg succeeded General Beauregard in command of the Confederate troops at Tupelo, Miss., about fifty miles south of Corinth, on
June 27th, 1862. The field returns of June 9th, a week after our army
reached Tupelo, reported it at 45,080. This return included the Army of
Mississippi, reënforced by the troops brought from Arkansas by Generals
Price and Van Dorn, together with detachments gathered from various
localities. About two thousand cavalry not included in this return also
belonged to the army. This was the maximum force General Bragg could
expect to concentrate at that point. General Halleck, immediately confronting Bragg with the armies of Grant, Pope, and Buell, had in and
about Corinth a force of 128,315 men, of which the field return of June
1st showed 108,538 present for duty. A division reporting 8682 for duty,
under the Federal General George W. Morgan, was at Cumberland Gap;
a division with 6411 for duty, under General Ormsby M. Mitchel, was
in north Alabama, and three brigades were located at Nashville, Murfreesboro', and other points in middle Tennessee. Buell soon started en
route to north Alabama, General Halleck remaining at or near Corinth
with seventy thousand men for duty, a force strong enough to hold

Corinth and west Tennessee, while Buell could menace or even invade Alabama or north Georgia.

The changed condition of the opposing armies during four months should now be considered. In January 1862, the confederates had held all of Tennessee and most of Kentucky and the Mississippi River from Columbus to the delta. Now, after a series of Confederate reverses, both States were virtually under the control of the armies under General Halleck, and the Federal flotilla sailed unmolested from St. Louis to Vicksburg. The Federal right was thrown forward into Mississippi. Its center occupied north Alabama, and its left was pressing the Confederates to the southern border of east Tennessee.

The Confederate problem was to devise some plan to turn the tide of disaster and recover at least a portion of our lost territory. Our soldiers had expected a battle at Corinth, in which they felt confident of as decisive a victory as was won by them on the first day of Shiloh; and the withdrawal to Tupelo had at last forced upon them a conviction that the numerical preponderance of the enemy was such that they could not expect to cope successfully with the combined armies then commanded by General Halleck.

Already the army had suffered much from sickness, and we could hardly expect any improvement while it remained idle in the locality where it had halted after its retreat from Corinth. An advance into west Tennessee would not afford protection to Alabama or Georgia. An advance into middle Tennessee by crossing the river at Florence, Decatur, or any neighboring point, would have the disadvantage of placing the Confederates between the armies of Grant and Buell under circumstances enabling these two commanders to throw their forces simultaneously upon General Bragg, who could not, in this event, depend upon any material cooperation from the army in east Tennessee under General Kirby Smith. There was another line for an aggressive movement. A rapid march through Alabama to Chattanooga would save that city, protect Georgia from invasion, and open the way into Tennessee and Kentucky without the disadvantage of an intervening force between the column commanded by Bragg and that under the orders of General Kirby Smith. This movement was determined upon and resulted in what is called the Kentucky Campaign of 1862.

Major-General E. Kirby Smith had reached Knoxville March 8th, 1862, and assumed command of the Confederate troops in east Tennessee. The returns for June reported his entire force at 11,768 infantry, 1055 cavalry and 635 artillery. The occupation of Cumberland Gap, June 18th, by a Federal division, and the approach of Buell's forces toward Chattanooga seriously threatened his department. General Bragg recognized the inadequacy of General Smith's force, and June 27th he transferred the division commanded by Major-General John P. McCown from Tupelo to Chattanooga. Forrest and John H. Morgan had already been sent into middle Tennessee and Kentucky and the operations of these enterprising officers materially lessened the pressure upon General Smith. Correspondence between Generals Bragg and Smith resulted in an order, dated July 21st, transferring the entire Army of Mississippi to Chattanooga. To mislead the enemy and to prevent an advance upon Tupelo, Bragg had, on the 19th, sent Colonel Joseph Wheeler with a brigade of cavalry into west Tennessee, and Brigadier-General Frank C. Armstrong with a like force into north Alabama. Wheeler's operations in west Tennessee may be briefly summarized as a rapid march from Holly Springs, Mississippi, to Bolivar, Tennessee; an attack upon the outposts at that place; the destruction of bridges on the line of communications of the troops at Bolivar and Jackson; a number of slight affair with the enemy's cavalry and the burning of quantity of cotton in transit to the North.

One week was thus occupied behind the enemy's lines, the main object of the movement being to create the impression of a general advance. On July 31st Bragg and Kirby Smith met at Chattanooga, and a joint movement into middle Tennessee was determined upon, Price and Van Dorn being left to confront Grant in northern Mississippi. On August 5th Bragg sent two of his brigades (Cleburne's and Preston Smith's) to General Smith at Knoxville. General C.L. Stevenson, with nearly nine thousand men, was ordered to watch the Federal General G.W. Morgan, who occupied Cumberland Gap. General Smith started on the 14th en route to Rogers's Gap, with 4 brigades, 6000 strong. The brigades of Preston Smith and B.J. Hill were commanded by General P.R. Cleburne and the brigades of McCray and McNair were under command of General T.J. Churchill. General Henry Heth, with a force nearly 4000 strong, was ordered to march direct to Barboursville by way of Big Creek Gap, and the army was preceded by 900 cavalry under Colonel John S. Scott. General Smith had at first contemplated cutting of the supplies of the garrison at Cumberland Gap, but learning that they were well provisioned, and seeing the difficulty of supplying his own troops in the poor and barren region of south-eastern Kentucky, he determined to push rapidly on to the rich blue-grass country in the central part of the State. This determination had been communicated to General Bragg, and a march toward Lexington was commenced.

On the evening of the 29th, having reached Madison County, Kentucky, Colonel Scott found the enemy about half way between the small village of Kingston and the town of Richmond. The force displayed and resistance offered indicated that they were resolved to contest any farther advance of the Confederates. Although his troops were quite weary and General Heth was far to the rear, General Smith determined upon an immediate attack. He was in the heart of Kentucky and the Confederate commander rightly judged that boldness was the surest road to victory.

Early on the 30th, General Cleburne, being in advance with his two brigades, found that the Federal force had moved forward and was in line of battle about a mile north of Kingston and probably five miles south of Richmond. The extreme advance-guard of the enemy, about six hundred yards in front of their main line, became engaged with Cleburne's leading brigade, commanded by Colonel Hill, but after a light brush retired upon the main body of the Federal army. Hill's brigade was soon formed in line behind the crest of a low ridge which was nearly parallel with and about five hundred yards south of the position occupied by the enemy. Cleburne also brought up Douglas's battery which he placed in a favorable position near the center of his line. A fire of artillery and infantry commenced, and Captain Martin, with a second battery having arrived, was also brought into action, and for two hours both infantry and artillery were engaged from their respective positions. General Mahlon D. Manson, who was in command of the Federal army before General Nelson arrived, and who commenced the battle, now pushed his left forward to turn our right. Cleburne met this with one regiment of Preston Smith's brigade, which had been formed behind a crest in his rear, but the persistence of the enemy in that quarter made it necessary to reënforce the right with all of the reserve brigade under Preston Smith.

In the meantime General Kirby Smith had reached the field with the two brigades (McCray's and McNair's) forming General Churchill's division. He promptly dispatched that officer with one brigade to turn the enemy's right. The Federal commander, apparently disregarding this movement, still boldly advanced his own left to carry out his plan of turning the Confederate flank. This well-conceived manœuvre at first seemed to endanger the Confederate army but Colonel Preston Smith with his brigade stood firm, and after a severe struggle checked and finally drove back the advancing enemy. General Cleburne, who up to this time had displayed both skill and gallantry, was severely wounded and left the field. General Churchill had now gained the enemy's right, and by a bold and determined charge threw the enemy into disorder.

Two miles farther north the Federal force made a stand, and McCray's gallant brigade, by a rapid march, struck their right, while Cleburne's division, now commanded by Colonel Preston Smith, moved to the attack in front. The celerity of McCray's movements brought him into action before the other troops reached the field, and he suffered from the concentration of a galling and destructive fire; but the approach of Preston Smith, with troops cheering as they advanced again, caused a rout of the Federal army, closely followed by our victorious soldiers. When in sight of the town of Richmond the enemy were seen forming for a final struggle upon a commanding ridge, which had been judiciously selected by the Federal commander, Major-General William Nelson, both of the enemy's flanks being protected by skirts of woods. General Smith promptly sent McNair's brigade again to turn the Federal flank, and with the remaining force attacked directly in front. A warm fusillade lasted a few moments, when the Federal army again retreated. Early in the morning Colonel Scott had been sent to gain the rear of the town. His arrival at this moment increased the dismay of the enemy and assisted materially in securing prisoners. The reports of the division and brigade commanders show that General Smith's entire force was about five thousand. The enemy supposed it much greater, their estimate including General Heth, but his division did not join General Smith until the day after the battle. Kirby Smith's loss was 78 killed, 372 wounded, and 1 missing.

Nelson in his report speaks of his own command on the Kentucky river as 16,000 strong, and the official report of casualties is given as 206 killed, 844 wounded, and 4303 captured. The Federal official reports admit that nine pieces of artillery and all their wagon trains were captured by the Confederates. General Manson contends that the Federals engaged did not exceed 6500.

Elated with success, and reënforced by about four thousand troops just arrived under Heth, the victorious army moved forward to Lexington, and was designated by its commander as "The Army of Kentucky." During the month of September the greater portion of the army remained in that vicinity.

On September 4th Colonel Scott, with a brigade of cavalry, was ordered to push on as near as practicable to Louisville, and to destroy the Louisville and Nashville Railroad. Heth, with a division of infantry and a brigade of cavalry marched north; some of his troops, on September 6th, reached the suburbs of Covington, but his instructions were not to make an attack upon the city. Smith used vigorous efforts to gather and concentrate supplies, arouse the people, and raise and organize troops for the Confederacy.

General George W. Morgan (Federal), who was left at Cumberland Gap with 8682 men, seeing these active movements in his rear, evacuated that position on September 17th and made his way through eastern Kentucky to the Ohio River at Greenupsburg, arriving there October 3d.

While these events were happening, Bragg had organized his army at Chattanooga into two wings. The right, commanded by General Polk, consisted of Cheatham's and Withers's divisions of infantry and Colonel Lay's brigade of cavalry. The left wing, commanded by General Hardee, consisted of Buckner's and Anderson's divisions of infantry and Wheeler's brigade of cavalry. This entire force, on August 27th, reported 27,816 officers and men for duty. On the 28th the army was fairly in motion, but up to this time General Bragg had not positively determined upon his plan of campaign, and much depended upon the course pursued by the Federal army.

As early as the 22d General Buell had established his headquarters at Decherd, on the Nashville Railroad, thirty miles north-west of Stevenson, and had all the supplies at Stevenson transferred to that place. Two parallel mountain ranges, running north-east and south-west, separated him from Chattanooga. A railroad, connecting McMinnville and Tullahoma, ran nearly parallel to the north-west slope of these mountain ranges. Already he had located General Thomas at McMinnville with Wood's and Ammen's divisions, while the divisions of Schoepf, McCook, and Thomas L. Crittenden were near the Nashville and Stevenson Railroad within easy call of headquarters of Decherd. Buell seemed impressed with the belief that Bragg's objective point was Nashville, and that he would take the short route over the mountain by way of

Altamont, which movement, if made, would have placed Bragg between the force under Thomas and the rest of Buell's army. To prevent this Buell, on the 23d, ordered these five divisions to concentrate at Altamont. General Thomas reached his destination on the 25th, but, finding no enemy to confront him and learning that there was no enemy on the mountains, the nearest Confederates being at Dunlap's in the Sequatchie Valley he reported these facts to Buell and returned to McMinnville. Crittenden's division halted near Pelham, and Schoepf at Hillsboro'. McCook pressed on and reached Altamont on the 29th, where, on the 30th, Wheeler attacked his outposts, and McCook retired down the mountain. The same day General Buell ordered his entire army to concentrate at Murfreesboro'.

By September 5th, the five divisions just mentioned had reached that place, together with all detachments from along the lines of railroad except Rousseau's division, which, being on the Nashville and Decatur Railroad, marched directly to Nashville.

The strength of Buell's forces during the months of July, August, and September was estimated by witnesses before the Buell Commission, in 1863, at from 45,000 to 59,309. His own returns for June, deducting the force at Cumberland Gap, showed 56,706 present for duty, and his October returns, with the same deduction, 66,595. General Buell presented a paper to the Commission which does not question any of these statements regarding strength, but states that he could not have concentrated more than 31,000 men at McMinnville to strike the Confederate forces as they debouched from the mountains; and the same paper estimated Bragg's army at 60,000, while his returns of August 27th showed but 27,816 officers and men for duty. These facts prove the large preponderance of the Federals.

At Murfreesboro' Buell heard of Nelson's defeat at Richmond, and without halting he marched to Nashville. On September 7th he intrusted General Thomas with the defense of that city with the divisions of Palmer, Negley and Schoepf, while with the infantry divisions of McCook, Crittenden, Ammen, Wood, Rousseau, and R.B. Mitchell, and a cavalry division under Kennett, General Buell determined to race with Bragg for Louisville.

It was a fair race, as on that day most of Bragg's army was south of the Cumberland River, at Carthage and Greensboro'. Bragg was nearest to Louisville by some twenty-five miles, but Buell had the advantage of a bridge at Nashville and the assistance of the railroad to aid in his march. With seven hundred cavalry, I hastened to strike and break the railroad at points between Bowling Green and Nashville, and otherwise sought to retard the northern march of the Federal army. By the 12th it was evident to Buell that no attack would be made on Nashville, and he ordered General Thomas to join him with his own division, which had been commanded by General Schoepf. Buell reached Bowling Green with his cavalry and two divisions of infantry on the 14th, and turned his column in the direction of Munfordville. I interposed my cavalry on the Munfordville road, and also on the roads leading to Glasgow and reported Buell's movements to Bragg. General Chalmers, with Bragg's advance, reached Munfordville at daylight on the 14th and learned that Colonel Scott, with a cavalry brigade, had demanded the surrender on the night previous. Chalmers was misinformed regarding the strength of the garrison and the character of the defensive works. He attacked with vigor, but was repulsed. He reported his force at 1913 men, and his loss at 35 killed and 253 wounded. On the 14th all of Buell's six divisions had reached Bowling Green, and on the 16th he advanced vigorously to succor the garrison at Munfordville, the head of his column being opposed by cavalry. Bragg, hearing of Chalmers's attack and of Buell's movements, ordered his entire army, which had rested two days at Glasgow, to start early on the 15th *en route* for Munfordville. On the next day he reached that place, boldly displayed his army and on the 17th at 2 P.M. the fort and garrison surrendered. The Federals reported their loss at 15 killed, 57 wounded, and 4076 prisoners. We also captured their armament, 10 pieces of artillery and 5000 stand of small-arms. As might be expected, the Confederate army was much elated, and were eager to grapple with the dispirited army under General Buell.

Bragg placed his troops in a strong position south of the river, using the fort as a part of his line of defense. My command was thrown forward to meet and skirmish with the enemy who, on the 19th, commenced preparations for an attack. On the 20th General Thomas joined the Federal army with his division. General Bragg, in referring to the situation of September 20th, wrote:

> With my effective force present reduced by sickness, exhaustion, and the recent affair before the intrenchments at Munfordville to half that of the enemy, I could not prudently afford to attack him there in his selected position.

If Kirby Smith's command had been ordered from *Lexington* to Munfordville even as late as the 12th, a battle with Buell could not have been other than a decided Confederate victory. Bragg at first had determined to fight with his four divisions, and no doubt would have done so had Buell advanced on the 17th, or 18th, or 19th. Early on the morning of the 18th, General Bragg sent for me and explained his plans. I never saw him more determined or more confident. The entire army was in the best of spirits. I met and talked with Generals Hardee, Polk, Cheatham, and Buckner; all were enthusiastic over our success, and our good luck in getting Buell where he would be compelled to fight us to such a disadvantage. It is true our back was to a river, but it was fordable at several places, and we felt that the objection to having it in our rear was fully compensated by the topographical features, which, with the aid of the fort, made our position a strong one for defense. So anxious was Bragg for a fight that he sent Buckner's division to the front in the hope that an engagement could thus be provoked; but after the arrival of General Thomas, Bragg did not deem it advisable to risk a battle with the force then under his command, believing that another opportunity would offer after being joined by Kirby Smith. He therefore withdrew to Bardstown, sending to me, who still confronted Buell, the followng order, dated September 20th, through General Hardee:

> General Bragg directs that, if possible, the enemy be prevented from crossing Green River tomorrow and General Hardee instructs me to say that he expects you will contest the passage of that river at Munfordville to that end.

Buell heard of Bragg's movements and pressed forward with determination. My small brigade of cavalry contested his advance on the 20th and 21st, in efforts to comply with the instructions from General Bragg. On the afternoon of the 21st, Buell's right approached the river above the town, and at the same time he pressed forward his line of battle so rapidly as almost to command the only ford by which I could cross Green River with both artillery and cavalry. Allen's 1st Alabama Regiment, being directly in front, was thrown into column and, charging gallantly, defeated the opposing cavalry and broke through their infantry. Among our killed was the noble Lieutenant-Colonel T.B. Brown, but the charge sufficiently checked the advance to enable the command to cross the ford in good order.

On the 22d, with a clear road to Louisville, Buell moved with celerity in that direction. My cavalry contested his advance, but the country was too open to allow of effective opposition with so small a force. On the 25th the leading Federal column reached the city, and the seven divisions were all up on the 27th. Bragg, Polk, and Hardee had been kept thoroughly informed of Buell's march and of the exposure of his flank, which presented an inviting opportunity for attack, but so worn and wearied was the condition of our army that these officers did not feel justified in attempting an aggressive movement. On the 8th Bragg left Bardstown with his staff to confer with Kirby Smith at Lexington, and then proceeded to Frankfort, where, on the 4th of October, a day was occupied in the installation of the Hon. Richard Hawes as Confederate Provisional Governor of the Commonwealth.

While these events were happening Buell was making active preparations for an aggressive campaign. On the 26th Major-General Wright, commanding the Department of the Ohio, went from Cincinnati to Louisville to confer with him, and on the 27th General Halleck issued an order placing Buell in command of the troops of both departments, then in Louisville. . . .

The above [48,776] was the reported strength of the Confederate troops when the campaign began, but to make sure and to compensate for any omitted cavalry let us add 1000, making the entire force, 49,776. The losses at Richmond and Munfordville were very slight, compared to the daily depletion caused by dropping out along the route. Some were allowed to organize in squads and make their way back to east Tennessee; some sought shelter among the kind and hospitable people; some struggled along with the ambulance trains, and some were left at temporarily established hospitals, one of which, containing two hundred inmates, was captured by the enemy at Glasgow.

This character of loss always attends a rapidly moving army, and its extent can be realized when we see that Hardee's wing left Chattanooga 12,825 strong, was reënforced by Cleburne's brigade early in October; yet, even with Cleburne included, Hardee, in stating officially the force with which he fought at Perryville, says: "Thinned by battle and long and arduous service, my effective force did not exceed 10,000 men." It will be seen, therefore, that these causes reduced the Confederate ranks in much greater proportion than they were increased by enlistments and other accretions, and General Bragg in his official report of the campaign asserts that we were able "at no time to put more than forty thousand men of all arms, and at all places in battle." This included Bragg's, Smith's, and Marshall's columns, and although it is probably true that their aggregate strength in August was 48,776, it would have been as difficult for Bragg and Smith to have concentrated that number as it would have been for Buell and Wright to have concentrated the 163,633 which they commanded. Even with such a force available to drive 40,000 men out of Kentucky, General Wright on the 16th appealed to the governors of Indiana, Illinois, Wisconsin, and Michigan for additional troops. What troops came in answer to these calls I could not venture to say; but leaving these and the troops in West Virginia under General Wright out of the calculation, our strength, even after Stevenson joined us, was less than half, and but little more than one-third that of the enemy, and that powerful enemy was directly on its base of supplies, with unlimited commissary and ordnance stores, while the Confederate army had no base, was living off the country and had no possibility of replenishing ammunition. Bragg felt very keenly the misfortune caused by his inability to concentrate and gain a victory over Buell before he should reach the reënforcements which awaited him at Louisville.

In writing to the Government, September 25th, Bragg says:

I regret to say we are sadly disappointed in the want of action by our friends in Kentucky. We have so far received no accession to this army. General Smith has secured about a brigade-not half our losses by casualties of different kinds. Unless a change occurs soon we must abandon the garden spot of Kentucky....

On September 18th, Kirby Smith writes to General Bragg:

The Kentuckians are slow and backward in rallying to our standard. Their hearts are evidently with us, but their blue-grass and fat-grass are against us. Several regiments are in process of organization, and if we remain long enough recruits will be found for all the disposable arms in our possession.

These letters illustrated why a victory over Buell was necessary.

Although Kentucky maintained her neutrality as long as it was possible, the chivalric spirit of her gallant sons was fully manifested at the earliest opportunity—each obeying only the dictates of his own convictions of duty. While thousands united their fortunes with the South, other and more thousands flocked to the standard of the North.

The proud old families—descendants of the pioneers of the Commonwealth—each sent sons to do battle in the opposing armies. Friends, neighbors, kinsmen, and even brothers bade each other adieu—one to the Northern army, the other to the Confederate. Wherever daring courage, rare intelligence, extraordinary fertility of resource, or fortitude under privation and suffering were displayed, Kentuckians were conspicuous, and when the fight was over and the battle-rent banner of the vanquished Confederacy furled about its shattered staff was buried in that grave from which a resurrection is no less unwished for than impossible, the survivors of the contest from that State returned to their homes with no feelings of animosity, no brooding hopes of vengeance to be wreaked upon their late opponents.

On October 1st Buell commenced his march from Louisville upon Bragg at Bardstown. On September 29th General Thomas had been assigned by President Lincoln to the command of the army but at Thomas's request the order was revoked, and he was announced in orders as second in command.

Buell organized his infantry into three army corps, of three divisions each. The First Corps on the left, under Major-General McCook, marched through Taylorsville. The Second Corps, under Major-General Crittenden, marched through Mount Washington, and the Third Corps, under Major-General Gilbert, which formed the Federal right took the route by way of Shepherdsville. General Sill, of McCook's corps, reënforced by Dumont's independent division, marched direct to Frankfort to threaten Kirby Smith.

> Skirmishing with the enemy's cavalry and artillery marked the movement of each column from within a few miles of Louisville. It was more stubborn and formidable near Bardstown, but the rear of the enemy's infantry retired from that place eight hours before our arrival, when his rear-guard of cavalry and artillery retreated after a sharp engagement with my cavalry. The pursuit and skirmishing with the enemy's rear-guard continued toward Springfield.

General Smith prepared to meet Sill and Dumont, and on October 2d Bragg ordered General Polk to move the entire army from Bardstown via Bloomfield toward Frankfort, and to strike Sill's column in flank while Smith met it in front. For reasons which were afterward explained that order was not complied with, but, on the approach of Buell, Polk marched via Perryville toward Harrodsburg, where he expected the entire army would be concentrated. General Smith, confronted by Sill and Dumont near Frankfort, had several times on the 6th and 7th called upon Bragg for reënforcements, and Withers's division of Polk's corps was ordered to him. Reports reached Bragg exaggerating the strength of the movement upon Frankfort. He was thus led to believe that the force behind Polk was not so heavy as represented, and on the evening of October 7th he directed him to form the cavalry and the divisions of Cheatham, Buckner, and Patton Anderson at Perryville, and vigorously attack the pursuing column. Since October 1st our cavalry had persistently engaged the two most advanced of Buell's columns.

The reader should now observe, by the map that McCook's corps approached Perryville by the road through Bloomfield, Chaplin, and Mackville, its general direction being nearly south-east. General Gilbert's corps approached by the road from Springfield, its general direction being east, but bearing north-east as it approached the town. Crittenden's corps, accompanied by General Thomas and preceded by cavalry having crossed Gilbert's line of march, was on a road which runs due east from Lebanon to Danville. At a point about five miles south-west of Perryville this road has a branch which turns north-east to that place. Now remember that our stores and supplies were at Bryantsville and Camp Dick Robinson about eighteen miles east of Perryville, and that Kirby Smith was at McCown's Ferry on the Kentucky River, *en route* for Versailles, menaced by two divisions under General Sill. Also observe the important feature that McCook was at Mackville during the night of the 7th, at which place a road forks, running east to Harrodsburg and thence to our depot at Bryantsville; and also consider that Mackville was as near Bryantsville as were our troops in front of Perryville.

On the 7th our cavalry fought with considerable tenacity, particularly in the evening, when the enemy sought to get possession of the only accessible supply of water. General Buell, in his report, says:

> The advanced guard, consisting of cavalry and artillery, supported toward evening by two regiments of infantry, pressed successfully upon the enemy's rear-guard to within two miles of the town, against a somewhat stubborn opposition.

After dark, at General Hardee's request, I went to his bivouac and discussed the plans for the following day. I explained to him the topography of the country and the location of Buell's columns. I understood from him that the attack would be made very early the next morning, and I endeavored to impress upon him the great advantage which must follow an early commencement of the action. An early attack on the 8th would have met only the advance of Gilbert's corps on the Springfield

road, which was four or five miles nearer to Perryville than any other
Federal troops, and their overthrow could have been accomplished with
little loss, while every hour of delay was bringing the rear divisions of
the enemy nearer to the front, besides bringing the corps of McCook and
Crittenden upon the field. I explained, also, that Thomas and Crittenden
on the Lebanon and Danville road could easily gain our rear, while all
our forces were engaged with McCook and Gilbert. For instance, if
Crittenden turned toward Perryville at the fork five miles from that place,
he would march directly in the rear of our troops engaged with Gilbert's
corps. If he kept on toward Danville and Camp Dick Robinson, our
position would be turned, and a rapid retreat to our depot of supplies,
closely followed by McCook and Gilbert, would be the inevitable result.
With equal ease, McCook, by marching from Mackville to Harrodsburg,
could reach our depot, thus turning our right flank.

The reader will plainly see that Perryville was not a proper place for
sixteen thousand men to form and await the choice of time and manner
of attack by Buell, with his tremendous army, and that every moment's
delay after daylight was lessening the probabilities of advantage to the
Confederates. The cavalry under my command was pressed forward at
dawn on the 8th, and skirmished with the outposts of the enemy until,
on the approach of a Federal brigade of cavalry supported by a line of
infantry, we charged, dispersing the cavalry, and, breaking through both
infantry and artillery drove the enemy from their guns and took 140
prisoners.

The Federal army was now being placed in line: McCook's corps on
the left, Gilbert's in the center, and Crittenden's corps, which reached
the field at 11 o'clock on the right, its flank being covered by Edward
M. McCook's brigade of cavalry. The management of the Federal right
wing was under the supervision of General Thomas.

General Bragg reached Perryville about 10 o'clock. General Liddell's
brigade, of Buckner's division, had been advanced with his left near the
Springfield road, and his skirmish line became engaged. The cavalry on
the Confederate left apparently being able to hold their own against the
enemy upon that part of the field, Cheatham's division, composed of
Donelson's, Stewart's, and Maney's brigades, was ordered to the right,
where, between 1 and 2 o'clock, with its right supported by cavalry, it
moved forward to the attack. Generals Hardee and Buckner, seeing
Cheatham fairly in action, ordered General Bushrod Johnson's and

Cleburne's brigades forward. There being considerable space between Cheatham's left and Buckner's right, General John C. Brown's and Colonel Jones's brigades, of Anderson's division, and General S.A.M. Wood's, of Buckner's division, had been placed in position to fill the vacancy. Adams's and Powell's brigades, of Anderson's division, were to the left of Buckner, and the line thus arranged with cavalry on both flanks gallantly advanced upon the enemy. Cheatham was first in action and was almost immediately exposed to a murderous fire of infantry and artillery which soon spread to the left of our line.

Our artillery, handled with great skill, told fearfully on the enemy who sought, when practicable, to take shelter behind stone walls and fences. Fortunately we were enabled to enfilade many of their temporary shelters with a well-directed fire from our batteries, and this, added to our musketry, was so effective that first one regiment, then another, and finally the entire Federal line, gave way before the determined onset of our troops.

At one time Cleburne and Johnson seemed checked for a moment, as they assailed a very strong position, the fire from which cut down our men and severely wounded General Cleburne. But encouraged by the steady advance on both right and left, these troops recovered from the shock, and with increased speed the entire line overran the enemy, capturing three batteries and a number of prisoners. Among the dead and wounded Federals lay one who, the prisoners told us, was General James S. Jackson, the commander of one of McCook's divisions. General Liddell, who had been placed in reserve followed the movement, and when the contest became warmest was sent to reënforce Cheatham, where he did valiant service.

During this sanguinary struggle, our line had advanced nearly a mile. Prisoners, guns, colors, and the field of battle were ours; not a step which had been gained was yielded. The enemy, though strongly reënforced, was still broken and disordered. He held his ground mainly because our troops were too exhausted for further effort. At one point just at dusk we captured a disorganized body, including a number of brigade and division staff-officers. Soon darkness came on and we rested on the field thus bravely won.

Our entire force engaged, infantry cavalry and artillery was but 16,000 men. Our loss was 510 killed, 2635 wounded, and 251 missing. Generals S.A.M. Wood and Cleburne were disabled, and a large proportion of higher officers were killed or wounded. Three of General Wood's staff were among the killed.

General Buell lost 916 killed, 2943 wounded, and 489 captured by the Confederates. General Jackson, commanding a division, and General Terrill and Colonel Webster, commanding brigades, were among the Federals killed, and Colonel Lytle was among the wounded.

At every point of battle the Confederates had been victorious. We had engaged three corps of the Federal army; one of these McCook's, to use Buell's language, was "very much crippled," one division, again to use his language, "having in fact almost entirely disappeared as a body."

After darkness had closed a battle, it was a custom to send messengers or notes to the nearest generals, detailing results, telling of this or that one who had fallen, and asking information from other portions of the field. Resting quietly on the ground, the army expected, and would gladly have welcomed, a renewal of the fight on the next day, but the accumulation of Buell's forces was such as not to justify further conflict in that locality. Kirby Smith was near Lawrenceburg with his own troops and Withers's division, and after full consultation it was determined to march to Harrodsburg, where it was hoped the entire Confederate force in Kentucky might be concentrated. I was directed with the cavalry to prevent an advance on the road leading to Danville. At night the troops withdrew to Perryville, and at sunrise continued the march. It was long after this when the Federal pickets began to reconnoiter, and it was fully 10 o'clock when, standing on the edge of the town, I saw the advance of the skirmish line of Buell's army. Bragg prepared for battle on the Harrodsburg road, only eight miles from Perryville, and awaited Buell's advance.

Two days elapsed, and the Federal army evinced no disposition to attack. A division of infantry and a brigade of cavalry fought me back to near Danville, and at the same time Buell formed with his right within four miles of that place, making a feint in Bragg's immediate front on the road leading from Perryville to Harrodsburg. Buell, no doubt, hoped to cut him off from the crossing of the Dick River near Camp Dick Robinson.

I sent General Bragg information of Buell's dispositions, whereupon he issued orders to his army and wrote me as follows:

HARRODSBURG, KY., October 10th, 1862.

COLONEL WHEELER. DEAR COLONEL: I opened your dispatch to General Polk regarding the enemy's movements. The information you furnish is very important. It is just what I needed and I thank you for it. This information leaves no doubt as to the proper course for me to pursue. Hold the enemy firmly till to-morrow. Yours, etc., BRAXTON BRAGG

Bragg had now determined to retreat to Knoxville by the way of Cumberland Gap. It was evident that Buell's large army would enable him to select his own time and position for battle unless Bragg chose to attack. Bragg already had 1500 sick and over 3000 wounded. A severe battle would certainly have increased the wounded to 4000 or 5000 more. The care of such a number of wounded would have embarrassed, possibly controlled, our movements.

Hardee states that he had but 10,000 men before the battle of Perryville, and Bragg said that the three divisions which fought that battle had but 14,500. If that was correct they had now but 11,000.

It was too hazardous to guard our depot of supplies and contend with the Federal forces within easy march. Our wagon trains were immense, and our artillery large in proportion to other arms.

The enemy pushed up close to Danville on the night of the 10th, but we easily held him in check until all our army had crossed Dick River. On the 11th we contended against a force of infantry which finally pressed us so warmly that we were compelled to retire east of Danville. Here the enemy was again driven back, and we held our position near the town.

Before day on the 13th I received the following appointment and instructions in a special order from General Bragg, dated Bryantsville:

Colonel Wheeler is hereby appointed chief of cavalry and is authorized to give orders in the name of the commanding general. He is charged under Major-General Smith with covering the rear of the army and holding the enemy in check. All cavalry will report to him and receive his orders.

Compliance with the above of course involved considerable fighting, but by using the cavalry to the best advantage, and adopting available expedients, the movement of our infantry and trains in retreat was unmolested. These engagements were constant, and were often warmly and bitterly contested.

The large trains of captured stores made the progress of our infantry very slow and the corps commanders sent frequent admonitions to me urging the importance of persistent resistance to Buell's advance. In crossing Big Hill, and at other points, the trains hardly averaged five miles a day and General Kirby Smith at one time regarded it as impossible for the cavalry to save them. In his letter to Bragg, on the 14th, he says: "I have no hope of saving the whole of my train"; and in his letter on the 15th he says: "I have little hope of saving any of the trains, and fear much of the artillery will be lost." But fortunately nothing was lost. Our cavalry at times dismounted and fought behind stone fences and hastily erected rail breastworks, and when opportunity offered charged the advancing enemy. Each expedient was adopted several times each day and when practicable the road was obstructed by felling timber. These devices were continually resorted to until the 22d, when the enemy ceased the pursuit, and early in November the cavalry force, which covered the retreat from Kentucky, reached middle Tennessee and was close to the enemy, less than ten miles south of Nashville.

The campaign was over. Buell was deprived of his command for not having defeated Bragg, who, in turn, was censured by the Southern people for his failure to destroy the Federal army commanded by Buell.

This campaign was made at a time when the opposing Governments hoped for more from their generals and armies than could reasonably be accomplished. The people of the South were misinformed regarding the resources at the disposal of Generals Bragg and Kirby Smith, and our first successes aroused expectations and hopes that the Kentucky movement would result in the defeat, or at least the discomfiture, of Buell's army, the possible invasion of the North, and certainly the recovery of Confederate power in the central and eastern portions of Kentucky and Tennessee. They were sorely disappointed when they heard of General Bragg's withdrawal through Cumberland Gap, and could not easily be convinced of the necessity of such a movement immediately following the battle of Perryville, which they regarded as a decisive victory. The censure which fell upon Bragg was therefore severe and almost universal. It somewhat abated after the prompt advance of the army to Murfrees-boro'; but to this day there are many who contend that Bragg should have defeated Buell and maintained himself in the rich and productive plains of Kentucky. On the other hand the Federal Government was, if possible, more severe in denunciation of General Buell, and held that, far from allowing General Bragg to cross the Tennessee River and the mountains into middle Tennessee, Buell should have anticipated these movements, occupied Chattanooga, and, as some even contended, marched his army toward Atlanta. The Government was convinced that he could easily have met and halted Bragg as he debouched from the mountains before entering middle Tennessee. It was emphatic in its assertion that ordinary celerity on the part of General Buell would have saved Munfordville and its garrison of 4200 men; that proper concentration would have destroyed the Confederate forces at Perryville, and that the plainest principles of strategy represented the opportunity of throwing forward a column to cut off Bragg's retreat via Camp Dick Robinson, or that at least after the commencement of the conflict at Perryville he should have pressed close to his antagonist and forced Bragg to continuous battle, contending, as they did, that superior numbers and proximity to his base gave the Federal commander advantages that, if properly improved, would have resulted in the destruction of the Confederate army.

Buell's strategy and tactics were the subject of Congressional investigation and inquiry by a military commission. With regard to the adverse criticisms on Bragg's campaign it must be admitted that there were opportunities, had they been improved, to cripple, if not to defeat, the Federal army.

The failure to "concentrate and attack" tells the story of the campaign. The first opportunity was on September 18th, when we caught Buell south of Munfordville. Bragg could not have attacked at Altamont, because it will be remembered that on August 30th, at the first appearance of our cavalry, the Federal force retreated from that place down the mountain. Neither could he have overtaken Buell's troops at McMinnville, because, fully three days before Bragg could have reached that place, Buell had ordered all his army to Murfreesboro'.

Those who contend that Bragg should have followed Buell to Nashville do not consider that he would have found him in a good position, strengthened by fortifications, and defended by 9 divisions of infantry and 1 of cavalry; his available force for duty then being 66,595.

After the surrender of the Federal fort at Munfordville, it became painfully apparent that a single mind should control the Confederate troops in Kentucky, and concentrate our entire force and attack the divided enemy; but a condition existed which has been repeated in military operations for four thousand years, and always with disastrous results. The troops in Kentucky had two commanders. The troops of two different departments were expected to coöperate.

Both Kirby Smith and Bragg were brave and skillful generals. The devotion of each to the cause in which they were enlisted was absolute, and their only ambition was to contribute to its success. In their characters the pettiness of personal rivalry could find no place, and either would willingly have relinquished to the other the honor of being the victor, if victory could only have been won.

It will be remembered how promptly, in the preceding June, General Bragg had weakened his own army and strengthened Smith's by sending McCown's division from Tupelo to Chattanooga, and again in August by sending the brigades of Cleburne and Preston Smith from Chattanooga to Knoxville; and again, when Smith was pressed at Frankfort, that Bragg reënforced him promptly with one of his best divisions. That Kirby Smith would, at any time, have been as ready and prompt to give Bragg any part or all of his army there can be no doubt, but when the decisive moment came, the two independent armies were more than one hundred miles apart, and neither commander could be informed of the other's necessities. Bragg and Smith conferred together, but neither commanded the other. If all the troops had belonged to one army Bragg would have ordered, and not conferred or requested.

To aggravate the difficulties inherent in the system of independent commands and divided responsibility, Brigadier-General Marshall, who had commanded in West Virginia, appeared upon the field of active operations with 2150 men. He was an able and distinguished man and determined in his devotion to the Confederacy. He wished to do his full duty but he appeared to feel that he could render more efficient service with a separate command than if trammeled by subordination to a superior commander; and his aversion to having any intervening power between himself and the President was apparent.

While General Smith was anxious to cooperate, he nevertheless, in reply to Bragg's request for cooperation, wrote indicating very forcibly that he thought other plans were more important; and, in fact, the only cooperative action during the campaign was Bragg's compliance with Smith's request to transfer to him two brigades on August 5th, and to transfer Withers's division to him on October 7th.

In reply to the question as to what one supreme commander could have done, I confidently assert he could have concentrated and attacked and beaten Buell on September 18th south of Munfordville. He could then have turned and marched to Louisville and taken that city. If it should be argued that this plan involved unnecessary marching on the part of Kirby Smith, who was then at Lexington, a supreme commander could have adopted the one which was contemplated by Bragg early in the campaign.

After the surrender of Munfordville he could by September 21st have reached Louisville with all the force in Kentucky, taken the city, and then risked its being held by a small garrison while making another concentration and attack upon Buell.

As an evidence of how easily we could have taken Louisville, it must be observed that on September 22d Buell sent Major-General Nelson orders containing these words:

> If you have only the force you speak of it would not, I should say, be advisable for you to attempt a defense of Louisville unless you are strongly intrenched; under no circumstances should you make a fight with his whole or mainforce. The alternative would be to cross the river or march on this side to the mouth of Salt River and bridge it so as to form a junction with me. . .

Nelson seemed to concur with Buell, and it was not until that officer was but a day's march from Louisville that Nelson telegraphed the fact to General Wright, saying, "Louisville is now safe; 'God and Liberty'"

In further corroboration of this, "Harper's History" p. 311, says:

> Just before the Federal army entered Louisville, on the 25th of September, the panic there had reached its height. In twenty-four hours more Nelson would have abandoned the city.

But suppose neither plan had been adopted, the next chance for a supreme commander of the Kentucky forces was to "concentrate and attack" Buell's flank while his army was strung out *en route* to Louisville. Elizabethtown would have been a good place, and had it been done with vigor about September 23d it certainly would have resulted in victory. But at this time General Smith's forces were all moving to Mount Sterling, 130 miles to the east of that place (Elizabethtown), and General Smith was asking, not ordering, General Marshall to cooperate with him. The next field upon which a supreme commander had an opportunity to concentrate and attack was at Perryville. Three hundred cavalry could have played with Generals Sill and Dumont around Frankfort, and every other soldier, except a few scouts, could then have struck Gilbert's corps as day dawned on the 8th of October.

Since, in the final result, we neither defeated Buell nor took Louisville, it is now evident that it was unfortunate Bragg did not foresee the end immediately after his victory at Munfordville. He could certainly have crippled Buell to some extent as he attempted his hazardous flank movement *en route* to Louisville, and then, by a rapid march, he could have reached and captured Nashville and returned and established himself at Bowling Green.

I have pointed out these lost opportunities as an additional proof of the adage, as old as war itself, "that one bad general is better than two good ones." The very fact that both the generals are good intensifies the evil; each, full of confidence in himself and determined to attain what he has in view, is unwilling to yield to any one; but if both are weak the natural indisposition of such men to exertion, their anxiety to avoid responsibility, and their desire in a great crisis to lean on some one, will frequently bring about the junction of two independent armies without any deliberately planned concert of action between the commanders. Both Bragg and Kirby Smith were men who had, to an eminent degree, those qualities that make good generals, and, once together with their armies upon the same field, victory would have been certain. Both fully appreciated the fact that, when an adversary is not intrenched, a determined attack is the beginning of victory. By this means Smith had been victorious at Manassas and at Richmond, Ky., and by vigorous attack Albert Sidney Johnston and Bragg had won at every point of battle at Shiloh, on the 6th of April. Later, the Confederate points of attack were Bragg's scene of victory the first day at Murfreesboro', and the boldness of his onset gave Bragg his great triumph at Chickamauga. Nothing was therefore wanting in Kentucky but absolute authority in one responsible commander. Coöperation should be stricken from military phraseology.

In writing to the Government on August 1st, after he had met General Smith, General Bragg says: "We have arranged measures for mutual support and effective cooperation." On August 8th Bragg writes to Smith: "I find myself in your department; without explanation this might seem an unjustifiable intrusion." While it is no doubt true that General Smith was at all times willing to yield to the authority of General Bragg, yet the fact that Smith was the commander of an independent department, receiving orders from and reporting directly to the President, made him primarily responsible to the Executive, and this limited the authority of General Bragg. Nevertheless the Kentucky campaign was attended with great results to the Confederacy. Two months of marches and battle by the armies of Bragg and Smith had cost the Federals a loss in killed, wounded, and prisoners of 26,530. We had captured 35 cannon, 16,000 stand of arms, millions of rounds of ammunition, 1700 mules, 300 wagons loaded with military stores, and 2000 horses. We had recovered Cumberland Gap and redeemed middle Tennessee and north Alabama. Yet expectations had been excited that were not realized, and hopes had been cherished that were disappointed; and therefore this campaign of repeated triumphs, without a single reverse, has never received—save from the thoughtful, intelligent, and impartial minority—any proper recognition.

B.P. STEELE

Charge of the First Tennessee at Perryville

With no stunning result save forcing the Confederates to abandon
Kentucky once more, Perryville was a terribly bloody battle with the
Confederates losing over 3000 men and the Federals suffering some
4000 casualties. Distinguishing itself on that "ensanguined" Kentucky
battlefield was the First Tennessee, called the Kid Glove Regiment, as
the unit primarily consisted of youths from Nashville and central
Tennessee.

> Far and wide on Perryville's ensanguined plain,
> The thunder and carnage of battle resounded;
> And there, over thousands of wounded and slain,
> Riderless steeds from battle's shock rebounded.
> Cheatham's division was fiercely attacking,
> And proudly from his men rose cheer after cheer,
> As before them McCook was sullenly backing,
> Gallantly fighting as he moved to the rear.
> On Cheatham's left, Stewart's guns roared and rattled,
> And in the center, Donelson onward bore;
> On the right, Maney's brigade charged and battled,
> Valiantly driving the stubborn foe before.
> 'Twas there, held in reserve, impatiently lay
> The First Tennessee, the "Knights of the Kid Glove,"
> Eager and chafing to join the bloody fray—
> Help their brave comrades, and their own powers prove.
> Soon was their impatient valor to be tried,
> Soon were they to charge to the cannon's grim mouth—
> Soon upon the battle's crimsoned wave to ride—
> Soon to prove themselves worthy "Sons of the South."

For soon, at headlong speed, there came dashing down—
His steed flecked with sweat and foaming at the mouth—
The warrior-bishop—he of the "Sword and Gown"—
Who with like devotion served God and the South.
Every eye and ear of that gallant band,
Was eager turned to catch the old hero's words;
On the guns more firmly clenched was every hand,
And from their scabbards quick leaped two score of swords;
For all knew by the flash of the old chief's eye,
That he had hot work for every trusty gun;
And ready was each man to fight and to die,
In the bloody work then and there to be done.
A moment along their solid ranks he glanced,
And with just pride his eagle-eye beamed o'er them—
Assured by their firm main, that when they advanced,
No equal numbered foe could stand before them.
He noted the firm set lip and flashing eye,
And on their sun-burnt cheeks the brave man's pallor;
And knew they had the spirit to "do or die,"
For Southern honor and with Southern valor.
Then pointing towards the cannon-crested height,
Where Loomis' guns volleyed in death-dealing wrath,
He seemed as a war-god gathering his might,
To hurl missiles of destruction on his path,
And with a look that plainly said, "You must win,
For the sake of the Sunny Land that bore you,"
He shouted above the battle's fierce din,
"Forward! and carry everything before you!"
Forth they sprang, four hundred, less fifty, all told;
And as their ranks were thinned by iron and lead,
With true discipline, fearless courage, and bold,
They closed their files and rushed on over the dead.
Towards the height, bristling in hostile array,
With unwavering line the heroes rushed on—
Oh! truly was it a glorious display
Of courage—worthy the fame the "Old Guard" won.
All *dressed by the right* with veteran skill,
They moved on their way with step steady and true,

And guns at shoulder, to the foot of the hill,
As if on parade, for the "soldiers in blue."
But then their muskets spoke, their wild shouts leaped,
As before them, in rout, a regiment fled;
Many of which their bullets halted and heaped
In bloody confusion, the wounded and dead.
Now more dreadful the carnage volleyed and roared,
A volcanic crater the hill's frowning crest,
Down whose bloody sides, death's fiery lava poured,
Sweeping the young and the brave upon its breast.
Like sear leaves before the autumn blast they sank,
But their undaunted comrades pressed on o'er them—
Pressed on, with quick, steady step and closed up rank,
Hurling death into the blue links before them.
Brave Loomis' support were veterans long tried,
And nobly did they second his fatal blows;
But their numbers and valor were all defied,
By the impetuous ranks of their Southern foes.
Loomis' gunners and horses went to the dust,
And his terrible war-dogs were hushed and still;
A few more quick bounds and a bayonet thrust,
And the "kid glove soldiers" had captured the hill.
But then came stern Rousseau, a Federal "brave,"
Rapidly sweeping down with his fine command,
And threw it like a torrent, wave upon wave,
Against the brave First's shattered and bleeding band.
But they met it as meets the breakers firm rock,
The wild, towering waves of the storm lashed sea—
Met it to hurl it back with a fearful shock—
Back, like the foiled, rock-broken waves of the sea.
But just then the cry was passed along the line,
"They are flanking by the left! fall back! fall back!"
Ah! 'twas then more brilliant did their valor shine,
As with face to the foe, they retraced their track.
Proudly their reluctant, backward way they bent,
With sullen, defiant mien, firm step and slow,
Sending back defiance and death as they went,
And moved more to the left in the plain below.

And then "forward!" was again the cheering cry,
And quickly did those noble Southerners respond;
They again sprang forward, and their shouts rose high,
As they swept the hill and the wide plain beyond.
And then, when the fierce, bloody conflict was o'er,
The heroes sank down with fighting sore wearied;
And wept that of their brave comrades, full ten score,
Were wounded or dead; *but the height had been carried.*

WILLIAM L.B. JENNY

"On to Vicksburg . . ."

In attempting to assail Vicksburg, Union commanders were faced with numerous difficulties; the swampy terrain made any assault down from the North an almost complete impossibility and the Confederates blocked most of the landings on the eastern bank of the Mississippi River. The quandary of how to get around Vicksburg in order to take the town occupied Federal planners for months. An eyewitness to these and subsequent events, William Jenny wrote an account of the attempts to take the Confederate stronghold entitled *Personal Recollections of Vicksburg.*

The division under A.J. Smith proceeded to destroy the railroad running from the west to Vicksburg, over which the Confederates under General Pemberton were receiving supplies. On December 26 the other three divisions, under command of General Sherman, ascended the Yazoo about thirteen miles, and were landed on the low bottom-lands between the Yazoo and the Walnut Hills. The troops moved forward with little opposition along Chickasaw Bayou until it turned and ran parallel with the bluffs, on which the enemy were posted in great numbers and in strong position. An assault which was immediately made demonstrated that the ground was too difficult and the enemy too well fortified to be dislodged. The only passage across this bayou was in front of General Morgan's division, and this passage was much in the nature of a breach, admitting only a few men at a time, and was swept by numerous guns of the enemy. The way was then across a broad and gently sloping bottom without cover to the foot of the hills, which had to be scaled under the fire of an enemy so securely posted that almost every man amounted to an army on his own account. It was then determined to try a night attack higher up the river at Haines's Bluff, which was also protected by a bayou at its foot known as "Skillet Goliah," and beyond which the troops must be landed in order to reach the high land. The landing and assault were intended to be made under cover of an attack by the gunboats. For this purpose 10,000 men were embarked on the transports, but the night was so intensely foggy that the boats could not move and the moon rendered no service whatever to such a movement. On learning the next morning that secrecy was no longer possible, the contemplated attack was abandoned as too hazardous and Sherman reembarked his troops, without opposition from the enemy on the night of January 2, 1863. At daylight the next morning Sherman, learning that General John A. McClernand was at the mouth of the Yazoo with orders from the President to assume command of the river expedition, left his troops all on board of the transports and promptly steamed down the river to report to the new commander. We waited with the boats lying against the river bank for about three hours, expecting every moment to see the enemy coming through the woods, but in this we were happily disappointed, and finally orders were received to proceed to Milliken's Bend, the enemy only showing himself as the last boat left the bank.

On January 5, 1863, the entire force then under command of McClernand left Milliken's Bend for Arkansas Post, which was surrendered after a combined attack by the gunboats and the army. The capture of Arkansas Post was an important event, resulting in the surrender of more than 5,000 men and a large number of guns and a quantity of munitions of war. The event was heralded by General McClernand as a great victory, although he really had but little to do with the details of it. After the gunboats had opened fire the attitude of McClernand became quite theatrical; but the reduction of that rebel stronghold was largely due to the skill and efficiency of the gunboats under Porter.

McClernand next proposed to push on to Little Rock, but peremptory orders were received from General Grant directing the return of the army under McClernand at once to the Mississippi River where Grant met the troops in person at Napoleon. After a conference with his subordinates, Grant returned to Memphis and ordered McClernand to proceed to Young's Point immediately opposite Vicksburg and there complete the canal that had been commenced long before and was known to Sherman's army as "Butler's Ditch." This canal had long been discussed and its completion seems to have been a pet idea of Mr. Lincoln.

As soon as a landing was made in the vicinity of Young's Point, Sherman and his staff rode over to inspect the canal, the completion of which, it was then expected, would give us possession of Vicksburg, and would, as often remarked at that time, "leave that city an inland town"; but all our hopes were doomed to utter disappointment. The line of the canal was soon reached, and as Sherman checked his horse on the bank he remarked, "It is no bigger than a plantation ditch." But this was not all. Both ends of the proposed canal were in slack water and its entire length was within the enfilading fire of the enemy's batteries at Vicksburg, which stretched along the bluff to Warrenton, a point quite as capable of being strongly fortified as any other in the vicinity of Vicksburg. It was soon learned that the proposed canal, if completed, could be of but little practical use. While we are discussing how it could happen that so trifling an affair could have been considered of such great importance that an army of 30,000 men should be collected to complete it, an orderly arrived with a peremptory order from McClernand to General Sherman, which read: "You will proceed immediately to blow up the bottom of the canal. It is important that this be done to-night, as to-morrow it may be too late." General Sherman handed me the order with instructions to go and do it. I read the order, and looked at General Sherman. There was a roguish twinkle in the general's eye, indicating that he knew as little what the order meant as I did. A few minutes later I met General McClernand, and with all the politeness and diplomacy at my command endeavored to obtain some definite instructions. My endeavor, however, to obtain information as to what the order really meant was futile. General McClernand, pursuant to his customary manner in those days, flew into a passion, exclaiming, "You can dig a hole, can't you? You can put powder into it, can't you? You can touch it off, can't you? Well, then, won't it blow up?" With these interrogatories ringing in my ears I rode away and a suppressed "Damn" was all the "blowing up" it received that night.

We subsequently learned that a steamboat captain, one of that ignorant class from whom so many absurdities in military affairs were derived, had told General McClernand that the bottom of the canal was a thin stratum of hard clay with sand below and that by exploding some powder in the sand the clay bottom would be shattered and washed out with untold quantities of sand by the rapidly rising river. No condition of the kind existed save in the turbid fancy and grotesque superstition of an over-officious Mississippi River steamboat captain. It was one of this class of captains who went to General Grant when the army was on the bluffs behind Vicksburg, and in all seriousness proposed to Grant that he should send north for all the steam fire-engines that could be obtained, back them up against the enemy's parapets, and wash Vicksburg into the river. This watery method of reducing the stronghold of Vicksburg was never tried. But inasmuch as we had been directed to complete the canal at Young's Point the work was commenced and pushed as rapidly as possible. It was nearly completed, when one night during a heavy rain the levee gave way at the upper end of the canal and inundated the whole of the lower Peninsula, driving the troops to the levee, where the tents were huddled together as closely as they could be pitched. Dredging machines were then tried, but our men were driven off by the enemy's guns; for although the attempt was made to carry on the work at night, the light of their fires exposed their positions as soon as they opened the boiler furnace doors.

It was at this time that the governor of one of the northwestern states made us a visit. He became the guest of General Sherman, and was entertained as became his high political station. He expressed to the general his great desire to hear the sound of a shell, and, in order to gratify his ambition, Sherman sent him under escort of Colonel Dayton to the dredge, where his curiosity to hear the whiz of a hostile shell was soon adequately satisfied, and this war governor thereupon fully and cheerfully expressed himself as quite ready to go home.

The army remained for nearly four months at Young's Point with the weather very disagreeable, and the troops, huddled together on the levee, by no means comfortable or very cheerful, although complaints were rarely ever uttered either by officers or men. There seemed to be a feeling pervading the rank and file that they were the vanguard in a campaign which would be successful, and for that reason whatever of hardship was necessary to the supreme purpose of the campaign was borne with a silent heroism which was at least grateful to General Sherman.

Some amusing incidents, however, relieved the monotony of our stay at Young's Point. It was during this time that Admiral Porter constructed a dummy gunboat from a large coal barge. This dummy was rigged up with smokestacks and sloping sides, and all were covered black with a coat of coal tar so that in the obscurity of darkness, or even of moonlight, she looked very much like an ironclad. One dark night some smoke-making combustibles were lighted below the smokestack, the dummy was pushed down the river as near the Vicksburg batteries as it was prudent to go, and was then set adrift in the middle of the steam, and floated silently and majestically down the current of the Father of Waters. As soon as this dummy was discovered the Confederate batteries one after another opened fire as she came in range, but the dummy behaved admirably and kept steadily on her course without returning a shot. When General Pemberton saw that what he supposed was a real ironclad was likely to run his batteries, he sent a swift messenger down the river to where the ironclad *Indianola*, which had been captured by the Confederates, was being repaired, with orders to blow her up; but when, later, the trick perpetrated by Porter with his dummy was discovered, Pemberton sent another messenger to countermand the order to destroy the *Indianola*. This messenger, however, was too late, for we heard the explosion which destroyed the *Indianola*. Not long after this event Admiral Farragut came up the river and anchored his fleet below Warrenton. Farragut was short of coal and provisions, and in order to supply him Admiral Porter loaded some barges with coal and provisions and sent them down the river as he had sent the dummy. These barges passed the Vicksburg batteries without notice and their contents were appropriated by Admiral Farragut. The next day a flag of truce was received from Vicksburg with General Cheatham in charge. After the business connected with this flag of truce had been concluded, General Cheatham remarked, "You Yanks make very good dummy gunboats and we wasted lots of powder and shot on one of them, but you must think us green if you expected to fool us a second time by the same trick. We saw your dummies last night, but we don't waste any more powder on such trash." We smiled pleasantly and bade them an affectionate goodbye, permitting them to go away in ignorance of the fact that the second lot of dummies were really engines of destruction, because they carried the sinews of war to the fleet below.

The numerous projects which were tried one after another for the purpose of reaching high ground in the rear of Vicksburg are known to everyone. One of these expeditions consisted of an endeavor to force the gunboats through the bayous up the Yazoo above Haines's Bluff, but when an effort was made to put this plan in execution it was discovered that the enemy had cut down trees across the bayou above and were doing the same below the gunboats, and that the Confederate sharpshooters from behind the trees killed or wounded almost every man that showed himself. In this situation Admiral Porter sent a colored man with a note to Sherman begging him to come to his relief. Sherman received this note about nine o'clock in the evening, and by midnight had embarked his troops and left the Mississippi. The enemy were soon driven away and some three hundred axes were captured, which were used to help clear the bayou behind the boats, which were backed out into the river. Sherman returned in the night, and the next morning Major Chase, commanding the battalion of the Thirteenth regulars, came to my room, carefully closed the door, looked around to see that we were alone, and in a manner that indicated that he had a great secret to impart, whispered to me, "I command a battalion of regulars,—I have been on an expedition,—I must write a report,—I want you to tell me where I have been, how I went there, what I did, and if I came back the same way I went, or if not, how I did get back." Major Chase was an old soldier who had won his shoulder-straps on a battlefield in Mexico, and this incident serves to illustrate how little even battalion commanders knew of what was being done at this time. Many of these moves on the Vicksburg chessboard were very bold in their conception, made with secrecy, energy, and rapidity and all failed from a combination of natural causes, very materially assisted by an active and watchful enemy.

General Grant finally decided to make a landing below the Vicksburg batteries, and a new canal was started farther up the river where a short cut would open into a system of bayous that would take small steamboats from a point below Warrenton. These bayous were filled with trees of young growth averaging about six inches in diameter.

I was sent with the One Hundred and Seventeenth Illinois, under command of Colonel Eldredge, to clear out these trees. For that purpose we made saw-frames in the shape of the letter A with a crosscut saw across the bottom, and hung them to the trees to be cut, by a pin at the apex. The saws were put in motion by ropes worked by men on rafts. We soon found, however, that our work was rendered especially dangerous by an enemy that did not carry rebel guns. Poisonous snakes were very numerous at that season of the year in that region, and frequently hung from the trees which stretched their branches across the water. A slight tap on the branch and the snake would fall, so that, in order to keep them out of our boats and rafts, we were obliged whenever we moved to station men forward with long poles to clear the track from snakes. With our force we cut off at a point six feet under the water about seven hundred trees per day but the trees were in great numbers and our progress was slow. One stern-wheeler forced her way through the bayou; but the next day the river began to fall and the passage of the bayous became impracticable.

Next came the running of the Vicksburg batteries, and a fleet was soon collected below Warrenton sufficient to transport the troops designed for the expedition in the rear of Vicksburg. The gunboats attacked the batteries at Grand Gulf, silencing the guns, but failing either to force the evacuation or the surrender of the works at that point. That night the attack was renewed, and under its cover the transports passed below and the next morning picked up a part of McClernand's corps, the Thirteenth, and ran up and down the river so that the enemy could form but little idea where the landing was to be attempted. After some maneuvering the troops were landed at Bruinsburg, and the balance of McClernand's corps was ferried over. By noon of May 1, 1863, 18,000 men were on the east bank of the Mississippi, with no enemy in sight. Grant's movements were so well planned, and conducted with so much celerity and skill, as to have caused the utmost confusion to the enemy's camp.

General Grierson was at this same time making his raid from La Grange to Baton Rouge, and this daring attempt had caused Pemberton to send various detachments from the Confederate army at Vicksburg in several different directions in an effort to intercept and capture Grierson. This added to the confusion of Pemberton and the army under him. In order to further increase the confusion in the mind of Pemberton, Grant, before he attempted to cross the river with his troops, wrote to Sherman at Milliken's Bend, saying: "If you will make a demonstration against Haines's Bluff it will help to confuse the enemy as to my intentions. I do not give this as an order, for the papers will call it another failure of Sherman to capture Haines's Bluff." When this letter was received by General Sherman he remarked, "Does General Grant think I care what the newspapers say?" and jumped into a boat at once and rowed to Porter's flagship, where Sherman and Porter then arranged a jolly lark.

Some of the newspaper correspondents had written that Sherman protested against the running of the batteries and the crossing of the river below Vicksburg, but Sherman made no protest, and later said to me, "The campaign was entirely Grant's conception, and when Grant told me he had decided to execute it I offered him my hearty support." It was at this time that Grant adopted the motto, "Waste no time in trying to shift the responsibility of failure from one to the other, but take things as you find them and make the best of them." In all his vocabulary Grant found no such word as "can't."

But to return to the lark on the Yazoo. Sherman spread his command over the decks of the transports, with orders that every man should be in sight and look as numerous as possible. Porter ordered every boat to get up steam, and even took a blacksmith shop in tow which he left behind a point near to and concealed from Haines's Bluff, with orders to fire up every forge and make all the smoke possible. The gunboats and transports whistled and puffed, and made all the noise they could. They showed themselves to the garrison at Haines's Bluff and then drifted back and landed the men, who were marched through the woods toward Haines's Bluff until they were seen by the enemy marched a mile or so down the river, and taken again on board the transports, to go through the same farce again. The boats were kept in movement up and down the Yazoo all night, as if they were bringing up more and more troops. As soon as Grant had effected his landing he sent word to Sherman, "All right; join me below Vicksburg."

Later we learned the good effect of the demonstration of Sherman and Porter. The commander at Haines's Bluff telegraphed to Pemberton: "The demonstration at Grand Gulf must be only a feint. Here is the real attack. The enemy are in front of me in force such as we have never seen before at Vicksburg. Send me reënforcements." Pemberton recalled troops marching against Grant, who had already reached the Big Black, and sent them by forced marches to Haines's Bluff. The citizens turned out with wagons and carriages to help along the stragglers. The Confederates had no sooner reached Haines's Bluff than the nature of Sherman's maneuvers was discovered, and they were marched back again, to arrive finally in front of Grant, tired out and half demoralized.

Pemberton had a force exceeding that of Grant's in number, but it was badly scattered and handled with little ability. Grant kept his forces well in hand, so that at Champion Hills he completely routed the enemy and drove the greater part across the Big Black into Vicksburg, cutting off Loring's division, which joined General Johnson at Jackson, without transportation or artillery.

You all know the details of that brilliant campaign, which had for its object to place the Union army in a position to invest Vicksburg, and at the same time have a base of supplies on the Yazoo River. In speaking of this afterwards, Sherman said: "Any good general will fight a battle when the chances are three to one of success. Grant will fight if the chances are two to three in his favor, but in this campaign he took all the chances of war against himself, and won."

The morning after the battle I rode across the field of Champion Hills. At a place where the fight had raged the fiercest, there remained a solitary house, with all its surroundings swept away as clean as if a cyclone had passed that way. On the front veranda stood a woman weeping. I was so near her, as I turned the corner of the house, that I could not avoid speaking. I expressed the hope that she had not been unnecessarily annoyed. "Annoyed!" said the good lady "a big battle passed by here yesterday." "Where were you?" I asked. "I was trembling with fright down cellar," she replied. *Annoyed* was in her opinion too mild a word for the occasion.

On the 18th of May 1863, Grant's army appeared in sight of the fortifications of Vicksburg, and on the 19th, when Sherman's corps was in position, a general assault was ordered at 2 P.M. which did not result with any success.

That night I was ordered to lay a pontoon across Chickasaw Bayou at the point crossed by Morgan's command some five months before, in the first move in Grant's campaign against Vicksburg. The supplies we had already received had come by way of Haines's Bluff, which had been abandoned with all its artillery the morning after the battle of Champion Hills. I started at 9 P.M. with a regiment that had been detailed to do the work. The troops were worn out and hungry, and when we had made half the distance the colonel commanding ordered his men to bivouac. At daylight next morning there was a grand hunt. A flock of sheep had been discovered and soldiers were chasing sheep in every direction. Soon mutton chops were broiling at a hundred fires made from fence rails. I protested against the long delay but the colonel insisted, stating that his men had not had a square meal since they crossed the Mississippi. At length the last bone was picked, and the march was resumed. On reaching the bayou, we found Lieutenant Freeman of General McClernand's staff, who, not having had a flock of sheep to consume, and looking for his breakfast to come from the Yazoo across that pontoon, had the bridge half completed. With the additional force I had brought the bridge was quickly finished, the wagon trains from the Yazoo commenced to cross, and the campaign of investment was complete.

A little incident occurred here. Lieutenant-Colonel McFeeley, then chief commissary and now commissary-general, came to the bank from the hills at a moment when the bridge was filled with wagons coming from the Yazoo. He was about to cross, when the guard said to him, "The orders are to pass but one-way at a time"; but McFeeley knowing that it was important, that he should reach the transports at once, and being impatient of delay, attempted to force his horse beside the wagons, when, in the middle of the bridge, the animal took fright and leaped with his rider into the middle of the muddy bayou. They both went out of sight, but were quickly pulled out on the opposite bank.

Another attack was made on the Vicksburg fortifications on the 22d. By noon, when it was evident to General Grant that the place could not be carried by assault, he received a note from General McClernand stating that he had taken three of the enemy's works, "that the flag of our beloved country floated over the stronghold of Vicksburg"; he asked for reënforcements and begged that the enemy be pushed at every point, so that he might not be overwhelmed. Grant read the note and handed it to Sherman, with the remark, "If I could only believe it." Sherman, however, favored a renewal of the assault, saying, "A corps commander would not write a misstatement over his own signature at such a time." Grant replied, "I do not know," but finally decided to renew the assault, with no other results than a heavy loss.

That night there were stirring times at Grant's headquarters, where most of the corps and division commanders were assembled. McClernand was spoken of in no complimentary terms. Rawlins ordered Major Bower to open the record book and charge a thousand lives to that ___ McClernand. Rawlins used strong language when the occasion required, and this was one of them.

The only works McClernand had captured were some advanced picket posts abandoned by the enemy before our line came in sight.

In due time the St. Louis *Democrat* arrived in camp containing a vain-glorious congratulatory order from McClernand to his corps, telling them in the most laudatory language what "bully boys" they were, and what they had done. It also asserted that "at Champion Hills, where they were truly the Champions, and at Vicksburg, where, had the other corps but done their duty the stronghold would now be ours." The publication of this untimely and indiscreet order created much excitement and indignation among the other corps. General Frank Blair wrote a letter to General Sherman and told him that if he and McPherson did not take it up, he, who had already made a campaign against another general officer, Fremont, would commence another against McClernand. Thereupon General Sherman and General McPherson each wrote a letter to General Grant, enclosing letters from their subordinates. Grant wrote to McClernand asking him if the order published in the St. Louis *Democrat* was substantially correct, and stating that he had not received a copy of the order as regulations required. McClernand replied that the order as published was correct, and that he was ready to maintain its statement; that he supposed a copy had been duly forwarded to headquarters, and charged his adjutant-general with the neglect.

Grant immediately relieved McClernand, and appointed General Ord to the command of the Thirteenth corps. The order relieving him was sent to McClernand by Lieutenant-Colonel J.H. Wilson, then of General Grant's staff, and later the General Wilson commanding the cavalry division that captured Jeff Davis.

There was a particular bit of malice in selecting Wilson to carry this order, for Wilson had been a boy in the town where McClernand had formerly lived, and McClernand had never lost an opportunity to annoy Wilson with reminiscences,—of no account were they not told in an unpleasant way. Wilson handed the order to McClernand, who threw it on his table unopened. Wilson stated that he was instructed to wait and see him read it. McClernand then read the order, and, after a few moments' silence, said to Wilson that he much doubted the authority of General Grant to relieve a general officer appointed by the President, but that he would not make a point of it, —a very wise conclusion on McClernand's part, since Grant had all the bayonets.

The departure of McClernand was a relief to the whole army and the appointment of General Ord materially increased the efficiency of the Thirteenth corps.

Grant enclosed McClernand's published order, the letters of Sherman, McPherson, and Blair, and his own order relieving McClernand and ordering him to return to Illinois and report to the adjutant-general, by letter, and ordered C.C. Chaffee, lieutenant of ordnance on his staff, to take them to Washington.

Chaffee was tenting with me at General Sherman's headquarters at the time, and, as he could not leave until the next morning, we spent the night together. Chaffee remarked that as General Grant had given him the papers unsealed, with the envelope gaping open, he evidently intended that he should read them; so, lying on his cot, by the light of a candle he read them aloud. Sherman's letter was very bitter; he said that it was "the first instance on record of a commanding general congratulating his troops on their defeat"; it was not, however, for the troops at all, but to make political capital to be used thereafter in Illinois. McPherson was more mild, but very sarcastic, and in his letter said, "Although born a warrior as he himself has said, he forgets one of the traits of a true soldier, generosity and justness to his companions in arms." McPherson alluded to a story often told at that time, that in a public speech in Illinois McClernand was said to have told his audience that "Some men were born to one walk in life, and some to another. Thank God, I [McClernand] was born a warrior insensible to fear."

The siege went on. There were so few engineering officers that Chief Engineer Captain Prime did not attempt to control the approaches, but let each brigade dig as they chose toward the enemy remarking that they were ready enough to dig in that direction. The engineers were mostly employed in preparing gabions and sap-rollers; in building batteries and in making parallels connecting the numerous zigzags, and in mining.

During the night pickets were advanced beyond the parallels by both parties. When no officers were within hearing the pickets would indulge in a friendly truce, and it was not unusual to hear, "Johnny!" "Hello, Yank!" "Don't shoot and I'll come out." "Come on." "Any tobacco, Johnny?" "Yes; have you any coffee, Yank?" Our men used to dry their coffee-grounds and exchange them with the "Rebs" for tobacco. "It isn't real strong, Johnny" they would say "but it will give you some *grounds* for calling that rye drink of yours coffee." They would also exchange newspapers, and every morning we had at headquarters the Vicksburg paper of the day before. Toward the latter part of the siege these newspapers were printed on the back side of cheap wall-paper.

By the end of June the approaches were within a few feet of the enemy's ditch at several points, and General Grant then ordered preparations to be made for a general assault on the 6th of July. The ditches in the immediate vicinity of the enemy were widened and straightened, and long lines of rifle-pits were built with sand-bag embrasures for riflemen to command the enemy's parapet, so that not a man might show himself above the rebel breastworks and live.

Pemberton saw all these preparations, and fearing an assault on the 4th which he felt must be successful, surrendered on the 3d, and the

Fourth of July was celebrated by the ceremony of the surrender,—the army marching with colors flying and bands playing, while on the river the fleets from above and below, with vessels decorated with flags, sailors in holiday dress, and guns firing, were united once again.

As soon as our men were relieved from duty they made friends with their late enemy separated into squads, and as usual commenced to boil coffee and fry hard-tack and bacon. At noon I rode inside the fortifications of Vicksburg.

The place seemed filled with a gigantic picnic; thousands of little parties were seated here and there on the ground, the "Yanks" playing the host. They were talking and laughing and telling the incidents of the siege, and comparing notes. I stopped several times to listen to some of the Confederate tales of what "You-uns" and "We-uns" did. I heard one "Reb" say "You outgeneraled us, you did. T'was General Starvation that outflanked us."

The fall of Vicksburg gave us Port Hudson and opened the Mississippi River from Canada to the Gulf.

ALBERT O. MARSHALL

Champion Hills and Black River

In order to attain his objective of finally taking Vicksburg, Grant boldly cut his lines of supply and communications and went tearing into Mississippi to the south of the town. After defeating the forces under Confederate General Joseph Johnston at the state capital, Jackson, on 14 May, the Federals learned from a Confederate courier turned Yankee spy that enemy forces from Vicksburg under John C. Pemberton were attempting to link up with Johnston's army to strike at Grant's rear. Rather than allow this event to pass, the Federal general struck at Pemberton as he moved to comply, defeating the Southerners decisively at Champion Hill on 16 May 1863. On the following day, Grant's troops crushed the Confederate force guarding a crossing of the Big Black River. Both battles enabled Grant to lay siege to the beleaguered Confederates in their entrenchments before Vicksburg. Serving with the 33rd Illinois Regiment at the time, Albert 0. Marshall wrote of his experiences in the campaign in his work *Army Life: From a Soldier's Journal.*

At an early hour on Saturday morning, May 16, 1863 our entire army was aroused, a hasty breakfast consisting of some coffee and hard tack eaten, and every thing put in readiness for the coming contest. The thick woods in our front covered the Confederate army lying there and waiting for us. The ground was broken and hilly as well as covered with a heavy growth of timber. Many capital positions could be selected by an army that chose to stand on the defensive. This was the course taken by the enemy. Between where we had camped for the night and the wooded hills where the rebels had taken their stand was some open ground.

Our army corps, the thirteenth, was the left of the advancing Union army. At an early hour, between seven and eight o'clock, and before we were fairly under way, we heard the first guns of the day's contest. It was commenced by the advance of our corps and to our extreme left. This first firing being thus to the left of our army suggested the probability that the enemy was attempting to pass from the immediate front of our army and probably looking for a way to escape instead of maintaining his fighting ground.

Our heavy infantry columns immediately went forward. As they did so the slight firing we had heard in front of our left passed along to our center and became somewhat heavier. It now became apparent that the rebels had determined to make a stubborn stand. Of course all the firing yet done had been only that of the advance skirmishers on both sides. The tell-tale stubbornness with which the rebel skirmishers stood their ground, in our front, plainly showed that heavy forces of the enemy were immediately behind them. A soldier, by observation, will learn so as to know when a strong force of the enemy is near at hand as plainly as an experienced sea captain, when upon the water, can tell when a fierce storm is approaching. As we neared the open woods in our front we formed in army line in the open fields and were all ready to march in and attack the waiting rebels.

Now a strange and wonderful day's experience opened before us. Although we were the first of the Union troops upon the ground, and within striking distance of the enemy, we lay still and made no forward move. A ten minutes' march would have brought us upon the main rebel line. The real battle had not yet commenced. We formed in line and waited. During the day all of the varied phases of the fierce battle could be noted by us.

Heavy firing soon told us that the real battle had commenced. Now a fierce artillery duel would be fought and then succeeded by the more desperate and stubborn conflict of small arms. Then a seeming lull in the contest would be again followed by the fierce roar of artillery and this again followed by an infantry contest. Up and down the line the thunder roar of the battle would go; at one time fierce at one point, then to quiet there and rage with increased fury at another. The heavy cloud of battle smoke, as the dark mass arose above the trees, also told its story of the fierce contest. Now and then we would plainly hear the wild cheers of the Northern boys as some of our troops would charge upon and carry some point held by the enemy. During all this time we lay still. No order for us to go forward was given.

As the hours passed by some of our impatient soldiers would leave the ranks and go forward into the woods and then return with news of the battle. From them and other sources we had almost continual information from the front. This was hardly necessary however, for we were so near that the smoke of battle, the firing guns and the varied sounds of the fierce struggle plainly told us of advances and retreats made. The progress of the battle was ever before us.

At last, after long waiting and much wondering why we were not permitted to go forward and share in the fierce conflict, the order to "Forward, march," was given. In a brief moment we were on the way. As we started the wild and advancing cheers that rose above the battle roar told us that the Union troops were making a fierce and successful charge upon the rebel lines. As we went in the battle was well-nigh over; we went into the woods and struck the right wing of the rebel army. It vanished before us like snow beneath the summer sun. Had we struck this wing of the rebel army an hour earlier it would have been thrown upon the enemy's center and the confusion that would then have overwhelmed them would have led to the destruction of the entire rebel army. As it was, at the time when we struck them, the Union troops under McPherson had made their last charge and driven in the main rebel line, so that all were now upon a fierce run to escape. Had we been soon enough the confusion in the rebel lines would have been so great that they could not have seen any open way of escape and they would have been obliged to throw down their arms and surrender *en masse*.

We drove all before us and then rushed on to the main road where the fiercest contest of the battle had been fought. The hill upon which the enemy had made his most desperate contest was thickly covered with the dead of both sides. Broken guns and ruin covered the field. Rebel artillery with its horses and men were here and there all heaped together in a mountain of death and ruin. Over this gory field we rushed, and on into the woods beyond where we struck all that was left of the rebel army. It was the last shot of the day. The frightened enemy hardly having courage to return our first fire. We cut the remains of the rebel army apart. The largest force was driven toward Vicksburg. The other part ran over the hills and went to the east. The Thirty-third had been given the advance of the reserve force as it went upon the field. The last guns fired in the battle of Champion Hills was by our men and at the force of the enemy we drove to the rear.

Many pieces of rebel artillery fell to our hands. Hosts of rebels surrendered as we advanced. These were left for others to guard, as we pushed on, rapidly following the retreating rebels. Letting those who had gone to the east pursue their way to escape or be captured by other Union forces as their fate might be, we pushed toward the west after the rebels who were retreating toward Vicksburg. Darkness soon ended our pursuit and we stopped for the night at Edwards' Station.

At night, as the full results of the battle became known, it was found that a great victory had been won by our troops.

Having become historical, and its general results being open to all who choose to refer to the pages of written history, it is not necessary to here recount at large the scenes and results of the battle of Champion Hills.

Sunday morning, May 17, 1963, found us ready to move forward as soon as it was light enough to march. We were now given the advance. A rapid march brought us within sight of the rebel works at Black River. The outside picket guards were driven in without difficulty.

The conditions for a stubborn defense were ample. The rebel position was a strong one. At this point Black River is a stream of considerable size. The wagon road to Vicksburg, as well as the railroad, here crosses the river. On the west side of Black River are some high bluffs. We were approaching from the east. Why the Confederates did not select these bluffs on the west side of the river as the place for their fortifications, it is hard to tell; they probably thought the position chosen preferable. It certainly was a mistake. Still, the place selected for their fortifications was by no means a weak one. Had not the west bank of Black River furnished stronger natural positions, that selected by the rebels would have been considered a wise selection. Some little distance from the east side of the main river was a channel of considerable width and depth. This virtually created an island, which lay between the main river and this channel or bayou. The island was the place selected by the enemy for his fortifications. The island was of sufficient size, and the ground being comparatively level and unbroken, it was probably selected by the rebels as a better place for the movement of troops than would have been the uneven hills upon the west side of the river. Again, east of the bayou was a smooth valley varying from half a mile to a mile in width. As the attacking force would have to pass over this level ground, the rebels doubtless thought that they could easily destroy all who attempted to approach, before their works could be reached.

A range of forts well supplied with heavy artillery had been built along the east side of the bayou. These had been connected with a complete chain of breastworks for the enemy's infantry. Thus an attacking force would have to first charge over a wide space of level ground; then pass a deep and wide stream of water, and then climb the rebel fortifications upon the bank of the channel before they could reach the well fortified rebels. What possessed the enemy to waste so much valuable strength in fighting in the open woods upon Champion Hills when Black River, so near at hand, afforded them such superior positions of defense, is, indeed, a marvel.

We were upon the skirmish line and consequently the first troops in sight of the enemy that morning. The position our company held was next to and upon the south side of the road running west toward Vicksburg. This brought us in front of the center and strongest part of the enemy's works. The valley between the rebel works and the small wood-covered hills was at this point a little over half a mile in width. The valley at this point had been a cultivated corn or cane field. The previous year's furrows ran parallel with the rebel works. The small hills back of this field were covered with a thick growth of underbrush. Had the enemy been thoughtful and industrious enough to have cut and burned all of the small trees and brush upon these hills as far back as heavy artillery could reach, it would have been of untold advantage to him. To our right the valley lessened in width so that the ground covered with trees reached nearer to the rebel works. To our left it continued to widen so that the rebel works upon that part of the line had at least a mile of level ground over which to fire.

Our early morning call had evidently greatly surprised the indolent enemy. As we, upon the skirmish line, came out of the woods and upon the level field in front of their works, we beheld wild confusion in the rebel lines. Evidently they had not yet all got up and finished their breakfast, much less formed into line ready to meet us. All were aroused and called into line. If we had been supported by a solid column, at that moment, we could no doubt have rushed over and taken the works before the enemy was prepared to defend them. But just then the Union troops at hand were only those of a small skirmish line of barely sufficient strength to feel of the enemy.

From the ground we were upon, all of the movements of the enemy could be plainly noted. Officers mounted in hot haste and rushed among the rebel soldiers to arouse and hurry them into position. Every movement of the enemy was plainly seen by us. We could note the strength of each rebel command and see to which part of the line it was sent. Probably no battle was ever before fought which was so completely seen from its commencement to its end as was the battle of Black River by those of us who were upon the advance skirmish line.

To get as near to the rebel works as we did upon such ground was wonderful. For any of us to live through the fight that ensued, holding the position we did, was a miracle. Our ability to advance so close to them was no doubt largely owing to the confusion in the enemy's ranks caused by our early approach. The first firing of the rebels was fearfully wild. They seemed only to put the muzzles of their guns over their breastworks and fire into the air at random. Such firing is more apt to hit those far in the rear as the bullets fall to the ground, than to trouble those who, like us, are near at hand. Now and then a gun in the hands of a cool-headed rebel would be fired with more judgment at our line. A few were hit. I supposed that I was one of the unfortunate ones. A rifle ball passed near enough to "burn" my face. I then knew by experience how it was with so many others who for a moment supposed they were hit, when they were not. I plainly felt a hole cut through my cheek. That the passing bullet had cut a deep, long gash through the side of my face I did not doubt. I immediately put up my hand to see how much of my cheek was left, and to my glad surprise found that the bullet had simply grazed and not cut me. Those who have experienced both, insist that at the first moment, a bullet that passes near enough to "burn" by the "hot wind" of a swift revolving bullet, produces a much sharper sting than that caused by a direct shot.

Our skirmish line pressed well forward, much farther than prudence would have permitted, and then each selected the best place he could find and lay upon the ground and commenced to load and fire as opportunity offered. Amidst thickly flying bullets it is surprising how small an elevation of ground a soldier can make available as breastwork. The rough plowing of the previous year's crop had left deep furrows and corresponding ridges, the best of which served us well during the hot fight in which we were engaged. The success with which a soldier can, under such circumstances, apparently sink into the ground and out of sight while loading his gun, can not be realized by those who have never seen it done.

Some of our artillery were soon in place on the hills behind us and commenced their work upon the enemy. The artillery was supported by the infantry columns. This heavy force on the higher ground in our rear soon claimed the entire attention of the rebels in our front. They no doubt also believed that all who had advanced on the skirmish line had been killed. These things combined caused us to be neglected by the enemy so that we were at liberty to load and fire at pleasure and almost unmolested. While it, no doubt, did far more harm in the rebel ranks, still the few guns on the skirmish line attracted no attention when mingled with the fierce firing of the two contending armies. And then our nearness to the rebel line made it difficult for them to look over their works to take effective aim at us. Even when the conditions of the ground are favorable, the experience of war is that most of the firing done carries the balls high above the effective point. Situated as we were, it was safe to calculate that the rebel bullets would pass above us. There being so much vacant space in the open air compared with the little space occupied by one individual, is the reason why so few are killed compared with the amount of lead shot in battle. The space occupied by a man is but a mere speck compared with all out doors, and there are a thousand chances to miss, to one to hit him with the ball of a random shot.

Our artillery had a capital position. The hills upon which our cannon were placed were within easy range of the rebel works. Our gunners were much better marksmen than those handling the rebel artillery. The thick underbrush completely covered the movements of our men. An entire battery would be run into position under cover of the thick young trees, careful aim taken and then altogether commence a rapid fire upon the rebel works. As soon as the rebel artillery began to get their guns bearing on the spot our men would run their guns to another point and the first notice of the change the enemy would get was another well-aimed volley. With different batteries doing this and a fine range of favorable ground to stand upon our artillery did most effective work. With our sharp-shooters on the skirmish line so near at hand to annoy every one who attempted to handle a rebel cannon, and our artillerymen so well improving their opportunities, the result of the artillery duel was favorable to the Union side. All things combined produced the strange result, that superior artillery protected by complete works was worsted by smaller guns in the open field. During the fight many of the protected rebel guns were dismounted, while our artillery out in the open field escaped with but little harm.

Thus the battle raged with our cannon in our rear, and the rebel guns in our front, both firing over us. We were fortunately low enough so that both sides fired their balls and shells above us. The smoke and confusion of the heavy contest also served to withdraw all attention from our skirmish line and left us free to use our trusty rifles to the best advantage. After the engagement had commenced in earnest, the greatest danger we were in was from imperfect shells which would burst on the way and from faulty charges of powder or misdirected guns which now and then sent iron and lead to plow the ground where we lay.

It would be useless to attempt to describe the terrific scenes of this fierce contest as viewed from the position we held between the two contending forces. The heavy battle smoke rapidly rising continually opened the entire scene to our view. Even in the hottest of the fight every move of the enemy could be noted by us. One rebel officer, mounted upon a powerful white horse, attracted unusual attention. As he first started at the beginning of the fight he appeared to be supported by a numerous staff. His daring was so reckless that he often became the mark our riflemen aimed at. As time passed swiftly on, one by one of his assistants were seen to be disabled. He rode until the last of his staff had fallen or left the field, and still the rider upon the white horse, within range of our guns, continued to inspire the rebel soldiers. At last, as it became plain that the day was soon to be ours, a desire seemed to spring up to let the reckless rider live, and he was permitted to ride away at the last unharmed. As the artillery battle reached its height, all incidents and individual matters were absorbed by the fierce grandeur of the terrific storm raging around and above us. For a time the cannon in front of us, the cannon behind us, the cannon around us, thundered and roared and poured forth their fierce storm of fire and shot. Look to the front, look to the rear, look everywhere and the red-mouthed artillery seemed opened upon us. Above us was the black cloud of battle smoke, through which crashed and burst and screamed the murderous shell and ball. But few ever looked upon what we saw during that hour, and lived to tell the tale of the day's conflict. Imagination has often suggested that the grandest place from which to view a battle scene would be from a stationary balloon anchored high above the field of battle, and from thence to look down upon both contending forces. Even this would not prove equal to the position we held, because the rising smoke would then obscure the view while with us, the dense cloud continually rose so that we could look beneath it and see the entire fury of the fierce conflict.

Although the gigantic grandeur of the conflict was created by the heavy artillery and the solid ranks of infantry in our rear, still the most effective work of the entire battle was done by the line of skirmishers, who, with their trusty rifles, had approached so near the rebel works. We held our ground during the entire battle. In fact it was better to do so than to have attempted to go back while so plainly within range of the rebel guns. I had a little experience in this. Near to me was John Spradling of our company. A piece of bursting shell struck him in the side or top part or his hip inflicting a fearful wound. He supposed that it was fatal and told us that he would soon die. His wound bled badly but his strength remained so well that he soon thought that if he could get medical aid there might still be a chance for him to live. If death is inevitable a soldier will die without a single word of complaint. While there is hope of life he is anxious to improve it. Spradling became wildly anxious to get back where his wound could be attended to before he bled to death. He desired me to help him. It was a dangerous undertaking. The artillery on both sides was still firing rapidly. Standing up incurred more danger from the balls and shells swiftly flying from both front and rear over our heads. The worst, however, was to slowly walk over so much exposed ground, and that in plain sight and range of the solid line of rebel riflemen. The hope was that they would not care to waste any shots at a crippled soldier and his assistant, going to the rear. I got our wounded comrade up and started. With my gun fastened upon one shoulder—a soldier never abandons his gun—I lent my other shoulder and arm to the wounded man. He was so injured that practically he could use only one foot to assist in the walk. Going back in this condition was slow and tedious. The hope of magnanimity on the part of the rebels was mis-placed. We had not gone far before the screeching rifle balls aimed at us commenced hissing by our ears. Spradling knew that he would die if he stayed upon the field. Another ball could do no more than kill him. He begged to go on. As a soldier who could yet be useful in front I ought not to have taken the chances. But who could withstand the pleading of a wounded soldier. And then who could tell what the result would be? The chances were even that he would be hit as soon as I. Then my mission toward the rear would be ended. A soldier's life makes all reckless of danger. All places in the midst of a fierce battle are dangerous. What great difference did it make, for us to go or stay? I told Spradling to brace up and we would continue until one or the other of us fell. It is not wild to say that, during our tedious journey, at least a thousand rifle balls aimed at us passed near, and, strange to say neither of us was touched. There must have been some special Providence that protected us. With much difficulty I managed to get back over the open ground, reached the woods, dragged our wounded comrade up over the hill and then back until we met a squad with their white badges and a stretcher, in whose hands I placed the wounded soldier and who carried him back to the field hospital where his wounds would be dressed.

Relieved of our wounded soldier I turned and immediately went forward to rejoin my comrades. It is usual in such cases to remain with the main line and not hazard the attempt to reach the skirmish line in front. Probably it would be more correct to state the fact that it is always usual in all battles for the entire skirmish line to fall back out of the way when the actual engagement commences. It was only owing to the peculiar condition of the ground upon which it was fought that in this battle we upon the skirmish line retained our advanced position and allowed the heavy firing to be done over our heads.

Many indications told us that the battle would soon be ended. Most of the rebel cannon had been silenced. The rebel infantry began to exhibit evidences of uneasiness. I was anxious to be in at the end. To go forward was of course far different from what my retreat had been. Being alone I could skip along lively. There was a chance to select the ground and now and then dodge behind some protection. In short, going back was not by any manner of means a matter of recklessness.

My return had been none too soon. I had hardly reached our skirmish line when the last move in the battle of Black River was made. It was a brisk, sharp and successful charge upon the rebel works. This is how it happened: The woods to our right ran well down toward the rebel works. Colonel Bailey of the Ninety-ninth Illinois—"old rough and ready number two," General Benton had called him after the battle of Magnolia Hills—was with the advance. In their zeal the Union soldiers had pressed to the verge of the woods which brought them near to the rebel works. It became right hot for our boys so near to the enemy's lines. They had no orders to go farther; in fact, had already pushed on farther than orders had been given for them to go. The proper thing to have done was to have fallen back to a less exposed position. Colonel Bailey was one of those awkward officers who could never learn military rules. His only idea of war was to pitch in and whip the enemy whenever and wherever he could be found. By his impetuosity he became the hero of the day's battle. Had his unauthorized movement failed he would probably have been at least dismissed from the army. No, he would not. Had it failed and he come out of it alive, he might have been tried by a court-martial, but that never would have happened. His rash act was bound to succeed or Colonel Bailey would have been killed in the attempt.

Finding it disagreeable to be so near the rebel works and seeing the effective fire upon his soldiers, Colonel Bailey became fighting mad and yelled out in thundering tones that rang along the line: "Boys, it is getting too d____ hot here. Let us go for the cussed rebels!" Before the last word was out of his mouth, with a drawn sword flashing in the air, he was on a fierce run toward the rebel works. With a wild hurrah his entire command joined him in the wild race. Others to the right and left, without a moment's delay or a single command, joined in the mad career, and thus with wild cheers the entire Union line joined in a charge upon the rebel works.

The disheartened Confederates having already suffered so severely and vividly remembering the fearful pounding they had received the day before at Champion Hills, at once gave up all hope of further defense and immediately abandoned their works, and were in a hot race to the rear before the Union troops had reached their lines. Crossing the bayou was no easy matter. In front of part of our line the water was only breast deep; through this the soldiers easily waded, holding their guns and cartridge boxes above the water. In some places the stagnant water was covered with drift-wood. Here some would jump from one log to another like rabbits. In places where the water was more open a soldier running up would jump on to a floating log and the momentum of the fierce run would carry both him and the log across so that he could jump dry shod upon the other side, before the log he thus used for a boat commenced to turn wrong side up. In front of us the water was deeper and wider, but as good fortune would have it, the rebels had only removed the planks from the bridge, leaving the narrow stringers still running over. Our company immediately jumped upon these stringers and ran across like squirrels. The rest of the skirmish line followed, and thus the Thirty-third was soon all inside of the rebel works, being the first troops inside the main part of the fort. Other troops came in hot haste. The rebels were gone. And the battle of Black River was ended.

A fine lot of rebel cannon was taken with the fort. Our boys had learned a little war experience from the fight of the day before. As we drove the enemy from some of his cannon at Champion Hills, we rushed forward without regard to the guns. When we afterward sent back for them we found that the troops who had followed us had taken possession of the captured cannon, and were thus entitled to the credit of their capture. The rule is, that if a command captures artillery it must retain possession of it, or else the next command coming up will have the right to claim it. Infantry troops can not always carry captured artillery along with them, nor stop in the midst of a fight to retain possession of it. To provide for these and other difficulties that might arise, the established rule has become for the troops who capture a cannon to have one of their men "straddle" it, that is, sit upon it as though on horseback. Then the command can go to any other work at hand, and the one soldier upon the gun will be recognized by the entire army as in full possession of it. Thus one man for each piece of artillery is all the regiment need leave to retain possession of captured cannon. Of course, should any of the enemy return, the "straddling" is ended, and it is again a fight for possession of the guns. We had profited by the Champion Hills lesson, and the result was that the captured rebel forts were full of Thirty-third boys "straddling" the captured cannon. Thus we were credited with the capture of cannon enough to supply a good sized army and were more than made even for the loss of those we had neglected to "straddle" at Champion Hills. The captured guns came near being a burden to us, there were so many of them that they could not be disposed of at once, so an entire company of our regiment was detailed to take care of the captured guns until they could be properly disposed of.

The rebels retreated across the river and went toward Vicksburg. One of their batteries took position upon the high bluffs on the west side of the river and fired a few rounds at us, but as soon as they saw one of our batteries getting into position to reply to them, they "limbered up" and scampered away. This was the last we saw of the rebels at Black River.

U.S. GRANT

Capturing Vicksburg

After a few bloody repulses, Grant found he could make little headway against the almost impenetrable earthworks surrounding Vicksburg. Thus, both sides settled down to a long drawn out siege in which the Federals continuously threw shells into the enemy ranks and the town itself. In less than two months, lacking food and supplies, with no hope of relief in sight, Pemberton decided to surrender, with Vicksburg capitulating on 4 July 1863. The fall of the town culminated Grant's most brilliant triumph and continued his spectacular rise to fame. His recollections of the siege are taken from *Personal Memories of U.S. Grant.*

I now determined upon a regular siege—to "outcamp the enemy" as it were, and to incur no more losses. The experience of the 22d convinced officers and men that this was best, and they went to work on the defenses and approaches with a will. With the navy holding the river, the investment of Vicksburg was complete. As long as we could hold our position the enemy was limited in supplies of food, men and munitions of war to what they had on hand. These could not last always.

The crossing of troops at Bruinsburg commenced April 30th. On the 18th of May the army was in rear of Vicksburg. On the 19th, just twenty days after the crossing, the city was completely invested and an assault had been made: five distinct battles (besides continuous skirmishing) had been fought and won by the Union forces; the capital of the State had fallen and its arsenals, military manufactories and everything useful for military purposes had been destroyed; an average of about one hundred and eighty miles had been marched by the troops engaged; but five days' rations had been issued, and no forage; over six thousand prisoners had been captured, and as many more of the enemy had been killed or wounded; twenty-seven heavy cannon and sixty-one field-pieces had fallen into our hands; and four hundred miles of the river, from Vicksburg to Port Hudson, had become ours. The Union force that had crossed the Mississippi River up to this time was less than forty-three thousand men. One division of these, Blair's, only arrived in time to take part in the battle of Champion's Hill, but was not engaged there; and one brigade, Ransom's of McPherson's corps, reached the field after the battle. The enemy had at Vicksburg, Grand Gulf, Jackson, and on the roads between these places, over sixty thousand men. They were in their own country where no rear guards were necessary. The country is admirable for defense, but difficult for the conduct of an offensive campaign. All their troops had to be met. We were fortunate, to say the least, in meeting them in detail: at Port Gibson seven or eight thousand; at Raymond, five thousand; at Jackson, from eight to eleven thousand; at Champion's Hill, twenty-five thousand; at the Big Black, four thousand.

A part of those met at Jackson were all that was left of those encountered at Raymond. They were beaten in detail by a force smaller than their own, upon their own ground.

Of the wounded many were but slightly so, and continued on duty. Not half of them were disabled for any length of time.

After the unsuccessful assault of the 22d the work of the regular siege began. Sherman occupied the right starting from the river above Vicksburg, McPherson the centre (McArthur's division now with him) and McClernand the left, holding the road south to Warrenton. Lauman's division arrived at this time and was placed on the extreme left of the line.

In the interval between the assaults of the 19th and 22d, roads had been completed from the Yazoo River and Chickasaw Bayou, around the rear of the army to enable us to bring up supplies of food and ammunition; ground had been selected and cleared on which the troops were to be encamped, and tents and cooking utensils were brought up. The troops had been without these from the time of crossing the Mississippi up to this time. All was now ready for the pick and spade. Prentiss and Hurlbut were ordered to send forward every man that could be spared. Cavalry especially was wanted to watch the fords along the Big Black and to observe Johnston. I knew that Johnston was receiving reënforcements from Bragg, who was confronting Rosecrans in Tennessee. Vicksburg was so important to the enemy that I believed he would make the most strenuous efforts to raise the siege, even at the risk of losing ground elsewhere.

My line was more than fifteen miles long, extending from Haines' Bluff to Vicksburg, thence to Warrenton. The line of the enemy was about seven. In addition to this, having an enemy at Canton and Jackson, in our rear, who was being constantly reënforced, we required a second line of defense facing the other way. I had not troops enough under my command to man these. General Halleck appreciated the situation and, without being asked, forwarded reënforcements with all possible dispatch.

The ground about Vicksburg is admirable for defense. On the north it is about two hundred feet above the Mississippi River at the highest point and very much cut up by the washing rains; the ravines were grown up with cane and underbrush, while the sides and tops were covered with a dense forest. Farther south the ground flattens out somewhat, and was in cultivation. But here, too, it was cut up by ravines and small streams. The enemy's line of defense followed the crest of a ridge from the river north of the city eastward, then southerly around to the Jackson road, full three miles back of the city; thence in a southwesterly direction to the river. Deep ravines of the description given lay in front of these defenses. As there is a succession of gullies, cut out by rains along the side of the ridge, the line was necessarily very irregular. To follow each of these spurs with intrenchments, so as to command the slopes on either side, would have lengthened their line very much. Generally therefore, or in many places, their line would run from near the head of one gully nearly straight to the head of another, and an outer work triangular in shape, generally open in the rear, was thrown up on the point; with a few men in this outer work they commanded the approaches to the main line completely. The work to be done, to make our position as strong against the enemy as his was against us, was very great. The problem was also complicated by our wanting our line as near that of the enemy as possible. We had but four engineer officers with us. Captain Prime, of the Engineer Corps, was the chief, and the work at the beginning was mainly directed by him. His health soon gave out, when he was succeeded by Captain Comstock, also of the Engineer Corps. To provide assistants on such a long line I directed that all officers who had graduated at West Point, where they had necessarily to study military engineering, should in addition to their other duties assist in the work.

The chief quartermaster and the chief commissary were graduates. The chief commissary, now the Commissary-General of the Army, begged off, however, saying that there was nothing in engineering that he was good for unless he would do for a sap-roller. As soldiers require rations while working in the ditches as well as when marching and fighting, and as we would be sure to lose him if he was used as a sap-roller, I let him off. The general is a large man; weighs two hundred and twenty pounds, and is not tall.

We had no siege guns except six thirty-two pounders, and there were none at the West to draw from. Admiral Porter, however, supplied us with a battery of navy-guns of large calibre, and with these, and the field artillery used in the campaign, the siege began. The first thing to do was to get the artillery in batteries where they would occupy commanding positions; then establish the camps, under cover from the fire of the enemy but as near up as possible; and then construct rifle-pits and covered ways, to connect the entire command by the shortest route. The enemy did not harass us much while we were constructing our batteries. Probably their artillery ammunition was short; and their infantry was kept down by our sharpshooters who were always on the alert and ready to fire at a head whenever it showed itself above the rebel works.

In no place were our lines more than six hundred yards from the enemy. It was necessary therefore, to cover our men by something more than the ordinary parapet. To give additional protection sand bags, bullet-proof, were placed along the tops of the parapets far enough apart to make loop-holes for musketry. On top of these, logs were put. By these means the men were enabled to walk about erect when off duty without fear of annoyance from sharpshooters. The enemy used in their defense explosive musket-balls, no doubt thinking that, bursting over our men in the trenches, they would do some execution; but I do not remember a single case where a man was injured by a piece of one of these shells. When they were hit and the ball exploded, the wound was terrible. In these cases a solid ball would have hit as well. Their use is barbarous, because they produce increased suffering without any corresponding advantage to those using them.

The enemy could not resort to our method to protect their men, because we had an inexhaustible supply of ammunition to draw upon and used it freely. Splinters from the timber would have made havoc among the men behind.

There were no mortars with the besiegers, except what the navy had in front of the city; but wooden ones were made by taking logs of the toughest wood that could be found, boring them out for six or twelve pound shells and binding them with strong iron bands. These answered as coehorns, and shells were successfully thrown from them into the trenches of the enemy.

The labor of building the batteries and intrenching was largely done by the pioneers, assisted by negroes who came within our lines and who were paid for their work; but details from the troops had often to be made. The work was pushed forward as rapidly as possible, and when an advanced position was secured and covered from the fire of the enemy the batteries were advanced. By the 30th of June there were two hundred and twenty guns in position, mostly light field-pieces, besides a battery of heavy guns belonging to, manned and commanded by the navy. We were now as strong for defence against the garrison of Vicksburg as they were against us; but I knew that Johnston was in our rear, and was receiving constant reënforcements from the east. He had at this time a larger force than I had had at any time prior to the battle of Champion's Hill.

As soon as the news of the arrival of the Union army behind Vicksburg reached the North, floods of visitors began to pour in. Some came to gratify curiosity; some to see sons or brothers who had passed through the terrible ordeal; members of the Christian and Sanitary Associations came to minister to the wants of the sick and the wounded. Often those coming to see a son or brother would bring a dozen or two of poultry. They did not know how little the gift would be appreciated. Many of the soldiers had lived so much on chickens, ducks and turkeys without bread during the march, that the sight of poultry, if they could get bacon, almost took away their appetite. But the intention was good.

Among the earliest arrivals was the Governor of Illinois, with most of the State officers. I naturally wanted to show them what there was of most interest. In Sherman's front the ground was the most broken and most wooded, and more was to be seen without exposure. I therefore took them to Sherman's headquarters and presented them. Before starting out to look at the lines—possibly while Sherman's horse was being saddled—there were many questions asked about the late campaign, about which the North had been so inperfectly informed. There was a little knot around Sherman and another around me, and I heard Sherman repeating, in the most animated manner, what he had said to me when we first looked down from Walnut Hills upon the land below on the 18th of May adding: "Grant is entitled to every bit of the credit for the campaign; I opposed it. I wrote him a letter about it." But for this speech it is not likely that Sherman's opposition would have ever been heard of. His untiring energy and great efficiency during the campaign entitle him to a full share of all the credit due for its success. He could not have done more if the plan had been his own.

On the 26th of May I sent Blair's division up the Yazoo to drive out a force of the enemy supposed to be between the Big Black and the Yazoo. The country was rich and full of supplies of both food and forage. Blair was instructed to take all of it. The cattle were to be driven in for the use of our army and the food and forage to be consumed by our troops or destroyed by fire; all bridges were to be destroyed, and the roads rendered as nearly impassable as possible. Blair went forty-five miles and was gone almost a week. His work was effectually done. I requested Porter at this time to send the marine brigade, a floating nondescript force which had been assigned to his command and which proved very useful, up to Haines' Bluff to hold it until reënforcements could be sent.

On the 26th I also received a letter from Banks, asking me to reënforce him with ten thousand men at Port Hudson. Of course I could not comply with his request, nor did I think he needed them. He was in no danger of an attack by the garrison in his front, and there was no army organizing in his rear to raise the siege.

On the 3d of June a brigade from Hurlbut's command arrived, General Kimball commanding. It was sent to Mechanicsburg, some miles northeast of Haines' Bluff and about midway between the Big Black and the Yazoo. A brigade of Blair's division and twelve hundred cavalry had already on Blair's return from the Yazoo, been sent to the same place with instructions to watch the crossings of the Big Black River, to destroy the roads in his (Blair's) front, and to gather or destroy all supplies.

On the 7th of June our little force of colored and white troops across the Mississippi, at Milliken's Bend, were attacked by about 3,000 men from Richard Taylor's trans-Mississippi command. With the aid of the gunboats they were speedily repelled. I sent Mower's brigade over with instructions to drive the enemy beyond the Tensas Bayou; and we had no further trouble in that quarter during the siege. This was the first important engagement of the war in which colored troops were under fire. These men were very raw, having all been enlisted since the beginning of the siege, but they behaved well.

On the 8th of June a full division arrived from Hurlbut's command, under General Sooy Smith. It was sent immediately to Haines' Bluff and General C.C. Washburn was assigned to the general command at that point.

On the 11th a strong division arrived from the Department of the Missouri under General Herron, which was placed on our left. This cut off the last possible chance of communication between Pemberton and Johnston, as it enabled Lauman to close up on McClernand's left while Herron intrenched from Lauman to the water's edge. At this point the water recedes a few hundred yards from the high land. Through this opening no doubt the Confederate commanders had been able to get messengers under cover of night.

On the 14th General Parke arrived with two divisions of Burnside's corps, and was immediately dispatched to Haines' Bluff. These latter troops—Herron's and Parke's—were the reënforcements already spoken of sent by Halleck in anticipation of their being needed. They arrived none too soon.

I now had about seventy-one thousand men. More than half were disposed across the peninsula, between the Yazoo at Haines' Bluff and the Big Black, with the division of Osterhaus watching the crossings of the latter river farther south and west from the crossing of the Jackson road to Baldwin's ferry and below.

There were eight roads leading into Vicksburg, along which and their immediate sides, our work was specially pushed and batteries advanced; but no commanding point within range of the enemy was neglected.

On the 17th I received a letter from General Sherman and one on the 18th from General McPherson, saying that their respective commands had complained to them of a fulsome, congratulatory order published by General McClernand to the 13th corps, which did great injustice to the other troops engaged in the campaign. This order had been sent North and published, and now papers containing it had reached our camps. The order had not been heard of by me, and certainly not by troops outside of McClernand's command until brought in this way. I at once wrote to McClernand, directing him to send me a copy of this order. He did so, and I at once relieved him from the command of the 13th army corps and ordered him back to Springfield, Illinois. The publication of his order in the press was in violation of War Department orders and also of mine.

On the 22d of June positive information was received that Johnston had crossed the Big Black River for the purpose of attacking our rear, to raise the siege and release Pemberton. The correspondence between Johnston and Pemberton shows that all expectation of holding Vicksburg had by this time passed from Johnston's mind. I immediately ordered Sherman to the command of all the forces from Haines' Bluff to the Big Black River. This amounted now to quite half the troops about Vicksburg. Besides these, Herron and A.J. Smith's divisions were ordered to hold themselves in readiness to reënforce Sherman. Haines' Bluff had been strongly fortified on the land side, and on all commanding points from there to the Big Black at the railroad crossing batteries had been constructed. The work of connecting by rifle-pits where this was not already done, was an easy task for the troops that were to defend them.

We were now looking west, besieging Pemberton, while we were also looking east to defend ourselves against an expected siege by Johnston. But as against the garrison of Vicksburg we were as substantially protected as they were against us. Where we were looking east and north we were strongly fortified, and on the defensive. Johnston evidently took in the situation and wisely I think, abstained from making an assault on us because it would simply have inflicted loss on both sides without accomplishing any result. We were strong enough to have taken the offensive against him; but I did not feel disposed to take any risk of losing our hold upon Pemberton's army while I would have rejoiced at the opportunity of defending ourselves against an attack by Johnston.

From the 23d of May the work of fortifying and pushing forward our position nearer to the enemy had been steadily progressing. At three points on the Jackson road, in front of Leggett's brigade, a sap was run up to the enemy's parapet, and by the 25th of June we had it undermined and the mine charged. The enemy had countermined, but did not succeed in reaching our mine. At this particular point the hill on which the rebel work stands rises abruptly. Our sap ran close up to the outside of the enemy's parapet. In fact this parapet was also our protection. The soldiers of the two sides occasionally conversed pleasantly across this barrier; sometimes they exchanged the hard bread of the Union soldiers for the tobacco of the Confederates; at other times the enemy threw over hand-grenades, and often our men, catching them in their hands, returned them.

Our mine had been started some distance back down the hill; consequently when it had extended as far as the parapet it was many feet below it. This caused the failure of the enemy in his search to find and destroy it. On the 25th of June at three o'clock, all being ready the mine was exploded. A heavy artillery fire all along the line had been ordered to open with the explosion. The effect was to blow the top of the hill off and make a crater where it stood. The breach was not sufficient to enable us to pass a column of attack through. In fact, the enemy having failed to reach our mine had thrown up a line farther back, where most of the men guarding that point were placed. There were a few men, however, left at the advance line, and others working in the countermine, which was still being pushed to find ours. All that were there were thrown into the air, some of them coming down on our side, still alive. I remember one colored man, who had been under ground at work when the explosion took place, who was thrown to one side. He was not much hurt, but terribly frightened. Some one asked him how high he had gone up. "Dun no, massa, but t'ink 'bout t'ree mile," was his reply. General Logan commanded at this point and took this colored man to his quarters, where he did service to the end of the siege.

As soon as the explosion took place the crater was seized by two regiments of our troops who were near by under cover, where they had been placed for the express purpose. The enemy made a desperate effort to expel them, but failed, and soon retired behind the new line. From here, however, they threw hand-grenades, which did some execution. The compliment was returned by our men, but not with so much effect. The enemy could lay their grenades on the parapet, which alone divided the contestants, and roll them down upon us; while from our side they had to be thrown over the parapet, which was at considerable elevation. During the night we made efforts to secure our position in the crater against the missiles of the enemy so as to run trenches along the outer base of their parapet, right and left; but the enemy continued throwing their grenades, and brought boxes of field ammunition (shells), the fuses of which they would light with port-fires, and throw them by hand into our ranks. We found it impossible to continue this work. Another mine was consequently started which was exploded on the 1st of July, destroying an entire rebel redan, killing and wounding a considerable number of its occupants and leaving an immense chasm where it stood. No attempt to charge was made this time, the experience of the 25th admonishing us. Our loss in the first affair was about thirty killed and wounded. The enemy must have lost more in the two explosions than we did in the first. We lost none in the second.

From this time forward the work of mining and pushing our position nearer to the enemy was prosecuted with vigor, and I determined to explode no more mines until we were ready to explode a number at different points and assault immediately after. We were up now at three different points, one in front of each corps, to where only the parapet of the enemy divided us.

At this time an intercepted dispatch from Johnston to Pemberton informed me that Johnston intended to make a determined attack upon us in order to relieve the garrison at Vicksburg. I knew the garrison would make no formidable effort to relieve itself. The picket lines were so close to each other—where there was space enough between the lines to post pickets—that the men could converse. On the 21st of June I was informed, through this means, that Pemberton was preparing to escape, by crossing to the Louisiana side under cover of night; that he had employed workmen in making boats for that purpose; that the men had been canvased to ascertain if they would make an assault on the "Yankees" to cut their way out; that they had refused, and almost mutinied, because their commander would not surrender and relieve their sufferings, and had only been pacified by the assurance that boats enough would be finished in a week to carry them all over. The rebel pickets also said that houses in the city had been pulled down to get material to build these boats with. Afterwards this story was verified: on entering the city we found a large number of very rudely constructed boats.

All necessary steps were at once taken to render such an attempt abortive. Our pickets were doubled; Admiral Porter was notified, so that the river might be more closely watched; material was collected on the west bank of the river to be set on fire and light up the river if the attempt was made; and batteries were established along the levee crossing the peninsula on the Louisiana side. Had the attempt been made the garrison of Vicksburg would have been drowned, or made prisoners on the Louisiana side. General Richard Taylor was expected on the west bank to cooperate in this movement, I believe, but he did not come, nor could he have done so with a force sufficient to be of service. The Mississippi was now in our possession from its source to its mouth, except in the immediate front of Vicksburg and of Port Hudson. We had nearly exhausted the country along a line drawn from Lake Providence to opposite Bruinsburg. The roads west were not of a character to draw supplies over for any considerable force.

By the 1st of July our approaches had reached the enemy's ditch at a number of places. At ten points we could move under cover to within from five to one hundred yards of the enemy. Orders were given to make all preparations for assault on the 6th of July. The debouches were ordered widened to afford easy egress, while the approaches were also to be widened to admit the troops to pass through four abreast. Plank, and bags filled with cotton packed in tightly were ordered prepared, to enable the troops to cross the ditches.

On the night of the 1st of July Johnston was between Brownsville and the Big Black, and wrote Pemberton from there that about the 7th of the month an attempt would be made to create a diversion to enable him to cut his way out. Pemberton was a prisoner before this message reached him.

On July 1st Pemberton, seeing no hope of outside relief addressed the following letter to each of his four division commanders:

> Unless the siege of Vicksburg is raised, or supplies are thrown in, it will become necessary very shortly to evacuate the place. I see no prospect of the former, and there are many great, if not insuperable obstacles in the way of the latter. You are, therefore, requested to inform me with as little delay as possible, as to the condition of your troops and their ability to make the marches and undergo the fatigues necessary to accomplish a successful evacuation.

Two of his generals suggested surrender, and the other two practically did the same. They expressed the opinion that an attempt to evacuate would fail. Pemberton had previously got a message to Johnston suggesting that he should try to negotiate with me for a release of the garrison with their arms. Johnston replied that it would be a confession of weakness for him to do so; but he authorized Pemberton to use his name in making such an arrangement.

On the 3d about ten o'clock A.M. white flags appeared on a portion of the rebel works. Hostilities along that part of the line ceased at once. Soon two persons were seen coming towards our lines bearing a white flag. They proved to be General Bowen, a division commander, and

Colonel Montgomery, aide-de-camp to Pemberton, bearing the following letter to me:

> I have the honor to propose an armistice for—hours, with the view to arranging terms for the capitulation of Vicksburg. To this end, if agreeable to you, I will appoint three commissioners, to meet a like number to be named by yourself, at such place and hour to-day as you may find convenient. I make this proposition to save the further effusion of blood, which must otherwise be shed to a frightful extent, feeling myself fully able to maintain my position for a yet indefinite period. This communication will be handed you under a flag of truce, by Major-General John S. Bowen.

It was a glorious sight to officers and soldiers on the line where these white flags were visible, and the news soon spread to all parts of the command. The troops felt that their long and weary marches, hard fighting, ceaseless watching by night and day in a hot climate, exposure to all sorts of weather, to diseases and, worst of all, to the gibes of many Northern papers that came to them saying all their suffering was in vain, that Vicksburg would never be taken, were at last at an end and the Union sure to be saved.

Bowen was received by General A.J. Smith, and asked to see me. I had been a neighbor of Bowen's in Missouri, and knew him well and favorably before the war; but his request was refused. He then suggested that I should meet Pemberton. To this I sent a verbal message saying that, if Pemberton desired it, I would meet him in front of McPherson's corps at three o'clock that afternoon. I also sent the following written reply to Pemberton's letter:

> Your note of this date is just received, proposing an armistice for several hours, for the purpose of arranging terms of capitulation through commissioners, to be appointed, etc. The useless effusion of blood you propose stopping by this course can be ended at any time you may choose, by the unconditional surrender of the city and garrison. Men who have shown so much endurance and courage as those now in Vicksburg, will always challenge the respect of an adversary and I can assure you will be treated with all the respect due to prisoners of war. I do not favor the proposition of appointing commissioners to arrange the terms of capitulation, because I have no terms other than those indicated above.

At three o'clock Pemberton appeared at the point suggested in my verbal message, accompanied by the same officers who had borne his letter of the morning. Generals Ord, McPherson, Logan and A.J. Smith, and several of my staff accompanied me. Our place of meeting was on a hillside within a few hundred feet of the rebel lines. Near by stood a stunted oak-tree, which was made historical by the event. It was but a short time before the last vestige of its body, root and limb had disappeared, the fragments taken as trophies. Since then the same tree has furnished as many cords of wood, in the shape of trophies, as "The True Cross."

Pemberton and I had served in the same division during part of the Mexican War. I knew him very well therefore, and greeted him as an old acquaintance. He soon asked what terms I proposed to give his army if it surrendered. My answer was the same as proposed in my reply to his letter. Pemberton then said, rather snappishly, "The conference might as well end," and turned abruptly as if to leave. I said, "Very well." General Bowen, I saw was very anxious that the surrender should be consummated. His manner and remarks while Pemberton and I were talking, showed this. He now proposed that he and one of our generals should have a conference. I had no objection to this, as nothing could be made binding upon me that they might propose. Smith and Bowen accordingly had a conference, during which Pemberton and I, moving a short distance away towards the enemy's lines, were in conversation. After a while Bowen suggested that the Confederate army should be allowed to march out with the honors of war, carrying their small arms and field artillery. This was promptly and unceremoniously rejected. The interview here ended, I agreeing, however, to send a letter giving final terms by ten o'clock that night.

CHARLES B. JOHNSON, M.D.

Treating the Wounded at Vicksburg

The post of surgeon in the field armies during the Civil War could hardly be considered an enviable one. Even then, modern warfare was capable of wounding men in most horrible ways while the art of healing had not advanced to provide much supplication for those wounded in combat. A surgeon in the Union ranks at Vicksburg, Charles B. Johnson related tales of horror and humor in his reminiscences entitled *Muskets and Medicine.*

At 2 P.M., May 19, an assault was made on the Confederate works at Vicksburg. This assault was unsuccessful, so far as capturing the stronghold was concerned, but resulted in giving the Federals an advanced position, which position was made secure by the use of the spade the succeeding night. Believing that the Confederates would not hold out against another determined assault, a second one was ordered at 10 A.M., May 22. This was opened by a terrific cannonade from all the Federal batteries; following this was an incessant rattle of musketry.

It was known at the hospital this charge was to be made, and the constant boom of cannon and continual roll of musketry firing after 10 in the forenoon all knew would soon bring in a frightful harvest of mangled and wounded. The slain would, of course, for the time at least, be left on the field. About 2 P.M. through the trees was seen a long train of ambulances approaching, all heavily loaded with mangled humanity. Upon reaching the hospital grounds two or three ambulances were backed up at once, and the wounded lifted or assisted out. One of the first that I assisted in taking from the ambulance was a tall, slender man, who had received a terrible wound in the top of his head; a minnie ball had, so to speak, plowed its way through the skull, making a ragged, gaping wound, exposing the brain for three or four inches. He lived but a moment after removal from the ambulance.

The captain of the company in which I enlisted was in another ambulance, mortally wounded, with a bullet in his brain. He lived a day or two in an unconscious stupor—a comatose state—as the doctors say. But the majority of the wounded were boys, young, brave, daring fellows, too often rash, and meeting death, or next to it, oftentimes from needless exposure.

One nice young fellow of eighteen the writer can never forget. He had been wounded in the bowels, and was sitting at the root of a large tree, resting his head against its trunk. His name was Banks, and knowing me well, he recognized me, and calling me by name, said: "Ah, I'm badly wounded." Already his lips were ashy pale, a clammy sweat was upon his face, and from the wound in his abdomen a long knuckle of intestine was protruding. A few hours more and young Banks was resting in the sleep of death. No danger from enemy's bullets now; the poor, senseless clay, which a little time before had been the dwelling place of joyous young life, nothing could harm more. By the quiet form sat the father, sad and heart-broken, himself a soldier, but the balance of his term of service would seem lonely and tedious.

Arms and legs of many in the ambulances were hanging useless and lying powerless by the sides of their owners, and soon the surgeons at several tables were kept busy removing mangled and useless limbs. As on all such occasions when there were a great many wounded on hand at one time, but little was done for the mortally injured, save to lay them in a comparatively comfortable position; those having mangled limbs and broken bones were first attended, while those with unextensive, simple flesh wounds were passed by till more serious cases were looked after. Judgment, however, in this direction was not always unerring, and I remember one man, with what seemed a slight wound of the foot, who was rather persistent in asking immediate attention; but the number of dangling limbs and gaping wounds calling for immediate care seemed to justify the surgeons in putting him off for a time. His case was attended to in due course, and later he was sent up the river to a large Memphis hospital, where, some weeks subsequently he was infected with hospital gangrene, and died from its effects. Of course, the delay in dressing his wound weeks before had nothing to do with the untoward result, but it did bring sharp criticism upon the surgeons.

All the afternoon and till late at night on May 22 did the surgeons work with the wounded; amputating limbs, removing balls, cleaning and washing wounds, ridding them of broken pieces of bone, bandaging them up and putting them in the best shape possible. A few were bruised from stroke of spent ball or piece of shell, and recovered in a few days. Long lines of wounded now occupied the shaded places, in the yard, and to attend to the wants of these kept all busy. Carbolic acid and other disinfectants were at that time not in use, and all wounds were at first treated with simple water dressings. Old muslin cloth or lint was saturated with cold water and applied to all fresh wounds. As soon as these began to supurate, simple cerate, a mild, soothing ointment, consisting of two parts of fresh lard and one of white wax, was applied. In most bullet wounds, the ball in entering the body carried before it little pieces of the clothing, leather of the belt or cartridge box, tin of the canteens or any such substance first struck by the missile. In nearly all instances these foreign substances were discharged in the form of little dark-colored bits of *débris*.

Every day the wounds were washed and freshly dressed. But, as the weather was warm, many wounds became infested with maggots. This looked horrible, but was not deemed specially detrimental. Two or three days' extra work was made by the large number of wounded, resulting from the assault of May 22. After this there was a constant accession of wounded men at the hospital, but only a few at a time.

One man received a wound from some sort of a large missile that made an extensive opening at the place of entrance, the fleshy part of the thigh, in which it buried itself deeply and could not be reached. In a day or two the limb all about the wound began to assume a greenish-yellow hue, and later the man died. Cutting into the wound after death revealed the presence of a copper-tap, more than an inch across, from a shell.

About a week after the siege began a young man from an Ohio regiment died from a wound, resulting from his own imprudence. The first day of the investment, while his regiment was drawn up in line, three or four miles from the enemy's works, there being some delay in the advance, the young man got some loose powder, ran it along in a little trail, covered this with dust and tried to fire it. As it did not ignite he was stooping over with his face close to the ground when the charge took fire. His face was badly burned, and later was attacked with erysipelas, from which death resulted. This seemed an inglorious way of yielding up one's life when the opportunities for dying gloriously for one's country were so plentiful and ready at hand.

As soon as communication by the Yazoo was opened up with the North, supplies in great abundance came in for the sick. In the way of eatables for the hospital were delicacies of various kinds, fruits, mild homemade wines, etc. Clothing for the sick and wounded was furnished in full quantities. This, for the most part, consisted of cotton garments for underwear, shirts, night-shirts, drawers, gowns, etc., nearly all of bleached muslin. Cotton goods were at the time expensive in the market, from the fact that the supply of the raw material by the South was stopped for the period during which the war continued.

Nearly all these things were donated by individuals and communities. Very many of the garments had the name of the donor stamped upon them with stencil plate. Quite a number of the articles seen by the writer had the name, now forgotten, of a lady with postoffice address at Janesville, Wis.

The assault of May 22 convinced all, officers and men alike, that Vicksburg was much more securely intrenched than had been supposed, and that the only way to capture it would be by siege. Accordingly all made up their minds to await the result patiently, but of the final fall of the stronghold no one entertained a doubt. Indeed, of ultimate triumph every man seemed from the start to have full confidence.

As before stated, after settling down to siege operations there were comparatively few wounded. Back of Swett's garden, under some small trees, the dead from the division hospital were buried. It was not possible to provide coffins, and so the dead were wrapped in blankets and covered over with earth—till their shallow graves were filled. As the siege progressed all the wounded and sick, who were able to be moved, were put in ambulances and conveyed to boats on the Yazoo River, from whence they went North.

Cane grew in abundance all about, and by cutting a number of these stocks, tying them together with strings, and putting the two ends on cross-pieces resting upon stakes driven in the ground, quite comfortable and springy cots were improvised for the hospital.

Swett's house had all the time been used as a place for storage of drugs and hospital supplies. Swett was a short, thick-set man with a rotund stomach and about fifty years old. He used to stand around and lean on his cane with much seeming complacency. In his yard were several bunches of fragrant jasmine in full bloom. This is a most beautiful and deliciously fragrant flower, scenting the air with its delightful odor.

In the timber all about were magnificent specimens of magnolia, having upon their branches, in May and June, long beautiful blossoms. Figs ripened in Swett's garden during the siege. These, while not liked by some when gathered fresh from the trees, by others were relished exceedingly. Thus, tree, flower and fruit lent something of their charms to assuage the horrors of war.

As soon as General Joseph E. Johnston discovered that Grant had securely invested Vicksburg, he began organizing a force to relieve the garrison. This force sought to attack Grant's rear on the line of the Big Black River. Grant, who by this time was receiving reënforcements from the North, was fully on the alert, and confronted Johnston with ample force to keep the latter at a safe distance from the operations against Vicksburg.

Meanwhile, all sorts of stories were in circulation—nearly all favorable, however, to the Federals. At one time it was rumored Port Hudson, some three hundred miles down the river, had capitulated to General Banks; at another, that the Confederates could not hold out longer; again, that Richmond was taken, and then that Washington had been captured by Lee.

Of nights the mortar boats from the river shelled Vicksburg, and sometimes, with one or more comrades, I would go out upon a high hill in front of the hospital from whence the bombardment could be seen. The mortar boats were, perhaps, eight miles distant, and first a flash would be seen, then the discharge of the mortar, next a streak of fire, followed by a burning fuse; this would rise away up in the air and finally descend, and, just before reaching the ground another flash, the explosion of the shell, broke upon the vision. Some time elapsed after the flash was seen before the report could be heard. The shells thrown by these mortar boats were of one and two hundred pounds caliber, and all through the siege were thrown at regular intervals during the night-time.

One cannon, belonging to the Confederates, received the appellation of "Whistling Dick." The ball from it passed through the air with a peculiar whistling noise that could be heard by all on the south-western aspect of the works. It was a fine breech-loading rifled cannon of English manufacture.

Toward the latter part of June rumors of the impending fall of Vicksburg pervaded the command, and later, as the National anniversary drew near, it was said a most determined assault would be made on the

4th of July. Finally preparations for this were in progress when, on the 3d of July, word came that the Confederates had already made propositions looking toward a surrender, and next day the 4th of July, Vicksburg, after withstanding a siege of forty-six days, capitulated.

The command, though long expecting this event, was almost wild with joy. Some surprise was, however, felt that the Confederates should have yielded on the day they did; the belief prevailed that they had, in some way gained an inkling of the intended assault and felt as though they could not withstand another determined effort on the part of the Federals. Up to date this was the most important success of the war. The number of men captured exceeded 30,000, with a vast quantity of small arms, cannon, heavy ordnance and munitions of all kinds. Indeed, more men capitulated at Vicksburg than were taken in one body at any other time during the war.

A day or two after I procured a pass and visited the city. It was alive with soldiers of both armies, all upon friendly relations, swapping yarns, telling experiences, trading curiosities, as if hostile words, much less shot and shell, had never passed between them. One tall young Confederate approached me and wanted to exchange a two-dollar Confederate note for the same amount in United States currency; he said, by way of explanation, that he would, in a few days, be going home over in Louisiana on his parole and wanted the "greenback" money to show his folks. This was, most probably not true; Confederate money was wholly valueless in the Union lines, and the United States currency was doubtless wanted for immediate use.

The various places of interest about the city were visited. The several roads passing from the city upon reaching the bluff, had roadways cut through this. In many places these cuts were twenty and thirty feet deep, and the walls of red clay perpendicular, or nearly so. But the clay composing these walls was of such tenacity that washings never occurred, and the sides of the cuts remained as durable as if built of stone.

From the sides of these walls of clay caves were cut in which for security some of the citizens passed much of their time. I visited several of these caves, and found two or three of them carpeted and neatly furnished. Many places were seen where the immense shells from the mortar fleet struck the earth. When these failed to explode a great round hole was made in the ground, and in case of explosion after striking the ground, a large excavation was the result.

The great guns along the river front—the Columbiads of 9-, 11- and 13-inch caliber—were visited. It was these that blockaded the river and made the passing of even heavily-armored vessels hazardous. Some of the Confederate soldiers belonging to the infantry were about one of these huge guns, and one of them said within ear-shot:

"I'll bet this 'ere old cannon's killed many a blue-belly."

Passing out toward the outworks a Confederate regiment, containing not many more men than a full company was seen draw up in line for inspection and roll-call, preparatory to completion of parole papers.

In conversation with the Confederates some said they had had enough of the war and hoped the South would make an end of it; others avowed their faith in ultimate success; the great majority, however, were non-committal regarding their notions of final success or failure.

The rifle-pits and works of the Confederates that crossed the railway and dirt road nearby were visited. The neighborhood of the dirt road seemed especially to have been the scene of most obstinate conflict; it ran along on a ridge and the approach was particularly well guarded. The space outside the Confederate works, between these and the Federal rifle-pits, was dotted all over with Union graves; if some dirt thrown over a soldier where he fell could be called a grave.

A day or two after the assault the Union dead were buried under a flag of truce. The weather being very warm, before this was attended to, decomposition had already begun and the consequent stench would soon grow intolerable. Under these circumstances both armies readily agreed to a short armistice for disposition of the dead. The time allowed was too short for regular interment, hence dirt was thrown over the dead bodies where they lay and in cases where they could be identified, a piece of board put at the head, upon which, in rude letters, were the names and commands of the fallen ones.

Wherever an elevation intervened between the Union lines and Confederate works the tracks of bullets through the grass and weeds were surprisingly thick and crossed and criss-crossed each other in various directions, and at one point there was hardly an inch of space but what had thus been marked. This was near the Jackson dirt road, where the Confederates had an enfilading fire and used it to most deadly advantage.

Immediately upon the fall of Vicksburg, an expedition was started against General Joe Johnston who, during the siege, had been threatening Grant from the rear and on the line of the Big Black River. Under a broiling July sun the Union soldiers took up the line of march and followed the Confederates under Johnston to Jackson, Miss., to which, for a time, they laid siege. Finally however, realizing that he was outnumbered, General Johnston evacuated his works at Jackson and permitted the Federals to take possession for a second time within two months.

Meanwhile, with the regimental surgeon I was assigned to duty at the Thirteenth Corps Hospital, which was in the near vicinity of a farmhouse, though the sick and wounded were in tents and everything needed for their comfort and care was on a much more commodious scale than had been possible at the Division Hospital, where I was on duty during the whole forty-five days of the siege. One peculiar method of prescribing was in vogue here: A number of favorite prescriptions for sundry diseases were put up in quantity and each given a number; consequently instead of having to write out a prescription and having it put up separately the surgeon had but to designate a given number, and in short order the patient would have the desired remedy.

During this period I, from time to time, secured a pass and visited Vicksburg, which was gradually settling down to the new order of things. The wharf at the river front, very soon after the Federal occupation, assumed a busy aspect. Steamboats with all needed supplies came down the river, I came near saying, in fleets. Many visitors came from the North, some to see friends in the army, some to see the newly captured stronghold, some to look up new fields for trade and speculation, and some came on the sad mission of, if possible, finding the bit of earth that hid from view the remains of fallen loved ones.

General Logan, who commanded within the limits of Vicksburg after its surrender, had his headquarters in the Court House, which, from its location on a high hill, was a conspicuous object. Over the dome of the Court House floated the flag of the 45th Illinois Infantry Volunteers, an organization that was given the advance when General Logan's Division entered Vicksburg after its surrender and took possession. The 45th Illinois was thus honored because its members, many of whom were miners, had, during the siege, performed a great deal of duty of an exceptionally hazardous nature.

Toward the end of the siege, J.W. Spurr, Company B, 145th Illinois Infantry Volunteers, became the hero of a most remarkable adventure. He, somehow, managed to get possession of an old Confederate uniform and going to the Mississippi River at the extreme left of our lines went in the water during a heavy rainstorm after night and swam north, past the pickets of both friend and foe. Then, upon going ashore he at once went to some Confederates who were gathered about a campfire and engaged them in conversation. Later he left them and went to a house and asked for something to eat which was refused in consequence of the fact that, at that particular time, eatables in Vicksburg were at a very high premium. Finally, however, with the persuasive influence of a five-dollar bill both food and lodging for the time being were secured.

Young Spurr's hostess was an Irish woman, who was found to be a Union sympathizer, and who proved her fidelity by warning her guest that he was being watched. Consequently, after spending three days in the beleaguered city the daring adventurer, after night, found his way to the river's bank south of the city, went in the water and swam and floated down past the pickets of foe and friend alike, and upon reaching the Union lines was promptly arrested, but upon establishing his identity was as promptly released.

It is, perhaps, not too much to say that this feat had few, if indeed any parallels in either army during the whole period of the Civil War's four years' history. That an eighteen-year-old boy on his own intitiative and impelled by nothing save curiosity and innate dare-deviltry should plan, undertake and successfully execute such a hazardous feat as that of young Spurr, is hard to believe. As to credibility, however, the reader can rest assured that the above is absolutely true, and can be verified by the best of evidence. J.W. Spurr, the hero of the adventure, is a well-preserved veteran, and has his home in Rock Island, Ill.

Chapter VI

CHANCELLORSVILLE

In late January of 1863, Major General Joseph Hooker inherited a demoralized and defeated Army of the Potomac from Ambrose Burnside who had led the force to disaster at Fredericksburg, Virginia, in December of the year before. In a short time, "Fighting Joe" had restored the Federal army into fighting condition, elevated the morale of his troops, and brazenly declared he would defeat Lee and take Richmond in short order. While the Yankee general could afford to make such statements of braggadocio from the safety of his encampment at Falmouth, Virginia, he found it would take more than words to beat the Confederate army even if his statements were backed up by 135,000 men. Engaging the enemy in the woods near Chancellorsville, Virginia, on 2-3 May 1863, Hooker lost his nerve and allowed the Army of the Potomac to record yet another loss at the hands of Robert E. Lee. Though the Confederates managed to win a major victory, the gallant Stonewall Jackson fell with a mortal wound. His presence was sorely missed in the battles to come.

FREDERICK L. HITCHCOCK

Hooker Takes Command

A major in the 132nd Regiment of the Pennsylvania Volunteer Infantry, Frederick L. Hitchcock was mustered in as an adjutant of the unit only to find himself in control of a large body of troops with hardly any experience in command. Winning its baptism by fire at Antietam and participating in the action at Fredericksburg, where Hitchcock received two wounds, the regiment went on to fight its final battle at Chancellorsville. After publishing his account of battlefield experiences as installments in a local paper, Hitchcock compiled the articles into a book, *War from the Inside,* from which this selection is taken.

General Burnside was relieved from command of the army on the 26th of January 1863, and was succeeded by Major-General Joseph Hooker. "Fighting Joe," as familiarly called, was justly popular with the army, nevertheless there was general regret at the retirement of Burnside, notwithstanding his ill success.

That there was more than the "fates" against him was felt by many and whether under existing conditions "Fighting Joe" or any one else was likely to achieve any better success was a serious question. However, all felt that the new commander had lots of fight in him, and the old Army of the Potomac was never known to "go back" on such a man. His advent as commander was signalized by a modest order announcing the fact, and matters moved on without a ripple upon the surface. Routine work, drills, and picket duty occupied all our time. Some of our men were required to go on picket duty every other day so many were off duty from sickness and other causes. Twenty-four hours on picket duty, with only twenty-four hours off between, was certainly very severe duty, yet the men did it without a murmur. When it is understood that this duty required being that whole time out in the most trying weather, usually either rain, sleet, slush, or mud, and constantly awake and alert against a possible attack, one can form an idea of the strain upon physical endurance it involved.

The chief event preceding the Chancellorsville movement was the grand review of the army by President Lincoln and staff. The exact date of this review I do not remember, but it occurred a short time before the movement upon Chancellorsville. Owing to the absence of Colonel Albright and the illness of Lieutenant-Colonel Shreve, the command of the regiment devolved upon me, and I had a funny experience getting ready for it. As a sort of preliminary drill, I concluded I would put the regiment through a practice review on our drill grounds. To do this properly, I had to imagine the presence of a reviewing officer standing before our line at the proper distance of thirty to forty yards. The ceremony involved opening the ranks, which brought the officers to the front of the line, the presenting arms, and dipping the colors, which the reviewing officer, usually a general, acknowledged by lifting his hat and gracefully bowing. I had reached the point in my practice drill where the "present arms" had been executed, and the colors lowered, and had turned to the front myself to complete the ceremony by presenting sword to my imaginary general, when lo! there rose up in front of me, in the proper position, a real reviewing officer in the shape of one of the worst looking army "bums" I ever saw. He assumed the position and dignified carriage of a major-general, lifted his dirty old "cabbage-leaf" cap, and bowed up and down the line with the grace and air of a Wellington, and then he promptly skedaddled. The "boys" caught the situation instantly and were bursting with laughter. Of course I didn't notice the performance, but the effort not to notice it almost used me up. This will illustrate how the army "bummer" never let an opportunity slip for a practical joke, cost what it might. This fellow was a specimen of this genus that was ubiquitous in the army. Every regiment had one or more. They were always dirty and lousy, a sort of tramp, but always on hand at the wrong time and in the wrong place. A little indifferent sort of service could be occasionally worked out of them, but they generally skulked whenever there was business on hand, and then they were so fertile of excuses that somehow they escaped the penalty and turned up again when the "business" was over. Their one specialty was foraging. They were born foragers. What they could not steal was not to be had, and this probably accounts in a measure for their being endured. Their normal occupation was foraging and, incidentally, Sancho Panza like, looking for adventure.

They knew more of our movements, and also of those of the enemy than the commanding general of either. One of the most typical of this class that I knew as a young fellow I had known very well before the war. He was a shining light in society, occupying a high and responsible business position. His one fault was his good fellowship and disposition to be convivial when off duty. He enlisted among the first, when the war broke out in 1861, and I did not see him again until one day one of this genus "bummer" strayed into our camp. He stuck his head into my tent and wanted to know how "Fred Hitchcock was." I had to take a long second look to dig out from this bunch of rags and filth my one-time Beau Brummel acquaintance at home. His eyes were bleared, and told all too surely the cause of the transformation. His brag was that he had skipped every fight since he enlisted. "It's lots more fun," he said, "to climb a tree well in the rear and see the show. It's perfectly safe, you know, and then you don't get yourself killed and planted. What is the use," he argued, "of getting killed and have a fine monument erected over you, when you can't see it nor make any use of it after it is done? Let the other fellows do that if they want to. I've no use for monuments." Poor fellow, his cynical ideas were his ruin. Better a thousand times had he been "planted" at the front, manfully doing his duty than to save a worthless life and return with the record of a poltroon, despised by himself and everybody else.

This review by President Lincoln and the new commander-in-chief, General Hooker, was, from a military spectacular point of view, the chief event of our army experience. It included the whole of the great Army of the Potomac, now numbering upward of one hundred and thirty thousand men, probably its greatest numerical strength of the whole war. Deducting picket details, there were present on this review, it is safe to say, from ninety thousand to one hundred thousand men. It was a remarkable event historically, because so far as I can learn it was the only time this great army was ever paraded in line so that it could be seen all together. In this respect it was the most magnificent military pageant ever witnessed on this continent, far exceeding in its impressive grandeur what has passed into history as the "great review" which preceded the final "muster out" at the close of the war in the city of Washington. At the latter not more than ten thousand men could have been seen at one time, probably not nearly so many for the eye could take in only the column which filled Pennsylvania Avenue from the Capitol to the

Treasury Building. Whereas, upon our review the army was first drawn up in what is known as three lines of "masses," and one glance of the eye could take in the whole army. Think of it! One hundred thousand men in one sweep of vision! If the word "Selah" in the Psalm means "stop! think! consider!" it would be particularly appropriate here.

A word now about the formation in "lines of masses." Each regiment was formed in column of divisions. To those unfamiliar with military terms, I must explain that this very common formation with large bodies of troops consists in putting two companies together as a division under the command of the senior officer, thus making of a regiment of ten companies a column of five divisions, each two-company front. This was known as "massing" the troops. When so placed in line they were called a line of "masses;" when marching, a column of "masses." It will be seen that the actual frontage of each regiment so formed was the width of two companies only, the other eight companies being formed in like manner in their rear. Now imagine four regiments so formed and placed side by side, fronting on the same line and separated from each other by say fifty feet, and you have a brigade line of masses. The actual frontage of a brigade so formed would be considerably less than that of a single regiment on dress parade. Now take three such brigades, separated from each other by say fifty feet, and you have a division line of masses. Three divisions made up an army corps. The army was formed in three lines of masses, of two corps each, on the large open plain opposite Fredericksburg, to the south and east of where the railroad crossed the river. Each of these lines of masses contained from seventy to eighty regiments of infantry, besides the artillery, which was paraded on the several lines of different intervals. I do not remember seeing any cavalry, and my impression is that this branch of the service was not represented. Some idea may be formed of the magnificence of this spectacle when I state that each of these lines of masses was more than a mile in length, and the depth of the three lines from front to rear, including the spaces between, was not less than four hundred yards, or about one-fifth of a mile. Each of the regiments displayed its two stands of silk colors, one the blue flag representing the State from which it came, the other the national colors. There were here and there a brace of these flags, very conspicuous in their brilliant newness, indicating a fresh accession to the army but, most of them were tattered and torn by shot and shell, whilst a closer look revealed the less conspicuous but more deadly slits and punctures of the minie-balls.

Now place yourself on the right of their army paraded for review and look down the long lines. Try to count the standards as the favoring wind lifts their sacred folds and caressingly shows you their battle scars. You will need to look very closely, lest those miniature penants, far away, whose staffs appear no larger than parlor matches protruding above lines of men, whose forms in the distance have long since merged into a mere bluish gray line, escape your eye. Your numbering will crowd the five hundred mark ere you finish, and you should remember that each of these units represented a thousand men when in the vigor and enthusiasm of patriotic manhood they bravely marched to the front. Only a fifth of them left? you say. And the others? Ah! the battle, the hospital, the prison-pen, the h-ll of war, must be the answer.

How can words describe the scene? This is that magnificent old battered Army of the Potomac. Look upon it; you shall never behold its like again. There have been and may yet be many armies greater in numbers, and possibly, in all the paraphernalia of war, more showy. There can never be another Army of the Potomac, with such a history. As I gazed up and down those massive lines of living men, felt that I was one of them, and saw those battle-scarred flags kissed by the loving breeze, my blood tingled to my very fingertips, my hair seemed almost to raise straight up, and I said a thousand Confederacies can't whip us. And here I think I grasped the main purpose of this review. It was not simply to give the President a sight of his "strong right arm," as he fondly called the Army of the Potomac, nor General Hooker, its new commander, an opportunity to see his men and them a chance to see their new chief— though both of these were included,—but it was to give the army a square look at its mighty self, see how large and how strong it really was, that every man might thereby get the same enthusiasm and inspiration that I did, and know that it simply could not be beaten. The enemy, it is not strange to say, were intensely interested spectators of this whole scene, for the review was held in full view of the whole of their army. No place could have been chosen that would better have accommodated their enjoyment of the picture, if such it was, than that open plain, exactly in their front. And we could see them swarming over Marye's Heights and the lines to the south of it, intently gazing upon us. A scene more resplendent with military pageantry and the soul-stirring assessories of war they will never see again. But did it stir their blood? Yes; but with bitterness only, for they must have seen that the task before them of successfully resisting the onslaughts of this army was impossible. Here was disclosed, undoubtedly, another purpose of this grand review, viz., to let the enemy see with their own eyes how powerful the army was with which they had to contend.

A remarkable feature of this review was the marvelous celerity of its formation. The various corps and subdivisions of the army were started on the march for the reviewing ground so as to reach it at about the same time. It should be remembered that most of them were encamped from four to eight miles away. Aides-de-camp with markers by the score were already in position on the plain when the troops arrived, so that there was almost no delay in getting into position. As our column debouched upon the field, there seemed an inextricable mass of marching columns as far as the eye could see. Could order ever be gotten out of it? Yet, presto! the right of the line fell into position, a series of blue blocks, and then on down to the far left, block after block, came upon the line with unerring order and precision, as though it were a long curling whiplash straightening itself out to the tension of a giant hand. And so with each of the other two lines. All were formed simultaneously. Here was not only perfection of military evolution, but the poetry of rhythmic movement. The three lines were all formed within twenty minutes, ready for the reviewing officers.

Almost immediately the blare of the trumpets announced the approach of the latter, and the tall form of the President was seen, accompanied by a large retinue, galloping down the first line. Our division was formed, as I recollect, in the first line, about three hundred yards from the right. The President was mounted on a large, handsome horse, and as he drew near I saw that immediately on his right rode his son, Robert Lincoln, then a bright-looking lad of fourteen to fifteen years, and little "Tad" Lincoln, the idol of his father, was on his left. The latter could not have been more than seven or eight years old. He was mounted on a large horse, and his little feet seemed to stick almost straight out from the saddle. He was round and pudgy and his jolly little body bobbed up and down like a ball under the stiff canter of his horse. I wondered how he maintained his seat, but he was really a better horseman than his father, for just before reaching our regiment there was a little summer stream ravine, probably a couple of yards wide, that had to be jumped. The horses took it all right, but the President landed on the other side with a terrific bounce, being almost unseated. The boys went over flying, little "Tad" in high glee, like a monkey on a mustang.

Of course, a might cheer greeted the President as he galloped down the long line. There was something indescribably weird about that huzzah from the throats of these thousands of men, first full, sonorous, and thrilling, and then as it rolled down that attenuated line gradually fading into a minor strain until it was lost in the distance, only to reappear as the cavalcade returned in front of the second line, first the faintest note of a violin, then rapidly swelling into the full volume, to again die away and for the third time reappear and die away as the third line was reviewed. The President was followed by a large staff dressed in full uniform, which contrasted strongly with his own severely plain black. He wore a high silk hat and a plain frock coat. His face wore that peculiar sombre expression we see in all his photographs, but it lighted up into a half-smile as he occasionally lifted his hat in acknowledgment of the cheering of the men.

About one hundred yards in rear of the President's staff came the new commanding general, "Fighting Joe." He was dressed in the full uniform of a major-general, and was accompanied by his chief of staff, Seth Williams—he who had held this position under every commander of the Army of the Potomac thus far—and a large and brilliant staff. There must have been fully twenty officers of various ranks, from his chief of staff, a general, down through all grades to a lieutenant, in this corps of staff officers. It was the first time I had seen General Hooker to know him. His personal appearance did not belie his reputation. He had a singularly strong, handsome face, sat his superb horse like a king, broad-shouldered and elegantly proportioned in form, with a large, fine head, well covered with rather long hair, now as white as the driven snow and flowing in the wind as he galloped down the line, chapeau in hand; he was a striking and picturesque figure. It was evident the head of the army had lost nothing in personal appearance by its recent change. The same cheering marked the appearance of "Fighting Joe" which had greeted the President, as he and staff galloped down and up and down through the three long lines.

Both reviewing cavalcades moved at a brisk gallop, and occupied only about twenty minutes covering the three miles of lines; and then the President and staff took position, for the marching review, some distance in front and about midway of the lines. Instantly the scene was transformed. The first line wheeled into column by brigades successively and headed by General Hooker and staff, moved rapidly forward. There were but few bands, and the drum corps had been consolidated into division corps. On passing the President, General Hooker took position by his side and remained throughout the remainder of the ceremony. The troops marched in columns of masses, in the same formation they had stood in line; that is, in column of two companies front and only six yards between divisions. This made a very compact mass of troops, quite unusual in reviews, but was necessary in order to avoid the great length of time that in the usual formation would have been required for the passing of this vast body of men. Yet in this close formation the balance of the day was nearly comsumed in marching past the President.

It must have been a trying ordeal to him, as he had to lift his hat as each stand of colors successively dipped in passing. Immediately on passing the President, the several brigades were wheeled out of the column and ordered to quarters. I remember that we returned to our camp, over a mile distant, dismissed the men, and then several of us officers rode back to see the continuation of the pageant. When we got back the second line was only well on its way, which meant that only about half the army had passed in review. We could see from fifteen to twenty thousand men in column—that is to say, about one army corps—at a time. The quick, vigorous step, in rhythmical cadence to the music, the fife and drum, the massive swing, as though every man was actually a part of every other man; the glistening of bayonets like a long ribbon of polished steel, interspersed with the stirring effects of those historic flags, in countless numbers, made a picture impressive beyond the power of description. A picture of the ages. How glad I am to have looked upon it. I could not remain to see the end. When finally I was compelled to leave the third line was marching. I can still see that soul thrilling column, that massive swing, those flaunting colors, the sheen of burnished steel! Majestic! Incomparable! Glorious!!!

DARIUS N. COUCH

The Chancellorsville Campaign

After entering the war as a colonel of the 7th Massachusetts Volunteer Regiment, Darius Couch had a close association with General George Brinton McClellan that won him the rank of Brigadier General and soon after a divisional command. Having proved his solid fighting ability in McClellan's Peninsular Campaign, Couch rose to the rank of major general wielding a division in the Antietam Campaign and the II Corps at Fredericksburg and Chancellorsville. After the latter battle, he asked to be relieved from the Army of the Potomac, only to be reduced to the command of Pennsylvania militia at Gettysburg and a division out West towards the end of the war. Taken from *Battles and Leaders of the Civil War*, his article describes the Federal command during the battle of Chancellorsville.

In the latter part of January, 1863, the Army of the Potomac under Burnside was still occupying its old camps on the left bank of the Rappannock, opposite Fredericksburg. After the failures under Burnside it was evident that the army must have a new commander. For some days there had been a rumor that Hooker had been fixed upon for the place, and on the 26th of January it was confirmed. This appointment, un-doubtedly, gave very general satisfaction to the army, except perhaps to a few, mostly superior officers, who had grown up with it, and had had abundant opportunities to study Hooker's military character; these be-lieved that Mr. Lincoln had committed a grave error in his selection. The army, from its former reverses, had become quite disheartened and almost sulky; but the quick, vigorous measures now adopted and carried out with a firm hand had a magical effect in toning up where there had been demoralization and inspiring confidence where there had been mistrust. Few changes were made in the heads of the general staff departments, but for his chief-of-staff Hooker applied for Brigadier-

General Charles P. Stone, who through some untoward influence at Washington, was not given to him. This was a mistake of the war dignitaries, although the officer finally appointed to the office, Major-General Daniel Butterfield, proved himself very efficient. Burnside's system of dividing the army into three grand divisions was set aside and the novelty was introduced of giving to each army corps a distinct badge, an idea which was very popular with officers and men.

Some few days after Mr. Lincoln's visit to the army in April I was again thrown with the President, and it happened in this wise. My pickets along the river were not only on speaking terms with those of the enemy on the other side of the river, but covertly carried on quite a trade in exchanging coffee for tobacco, etc. This morning it was hallooed over to our side: "You have taken Charleston," which news was sent to head-quarters. Mr. Lincoln hearing of it wished me to come up and talk the matter over. I went and was ushered into a side tent, occupied only by himself and Hooker. My entrance apparently interrupted a weighty conversation, for both were looking grave. The President's manner was kindly, while the general, usually so courteous, forgot to be convention-ally polite. The Charleston rumor having been briefly discussed, Mr. Lincoln remarked that it was time for him to leave. As he stepped toward the general, who had risen from his seat, as well as myself, he said: "I want to impress upon you two gentlemen in your next fight,"—and turning to me he completed the sentence,—"put in all of your men"—in the long run a good military maxim.

The weather growing favorable for military operations, on April 12th were commenced those suggestive preliminaries to all great battles, clearing out the hospitals, inspecting arms, looking after ammunition, shoeing animals, issuing provisions, and making every preparation nec-essary to an advance. The next day, the 13th, Stoneman was put in motion at the head of ten thousand finely equipped and well organized cavalry to ascend the Rappahannock and swinging around to attack the Confederate cavalry wherever it might be found and "Fight! fight! fight!" At the end of two days' march Stoneman found the river so swollen by heavy rains that he was constrained to hold up, upon which Hooker suspended his advance until the 27th. This unexpected delay of the cavalry seemingly deranged Hooker's original plan of campaign. He had hoped that Stoneman would have been able to place his horsemen on the railroad between Fredericksburg and Richmond, by which Lee received his supplies, and make a wreck of the whole structure, compelling that general to evacuate his stronghold at Fredericksburg and vicinity and fall back toward Richmond.

I estimate the grand total of Hooker's seven corps at about 113,000 men ready for duty, although the date from which the conclusion is arrived at are not strictly official. This estimate does not include the cavalry corps of not less than 11,000 duty men, nor the reserve artillery, the whole number of guns in the army being 400. Lee's strength in and around Fredericksburg was placed at between 55,000 and 60,000 not including cavalry. It is not known if Hooker's information concerning the Confederate force was reliable, but Peck, operating in front of Norfolk, notified him that two of Lee's divisions under Longstreet were on the south side of the James. The hour was, therefore, auspicious for Hooker to assume the offensive, and he seized it with a boldness which argued well for his fitness to command. The aim was to transfer his army to the south side of the river, where it would have a manoeuvring footing not confronted by intrenched positions. On the 27th of April the Eleventh and Twelfth corps were set in motion for Kelly's Ford, twenty-five miles up the Rappahannock, where they concentrated on the evening of the 28th, the Fifth, by reason of its shorter marching distance, moving on the 28th. The object of the expedition was unknown to the corps commanders until communicated to them after their arrival at the ford by the commanding general in person. The Eleventh Corps crossed the Rappahannock, followed in the morning by the Twelfth and Fifth corps—the two former striking for Germanna Ford, a crossing of the Rapidan, the latter for Ely's Ford, lower down the same stream. Both columns, successfully effecting crossings with little opposition from the enemy's pickets, arrived that evening, April 30th, at the point of concentration, Chancellorsville. It had been a brilliantly conceived and executed movement.

In order to confound Lee, orders were issued to assemble the Sixth, Third, and First corps under Sedgwick at Franklin's Crossing and Pollock's Mill, some three miles below Fredericksburg, on the left, before daylight of the morning of the 29th, and throw two bridges across and hold them. This was done under a severe fire of sharp-shooters. The Second Corps, two divisions, marched on the 28th for Banks's Ford, four miles to the right; the other division, Gibbon's, occupying Falmouth, near the river-bank, was directed to remain in its tents, as they were in full view of the enemy, who would readily observe their withdrawal. On the 29th the two divisions of the Second Corps reached United States Ford, held by the enemy; but the advance of the right wing down the river uncovered it, whereupon a bridge of pontoons was thrown across and the corps reached Chancellorsville the same night as the Fifth, Eleventh, and Twelfth. The same day, the 30th, Sedgwick was instructed to place a corps across the river and make a demonstration upon the enemy's right, below Fredericksburg, and the Third Corps received orders to join the right wing at Chancellorsville, where the commanding general arrived the same evening, establishing his headquarters at the Chancellor House, which, with the adjacent grounds, is Chancellorsville. All of the army lying there that night were in exuberant spirits at the success of their general in getting "on the other side" without fighting for a position. As I rode into Chancellorsville that night the general hilarity pervading the camps was particularly noticeable; the soldiers, while chopping wood and lighting fires, were singing merry songs and indulging in peppery camp jokes.

The position at Chancellorsville not only took in reverse the entire system of the enemy's river defense, but there were roads leading from it directly to his line of communication. But in order to gain the advantages now in the commanding general's grasp he had divided his army into two wings, and the enemy, no ordinary enemy, lay between them. The line of communication connecting the wings was by way of United States Ford and twenty miles long. It was of vital importance that the line be shortened in order to place the wings within easy support of each other. The possession of Banks's Ford, foreshadowed in the instructions given to Slocum, would accomplish all that at present could be wished.

There were three roads over which the right wing could move upon Fredericksburg: the Orange turnpike, from the west, passed through Chancellorsville, and was the most direct; the United States Ford road, crossing the former at Chancellorsville, became the Plank road, bent to the left and united with the turnpike five miles or so from Chancellorsville; the third road fell back from Chancellorsville toward the Rappahannock, passed along by Banks's Ford, six miles distant, and continued to Fredericksburg. That wing was ready for the advance at an early hour in the morning of May 1st, but somehow things dragged; the order defining the movement, instead of being issued the previous night, was not received by the corps commanders, at least by me, until hours after light. Meade was finally pushed out on the left over the Banks's Ford and turnpike roads, Slocum and Howard on the right along the Plank road, the left to be near Banks's Ford by 2 P.M., the right at the junction of its line of movement with the turnpike at 12 P.M. No opposition was met, excepting that the division marching over the turnpike came upon the enemy two or three miles out, when the sound of their guns was heard at Chancellorsville, and General Hooker ordered me to take Hancock's division and proceed to the support of those engaged. After marching a mile and a half or so I came upon Sykes, who commanded, engaged at the time in drawing back his advance to the position he then occupied. Shortly after Hancock's troops had got into a line in front, an order was received from the commanding general "to withdraw both divisions to Chancellorsville." Turning to the officers around me, Hancock, Sykes, Warren, and others, I told them what the order was, upon which they all agreed with me that the ground should not be abandoned, because of the open country in front and the commanding position. An aide, Major J.B. Burt, dispatched to General Hooker to this effect, came back in half an hour with positive orders to return. Nothing was to be done but carry out the command, though Warren suggested that I should disobey, and then he rode back to see the general. In the meantime Slocum, on the Plank road to my right, had been ordered in, and the enemy's advance was between that road and my right flank. Sykes was first to move back, then followed by Hancock's regiments over the same road. When all but two of the latter had withdrawn, a third order came to me, brought by one of the general's staff: "Hold on until 5 o'clock." It was then perhaps 2 P.M. Disgusted at the general's vacillation and vexed at receiving an order of such tenor, I replied with warmth unbecoming in a subordinate: "Tell General Hooker he is too late, the enemy are already on my right and rear. I am in full retreat."

The position thus abandoned was high ground, more or less open in front, over which an army might move and artillery be used advantageously; moreover, were it left in the hands of an enemy, his batteries, established on its crest and slopes, would command the position at Chancellorsville. Everything on the whole front was ordered in. General Hooker knew that Lee was apprised of his presence on the south side of the river, and must have expected that his enemy would be at least on the lookout for an advance upon Fredericksburg. But it was of the utmost importance that Banks's Ford should fall into our hands, therefore the enemy ought to have been pressed until their strength or weakness was developed; it would then have been time enough to run away.

Mott's Run, with a considerable brushy ravine, cuts the turnpike three-forths of a mile east of Chancellorsville. Two of Hancock's regiments, under Colonel Nelson A. Miles, subsequently the Indian fighter, were directed to occupy the ravine. Continuing my way through the woods toward Chancellorsville, I came upon some of the Fifth Corps under arms. Inquiring for their commanding officer, I told him that in fifteen minutes he would be attacked. Before finishing the sentence a volley of musketry was fired into us from the direction of the Plank road. This was the beginning of the battle of Chancellorsville. Troops were hurried into position, but the observer required no wizard to tell him, as they marched past, that the high expectations which had animated them only a few hours ago had given place to disappointment. Proceeding to the Chancellor House, I narrated my operations in front to Hooker, which were seemingly satisfactory as he said: "It is all right, Couch, I have got Lee just where I want him; he must fight me on my own ground." The retrograde movement had prepared me for something of the kind, but to hear from his own lips that the advantages gained by the successful marches of his lieutenants were to culminate in fighting a defensive battle in that nest of thickets was too much, and I retired from his presence with the belief that my commanding general was a whipped man. The army was directed to intrench itself. At 2 A.M. the corps commanders reported to General Hooker that their positions could be held; at least so said Couch, Slocum, and Howard.

Until after dark on May 1st the enemy confined his demonstrations to finding out the position of our left with his skirmishes. Then he got some guns upon the high ground which he had abandoned as before mentioned, and cannonaded the left of our line. There were not many casualties, but that day a shell severely wounded the adjacent-general of the Second Corps, now General F.A. Walker. Chancellorville was a strategic point to an offensive or retreating army, as roads diverged from it into every part of Virginia; but for a defensive position it was bad, particularly for such an army as Hooker had under him, which prided itself upon its artillery, which was perhaps equal to any in the world. There were no commanding positions for artillery, and but little open country to operate over; in fact, the advantages of ground for this army were mainly with the attacking party.

During the 29th and 30th the enemy lay at Fredericksburg observing Sedgwick's demonstrations on the left, entirely unconscious of Hooker's successful crossing of the right wing, until midday of the latter date, but that night Lee formed his plan of operations for checking the farther advance of the force which had not only turned the left flank of his river defenses but was threatening his line of communication with Richmond as well as the rear of his center at Fredericksburg. Stonewall Jackson, who was watching Sedgwick, received instructions to withdraw his corps, march to the left, across the front of Hooker's intrenched position, until its right flank was attained, and assault with his column of 22,000 men, while his commanding general would, with what force he could spare, guard the approach to Fredericksburg.

On the morning of May 2d our line had become strong enough to resist a front attack unless made in great force; the enemy had also been hard at work on his front, particularly that section of it between the Plank road and turnpike. Sedgwick, the previous night, had been ordered to send the First Corp (Reynolds's) to Chancellorsville. At 7 A.M. a sharp cannonade was opened on our left, followed by infantry demonstrations of no particular earnestness. Two hours later the enemy were observed moving a mile or so to the south and front of the center, and later the same column was reported to the commander of the Eleventh Corps by General Devens, whose division was on the extreme right flank. At 9:30 A.M. a circular directed to Generals Slocum and Howard called attention to this movement and to the weakness of their flanks.

At 11 A.M. our left was furiously cannonaded by their artillery, established on the heights in front of Mott's Run, followed by sharp infantry firing on the fronts of the Second and Twelfth corps. As time flew along and no attack came from the enemy seen moving in front, Hooker conceived that Lee was retreating toward Gordonsville. There was color for this view, as the main road from Fredericksburg to that point diverged from the Plank road two miles to the left of Chancellorsville, and passed along his front at about the same distance. Hooker therefore jumped at the conclusion that the enemy's army was moving into the center of Virginia. But instead of the hostile column being on the Gordonsville road in retreat, it was Stonewall's corps moving on an interior neighborhood road, about one mile distant, and in search of our right flank and rear. At 2 P.M. I went into the Chancellor House, when General Hooker greeted me with the exclamation: "Lee is in full retreat toward Gordonsville, and I have sent out Sickles to capture his artillery." I thought, without speaking it: "If your conception is correct, it is very strange that only the Third Corps should be sent in pursuit." Sickles received orders at 1 P.M. to take two divisions, move to his front and attack, which he did, capturing some hundreds of prisoners. The country on the front being mostly wooded enabled the enemy to conceal his movements and at the same time hold Sickles in check with a rear-guard, which made such a show of strength that reënforcements were called for and furnished. In the meantime Jackson did not for a moment swerve from his purpose, but steadily moved forward to accomplish what he had undertaken.

It was about 5:30 in the evening when the head of Jackson's column found itself on the right and rear of the army, which on that flank consisted of the Eleventh Corps, the extreme right brigade receiving its first intimation of danger from a volley of musketry fired into their rear, followed up so impetuously that no efficient stand could be made by the brigades of the corps that successively attempted to resist the enemy's charge. When General Hooker found out what that terrific roar on his right flank meant he quickly mounted and flew across the open space to meet the onset, passing on his way stampeded pack-mules, officers' horses, caissons, with men and horses running for their lives. Gathering up such troops as were nearest to the scene of action, Berry's division from the Third Corps, some from the Twelfth, Hays's brigade of the Second, and a portion of the Eleventh, an effectual stand was made. Pleasonton, who was returning from the front, where he had been operating with Sickles (at the time Jackson attacked), taking in the state of things, rapidly moved his two regiments of cavalry and a battery to the head and right flank of the enemy's advance columns, when, making a charge and bringing up his own guns, with others of the Eleventh and Third Corps, he was enabled to punish them severely.

Pickets had been thrown out on Howard's flank, but not well to the right and rear. I suspect that the prime reason for the surprise was that the superior officers of the right corps had been put off their guard by adopting the conjecture of Hooker, "Lee's army is in full retreat to Gordonsville," as well as by expecting the enemy to attack precisely where ample preparations had been made to receive him. It can be emphatically stated that no corps in the army, surprised as the Eleventh was at this time, could have held its ground under similar circumstances.

At half past two that afternoon the Second Corps' lines were assaulted by artillery and infantry. Just previous to Jackson's attack on the right a desperate effort was made by Lee's people to carry the left at Mott's Run, but the men who held it were there to stay. Hooker, desiring to know the enemy's strength in front of the Twelfth Corps, advanced Slocum into the thicket, but that officer found the hostile line too well defended for him to penetrate it and was forced to recall the attacking party. When night put an end to the fighting of both combatants, Hooker was obliged to form a new line for his right flank perpendicular to the old one and barely half a mile to the right of Chancellorsville. Sickles was retired, with the two columns, from his advanced position in the afternoon to near where Pleasonton had had his encounter, before mentioned, some distance to the left of the new line of our right flank and close up to the enemy. The situation was thought to be a very critical one by General Hooker, who had simply a strong body in front of the enemy but without supports, at least near enough to be used for that purpose. At the same time it was a menace to Jackson's right wing or flank. Before midnight some of the latter's enterprising men pushed forward and actually cut off Sickles's line of communication. When this news was carried to Hooker it caused him great alarm, and preparations were at once made to withdraw the whole front, leaving General Sickles to his fate; but that officer showed himself able to take care of his rear, for he ordered after a little while a column of attack, and communication was restored at the point of the bayonet.

The situation of Jackson's corps on the morning of May 3d was a desperate one, its front and right flank being in the presence of not far from 25,000 men, with the left flank subject to an assault of 30,000, the corps of Meade and Reynolds, by advancing them to the right, where the thicket did not present an insurmountable obstacle. It only required that Hooker should brace himself up to take a reasonable, common-sense view of the state of things, when the success gained by Jackson would have been turned into an overwhelming defeat. But Hooker became very despondent. I think that his being outgeneraled by Lee had a good deal to do with his depression. After the right flank had been established on the morning of the 3d by Sickles getting back into position, our line was more compact, with favorable positions for artillery and the reserves were well in hand. Meade had been drawn in from the left and Reynolds had arrived with the First Corps. The engineers had been directed on the previous night to lay out a new line, its front a half mile in rear of Chancellorsville, with the flanks thrown back,—the right to the Rapidan, a little above its junction with the Rappahannock, the left resting on the latter river. The Eleventh Corps, or at least that portion which formed line of battle, was withdrawn from the front and sent to the rear to reorganize and get its scattered parts together, leaving the following troops in front: one division of the Second Corps on the left from Mott's Run to Chancellorsville, the Twelfth Corps holding the center and right flank, aided by the Third Corps and one division of the Second Corps (French's), on the same flank; the whole number in front, according to my estimate, being 37,000 men. The First and Fifth corps in reserve numbered 30,000, and, placing the number of reliable men in the Eleventh Corps at 5000, it will be seen that the reserves nearly equaled those in line of battle in front.

After the day's mishaps Hooker judged that the enemy could not have spared so large a force to move around his front without depleting the defenses of Fredericksburg. Accordingly, at 9 P.M., an imperative order was sent to the commander of the left wing to cross the river at Fredericksburg, march upon Chancellorsville, and be in the vicinity of the commanding general at daylight. But Sedgwick was already across the river and three miles below Fredericksburg. It was 11 P.M., May 2d, when he got the order, and twelve or fourteen miles had to be marched over by daylight. The night was moonlight, but any officer who has had experience in making night marches with infantry will understand the vexatious delays occurring even when the road is clear; but when, in addition, there is any enemy in front, with a line of fortified heights to assault, the problem which Sedgwick had to solve will be pronounced impossible of solution. However, that officer set his column in motion by flank, leaving one division that lay opposite the enemy, who were in force to his left. The marching column, being continually harassed by skirmishers, did not arrive at Fredericksburg until daylight. The first assault upon the heights behind the town failed. Attempts to carry them by flank movements met with no success. Finally a second storming party was organized, and the series of works were taken literally at the point of the bayonet, though at heavy loss. It was then 11 A.M. The column immediately started for Chancellorsville, being more or less obstructed by the enemy until its arrival near Salem Heights, 5 or 6 miles out, where seven brigades under Early, six of which had been driven from the defenses of Fredericksburg, made a stand in conjunction with supports sent from Lee's army before Chancellorsville. This was about the middle of the afternoon, when Sedgwick in force attacked the enemy. Though at first successful, he was subsequently compelled to withdraw those in advance and look to his own safety by throwing his own flanks so as to cover Banks's Ford, the friendly proximity of which eventually saved this wing from utter annihilation.

At about 5 A.M., May 3d, fighting was begun at Chancellorsville, when the Third (Sickles's) Corps began to retire to the left of our proper right flank, and all of that flank soon became fiercely engaged, while the battle ran along the whole line. The enemy's guns on the heights to our left, as well as at every point on the line where they could be established, were vigorously used, while a full division threw itself on Miles at Mott's Run. On the right flank our guns were well handled, those of the Twelfth Corps being conspicuous, and the opposing lines of infantry operating in the thicket had almost hand-to-hand conflicts, capturing and recapturing prisoners. The enemy appeared to know what he was about, for pressing the Third Corps vigorously he forced it back, when he joined or rather touched the left of Lee's main body, making their line continuous from left to right. Another advantage gained by this success was the possession of an open field, from which guns covered the ground up to the Chancellor House. Upon the south porch of that mansion General Hooker stood leaning against one of its pillars, observing the fighting, looking anxious and much careworn. After the fighting had commenced I doubt if any orders were given by him to the commanders on the field, unless, perhaps, "to retire when out of ammunition." None were received by me, nor were there any inquiries as to how the battle was going along my front. On the right flank, where the fighting was desperate, the engaged troops were governed by the corps and division leaders. If the ear of the commanding general was, as he afterward stated, strained to catch the sound of Sedgwick's guns, it could not have heard them in the continuous uproar that filled the air around him; but as Sedgwick, who was known as a fighting officer, had not appeared at the time set—daylight—nor for some hours after, it was conclusive evidence that he had met with strong opposition, showing that all of Lee's army was not at Chancellorsville, so that the moment was favorable for Hooker to try his opponent's strength with every available man. Moreover, the left wing might at that very time be in jeopardy, therefore he was bound by every patriotic motive to strike hard for its relief. If he had remembered Mr. Lincoln's injunction ("Gentlemen, in your next fight put in all of your men"), the face of the day would have been changed and the field won for the Union arms.

Not far from 8:30 A.M. the headquarters pennants of the Third and Twelfth corps suddenly appeared from the right in the open field of Chancellorsville; then the Third began to fall back, it was reported, for want of ammunition, followed by that portion of the Twelfth fighting on the same flank, and the division of the Second Corps on its right. It is not known whether any efforts were made to supply the much needed ammunition to the Third as well as the Twelfth Corps, whose ammunition was nearly used up when it retired. My impression is that the heads of the ordnance, as well as of other important departments, were not taken into the field during this campaign, which was most unfortunate, as the commanding general had enough on his mind without charging it with details. The open field seized by Jackson's old corps after the Third Corps drew off was shortly dotted with guns that made splendid practice through an opening in the wood upon the Chancellor House, and everything else, for that matter, in the neighborhood. Hooker was still at his place on the porch, with nothing between him and Lee's army but Geary's division of the Twelfth and Hancock's division and a battery of the Second Corps. But Geary's right was now turned, and that flank was steadily being pressed back along his intrenched line to the junction of the Plank road and the turnpike, when a cannon-shot struck the pillar against which Hooker was leaning and knocked him down. A report flew around that he was killed. I was at the time but a few yards to his left, and dismounting, ran to the porch. The shattered pillar was there, but I could not find him or any one else. Hurrying through the house, finding no one, my search was continued through the back yard. All the time I was thinking, "If he is killed, what shall I do with this disjointed army?" Passing through the yard I came upon him, to my great joy, mounted, and with his staff also in their saddles. Briefly congratulating him on his escape—it was no time to blubber or use soft expressions—I went about my own business. This was the last I saw of my commanding general in front. The time, I reckon, was from 9:15 to 9:30 A.M., I think nearer the former than the latter. He probably left the field soon after his hurt, but he neither notified me of his going nor did he give any orders to me whatever. Having some little time before this seen that the last stand would be about the Chancellor House, I had sent to the rear for some of the Second Corps batteries, which had been ordered there by the commanding general, but word came back that they were so jammed in with other carriages that it was impossible to extricate them. General Meade, hearing of my wants, kindly sent forward the 5th Maine battery belonging to his corps. It was posted in rear of the Chancellor House, where the United States Ford road enters the thicket. With such precision did the artillery of Jackson's old corps play upon this battery that all of the officers and most of the non-commissioned officers and men were killed or wounded. The gallant Kirby, whose guns could not be brought up, was mortally wounded in the same battery of which I had for the time placed him in command, and my horse was killed under me while I was trying to get some men to train a gun on the flank of the force then pushing Geary's division. The enemy, having 30 pieces in position on our right, now advanced some of his guns to within 500 or 600 yards of the Chancellor House, where there were only four of Pettit's Second Corps guns to oppose them, making a target of that building and taking the right of Hancock's division in reverse, a portion of which had been withdrawn from its intrenchments and thrown back to the left to meet the enemy should he succeed in forcing Mott's Run. This flank was stoutly held by Colonel Miles, who, by the bye, had been carried off the field, shot through the body. Lee by this time knew well enough, if he had not known before, that the game was sure to fall into his hands, and accordingly plied every gun and rifle that could be brought to bear on us. Still everything was firmly held excepting Geary's right, which was slowly falling to pieces, for the enemy had his flank and there was no help for it. Riding to Geary's left, I found him there dismounted, with sword swinging over his head, walking up and down, exposed to a severe infantry fire, when he said: "My division can't hold its place; what shall I do?" To which I replied: "I don't know, but do as we are doing; fight it out."

It was not then too late to save the day. Fifty pieces of artillery or even forty, brought up and run in front and to the right of the Chancellor House, would have driven the enemy out of the thicket, then forcing back Geary's right, and would have neutralized the thirty guns to the right which were pounding us so hard. But it is a waste of words to write what might have been done. Hooker had made up his mind to abandon the field, otherwise he would not have allowed the Third and part of the Twelfth Corps to leave their ground for want of ammunition. A few minutes after my interview with Geary a staff-officer from General Hooker rode up and requested my presence with that general. Turning to General Hancock, near by, I told him to take care of things and rode to the rear. The Chancellor House was then burning, having been fired in several places by the enemy's shells.

At the farther side of an open field, half a mile in the rear of Chancellorsville, I came upon a few tents (three or four) pitched, around which, mostly dismounted, were a large number of staff-officers. General Meade was also present, and perhaps other generals. General Hooker was lying down I think in a soldier's tent by himself. Raising himself a little as I entered, he said: "Couch, I turn the command of the army over to you. You will withdraw it and place it in the position designated on this map," as he pointed to a line traced on a field-sketch. This was perhaps three-quarters of an hour after his hurt. He seemed rather dull, but possessed of his mental faculties. I do not think that one of those officers outside of the tent knew what orders I was to receive, for on stepping out, which I did immediately on getting my instructions, I met Meade close by, looking inquiringly as if he expected that finally he would receive the order for which he had waited all that long morning "to go in." Colonel N.H. Davis broke out: "We shall have some fighting now." These incidents are mentioned to show the temper of that knot of officers. No time was to be lost, as only Hancock's division now held Lee's army. Dispatching Major John B. Burt, with orders for the front to retire, I rode back to the thicket, accompanied by Meade, and was soon joined by Sickles, and after a little while by Hooker, but he did not interfere with my dispositions. Hancock had a close shave to withdraw in safety, his line being three-fourths of a mile long, with an exultant enemy as close in as they dared, or wished, or chose to be, firing and watching. But everything was brought off, except five hundred men of the Second Corps who, through the negligence of a lieutenant charged by Hancock with the responsibility of retiring the force at Mott's Run, were taken prisoners. However, under the circumstances, the division was retired in better shape than one could have anticipated. General Sickles assisted in getting men to draw off the guns of the Maine battery before spoken of. General Meade wished me to hold the strip of thicket in rear of Chancellorsville, some six hundred yards in front of our new line of defense. My reply was: "I shall not leave men in this thicket to be shelled out by Lee's artillery. Its possession won't give us any strength. Yonder [pointing to the rear] is the line where the fighting is to be done."

Hooker heard the conversation, but made no remarks. Considerable bodies of troops of different corps that lay in the brush to the right were brought within the lines, and the battle of Chancellorsville was ended. My pocket diary, May 3d, has the following: "Sickles opened at 5 A.M. Orders sent by me at 10 for the front to retire; at 12 M. in my new position"; the latter sentence meaning that at that hour my corps was in position on the new or second line of defense.

As to the charge that the battle was lost because the general was intoxicated, I have always stated that he probably abstained from the use of arden spirits when it would have been far better for him to have continued in his usual habit in that respect. The shock from being violently thrown to the ground, together with the physical exhaustion resulting from loss of sleep and the anxiety of mind incident to the last six days of the campaign, would tell on any man. The enemy did not press us on the second line, Lee simply varying the monotony of watching us by an occasional cannonade from the left, a part of his army having been sent to Salem Church to resist Sedgwick. Sedgwick had difficulty in maintaining his ground, but held his own by hard fighting until after midnight, May 4th-5th, when he recrossed at Banks's Ford.

Some of the most anomalous occurrences of the war took place in this campaign. On the night of May 2d the commanding general, with 80,000 men in his wing of the army, directed Sedgwick, with 22,000 to march to his relief. While that officer was doing this on the 3d, and when it would be expected that every effort would be made by the right wing to do its part, only one-half of it was fought (or rather half-fought, for its ammunition was not replenished), and then the whole wing was withdrawn to a place where it could not be hurt, leaving Sedgwick to take care of himself.

At 12 o'clock on the night of the 4th-5th General Hooker assembled his corps commanders in council. Meade, Sickles, Howard, Reynolds, and myself were present; General Slocum, on account of the long distance from his post, did not arrive until after the meeting was broken up. Hooker stated that his instructions compelled him to cover Washington, not to jeopardize the army, etc. It was seen by the most casual observer that he had made up his mind to retreat. We were left by ourselves to consult, upon which Sickles made an elaborate argument, sustaining the views of the commanding general. Meade was in favor of fighting, stating that he doubted if we could get off our guns. Howard was in favor of fighting, qualifying his views by the remark that our present situation was due to the bad conduct of his corps, or words to that effect. Reynolds, who was lying on the ground very much fatigued was in favor of an advance. I had similar views to those of Meade as to getting off the guns, but said I "would favor an advance if I could designate the point of attack." Upon collecting the suffrages, Meade, Reynolds, and Howard voted squarely for an advance, Sickles and myself squarely no; upon which Hooker informed the council that he should take upon himself the responsibility of retiring the army to the other side of the river. As I stepped out of the tent Reynolds, just behind me, broke out, "What was the use of calling us together at this time of night when he intended to retreat anyhow?"

On the morning of May 5th, corps commanders were ordered to cut roads, where it was necessary, leading from their positions to the United States Ford. During the afternoon there was a very heavy rainfall. In the meantime Hooker had in person crossed the river, but, as he gave orders for the various corps to march at such and such times during the night, I am not aware that any of his corps generals knew of his departure. Near midnight I got a note from Meade informing me that General Hooker was on the other side of the river, which had risen over the bridges, and that communications was cut off from him. I immediately rode over to Hooker's headquarters and found that I was in command of the army if it had any commander. General Hunt, of the artillery, had brought the information as to the condition of the bridges, and from the reports there seemed to be a danger of losing them entirely. After a short conference with Meade I told him that the recrossing would be suspended, and that "we would stay where we were and fight it out," returning to my tent with the intention of enjoying what I had not had since the night of the 30th ultimo—good sleep; but at 2 A.M., communication having been reëstablished, I received a sharp message from Hooker, to order the recrossing of the army as he had directed and everything was safely transferred to the north bank of the Rappahannock.

In looking for the causes of the loss of Chancellorsville, the primary ones were that Hooker expected Lee to fall back without risking battle. Finding himself mistaken he assumed the defensive, and was out-generaled and became demoralized by the superior tactical boldness of the enemy.

E.P. ALEXANDER

Lee Triumphant

One of the most continuously valued eyewitness histories of the Civil War is *Military Memoirs of a Confederate* by Edward Porter Alexander. After serving stints as a signal officer and chief of ordnance in the Confederate Army of Northern Virginia, E.P. Porter went on to serve in the artillery where he rose to the rank of Brigadier General. After the war, he wrote his memoirs in a style that achieved historical accuracy and spurned the romanticism of his age. This selection on the battle of Chancellorsville was taken from his famous book.

Each commander planned to take the initiative. Hooker knew that he had double Lee's infantry, and great superiority in artillery, and he desired only to get at Lee away from breastworks. On April 13 he ordered Stoneman's cavalry upon a raid to Lee's rear, which expedition was to be the opening of his campaign. A rain-storm on the 14th, lasting 36 hours, halted the movement, after its leading brigade had forded the Rappahannock. The brigade was recalled, having to swim horses across the fast-rising river, and two weeks elapsed before the movement could be renewed. It was intended that Stoneman should destroy the railroads, which would force Lee to retreat. Stoneman should then harass and delay him as he fell back, pursued by Hooker.

Lee's proposed campaign was another invasion; this time of Pa. He could neither attack Hooker, nor even threaten his rear across the Rappahannock. But he could again sweep the Valley and cross the Potomac; and beyond, both Lee and Jackson imagined great possibilities. Three months later the opportunity offered, and Lee put it to the test; but his great lieutenant, Jackson, was no longer at the head of his 2d corps.

On April 29, Lee found himself anticipated by Hooker's having, the night before, laid pontoon bridges across the Rappahannock, below Deep Run, at the site of Franklin's crossing in Dec. Hooker had commenced his movement, on the 27th, by going with the 5th, 11th, and

238

l2th corps to cross the Rappahannock at Kelly's Ford, above the mouth of the Rapidan, 27 miles from Fredericksburg. A picket, at this point, was driven off, a pontoon bridge laid, and the whole force, about 42,000 men, was across the river on the 29th, when the 6th corps, under Sedgwick, was crossing in front of Jackson. Hooker immediately pushed his force by two roads from Kelly's to Germanna and Ely's fords of the Rapidan—about 11 miles off, and, on arriving, the troops forded, although the water was nearly shoulder deep. The fording was kept up all night by light of large bonfires, and the next morning the march of Chancellorsville, six miles away was resumed.

Meanwhile, two divisions of the 2d corps had moved up from Fredericksburg to United States Ford, where they laid a pontoon bridge about noon on the 30th. By 9 P.M. they had crossed and united with the 5th, 11th, and 12th corps at Chancellorsville. No resistance had been encountered anywhere, but that of picket forces. Hooker, in 84 hours, had covered about 45 miles, crossing two rivers, and had established a force of 54,000 infantry and artillery upon Lee's flank at Chancellorsville. Hooker was naturally elated at his success, and issued an order to his troops, congratulating them, and announcing that now:

> the enemy must either ingloriously fly or come out from behind his defenses, and give us battle on our own ground, where certain destruction awaits him.

And, indeed, if a general may ever be justified in enumerating his poultry while the process of incubation is incomplete, this might be an occasion. He was on the left flank and rear of Lee's only strong position with a force fully equal to Lee's, while another equal force threatened Lee's right. And somewhere in Lee's rear—between him and Richmond—was Stoneman with 10,000 sabres, opposed only by two regiments of cavalry, tearing up the railroads and waiting to fall upon Lee's flank when he essayed the retreat which Hooker confidently expected to see. He had said to those about him that evening:

> The rebel army is now the legitimate property of the Army of the Potomac. They may as well pack up their haversacks and make for Richmond, and I shall be after them.

But Hooker had made one mistake, and it was to cost him dearly. He had sent off, with Stoneman, his entire cavalry force, except one brigade. This proved insufficient to keep him informed of the Confederate movements, even though their efforts were supplemented by many signal officers with lookouts and field telegraphs, and by two balloons.

It was during the morning of the 30th, that Lee learned that Hooker had divided his army, and that one-half of it was already at Chancellorsville, while most of the remainder was in his front. By all the rules of war, one-half or the other should be at once attacked, and as Sedgwick's was the nearest, and Lee's whole force was already concentrated, Jackson at first proposed to attack Sedgwick. Lee, however, thought the position impregnable, and Jackson, after careful reconnoissance, came to the same conclusion. Orders were then at once prepared to march and attack Hooker before he could move from Chancellorsville. Early with his division, Barksdale's brigade, Pendleton's artillery reserve, and the Washington artillery, in all about 10,000 men, were left to hold the lines before Fredericksburg. These covered about six miles, and the force averaged about one man to each yard, and nine guns to each mile. About midnight on the 30th, Jackson marched from Hamilton's Crossing with his three remaining divisions, under A.P Hill, Rodes, and Colston. He was joined on the road in the morning by Lee with the remaining brigades of McLaws, and by Anderson's division, and Alexander's battalion of artillery.

Jackson's three divisions numbered about 25,000, Anderson's division about 8000, and three brigades of McLaws about 6000. Thus, Lee had in hand nearly 40,000 men, with which to attack Hooker at Chancellorsville, where Hooker now had four corps the 3d, 5th, 11th, and 12th—and two divisions of the 2d; a total effective of about 72,000 infantry and artillery, and was intrenching himself.

Chancellorsville was situated about a mile within the limits of a tract called the Wilderness. It stretched some 12 or 14 miles westward along the Rapidan and was some 8 or 10 miles in breadth.

The original forest had been cut for charcoal many years before, and replaced by thick and tangled smaller growth. A few clearings were scattered at intervals, and a few small creeks drained it. Chancellorsville was merely a brick residence at an important junction of roads, with a considerable clearing on the west. Three roads ran toward Fredericksburg: the old turnpike most directly; the Plank road to its right, but uniting with the Turnpike at Tabernacle Church—about halfway; the River road to the left, by a roundabout course passing near Banks Ford of the Rappahannock.

Hooker's line of battle ran from Chancellorsville, about two miles northeastward to the Rappahannock, covering United States Ford. Westward it covered the Plank road for about three miles, ending in a short offset northward. Intrenchment was quickly done by cutting abattis, or an entanglement, in front, and throwing up slight parapets, or piling breastworks of logs. About 11 A.M., however, Hooker prepared to resume his advance, and ordered the 5th and 12th corps to move out on the three roads toward Fredericksburg and establish a line in the open-country beyond the Wilderness. Griffin's and Humphreys's divisions of the 5th were sent down the River road, on the left, Sykes's division down the Turnpike in the centre, and the 12th corps, under Slocum, down the Plank road on the right.

Meanwhile, Lee and Jackson disposed Anderson's division for an advance, covering both the Pike and the Plank roads. Wilcox's and Mahone's brigades, with Jordan's battery of Alexander's battalion, moved upon the former; Wright's, Perry's, and Posey's brigades, with the remainder of Alexander's battalion, on the latter. McLaws's division moved by the Pike, and Lee, with Jackson's three divisions, followed the Plank road. Thus the two armies were marching toward each other on these two roads, while on the River road two of the Federal Divisions were marching toward Banks Ford, which was at this time undefended, although some intrenchments had been erected there. The possession of Banks Ford by Hooker would shorten the distance between Chancellorsville and his left wing under Sedgwick, by several miles.

The advancing forces first came into collision on the Pike. Sharp fighting followed, Semmes's brigade coming up on the left of Mahone and bearing the brunt of it against Sykes's regulars. Sykes's orders had been, however, only to advance to the first ridge beyond the forest, and he maintained his position there, though menaced by the extension of the Confederate lines beyond his flank, until orders were received from Hooker to withdraw to the original position within the forest. Similar orders were also sent to Slocum on the Plank road, and to Griffin and Humphreys who had advanced, nearly five miles down the River road, entirely unopposed, and who were within sight of Banks Ford when the orders for the counter-march reached them. Slocum's corps had not become seriously engaged, but its skirmishers had been driven in and its right flank threatened by Wright's brigade. This advanced upon the line of an unfinished railroad, which, starting from Fredericksburg, ran through the Wilderness generally a mile or two south of the Plank road.

Up to the moment of the withdrawal of his troops, Hooker's campaign had been well planned and well managed, and its culmination was now at hand in the open field—as he had desired. He could scarcely hope for more propitious circumstances, and, by all the rules of the game, a victory was now within his grasp. His lieutenants received the order to fall back with surprise and regret. The advance, upon both the Plank road and the Pike, had cleared the forest and reached fairly good positions. An officer was sent to Hooker to explain and request permission to remain, but he returned in a half hour, with the orders repeated.

Hooker has been severely blamed for these orders, subverting all the carefully prepared plans only published to the army that morning. It is interesting to learn the cause. Reports from the balloons and signal officers had informed him of the march of a force toward Chancellorsville, estimated at two corps. Rumors had also been brought by deserters, the night before, that Hood's division had rejoined Lee, coming from Suffolk, but Hooker's information from Fortress Monroe should have shown that to be impossible. There is no sign of any hesitation upon his part until 2 P.M. At that hour he wired Butterfield, his chief of staff at Falmouth:

> From character of information have suspended attack. The enemy may attack me,—I will try it. Tell Sedgwick to keep a sharp lookout, and attack if he can succeed.

This despatch makes clear Hooker's mind. He realized from the rapid manner of Lee's approach, and from the sounds of battle already heard, both on the Pike and the Plank road, that Lee meant to attack. He had confidently expected Lee to retreat without battle, and finding him, instead, so quick to take the aggressive, he lost his nerve and wished himself back on the line he had taken around Chancellorsville, where he would enjoy the great advantage of acting upon the defensive. He had seen in Dec. the enormous advantage which even slight breastworks could confer, and now he saw the chance of having his battle a defensive one behind intrenchments. It was surely the safest game to play, and Hooker is fully justified in electing to play it. No remonstrances shook his confidence in the least. He said to Couch,

> It is all right, Couch, I have got Lee just where I want him. He must fight me on my own ground.

Orders were given to intrench, and work was at once begun with abundance of men and tools, and it was pushed during most of the night. Couch says,

> At 2 A.M. the corps commanders reported to Gen. Hooker that their positions could be held; at least so said Couch, Slocum, and Howard.

Indeed, no better field fortification can be desired than what it was the quickest to build in the Wilderness. A wide belt of dense small growth could be soon felled in front of shallow ditches, with earth and log breastworks. Any charging line is brought to a halt by the entanglement, and held under close fire of musketry and canister, while the surrounding forest prevents the enemy from finding positions to use his own artillery.

So the corps commanders, responsible only for the front of their own lines, might truly report that their positions could be held. Yet the line, as a whole, may have a weak feature. This was the case here. Its right flank "rested in the air," and was not even covered by a curtain of cavalry.

Hooker, however, was not entirely blind to this weakness of his line. He inspected it early next morning, May 2, and ordered changes and enjoined vigilance which might have saved him from the surprise of the afternoon, had he not, like Pope in his campaign of the previous fall, failed to fathom the boldness of Lee's designs even after discovering the Confederate movements.

Lee appreciated that Hooker's withdrawal into the Wilderness was not forced, but to fortify and concentrate. He could, therefore, lose no time in finding how and where he might attack. Until nightfall the skirmishes were pushed forward everywhere, in order to locate the exact position of the enemy.

The result is briefly given in Lee's report, as follows:

> The enemy had assumed a position of great natural strength, surrounded on all sides by a dense forest, filled with a tangled undergrowth, in the midst of which breastworks of logs had been constructed, with trees felled in front so as to form an

almost impenetrable abattis. His artillery swept the few narrow roads by which his position could be approached from the front, and commanded the adjacent woods.

Hooker had, indeed manoeuvred Lee out of his position without a battle. There was now nothing left but to attack the greatly superior force in the impregnable position, or to attempt a retreat already dangerously delayed. But presently there came some more cheerful news. Fitzhugh Lee, who held the extreme left of our cavalry, had also reconnoitred the enemy, and had discovered that his right flank was in the air.

The one chance left to Lee was to pass undiscovered entirely across the enemy's front and turn his right flank. The enterprise was of great difficulty and hazard. To try it and fail meant destruction. For the army, already divided, must now be further subdivided, and the largest fraction placed in a position whence retreat would be impossible. Only a very sanguine man could even hope that 15 brigades, with over 100 guns, could make a march of 14 miles around Hooker's enormous army without being discovered. The chance, too, must be taken of aggressive action by the enemy at Fredericksburg or Banks Ford, even if Hooker himself did nothing during the eight hours in which the flanking force would be out of position in a long defile through the forest.

But no risks appalled the heart of Lee, either of odds, or position, or of both combined. His supreme faith in his army was only equalled by the faith of his army in him. The decision to attack was quickly made and preparations begun. Wilcox's brigade was ordered to Banks Ford to hold the position. This precaution was well taken, for after midnight of the 1st, Hooker ordered Reynolds's corps to leave Sedgwick and join the army at Chancellorsville. Reynolds started at sunrise and marched by Banks Ford, where he expected to find a bridge. But, as has been told, Griffin's and Humphreys's divisions, after being within sight on the afternoon of the 1st, had been recalled. Wilcox, at dawn on the 2d, had occupied the trenches. So Reynolds, arriving after sunrise and seeing Confederates in possession, continued his march on the north side, and crossed at United States Ford.

Anderson's four remaining brigades, with McLaws's three, were ordered to intrench during the night. Jackson with his three divisions, his own artillery, and Alexander's battalion of Longstreet's corps, were assigned to make the march through the Wilderness and turn Hooker's right.

Lee himself would remain with McLaws's and Anderson's troops, and occupy the enemy while the long march was made. Cheering was forbidden, and stringent measures taken to keep the column closed. Fitz-Lee with his cavalry, would precede the infantry and cover the flank. Two hours after sunrise, Lee, standing by the roadside, watched the head of the column march by, and exchanged with Jackson the last few words ever to pass between them. Rodes's division led the column, Colston's division followed, and A.P. Hill's brought up the rear.

The sun rose on May 2 a few minutes after five, and set at 6:50 P.M. The moon was full that night. The march led by a cross-roads near the Catherine Furnace, thence southward for over a mile and then southwestward for two miles before turning west and striking the Brock road within another mile. At the cross-road, the line of march was nearest the Federal lines and was most exposed. Here the 23d Ga. regiment of Colquitt's brigade, Rodes's division, was left to cover the rear.

When the line of march reached the Brock road, it turned southward for about a mile, and then, almost doubling back upon itself, it took a woods road running a trifle west of north, nearly parallel to the Brock road itself, and coming back into it about three miles north of the point at which it was first entered. This made a route two miles longer than would have been made by turning northward when the Brock road was first reached. And as the part of the road was farthest of all from the enemy (over three miles), and in the densest woods, it would seem that two miles might have been saved, had there been time and opportunity for reconnoissance.

Where the Brock road crossed the Plank road, the column halted, while Fitz-Lee took Jackson to the front to a point whence he could see the Federal lines, with arms stacked, in bivouac behind their intrenchments, and utterly unconscious of the proximity of an enemy. Until that moment it had been uncertain exactly where Jackson would attack. But he now saw that by following the Brock road about two miles farther he would get upon the old turnpike, beyond the enemy's flank, and could take it in the rear. So the march was at once resumed to reach that position. But Paxton's brigade of Colston's division was here detached and placed with the cavalry, in observation on the Plank road, and did not rejoin its division until near midnight.

The head of the column made about two and a half miles an hour, the rear about one and a half, for in spite of all efforts the column lost distance. During the day there were three halts for rest of perhaps twenty minutes each. There were no vehicles except the artillery, ambulances, and ammunition wagons. These, marching each behind its division, made the column 10 miles in length, of which the infantry occupied over six. The head, marching at about 6 A.M., reached the deploying point

on the turnpike by 4 P.M. The distance had proven greater than anticipated, and time was now of priceless value.

Meanwhile the movement, though misunderstood, had been detected
by the enemy. About a mile southwest of Chancellorsville was a settlement called Hazel Grove, on a cleared ridge. From this ridge, about 8
A.M., Birney, of Sickles's corps, discovered a column of infantry, trains,
and artillery passing his front. He brought up a battery and opened on
the train at a range of 1600 yards, throwing it into much confusion, and
compelling it to find other routes around the exposed point. Jackson sent
a battery to reply and check the enemy from advancing. Sickles came to
Birney's position and observed Jackson's column. His official report
says:—

> This continuous column—infantry, artillery, trains, and ambulance—
> was observed for three hours, moving apparently in a southerly direction
> toward Orange C.H., on the O.&A.R.R. or Louisa C.H. on the Va. Cen.
> The movement indicated a retreat on Gordonsville, or an attack upon our
> right flank—perhaps both, for if the attack failed, the retreat would be
> continued. At noon I received orders to advance cautiously toward the
> road followed by the enemy, and attack his columns.

Sickles advanced Birney's division, which engaged an outpost on the
flank and captured a regiment, the 23d GA. the two rear brigades, under
Thomas and Archer, with Brown's battalion of artillery, were halted for
an hour in observation, but were not engaged, and then followed on after
the column. They were only able to overtake it, however, after night.

It was about 4 P.M. when the head of Jackson's column began its
deployment on both sides of the Plank road, beyond Hooker's right, in
the tangled forest; and it was nearly 6 P.M. when eight of the 12 brigades
now in his column, had formed in two lines of battle, and one of the
remaining four in a third line. Meanwhile Sickles, though now unopposed in front, had brought up Whipple's division of his own corps, and,
having asked for reinforcements, had also received Barlow's brigade from
the right flank of the 11th corps, Williams's division of the 12th corps,
and three regiments of cavalry and some horse artillery under Pleasonton.
Posey's brigade held the left flank of Lee's line of battle in Hooker's front,
while Jackson conducted the flanking movement. Posey had a strong
force of skirmishers in front, which became hotly engaged with the left
flank of Sickles's advance, when it engaged Jackson's rear-guard. While
bringing up their reinforcements, the Federals made several efforts to

carry Posey's position, but were always repulsed. Sickles then planned to outflank and surround it, but he had been so slow that, before he was ready to act, Jackson had attacked, and Sickles was hastily recalled.

Otherwise there might have been a strange spectacle. Sickles might have routed Anderson at the same time that Jackson was routing Howard. For he was on Anderson's flank with over 20,000 infantry, a brigade of cavalry, and some horse artillery He wandered off, however, to the south and west, for miles, where there was no enemy before him.

Along the front of Lee's line the six brigades present of Anderson's and McLaws's divisions, aided by their artillery, had spent the day in more or less active skirmishing and cannonading with the enemy. Where the enemy showed a disposition to advance, the Confederates were well satisfied to lie quiet and repel them, as on the left in front of Posey. But on the Confederate right the Federal skirmish-line, under Col. Miles, being strongly posted and showing no disposition to advance, it was wise to be moderately aggressive and keep the enemy in hopes of an attack. Kershaw and Semmes did this handsomely throughout the day, though the threat of Sickles's movements caused Lee to draw his troops to his left, and reduce his right to less than a full line.

About 6 P.M., the sun being then about one hour high, Jackson gave the signal to Rodes to move forward. His brigades were in the following order from left to right: Iverson, O'Neal, Doles, and Colquitt, with Ramseur's brigade 100 yards in rear of Colquitt on the right. Colston's three brigades formed in line with Ramseur, and in the following order from the left: Nichols, Jones, Warren. About half of each division was on each side of the pike, and two Napoleons of Breathed's horse artillery stood in the pike ready to follow the skirmishers. Two hundred yards behind Colston, A.P. Hill had deployed Pender on the left of the pike. Lane, McGowan, and Heth were coming in column down the pike. Archer and Thomas were following, but some miles behind. Jackson had made his play so far with fair success, and he now stood ready with over 20,000 men to surprise Howard's 13,000. He was sure of an important victory, but the fruits to be reaped from it would be limited for two reasons.

1st. Two brigades were some hours behind, for Archer, without orders, had taken them to protect the rear. 2d. There were now but two hours of daylight left, and only in daylight can the fruits of victories be gathered. The question is suggested whether or not time had been anywhere lost unnecessarily. It would seem that 12 hours should not be needed to march 14 miles and form 20,000 men in line of battle. Briefly, it may be said, that with good broad roads, or with troops formed, ready to march at the word, and disciplined to take mud holes and obstructions without loss of distance, two hours could have been saved. But none of these conditions existed. Especially was time lost in the morning in getting the column formed.

Rodes reports it about 8 A.M. before the start was made. Further on, his report notes, "a delay was caused by an endeavor on our part to entrap some Federal cavalry." There may have been, during the morning, lack of appreciation of the value, even of the minutes, in an enterprise of the character now on foot, and an inadequate idea of the distance to be covered.

Some time was also lost in deploying Pender's brigade in the third line just before the charge was ordered. It would have saved a half-hour of great value to have ordered the charge as soon as the 2d line was formed, and allowed A.P. Hill's division to follow Rodes and Colston in column from the first, as they actually did at last. For, after advancing some distance through the tangled undergrowth, Pender's brigade was brought back to the road and placed at the head of the column for the rest of the advance.

It was nearly 6 P.M. when the signal for the advance was given by a bugle, and taken up and repeated for each brigade by bugles to the right and left through the woods. But the sounds seem to have been smothered in the forest, for the Federal reports make no mention of them. Their first intimation of anything unusual was given by wild turkeys, foxes, and deer, startled by the long lines of infantry and driven through the Federal camps. Then came shots from the Federal pickets, and then the guns on the turnpike opened and were soon followed by Confederate volleys and yells, impressing upon the enemy the fact that an overwhelming force had surprised them. Nevertheless, a gallant effort at resistance was made. The extreme right of the Federals was held by Von Gilsa's brigade of four regiments, about 1400 strong, which was formed, a half facing south and half facing west. They stood to fire three volleys, but by that time the Confederate lines were enveloping their flanks, and enfilade and reverse fire was being opened upon them. Only prompt flight could save the brigade from annihilation. After the third volley the brigade very wisely took to its heels and made its escape with a loss of

264 killed, wounded, and captured. Two guns with Von Gilsa were also captured. The next brigade to the left, McLean's, endeavored to change front. But it did not take long for the stern facts of the situation to become clear to every man of the brigade. As the canister fire of the Confederate guns was added to the enfilade fire of the Confederate infantry, this brigade also dissolved into a mass of fugitives, and two more guns, serving with them, were captured. But that they had fought well is shown by their losses, which were 692 out of about 2500. The division commander and four out of five regimental commanders were killed or wounded.

For a while, now, the fight degenerated into a foot race. Howard's original force of 13,000 had been reduced to 10,000 by the sending off of Barlow's large brigade. Of the 10,000, in a half-hour 4000 had been routed. The Confederates, recognizing the importance of pushing the pursuit, exerted themselves to the utmost. The lines broke into the double-quick wherever the ground was favorable, stopping only to fire at fugitives, or when completely out of breath. The horse artillery kept nearly abreast, and directed its fire principally at the Federal batteries which endeavored to cover the retreat. Some of these were fought gallantly, and some were overrun and captured. More might have been, and more prisoners taken, but for a blunder by Colquitt. His brigade was on the right of the front line, and its advance was least obstructed either by woods or the enemy. It could have moved most rapidly, and might have narrowed the enemy's avenue of escape.

Jackson's instructions had been explicit. Rodes's report says:—

> Each brigade commander received positive instructions which were well understood. The whole line was to push ahead from the beginning, keeping the road for its guide.... Under no circumstances was there to be any pause in the advance.

Ramseur's brigade was ordered to move in rear of Colquitt's and to support it. Colquitt, early in the advance, halted to investigate a rumor of a body of the enemy on his right flank, which proved to be a small party of cavalry. He delayed so that neither his brigade or Ramseur's rejoined the line until late at night.

Thus two brigades, by disregard of instructions and without need, were kept entirely out of action during the whole afternoon. So it happened that five of Jackson's 15 brigades (Thomas, Archer, Paxton, Colquitt and Ramseur) were missing from his line of battle during the whole afternoon, and, as A.P. Hill's four remaining brigades were not deployed until after dark, only six brigades were in the attack and pursuit of the 11th corps: to wit, Rodes, Doles, and Iverson of Rodes's division, and Jones, Warren, and Nichols of Colston's division. The great advantage of the Confederates lay in their being able to bring the centre of their line of battle against the flank of the enemy's line. This overwhelmed the two right brigades in a very short while, as we have seen, and the line pushed rapidly on, hoping to overwhelm the succeeding brigades likewise, one at a time.

The next division was Schurz's of two brigades, in line of battle along the Plank road, with two batteries which took positions and fired on the approaching Confederates. Schurz endeavored to form at right angles to their approach, but the mass of fugitives with wagons, ambulances, beef cattle, etc., entirely overwhelmed some of his regiments, and only two or three isolated ones were able to march in good order, and, facing about, to fire from time to time at their pursuers.

Next, at Dowdall's tavern, was a line of rifle-pits at right angles to the Plank road, and already occupied by Buschbeck's brigade of Von Steinwehr's division, the last of Howard's corps—its companion brigade, Barlow's, being away with Sickles. Three or four batteries were here established upon the line, and to it were rallied numbers of fugitives. At last an organized resistance was prepared. When the Confederates approached, in very scattered shape, they met a severe fire, and the advance was checked. Had Colquitt here been on the Confederate right with his and Ramseur's brigades, an opportunity was offered for a large capture. It might have been accomplished by the force at hand with a little delay. But they were already flushed with victory and would not be denied. After a sharp fight of perhaps 20 minutes, Colston's second line merged into the first, and the two lines pushed forward everywhere. The Federal artillery foresaw the end and fled, five guns being too late and captured. Buschbeck followed in fairly good order, but preceded by a stampede of troops and trains, principally down the Plank road, though a part diverged to the left by a road to the White House, called the Bullock road.

The casualties in Schurz's division were 919. In Buschbeck's brigade were 483. The total loss of Howard's corps was: killed, 217; wounded, 1221; missing, 974; total, 2412; only about 20 percent of the corps.

It was a very trifling loss, compared with what it might have been had all of Jackson's troops been upon the field, and had his orders been strictly observed.

The casualties of the Confederates are not known, their returns consolidating all separate actions together.

Much undeserved obloquy was heaped upon the 11th corps for their enforced retreat. No troops could have acted differently. All of their fighting was of one brigade at a time against six. With the capture of the Buschbeck position, the fighting of the day practically ceased. The Confederate troops were at the limit of exhaustion and disorganization. Daylight was fading fast, and commands badly intermingled. The pursuit was kept up, however, for some distance, although the enemy was no longer in sight. A few hundred yards beyond the Buschbeck position, the Plank road entered a large body of forest, closing on both sides of the road for nearly a mile before the open Chancellorsville plateau is reached. At the entrance of the wood a single Federal gun, with a small escort, was formed as a rearguard, and followed the retreat to Chancellorsville without seeing any pursuers.

A notable case of acoustic shadows occurred during this action. Sickles, some two and a half miles away, heard nothing of the attack upon Howard until word was brought him, which he at first refused to believe. At 6:30 P.M., Hooker sat on the veranda of the Chancellorsville house in entire confidence that Lee was retreating to Gordonsville and that Sickles was "among his trains." Faint sounds of distant cannonading were at first supposed to come from Sickles. Presently, an aid looking down the road with his glass suddenly shouted, "My God! here they come." All sprang to their horses and, riding down the road, met, in a half-mile, the fugitive rabble of Howard's corps, and learned that Jackson, with half of Lee's army, had routed the Federal flank. Had there been some hours of daylight, Hooker's position would have been critical. For Lee and Jackson were now less than two miles apart, and between them were of infantry less than two divisions; Geary's of the 12th corps in front of Lee, and two brigades of Berry's of the 3d, near the path of Jackson.

But darkness puts an embargo upon offensive operations in a wooded country. Troops may be marched during the night, where there is no opposition, but the experiences of this occasion will illustrate the difficulty of fighting, even when the moon is at its best. The night restored to the Federals nearly all the advantages lost during the day. Hooker acted promptly and judiciously. Urgent recalls were sent for Sickles and his entire force. His advance had gone two miles to the front and was preparing to bivouac, when orders overtook it. It did not reach the field until after 10 P.M.

The force first available against Jackson was the artillery of the 12th corps, for which a fine position was offered along the western brow of the Chancellorsville plateau, south of the Plank road. This position was known as Fairview, and it now became the key-point of the battle. In front of it the open ground extended about 600 yards to the edge of the forest. A small stream, between moderate banks at the foot of the plateau, offered shelter for a strong line of infantry in front of the guns. Here, within an hour, was established a powerful battery of 34 guns, and during the night all were protected by parapets. The position was essentially like the Confederate position at Marye's Hill before Fredericksburg, but on a larger scale. The forest in front offered no single position for a Confederate gun.

Only from one point could it be assailed by artillery. Across the stream in front, about 1000 yards obliquely to the left, was the small settlement called Hazel Grove, occupying some high open fields, from which, as has been told, Birney had that morning discovered Jackson's march. Hazel Grove offered excellent positions for attacking the Fairview lines, but Hazel Grove was itself within the Federal lines, and, about sundown, was occupied by a few cavalry with some artillery of the 3d corps, and some miscellaneous trains.

The only Federal infantry near at hand when the fugitives reached Chancellorsville were Carr's and Revere's brigades of Berry's division of the 3d corps. These brigades were formed in line of battle in the forest north of the Plank road, with their left resting on the guns at Fairview. Here they promptly set to work to intrench themselves in the forest across the Plank road, and to cut an abattis in front. They were soon reënforced by Hays's brigade of French's division of the 2d corps, and later by Mott's, the remaining brigade of Berry's division, which had been guarding bridges at United States Ford.

Meanwhile, as darkness fell, the Confederate pursuit died out upon entering the forest beyond the open lands about Dowdall's tavern. The cessation was not voluntary on Jackson's part, but it was necessary that Rodes's and Colston's divisions should be re-formed, and that Hill's division should take the lead. It had followed the pursuit, marching in column, and was in good order and comparatively fresh. The other divisions were broken, mingled, and exhausted, and several brigades were far behind. During the long pause in the advance, while Hill's brigades filed into the woods to the right and left, and the disorganized brigades were withdrawn to re-form, Jackson impatiently supervised and urged forward the movements. It is possible that he proposed to push his attack down the Bullock road which, a short distance ahead, diverged to the left, toward the river, instead of following the Plank road to Chancellorsville, as he had said to Hill: "Press them, Hill! Press them! Cut them off from United States Ford." It would, however, have been an error to make such a diversion, for the attack would have met an overwhelming force. Its only hope of success was to reunite with Lee at Chancellorsville with the least delay. Meanwhile, partaking of the impatience of Jackson, his chief of artillery, Col. Crutchfield, pushed some guns forward on the Plank road, and opened a random fire down it toward Chancellorsville, now less than a mile away.

It was an unwise move, for it provoked a terrific response from the 34 guns now in position upon Fairview plateau. The Plank road was now crowded with troops and artillery in column, and the woods near it were full of the reorganizing brigades. Under such a fire, even in the dim light of the rising moon, great confusion soon resulted, and although casualties were few, it became necessary to discontinue our fire before order could be restored and the formation of the line of battle be resumed.

Lane's N.C. brigade was at the head of Hill's division. One regiment, the 33d, was deployed and sent some 200 yards ahead as skirmishers, and the other four formed line of battle with the centre on the Plank road in the following order from left to right: 28th, 18th, 37th, 7th. The Bullock road here diverged to the left, toward United States Ford, but the enemy was evidently close in front, and Jackson said to Lane, "Push right ahead, Lane. Right ahead."

While the formation was still in progress, Jackson, followed by several staff-officers and couriers, rode slowly forward upon an old road, called the Mountain road, which left the Bullock to its left near the Plank road, and ran parallel to the latter, about 80 yards distant, toward Chancellorsville.

Up this road the party advanced for 100 or 200 yards, but not passing the 33d N.C. skirmish-line. They then halted and listened for a while to the axes of the Federals, cutting abattis in the forest ahead. Beyond the Plank road, the Federal troops who had been off with Sickles were now returning, and were slowly working their way to reoccupy some breast-works which had been built the night before in the forest south of the Plank road. Between their skirmishers and those of the 33d N.C. on their side of the Plank road, there suddenly began some firing. The fire spread rapidly in both directions, along the picket-lines, and was presently taken up by Federal regiments and lines of battle in the rear. Jackson, at the head of his party, was slowly retracing his way back to his line of battle, when this volley firing began. Maj. Barry, on the left of the 18th N.C., seeing through the trees by the moonlight a group of horsemen moving toward his line, ordered his left wing to fire. Two of the party were killed, and Jackson received three balls; one in the right hand, one through the left wrist and hand, and one shattering the left arm between shoulder and elbow.

The reins were dropped, and the horse, turning from the fire, ran into overhanging limbs which nearly unhorsed him; but, recovering the rein, he guided into the Plank road where Capt. Wilbourn of his staff helped him off. Meanwhile, the enemy had advanced guns to their skirmish-line, and presently began to sweep the Plank road with shell and canister. A litter was brought and Jackson placed in it, but a bearer was shot, and Jackson fell heavily on his wounded side. With great difficulty he was finally gotten to an ambulance, which already held his chief of artillery, Col. Crutchfield, with a shattered leg.

During the night Jackson's left arm was amputated, and the next day he was taken in an ambulance via Spottsylvania, to a small house called Chandler's, near Guinea Station. For a few days his recovery was expected, but pneumonia supervened, and he died on May 10. In his last moments his mind wandered, and he was again upon the battle-field giving orders to his troops: "Order A.P. Hill to prepare for action. Pass the infantry to the front. Tell Maj. Hawks—" There was a pause for some moments, and then, calmly, the last words, "Let us pass over the river, and rest under the shade of the trees."

Jackson's fall left A.P. Hill in command, but Hill was himself soon disabled by a fragment of shell, and sent for Stuart. Rodes ranked Stuart, but the latter was not only best known to the army, but was of great popularity, and Rodes cheerfully acquiesced. His whole career, until his death at Winchester, Sept. 19, '64, was brilliant, and justifies the belief that he would have proven a competent commander, but, as will be seen, Stuart's conduct, upon this occasion, was notably fine. A little before dark, Stuart, with Jackson's consent, had taken his cavalry and a regiment of infantry and started to attack the camps and trains of the enemy near Ely's Ford. He had reached their vicinity and was forming for the assault, when one of Jackson's staff brought the message of recall. He ordered the command to fire three volleys into the nearest camp and then to withdraw, while he rode rapidly back—about five miles—and took command between 10 and 11 P.M.

There was but one course to take—to make during the night such preparation as was possible, and, at dawn, to renew the attack and endeavor to break through the enemy's line and unite with Lee at Chancellorsville. The wounding of Crutchfield had left me the senior artillery officer present, and I was sent for, and directed to reconnoitre, and to post before dawn as many guns as could be used. I spent the night in reconnoissance and, beside the Plank road, could find but one outlet through the forest, a cleared vista some 200 yards long and 25 wide, through a dense pine thicket, opening upon a cleared plateau held by the enemy. This plateau afterward proved to be the Hazel Grove position, and I concentrated near it several batteries.

One of Jackson's engineers was sent by a long detour and found Lee before daylight and explained to him Stuart's position and plans, that he might, during the action, extend his left and seek a connection with our right. During the night, the brigades in rear rejoined, and the three divisions were formed for the attack in the morning, with Hill's division in front, Colston's in a second line, and Rodes's in a third.

Two brigades on Hill's right were placed obliquely to the rear, to present a front toward that flank.

When Hooker found that the Confederate attack had come to a standstill in front of the Fairview line, with Sickles near Hazel Grove upon its right flank, he ordered Sickles to move forward by the moonlight, and attack. Birney's division, in two lines with supporting columns, about midnight, advanced from Hazel Grove upon the forest south of the Plank road and in front of the Fairview position. The left wing of this force grazed the skirmishers of McGowan and struck the right flank of Lane's brigade, of which two and a half regiments became sharply engaged. But the whole Federal advance glanced off, as it were, and, changing its direction, it turned toward the Federal line in front of Fairview, where it approached the position of Knipe's and Ruger's brigades of Williams's division of the 12th corps.

Hearing their noisy approach, and believing them to be Confederates, the Fairview guns and infantry opened fire upon the woods, while the approaching lines were still so distant that they were unable to locate their assailants, and supposed the fire to come from the Confederate line. And now for a long time, for one or perhaps two hours, the Confederates listened to a succession of furious combats in the forest in their front, accompanied by heavy shelling of the woods, volleys of musketry, and a great deal of cheering. Our pickets and skirmish-lines were forced sometimes to lie down or seek protection of trees from random bullets, but we had no other part in it. It extended northward sometimes even across the Plank road. And the official reports of many Federal officers give glowing accounts of the repulse of desperate Confederate attacks, and even of the capture of Confederate guns. These stories were founded on the finding of some Federal guns, which had been abandoned in one of the stampedes of the afternoon.

Col. Hamlin's book says:

Some of the reports of this midnight encounter are missing, and their publication will throw much light on the details. On the Federal side it was undoubtedly a mixed-up mess, and some of the regiments complain of being fired into from the front and from both.... At all events, after reading the reports of Gen. Sickles at the time, and his statement a year afterward to Congress... the brilliant array of gallant troops in the moonlight... the bold attack... the quick return of one of the columns to be stopped by the bayonets of the 63d Pa.... the advance of the other column deflecting to the right, until it met Gen. Slocum in person... certainly there is occasion for a slight smile on the part of the reader. And this smile may be lengthened on reading the story of Gen. De Trobriand, who was a participator, or the account left by Col. Underwood of the 23d Mass., who returned from the depths of the wilderness in time to witness and describe the ludicrous scene.

Hooker had little cause for apprehension after darkness had come to his relief, yet the shock to his overconfidence had been so severe that his only new dispositions were defensive. Yet he had over 60,000 fresh troops present, while Lee had on the east but about 16,000 and on the west about 24,000.

His first care was to order the intrenchment of an interior line, upon which he could fall back in case Stuart forced his way through to a junction with Lee. A short line was quickly selected, of great natural strength, behind Hunting Run on the west, and behind Mineral Spring Run on the east, with both flanks resting on the river and covering his bridges. This line will be more fully described and referred to later. It took in the White House, some three fourths of a mile in the rear of Chancellorsville, and was probably the strongest field intrenchment ever built in Va. Next, Hooker sent orders to Sedgwick at 9 P.M., as follows:

> The major-general, commanding, directs that you cross the Rappahannock at Fredericksburg on receipt of this order, and at once take up your line of march on the Chancellorsville road until you connect with him, and will attack and destroy any force you may fall in with on your road.
>
> You will leave all your trains behind, except pack trains of your ammunition, and march to be in the vicinity of the general at daylight. You will probably fall upon the rear of the forces commanded by Gen. Lee, and between you and the major-general, commanding, he expects to use him up. Send word to Gen. Gibbon to take possession of Fredericksburg. Be sure not to fail.

These orders were good, and would have insured victory, had they been carried out. And Hooker took a further precaution, most desirable whenever important orders are issued. He despatched a competent staff-officer, Gen. Warren, his chief engineer, to supervise their execution. Unfortunately for him, however, under the conditions it proved impossible to execute the orders within the time set, as will be told later. Here it is only necessary to note that Sedgwick was never able to get near Chancellorsville.

Even as the field stood, with or without the arrival of Sedgwick, the battle was still Hooker's, had he fought where he stood. But about dawn he made the fatal mistake of recalling Sickles from the Hazel Grove position, which he was holding with Whipple's and Birney's divisions, and five batteries. There has rarely been a more gratuitous gift of a battle-field. Sickles had a good position and force enough to hold it, even without reenforcements, though ample reenforcements were available. The Federal line was longer and overlapped ours on its right, and our only opportunity to use artillery was through the narrow vista above referred to, which was scarcely sufficient for four guns, and had but a very restricted view.

Had Stuart's attack been delayed a little longer, our right flank might have marched out upon Hazel Grove plateau without firing a shot. A Federal battery, supported by two regiments, had been designated as a rear-guard, and it alone occupied the plateau when our advance was made, though the rear of the retiring column was still near.

Stuart's men, when the lines were finally formed, got from two to three hours' rest before dawn. About that time, cooked rations were brought up. Before the distribution, however, was finished, Archer's and McGowan's brigades were moved forward, from their retired positions as the right flank, to straighten the line. They soon came upon a picket-line of the enemy, and sharp firing began. Stuart, without waiting further, ordered the whole line to the attack.

Archer's brigade, about 1400 strong, in advancing through the pine thickets, drifted to the right, and gradually opened a gap between it and McGowan's brigade, emerging from the forest alone, and in front of the enemy's rear-guard. A sharp action ensued, while Archer extended his right and threatened the enemy's rear, forcing the battery to retreat. He then charged and captured 100 prisoners, and forced the abandonment of four of the guns.

He attempted to push his advance much farther, but was checked by the fire of the enemy's artillery and of the rear brigade, Graham's, of Sickles's column. After two efforts, realizing that his force was too small, and leaving one of his captured guns, he fell back to Hazel Grove ridge, about 6:30 A.M. This was now being occupied rapidly by our guns. Thus, so easily that we did not at once realize its great value, we gained space for our batteries, where we soon found that we could enfilade the enemy's adjacent lines.

Meanwhile, the first assault had been made along the whole line by Hill's division. The enemy's advanced line crossed the Plank road and was held by Williams's division of the 12th corps, Berry's of the 3d corps, and Hays's brigade of the 2d corps. In rear of the front line was a second line near the edge of the forest. Across the small stream and along the edge of the elevated plateau, their artillery had been strongly intrenched during the night, making a third line. The two divisions from Hazel Grove, with their four batteries, were brought up in rear of the forces already holding the front to the west. This whole front from north to south was scarcely a mile and a quarter long. It was defended by about 25,000 men, and it was being attacked by about an equal number. The Confederates, however, had the hot end of the affair, in having to take the aggressive and advance upon breastworks protected by abattis and intrenched guns.

In his first assault, however, Hill's division, now commanded by Heth, after a terrific exchange of musketry, succeeded in driving the Federals from the whole of their front line. They followed the retreating enemy, and attacked the second line, where the resistance became more strenuous. On the extreme right, Archer's brigade had now fallen back to Hazel Grove, where it remained, supporting the guns now taking position there. This left McGowan's flank uncovered, and a Federal force attacked it, and drove it back to the captured line. This uncovered Lane's brigade, and it was also forced to fall back. On the left of the Plank road, the advance of Thomas beyond the enemy's first line met both a stronger second line and a flank attack, his left being in the air. After an hour's hard fighting, the whole line was forced back to the captured breastworks, with severe losses. It was clear that extreme efforts would be needed to drive the enemy from his position. Stuart ordered 30 additional guns to Hazel Grove, and brought forward both the second and third lines, putting in at once his last reserves. It would be useless to follow in detail the desperate fighting which now ensued and was kept up for some hours. The Federal guns on the Fairview heights were able to fire over the heads of two lines of infantry, and other batteries aided from the new position in which Hooker had now established the 1st, 2d, and 5th corps. This was so near on our left that Carroll's and McGregor's brigades of the 2d corps, with artillery, were sent forward to attack our flank, and were only repulsed after such fighting that they lost 367 men. With the aid of our second and third lines, fresh assaults were made on both sides of the Plank road, and now the enemy's second lines were carried. But his reserves were called upon, and again our lines were driven back, and countercharges south of the road again penetrated the gap between McGowan and Archer. Paxton's brigade was brought across from the north and restored the situation at a critical moment, Paxton, however, being killed. Some of our brigades were now nearly fought out, the three divisions being often massed in one, and the men could only be moved by much example on the part of their officers. Stuart himself was conspicuous in this, and was everywhere encouraging the troops with his magnetic presence and bearing, and singing as he rode along the lines, "Old Joe Hooker, won't you come out the Wilderness." There can be no doubt that his personal conduct had great influence in sustaining the courage of the men so that when, at last, our artillery had begun to shake the Federals' lines, there was still the spirit to traverse the bloody ground for the fourth time and storm the Fairview batteries.

Guns had been brought to Hazel Grove from all the battalions on the field—Pegram's, Carter's, Jones's, McIntosh's, and Alexander's. Perhaps 50 guns in all were employed here, but less than 40 at any one time, as guns were occasionally relieved, or sent to the rear to refill. Their field of fire was extensive, being an oblique on both the enemy's artillery and infantry. Some ground having been gained on the Plank road, Cols. Jones and Carter had also been able to establish 10 rifle guns there, which enfiladed the Plank road as far as the Chancellorsville house.

About nine o'clock, the Federal artillery fire was perceptibly diminished. Many of their guns were running short of ammunition, and fresh ammunition was not supplied. Sickles asked for it, and for reenforcements, but none were sent. It would seem that Hooker preferred to lose the Chancellorsville plateau entirely, and fall back into his new position, which was like a citadel close at hand, rather than risk fighting outside of it.

At Stuart's last charge, the Federal lines yielded with but moderate resistance. The guns in the Fairview intrenchments abandoned them, and fell back to the vicinity of the Chancellorsville house.

The guns at Hazel Grove moved forward across the valley and occupied the deserted Federal positions, here making connection with Anderson's division which Lee was extending to his left to meet them. They were soon joined by Jordan's battery of my own battalion, which had been serving with Anderson.

The enemy, driven out of their fortified lines, attempted to make a stand near the Chancellorsville house, but it was a brief one. There were no breastworks here to give shelter, and their position was now so contracted that our guns from three directions crossed their fire upon it. Hooker, in the porch of the Chancellorsville house, was put *hors de combat* for two or three hours by a piece of brick torn from a pillar by a cannon-shot. No one took command in his place, and for a while the army was without a head. Meanwhile, McLaws and Anderson had seen the enemy withdrawing from their fronts and pressed forward at the same time that Stuart's infantry crowned the plateau from the west. Some prisoners were cut off and captured on each flank, and a few guns also fell into our hands, but, as a whole, the enemy's withdrawal was orderly and well managed, and with less loss than might have been expected.

One sad feature of the occasion was that the woods on the north of the road were set on fire by shells, and the dry leaves spread the fire rapidly, although the trees and undergrowth did not burn. Efforts were made to remove the wounded, but the rapid spread of the fire prevented, and some of the wounded of both armies were burned.

About 10 A.M., Lee, advancing with McLaws's division, met Stuart with Jackson's corps near the site of the Chancellorsville house, now only a smoking ruin, for our shells had set it on fire. It was, doubtless, a proud moment to Lee, as it was to the troops who greeted him with enthusiastic cheering.

Lee, by no means, intended the battle to end here. Both infantry and artillery were ordered to replenish ammunition and renew the assault, but there came news from the rear, which forced a change of programme. Sedgwick's corps had broken through the flimsy line in front of it, and was now moving up the Plank road. With all his audacity Lee could not venture to attack five corps intrenched in his front, while Sedgwick came up in his rear.

The story of events at Chancellorsville must now pause, as the action there paused, while that is told of Sedgwick's venture against Lee's rear.

Hooker had sent urgent orders the night before to Sedgwick to come to his help, and a staff-officer, Warren, to supervise their execution. But Sedgwick, though already on the south side of the river, which Hooker did not seem to know, was three miles below Fredericksburg, near the scene of Franklin's crossing in Dec. He had been under orders to advance toward Richmond on the Bowling Green road, and had disposed his troops accordingly.

To advance up the Plank road, it was necessary to march to Fredericksburg and force the Confederate lines on Marye's Hill. These lines were held from Taylor's Hill to the Howison house, about three miles, by only two brigades, Barksdale's and Hays's, with a small amount of artillery. The regiments were strung out in single rank, the men sometimes yards apart, and with wide intervals at many places between regiments. On Marye's Hill, two regiments, the 18th and 21st Miss., with six-guns of the Washington Arty. and two under Lt. Brown of Alexander's Bat., were distributed from the Plank road to Hazel Creek, about a half-mile.

Sedgwick had marched at midnight with a good moon, but his progress was slow, for the Confederate pickets annoyed it. By daylight he was in Fredericksburg, and his batteries from both banks of the river and from the edge of the town opened on the Confederates. Sedgwick had been informed by Hooker that the Confederate force left at Fredericksburg was very small, and, without delay, he sent forward four regiments from Wheaton's and Shaler's brigades to charge the works in front of Marye's Hill. It was sending a boy on a man's errand. The Confederate infantry reserved its fire until the enemy were within 40 yards, when they opened and quickly drove them back. A second assault was made, but with similar result. Sedgwick was now convinced that a heavy force confronted him, and he waited for Gibbon's division of the 2d corps. This had just crossed from Falmouth, and it made an effort upon the extreme Confederate left. It proved futile on account of the canal along the front at that part of the field, which was defended by three regiments of Hays's brigade of Early's division, hurried there by Early on seeing the enemy's preparations.

Soon afterward, Wilcox's brigade came to the scene from Banks Ford, where it had been in observation on the 2d. At dawn on the 3d, Wilcox noted that the enemy's pickets on the north side were wearing haversacks, and correctly guessed that the forces opposite were leaving for Chancellorsville. He was preparing to march in the same direction, when a messenger brought word of the advance of Gibbon's division. Thereupon leaving a picket of 50 men and two guns in observation at Banks Ford, Wilcox marched to Taylor's Hill.

About 10 A.M., Gibbon having reported that an attack on our extreme left was impracticable, and Howe's division, making no progress east of Hazel Run, Sedgwick had no recourse but to renew his attack upon Marye's Hill by main force. He accordingly prepared a much stronger assault than that of the morning. Newton's division, supported by Burnham's brigade, was to attack Marye's Hill, while Howe's division assaulted Lee's Hill beyond Hazel Run.

This force numbered about 14,000 men, with an abundant artillery. Across Hazel Creek were seven guns of Cutt's and Cabell's battalions, and the two remaining regiments of Barksdale's brigade and one LA. of Hays's brigade.

About 11 A.M., both Newton and Howe renewed the assault. Newton advanced rapidly through the fire of the few Confederate guns, but recoiled soon after the infantry opened, although Barksdale's line was so thin that it scarcely averaged a man to five feet of parapet. Some of the

Federal regiments, however, suffered severely, and a number of killed and wounded were left near the Confederate line.

This, by a strange piece of good nature on the part of one of our best officers, proved our undoing. When Newton's line was beaten back, the firing on both sides nearly ceased, and some Federal officer sent forward a flag of truce. No Federal report mentions this incident. The flag was probably sent by only a brigade commander, for the fighting, by Howe's division, across Hazel Run, was kept up without cessation. Col. Griffin of the 18th Miss. received the flag. The officer bearing it asked to be allowed to remove his dead and wounded in Griffin's front. Without referring to his brigade commander, Griffin granted the request, and, still more thoughtlessly allowed his own men to show themselves while the wounded were being delivered. The enemy, to their great surprise, discovered what a small force was in their front.

They lost little time in taking advantage of the information. The action was reopened, and now a charge was made with a rush, and the enemy swarmed over our works. The Mississippians had no chance to escape, but fought with butts of guns and bayonets, and were mostly captured, with the loss of about 100 killed and wounded. The casualties in Newton's division and Burnham's brigade, in the whole battle, were about 1200, of which probably 900 fell in this affair. All of the guns on the hill were captured, Brown's section last of all, firing until surrounded.

Meanwhile, Howe's division had a full mile to traverse before reaching the Confederate lines. Instead of a charge, their progress was a slow advance under cover of heavy artillery fire. Before they reached the Confederate line, Newton's division had made its second charge and was in possession of Marye's Hill. Thereupon, Early, who was in command, ordered the withdrawal of his whole division, and the formation of a new line of battle across the Telegraph road, about two miles in the rear. Here he concentrated Gordon's, Hoke's, and Smith's brigades, with the remnants of Barksdale's. Hays's brigade had been cut off with Wilcox, and these two brigades were in position to delay Sedgwick in advancing upon the Plank road toward Chancellorsville. But Hays, under orders from Early, crossed the Plank road before Sedgwick had made any advance. Wilcox then took position with four guns across the Plank road, and delayed the enemy's advance as much as possible, while he fell back slowly to Salem Church, where he had been notified that McLaws would meet him with reinforcements. He reached this point about 3 P.M., meeting there Wofford's, Semmes's, Kershaw's, and Mahone's brigades, under McLaws. The five brigades rapidly formed a single line of battle across the Plank road. Wilcox's brigade held the centre, with the 14th and 11th Ala. on the left of the Plank road, and the 10th and 8th on the right. The 9th Ala. was in reserve a short distance in rear of the 10th. Four guns were posted across the Plank road, and a company of infantry was put in Salem Church, and one in a schoolhouse a short distance in front. Kershaw's brigade was on the right of Wilcox, and Wofford on right of Kershaw; Semmes's brigade was on Wilcox's left, and Mahone's brigade was on the left of Semmes.

In front of the line of battle stretched a fringe of dense young wood, some 200 yards wide, and beyond that, for perhaps a half-mile, were open fields, which extended with a few interruptions on each side of the Plank road back to Fredericksburg, about four miles. Sedgwick had been delayed over four hours in traversing that distance.

About 4:30 P.M., Sedgwick established a battery 1000 yards in front of Wilcox, and opened fire. The Confederate artillery was nearly out of ammunition, and after a few rounds it was withdrawn. Encouraged by this, the Federals now sent forward Brooks's division, formed across the road in two lines, with Newton's division in the same formation upon Brooks's right.

Now ensued one of the most brilliant and important of the minor affairs of the war. McLaws had reached the field and assumed the command, but credit is also due to Wilcox, who had delayed many times his number for several hours, and gained time for reinforcements to arrive.

The story of the battle may be told very briefly. North of the road, opposite the 14th and 11th Ala., was Torbert's Jersey brigade under Brown, in a double line. On the south, opposite the 8th, 9th, and 10th Ala., was Bartlett's brigade, one of the best in the Federal army, which boasted that it had never been repulsed, and had never failed to hold any position it was ordered to occupy.

The strength of the Confederate position consisted in the thick undergrowth which completely hid their lines, lying down on the crest of a slight ridge in rear of the woods. These were held by skirmishers during the enemy's approach across the open. When the artillery was withdrawn, it left a gap of about 50 yards between the 11th Ala., on the left of the road and the 10th on the right. Bartlett's brigade advanced gallantly through the severe skirmish fire, fought through the strip of woods, drove the company from the church, and cut off the one in the schoolhouse. Pushing on and overlapping the left of the 10th Ala., they enfiladed it, broke its line, and drove it back in confusion. The 8th Ala., under Lt.-Col. Herbert, on the right of the 10th, however, did not break, but threw back its three left companies, and brought an enfilade fire on the enemy's further advance. The 9th Ala., being in reserve a little in rear of the 10th, rose from the ground, and, giving the enemy a volley charged them and drove them back.

Brown's brigade, on the opposite side of the road, had a wider body of woods to cross, and had not advanced as far as Bartlett. But when Bartlett was driven back, Wilcox's whole brigade joined in the counter-stroke. Bartlett's first line was followed so rapidly that the prisoners in the schoolhouse were liberated, and the rush of the fugitives and the quick pursuit overwhelmed the second line, giving it no chance to make a stand.

Across the Plank road, Semmes's two right regiments, the 10th and 51st Ga., joined the 14th and 11th Ala., and these four regiments, meeting the Jersey brigade in the woods, drove it back in such a direction that the fugitives from each side of the Plank road converged upon the road. The Confederates in pursuit said that they had never had such crowds to fire upon. The pursuit was dangerously prolonged, but fortunately the enemy contented himself by checking it, and the Confederates then slowly withdrew. Long-range firing, however, was kept up until night.

Bartlett's brigade reported a loss in this attack of 580 officers and men out of less than 1500 men. Brown's brigade reported a loss of 511.

Wilcox's brigade lost 75 killed, 372 wounded, and 48 missing, a total of 495. The losses of Semmes's brigade are included with the campaign losses. One of its regiment, however, the 10th Ga., reports for this day: 21 killed, 102 wounded, and 5 missing, a total of 128 out of 230 present. In the morning at Chancellorsville, this regiment had received the surrender of the 27th Conn., which had been on picket and was cut off by the capture of Chancellorsville. During this charge it also captured 100 prisoners. While this action was going on, Early had formed line of battle to resist an advance of the enemy upon the Telegraph road, and was bringing up his extreme right from Hamilton's Crossing. It was about night when his whole division was concentrated.

The enemy was holding Gibbon's entire division idle in Fredericksburg, guarding the pontoon bridges to Falmouth. Had Gibbon moved up on Sedgwick's flank to Banks Ford, his division would have counted for something in the next day's affairs. His force was just what Segwick needed to enable him to hold his ground.

Returning now to Chancellorsville, we have to note a movement which involved an unfortunate Confederate delay on the next day—a delay which enabled Sedgwick's corps to escape scot-free from a position which should have cost him all his artillery and half his men. The River road, from Chancellorsville to Fredericksburg via Banks Ford, was left unoccupied when Hooker took refuge in his fortified lines on the morning of the 3d. Anderson, with his three remaining brigades,—Wright's, Perry's and Posey's,—was sent at 4 P.M. to watch that road, and threaten the enemy upon that flank. Two hours after sunrise on the 4th, Heth arrived with three brigades to relieve Anderson, who was now ordered to proceed to Salem Church, about six miles, and report to McLaws, which he did about noon. This sending Anderson to reënforce McLaws might have been done the afternoon before. He would then have been on hand at the earliest hour for the joint attack upon Sedgwick, on the 4th, which is now to be described.

The events of the morning of the 4th had been as follows: No communication had been received by Sedgwick from Hooker, and he was still under orders to come to Chancellorsville. But at an early hour, movements of Early's troops were discovered in his rear, and, instead of advancing, Sedgwick had deployed Howe's division perpendicular to the Plank road facing to his rear, and stretching to the river above Banks Ford, where pontoon bridges had been laid the afternoon before. Sedgwick's scouts had reported that "a column of the enemy, 15,000 strong, coming from the direction of Richmond, had occupied the heights of Fredericksburg, cutting him off from the town." He at once abandoned all idea of taking the aggressive, and only wished himself safely across the river. But he did not dare to attempt a crossing, except under cover of night. His lines were too long, and were weak in plan, as they faced in three directions,—east, south, and west. But he dared not venture a change, for fear of precipitating an attack. When at last he received a despatch from Hooker, its noncommital advice was not encouraging. It said:

Everything snug here. We contracted the lines a little and repulsed the last assault with ease. Gen. Hooker wishes them to attack him tomorrow, if they will. He does not desire you to attack them again in force, unless he attacks him at the same time. He says you are too far away for him to direct. Look well to the safety of your corps, and keep up communication with Gen. Benham at Banks Ford and Fredericksburg. You can go to either place if you think it best to cross. Banks Ford would bring you in supporting distance of the main body, and would be better than falling back to Fredericksburg.

A little later Hooker sent another message, urging Sedgwick, if possible, to hold a position on the south bank, to which Sedgwick replied:

The enemy threatens me strongly on two fronts. My position is bad for such attack. It was assumed for attack, not for defense. It is not improbable that the bridges at Banks Ford may be sacrificed. Can you help me strongly if I am attacked?

No answer to his inquiry appears, and Sedgwick stood on the defensive, awaiting nightfall. Meanwhile, early in the morning, Early's division, with Barksdale's brigade, had moved down upon Mayee's Hill, which they found held by a picket force only, and easily occupied. An advance was attempted into Fredericksburg, but it was found with barricades across the streets held by one of Gibbon's brigades, supported by two other brigades and a number of guns on the north bank. Early then sent to communicate with McLaws and endeavor to arrange a joint attack upon Sedgwick, but received information that Anderson's division was coming, and was himself sent for to meet Lee.

Before leaving Chancellorsville that morning, Lee had examined Hooker's lines with the view of assaulting at once, but their strength made it imprudent to do so while Sedgwick was still south of the river. So he next set out to dispose of Sedgwick, that he might then concentrate his whole force to attack Hooker.

Probably no man ever commanded an army and, at the same time, so entirely commanded himself, as Lee. This morning was almost the only occasion on which I ever saw him out of humor. It was when waiting the arrival of Anderson, with his three brigades from the River road, after being relieved by Heth. Anderson was in no way to blame for the delay, but he should have been relieved the afternoon before, which would have let him move during the night.

Some delay was inevitable, as Sedgwick's peculiar rectangular formation was not readily understood. It was about three miles in extent, and occupied high ground, with a wide, open valley in its front, forcing a development of our line of nearly six miles to cover its three fronts. An entire day would have been none too much to devote to the attack, if the fruits of victory were to be reaped. Although Lee urged all possible speed, it was 6 P.M. when the advance commenced. Sunset was at seven. Darkness fell before the lines could be gotten into close action. In the dusk, two of Early's brigades, Hoke's and Hays's, fired into each other by mistake, and were thrown into confusion. Both had to be withdrawn and re-formed. The enemy was, however, forced back to the vicinity of Banks Ford, and had there then been daylight to bring up our batteries, there might have been large captures. Upon McLaws's front, ranges were marked by daylight for firing upon Banks Ford and some guns were kept firing all night. But all that was possible amounted only to annoyance. It was again illustrated that afternoon attacks seldom reap any fruits of victory.

It was with great elation on the morning of the 5th, that our guns fired the two last shots across the Rappahannock at Sedgwick's retreating columns. But orders, soon received from headquarters, indicated that our commander was not yet satisfied. Early's division and Barksdale's brigade were directed to remain in observation at Banks Ford and Fredericksburg,—which has also been evacuated by Gibbon's division during the previous night,—while all the rest of the army was ordered to return to the front of Hooker's lines near Chancellorsville, which Lee intended to assault on the morrow with his whole force.

What was known of the enemy's position gave assurance that the task would be the heaviest which we had ever undertaken. Hooker now had his entire army concentrated, and, allowing for his losses, must have had fully 90,000 men to defend about five miles of breastworks. These he had had 48 hours to prepare, with all the advantages for defense which the Wilderness offered. Lee would scarcely be able to bring into action 35,000 under all the disadvantages imposed by the Wilderness upon the offensive and by two streams which on the southeast and northwest covered three-fourths of the enemy's front. Behind these streams both flanks rested securely upon the river. The attack would have to be made everywhere squarely in front, and our artillery would be unable to render any efficient help. When, upon the 6th, we found the lines deserted and the enemy gone, our engineers were amazed at the strength and completeness of the enemy's intrenchments. Impenetrable abattis covered the entire front, and the crest everywhere carried head-logs under which the men could fire as through loopholes. In rear, separate structures were provided for officers, with protected outlooks, whence they could see and direct without exposure.

Four of Hooker's corps had suffered casualties averaging 20 per cent, but three, the 1st, 2d, and 5th, had scarcely been engaged. It must be conceded that Lee never in his life took a more audacious resolve than when he determined to assault Hooker's intrenchments. And it is the highest possible compliment to the army commanded by Lee to say that there were two persons concerned who believed that, in spite of all the odds, it would have been victorious. These two persons were Gens. Lee and Hooker. For Hooker was already hurrying his preparations to retreat during the coming night. Clearly, this decision was the mistake of his life.

During the afternoon of the 5th, there came on one of the remarkable storms which on many occasions closely followed severe engagements. The rainfall was unusually heavy and continued long after dark, converting roads into quagmires, rivulets into torrents, and causing great discomfort to man and beast. But its occurrence was advantageous to the Confederates, as it prevented their pressing upon the enemy's impregnable line, and it hurried the efforts of the Federals to cross the river, as rapidly rising waters overflowed the approaches to their bridges. Before the rain, I had found positions for several guns close upon the riverbank, partly around a bend below the Federal left, giving an oblique fire upon some of their batteries. During the night we constructed pits, and, at early dawn, were putting the guns in them, when we were suddenly fired upon by guns square upon our own flank and across the river. A lieutenant had his ankle smashed, some horses were killed, and some dismounted limber chests were exploded, before all could be gotten under cover in the pits. From these we could make no reply, as they faced Hooker's lines, and we could only lie close and wait for more daylight. This revealed that the enemy had abandoned his works during the night and recrossed the river. To retaliate I brought up seven other guns, under cover of a wood, and engaged the enemy for a half-hour, inflicting "some loss in killed and wounded," as reported by Gen. Hunt, with no further loss to ourselves, but the wheel of a gun. Finding by then that the battle was over and no enemy left on our side of the river, the guns were gradually withdrawn and camps were sought in another severe rainstorm, which came up about 5 P.M. and lasted far into the night.[1]

The battle made by Stuart on the 3d, has rarely been surpassed, measured either by the strength of the lines carried or by the casualties suffered in so brief a period. In Colston's division four brigades lost eight brigade commanders, three killed and five disabled. Three out of six of the division staff fell. In Pender's brigade of Heth's division, six out of ten field-officers were killed or wounded. Our brigades rarely came to the field 2000 strong, and casualties of 600 to a brigade were rarely reached even in battles prolonged over a day. Here within six hours, five of the 15 brigades lost over 600 in killed and wounded each: Lane's N.C. brigade losing 786; Colston's N.C. and Va. losing 726; Pender's N.C., 693.

The battle of Chickamauga is generally called the bloodiest of modern battles. The losses given by Livemore are 22 percent in the Federal army and 25 percent in the Confederate, in two days' fighting. Jackson's three divisions had a paper strength of 26,661, and their losses were 7158, about 27 per cent. They were, doubtless, over 30 percent of the force actually engaged. The losses in the 3d and 12th Federal corps, which composed the principal part of our opponents, were less, as they fought behind breastworks. Their strength on paper was 32,171. Their losses were 4703, being about 15 percent of the paper strength and probably 18 percent of the actual.

Had Gen. Lee been present on the left, during the Sunday morning attack, and seen Stuart's energy and efficiency in handling his reserves, inspiring the men by his contagious spirit, and in the cooperation of artillery, with the infantry, he might have rewarded Stuart on the spot by promoting him to the now vacant command of Jackson's corps. Ewell, who did succeed Jackson, was always loved and admired, but he was not always equal to his opportunities, as we shall see at Gettysburg. Stuart's qualities were just what were needed, for he was young, he was not maimed, and he had boldness, persistence, and magnetism in very high degree. Lee once said that he would have won Gettysburg, had he had Jackson with him. Who so worthy to succeed Jackson as the man who had successfully replaced him on his last and greatest field?

---

1 A reminiscence of that night is the finding of our camp in the heaviest of the rain and blackest of the darkness by a lost ambulance carrying a Virginian colonel, whose leg had been amputated on the field. He was taken out and fed, slept on the crowded floor of our tent, and next morning was started for a hospital in fine spirits in spite of his maimed condition.

D. AUGUSTUS DICKERT

Routing the Yankees

The Battle of Chancellorsville proved to be one of Lee's most stunning victories of the war as well as a testament to his audacity and tactical brilliance. Heavily outnumbered by Hooker in the depths of the Wilderness, Lee divided his forces and sent Jackson's corps against the Federal right on a flank attack to roll up the enemy line while the rest of the Confederate force occupied the attention of Hooker's front. The next day, Lee vigorously engaged the Army of the Potomac convincing its commander to withdraw across the Rappahannock River even though most of his troops had not yet been engaged. A captain in the 3rd South Carolina Regiment of Brigadier General Joseph B. Kershaw's Brigade, D. Augustus Dickert was in the ranks at the time of this bloody confrontation and wrote an account of the battle in his *History of Kershaw's Brigade*.

On the morning of April 29th the soldiers were aroused from their slumbers by the beating of the long roll. What an ominous sound is the long roll to the soldier wrapped in his blanket and enjoying the sweets of sleep. It is like a fire bell at night. It denotes battle. It tells the soldier the enemy is moving: it means haste and active preparation. A battle is imminent. The soldiers thus roused, as if from their long sleep since Fredericksburg, feel in a touchous mood. The frightful senses of Fredericksburg and Marye's Hill rise up before them as a spectre. Soldiers rush out of their tents, asking questions and making suppositions. Others are busily engaged folding blankets, tearing down tents, and making preparations to move: companies formed into regiments and regiments into brigades. The distant boom of cannon beyond the Rappahannock tells us that the enemy is to cross the river again and try conclusions with the soldiers of Lee. All expected a bloody engagements for the Federal Army had been greatly recruited under excellent discipline, and headed by Fighting Joe Hooker. He was one of the best officers in that army and he himself had boasted that his was the "finest army that had ever been organized upon the planet." It numbered one hundred and thirty-one thousand men of all arms, while Lee had barely sixty thousand. We moved rapidly in the direction of Fredericksburg. I never saw Kershaw look so well. Riding his iron-gray at the head of his columns, one could not but be impressed with his soldierly appearance. He seemed a veritable knight of old. Leading his brigade above the city he took position in the old entrenchments.

Before reaching the battle line, the enemy had already placed pontoons near the old place of landing, crossed over a portion of their army and was now picketing on the south side of the river. One company from each regiment was thrown out as sharp shooters or skirmishers under Captain Goggans, of the Seventh, and deployed in the valley below where we could watch the enemy. My company was of the number. Nothing was done during the day but a continual change of positions. We remained on the skirmish line during the night without fire or without any relief, expecting an advance next morning, or to be relieved at least. The sun was obscured by the densest fog the following morning I almost ever witnessed. When it cleared up, about 10 o'clock, what was our astonishment—to find no enemy in our front, nor friends in our rear. There were, however, some Federals opposite and below the city but they belonged to another division. We could hear occasional cannonading some miles up the Rappahannock. By some staff officers passing, we ascertained that Hooker had withdrawn during the night in our front, recrossed the river at Ely's and Raccoon fords, or some of the fords opposite the Wilderness. This was on Friday May the first. After a consultation with the officers of our detachment, it was agreed to evacuate our position and join our regiments wherever we could find them. We had no rations, and this was one of the incentives to move. But had the men been supplied with provisions, and the matter left to them alone, I doubt very much whether they would have chosen to leave the ground now occupied, as we were in comparative safety and no enemy in sight, while to join our commands would add largely to the chances of getting in battle. I am sorry to say a majority of the officers were of that opinion, too. Some brought to bear one of Napoleon's maxims I had heard when a boy, "When a soldier is in doubt where to go, always go to the place you hear the heaviest firing," and we could indistinctly hear occasional booming of cannon high up the river, indicating that a part of the army at least was in that direction.

So we moved back and over the breastworks, on to the plank road leading to Orange Court House. Making our way keeping together as a battalion, up that road in the direction of the Wilderness, near noon we could hear the deep bay of cannon, now distant and indistinct, then again more rapidly and quite distinguishable, showing plainly that Lee was having a running fight. Later in the day we passed dead horses and a few dead and wounded soldiers. On every hand were indications of the effects of shot and shell. Trees were shattered along the road side, fences torn down and rude breastworks made here and there, the evidence of heavy skirmishing in our front. Lee was pressing the advance guard that had crossed at one of the lower fords back on the main army, crossing then at fords opposite and above the Chancellor's House. Near sundown the firing was conspicuously heavy, especially the artillery. The men of most of the companies evinced a desire to frequently rest, and in every way delay our march as much as possible. Some of the officers, too, joined with the men and offered objections to rushing headlong into battle without orders. I knew that our brigade was somewhere in our front, and from the firing I was thoroughly convinced a battle was imminent, and in that case our duty called us to our command. Not through any cowardice, however, did the men hesitate, for all this fiction written about men's eagerness for battle, their ungovernable desire to throw themselves upon the enemy, their great love of hearing the bursting of shells over their heads, the whizzing of minnie balls through their ranks is all very well for romance and on paper, but a soldier left free to himself, unless he seeks notoriety or honors, will not often rush voluntarily into battle, and if he can escape it honorably, he will do it nine times out of ten. There are times, however, when officers, whose keen sense of duty and honorable appreciation of the position they occupy will lead their commands into battle unauthorised, when they see the necessity, but a private who owes no obedience nor allegiance only to his superiors, and has no responsibility, seldom ever goes voluntarily into battle; if so, once is enough.

Under these circumstances, as the sun was near setting, we learned from some wounded soldier that Kershaw was moving in line of battle to the left of the plank road. Another Captain and myself deserted our companions and made our way to our regiments with our companies. As we came upon it, it was just moving out from a thicket into an open field under a heavy skirmish fire and a fierce fire from a battery in our front. We marched at a double-quick to rejoin the regiment, and the proudest moments of my life, and the sweetest words to hear, was as the other portion of the regiment saw us coming they gave a cheer of welcome and shouted, "Hurrah! for the Dutch; the Dutch has come; make way to the left for the Dutch," and such terms of gladness and welcome, that I thought, even while the "Dutch" and its youthful commander were but a mere speck of the great army, still some had missed us, and I was glad to feel the touch of their elbow on the right and left when a battle was in progress.

Companies in the army like school boys, almost all have "nick-names." Mine was called the "Dutch" from the fact of its having been raised in that section of the country between Saluda River and the Broad, known as "Dutch Fork." A century or more before, this country just above Columbia and in the fork of the two rivers, was settled by German refugees, hence the name "Dutch Fork."

After joining the regiment, we only advanced a little further and halted for the night, sleeping with guns in arms, lest a night attack might find the troops ill prepared were the guns in stack. We were so near the enemy that fires were not allowed, and none permitted to speak above a whisper. Two men from each company were detailed to go to the rear and cook rations. It is not an easy task for two men, who had been marching and fighting all day to be up all night cooking three meals each for thirty or forty men, having to gather their own fuel, and often going half mile for water. A whole day's ration is always cooked at one time on marches, as night is the only time for cooking. The decrees of an order for a detail are inexorable. A soldier must take it as it comes, for none ever know but what the next duties may be even worse than the present. As a general rule, soldiers rarely ever grumble at any detail on the eve of an engagement, for sometimes it excuses them from a battle, and the old experienced veteran never refuses that.

At daylight a battery some two hundred yards in our front opened a furious fire upon us, the shells coming uncomfortably near our heads. If there were an infantry between the battery and our troops, they must have laid low to escape the shots over their heads. But after a few rounds they limbered up and scampered away. We moved slowly along with heavy skirmishing in our front all the morning of the second. When near the Chancellor's House, we formed line of battle in a kind of semicircle, our right resting on the river and extending over the plank road, Kershaw being some distance to the left of this road, the Fifteenth Regiment occupying the right. Here we remained for the remainder of the day. We heard the word coming up the line, "No cheering, no cheering." In a few moments General Lee came riding along the lines, going to the left. He had with him quite a number of his staff and one or two couriers. He looked straight to the front and thoughtful, noticing none of the soldiers who rushed to the line to see him pass. He no doubt was then forming the masterful move, and one, too, in opposition to all rules or order of military science or strategy, "the division of his army in the face of the enemy," a movement that has caused many armies, before, destruction and the downfall of its commander. But nothing succeeds like success. The great disparity in numbers was so great that Lee could only watch and hope for some mistake or blunder of his adversary or by some extraordinary strategic manoeuvre on his own part, gain the advantage by which his opponent would be ruined. Hooker had one hundred and thirty thousand men, while Lee had only sixty thousand. With this number it seemed an easy task for Hooker to threaten Lee at Fredericksburg, then fall upon him with his entire force at Chancellorsville and crush him before Lee could extricate himself from the meshes that were surrounding him, and retreat to Richmond. The dense Wilderness seemed providential for the movement upon which Lee has now determined to stake the fate of his army and the fortunes of the Confederacy. Its heavy thick undergrowth entirely obstructed the view and hid the movements to be made. Jackson, with Rhodes, Colston's, and A.P. Hill's Divisions, were to make a detour around the enemy's right, march by dull roads and bridle paths through the tangled forest and fall upon the enemy's rear, while McLaws, Anderson's and Early's Divisions were to hold him in check in front. Pickett's Division had, before this time, been sent to Wilmington, N.C., while Ransom's Division, with Barksdale's Mississippi Brigade, of McLaws' Division, were to keep watch of the enemy at Fredericksburg. The Federal General, Stoneman, with his cavalry was then on his famous but disastrous raid to Richmond. Jackson commenced his march early in the morning, and kept it up all day turning back towards the rear of the enemy when sufficiently distant that his movement could not be detected. By marching eighteen or twenty miles he was then within three miles of his starting point. But

Hooker's Army stood between him and Lee. Near night Jackson struck the enemy a terrific blow near the plank road, just opposite to where we lay and the cannonading was simply deafening. The shots fired from some of the rifled guns of Jackson passed far overhead of the enemy and fell in our rear. Hooker, bewildered and lost in the meshes of the Wilderness, had formed his divisions in line of battle in echelon, and moved out from the river. Great gaps would intervene between the division in front and the one in rear. Little did he think an enemy was marching rapidly for his rear, another watching every movement in front, and those enemies, Jackson and Lee unknown to Hooker, his flank stood exposed and the distance between the columns gave an ordinary enemy an advantage seldom offered by an astute General, but to such an enemy as Jackson it was more than he had hoped or even dared to expect. As he sat watching the broken columns of the enemy struggling through the dense undergrowth, the favorable moment came. Seizing it with promptness and daring, so characteristic of the man, he, like Napoleon at Austerlitz, when he saw the Russians passing by his front with their flanks exposed, rushed upon them like a wild beast upon its prey turning the exposed column back upon its rear. Colston, commanding Jackson's old Division, led the attack, followed by A.P. Hill. Rhodes then fell like an avalanche upon the unexpectant and now thoroughly disorganized divisions of the retreating enemy. Volley after volley was poured into the seething mass of advancing and receding columns. Not much use could be made of artillery at close range, so that arm of the service was mainly occupied in shelling their trains and the woods in rear. Until late in the night did the battle rage in all its fury. Darkness only added to its intensity, and the fire was kept up until a shot through mistake lay the great Chieftain, Stonewall Jackson, low. General A.P. Hill now took command of the corps, and every preparation was made for the desperate onslaught of to-morrow. By some strange intuition peculiar to the soldier, and his ability to gather news, the word that Jackson had fallen burst through the camp like an explosion, and cast a gloom of sorrow over all.

As our brother South Carolinians, of McGowan's Brigade, were on the opposite side of us, and in the heat of the fray, while we remained idle, I take the liberty of quoting from "Caldwell's History" of that brigade a description of the terrible scenes being enacted on that memorable night in the Wilderness in which Jackson fell:

"Now it is night. The moon a day or two past full, rose in cloudless sky and lighted our way. We were fronted, and then advanced on the right of the road into a thick growth of pines. Soon a firing of small arms sprang up before us, and directly afterwards the enemy's artillery opened furiously bearing upon us. The scene was terrible. Volley after volley of musketry was poured by the Confederate line in front of us upon the enemy. The enemy replied with equal rapidity; cheer, wild and fierce, rang over the whole woods; officers shouted at the top of their voices, to make themselves heard; cannon roar and shells burst continuously. We knew nothing, could see nothing, hedged in by the matted mass of trees. Night engagements are always dreadful, but this was the worse I ever knew. To see your danger is bad enough, but to hear shells whizzing and bursting over you, to hear shrapnell and iron fragments slapping the trees and cracking off limbs, and not know from whence death comes to you, trying beyond all things. And here it looked so incongruous—below raged, thunder, shout, shriek, slaughter—above soft, silent, smiling moonlight peace!"

The next morning A.P. Hill was moving early, but was himself wounded, and General Jeb. Stuart, of the cavalry, took command. The fighting of Jackson's Corps to-day surpassed that of the night before, and after overcoming almost insurmountable obstacles, they succeeded in dislodging Hooker from his well fortified position.

Kershaw remained in his line of battle, keeping up a constant fire with his skirmishers. An advance upon the Chancellor's House was momentarily expected. The long delay between the commencement of Jackson's movement until we heard the thunder of his guns immediately in our front and in rear of the enemy, was taken up in conjecturing, "what move was next." All felt that it was to be no retreat, and as we failed to advance, the mystery of our inactivity was more confounding. Early next morning, however, the battle began in earnest. Hooker had occupied the night in straightening out his lines and establishing a basis of battle, with the hope of retrieving the blunder of the day before. Stuart (or rather A.P. Hill, until wounded) began pressing him from the very start. We could hear the wild yells of our troops as line after line of Hooker's were reformed, to be brushed away by the heroism of the Southern troops. Our skirmishers began their desultory firing of the day before. The battle seemed to near us as it progressed, and the opening around Chancellor's House appeared to be alive with the enemy's artillery. About two o'clock our lines were ordered forward, and we made our way through the tangled morass, in direction of our skirmish line. Here one of the bravest men in our regiment was killed, private John Davis, of the "Quitman Rifles." He was reckless beyond all reason. He loved danger for danger's sake. Stepping behind a tree to load (he was on skirmish line) he would pass out from this cover in plain view, take deliberate aim, and fire. Again and again he was entreated and urged by his comrades to shield himself, but in vain. A bullet from the enemy's sharp-shooters killed him instantly.

A singular and touching incident of this family is here recorded. David had an only brother, who was equally as brave as John and younger, James, the two being the only children of an aged but wealthy couple, of Newberry County. After the death of John, his mother exerted herself and hired a substitute for her baby boy, and came on in a week after the battle for the body of her oldest son and to take James home with her, as the only hope and solace of the declining years of this aged father and mother. Much against his will and wishes, but by mother's entreaties and friends' solicitations, the young man consented to accompany his mother home. But fate seemed to follow them here and play them false, for in less than two weeks this brave, bright, and promising boy lay dead from a malignant disease.

As our brigade was moving through the thicket in the interval between our main line and the skirmishers, and under a heavy fire, we came upon a lone stranger sitting quietly upon a log. At first he was thought an enemy, who in the denseness of the under-growth had passed our lines on a tour of observation. He was closely questioned, and it turned out to be Rev. Boushell, a Methodist minister belonging to one of McGowan's South Carolina regiments, who became lost from his command in the great flank movement of Jackson (McGowan's Brigade belonged to Jackson's Corps), and said he came down "to see how the battle was going and to lend aid and comfort to any wounded soldier should he chance to find one in need of his services."

The batteries in our front were now raking the matted brush all around and overhead, and their infantry soon became aware of our presence, and they, too, began pouring volleys into our advancing column. The ranks became confused, for in this wilderness we could not see twenty paces in front. Still we moved forward with such order as was under the conditions permissible. When near the turn-pike road General Kershaw gave the command to "charge." The Fifteenth raised the yell;

then the Third dashed forward; the Seventh was somewhat late on account of the almost impassable condition of the ground, but still it and the Third Battalion, with the Second on the left, made a mad rush for the public road, and entered it soon after the Fifteenth and Third. A perfect sea of fire was in our faces from the many cannon parked around the Chancellor House and graping in all directions but the rear. Lee on the one side and Stuart on the other had closed upon the enemy, their wings joining just in front of the house. Some of the pieces of the enemy's artillery were not more than fifty yards in our front, and the discharges seemed to blaze fire in our very ranks. Infantry, too, was there massed all over the yard, and in rear of this one vast, mingling, moving body of humanity, dead horses lay in all directions, while the dead and wounded soldiers lay heaped and strewn with the living. But a few volleys from our troops in the road soon silenced all opposition from the infantry, while cannoneers were hitching up their horses to fly away. Some were trying to drag away their caissons and light pieces by hand, while thousands of "blue coats," with and without arms, were running for cover to the rear. In less than twenty minutes the firing ceased in our front, and men were ordered to prepare breastworks. Our soldiers, like the beaver, by this time had become accustomed to burrow in the ground as soon as a "halt" was made. A shovel and a spade were carried at all times by each company to guard against emergencies. The bursting of a shell near my company caused a fragment to strike one of my own men on the shoulder. He claimed to be desperately wounded, and wished to go to the hospital. I examined him hastily to see if I could give him any assistance. He claimed his shoulder was broken. Just then the order was given to "commence to fortify." "G.," the wounded man, was the first to grasp the shovel, and threw dirt with an energy that caused my Orderly Sergeant, a brave and faithful soldier, but who never allowed the comic side of any transaction to pass him, to say: "Captain, look at the 'wild pigeon;' see how he scratches dirt." All soldiers carried a "nick-name," a name given by some physical disability or some error he had made, or from any circumstance in his life out of the usual order. Hardly had we taken possession of the turn-pike road and began fortifying, than the sound of shells down the river was heard, and we were hurriedly marched down the road. McLaws' and Anderson's Divisions were double-quicked down the turnpike road and away from the battle to meet Sedgwick, who had crossed the Rappahannock at Fredericksburg, stormed Mayree's

Height's, routed and captured the most of Barksdale's Mississippi Brigade, and was making his way rapidly upon Lee's rear.

This Battle of Chancellorsville certainly had its many sides, with its rapid marching, changing of positions, and generalship of the highest order. On the day before Jackson had gone around the right flank of Hooker and fell upon his rear, while to-day we had the novel spectacle of Sedgwick in the rear of Lee and Stuart in rear of Hooker. No one can foretell the result of the battle, had Hooker held his position until Sedgwick came up. But Lee's great mind ran quick and fast. He knew the country and was well posted by his scouts of every move and turn of the enemy on the chess-board of battle. Anderson, with his division, being on our right, led the advance down the road to meet Sedgwick. We passed great parks of wagons (ordnance and commissary) on either side of the road. Here and there were the field infirmaries where their wounded were being attended to and where all the surplus baggage had been stacked before the battle.

On reaching Zoar Church, some five miles in rear, we encountered Sedgwick's advance line of skirmishers, and a heavy fusilade began. Anderson formed line of battle on extreme right, and on right of plank road, with the purpose of sweeping round on the enemy's left. McLaws formed on left of the corps, his extreme left reaching out toward the river and across the road; Kershaw being immediately on the right of the road, with the Second resting on it, then the Fifteenth, the Third Battalion, the Eighth, the Third, and the Seventh on the right. On the left of the road leading to Fredericksburg was a large open field extending to the bluff near the river; on the right was a dense thicket of pines and undergrowth. In this we had to form. The Seventh experienced some trouble in getting into line, and many camp rumours were afloat a few days afterwards of an uncomplimentary nature of the Seventh's action. But this was all false, for no more gallant regiment nor better officered, both in courage and ability, was in the Confederate service than the "bloody Seventh." But it was the unfavorable nature of the ground, the difficulties experienced in forming a line, and the crowding and lapping of the men that caused the confusion.

Soon after our line of battle was formed and Kershaw awaiting orders from McLaws to advance, a line of support came up in our rear, and mistaking us for the enemy, commenced firing upon us. Handkerchiefs went up, calls of "friends," "friends," but still the firing continued. One

Colonel seeing the danger—the enemy just in front, and our friends firing on us in the rear—called out, "Who will volunteer to carry our colors back to our friends in rear?" Up sprang the handsome and gallant young Sergeant Copeland, of the "Clinton Divers," (one of the most magnificent and finest looking companies in his service, having at its enlistment forty men over six feet tall), and said, "Colonel, send me." Grasping the colors in his hand, he carried them, waving and jesticulating in a friendly manner, until he convinced the troops that they were friends in their front.

While thus waiting for Anderson to swing around the left of the enemy, a desperate charge was made upon us. The cannonading was exceedingly heavy and accurate. Great trees all around fell, snapped in twain by the shell and solid shot, and many men were killed and wounded by the falling timber. Trees, a foot in diameter, snapped in two like pipe stems, and fell upon the men. It was growing dark before Anderson could get in position, and during that time the troops never experienced a heavier shelling. It was enough to make the stoutest hearts quake. One of my very bravest men, one who had never failed before, called to me as I passed, "Captain, if I am not here when the roll is called, you may know where I am. I don't believe I can stand this." But he did, and like the man he was, withstood it. Another, a young recruit, and under his first fire, almost became insane, jumping upon me and begging "for God's sake" let him go to the rear. I could not stand this piteous appeal, and knowing he could not be of any service to us in that condition, told him "to go." It is needless to say he obeyed my orders. Dr. Evans, our surgeon, told me afterwards that he came to his quarters and remained three days, perfectly crazy. At last the order came after night to advance. In a semicircle we swept through the thicket; turning, we came into the road, and over it into the opening in front. The enemy was pushed back into the breastworks on the bluff at the river. These breastworks had been built by our troops during the Fredericksburg battle, and afterwards to guard and protect Raccoon and Ely's fords, just in rear. As night was upon us, and the enemy huddled before us at the ford, we were halted and lay on the field all night. This was the ending of the battle of Chancellorsville.

Next morning the sun was perfectly hidden by a heavy fog, so much so that one could not see a man twenty yards distant. Skirmishers were thrown out and our advance made to the river, but nothing was found on this side of the river but the wounded and the discarded rifles and munitions of war. The wounded lay in all directions, calling for help and heaping curses upon their friends, who had abandoned them in their distress. Guns, tent flies, and cartridge boxes were packed up by the wagon loads. Hooker's Army was thoroughly beaten, disheartened, and disorganized. Met and defeated at every turn and move, they were only too glad to place themselves across the river and under the protection of their siege guns on Stafford's Heights. Hooker's losses were never correctly given, but roughly computed at twenty-five thousand, while those of Lee's were ten thousand two hundred and eighty-one. But the Confederates counted it a dear victory in the loss of the intrepid but silent Stonewall Jackson. There was a magic in his name that gave enthusiasm and confidence to the whole army. To the enemy his name was a terror and himself an apparition. He had frightened and beaten Banks out of the Shennandoah Valley, had routed Fremont, and so entangled and out-generaled Seigle that he was glad to put the Potomac between himself and this silent, mysterious, and indefatigable chieftain, who often prayed before battle and fought with a Bible in one hand and a sword in the other. He came like a whirlwind upon the flank of McClellan at Mechanicsville, and began those series of battles and victories that terminated with the "Little Giant" being hemmed in at Drury's Bluff and Malvern Hill. While Pope, the "Braggart," was sweeping the fields before him in Northern Virginia, and whose boast was he "saw only the enemy's back," and his "headquarters were in the saddle," Jackson appeared before him like a lion in his path. He swings around Pope's right, over the mountains, back through Thoroughfare Gap: he sweeps through the country like a comet through space, and falls on Pope's rear on the plains of Manassas, and sent him flying across the Potomac like McDowell was beaten two years before. While pursuing the enemy across the river and into Maryland, he turns suddenly, recrosses the river, and stands before Harper's Ferry, and captures that stronghold with scarcely a struggle. All this was enough to give him the sobriquet of the "Silent Man," the man of "mystery," and it is not too much to say that Jackson to the South was worth ten thousand soldiers, while the terror of his name wrought consternation in the ranks of the enemy.

W. F. RANDOLPH

Jackson's Mortal Wound

Though the Confederates had managed to win a great victory at Chancellorsville, the seeds of defeat were sown when Stonewall Jackson was mortally wounded when he was accidentally fired upon by some of his own men while reconnoitering the battlefield on the evening of 2 May 1863. Historians still ponder what effect Jackson's presence at Gettysburg might have had on that battle and the entire war. Jackson died from his wound on 10 May. A member of Jackson's bodyguard, Captain W.F. Randolph was present at Jackson's fatal shooting. His account originally appeared in the Greeneville News Times and later in the *Southern Society Historical Papers*.

It is not the purpose of the writer of this article to give a detailed account of the memorable battle of Chancellorsville, which has been so often described by pens more felicitous than mine, but only to give some few incidents of the first two days leading up to the terrible catastrophe, which was the closing scene of one of the most brilliant and successful movements in the history of any war.

The writer was, during these two days, attached to the person of General Jackson, and only left his side occasionally as the bearer of orders to his division commanders.

During the winter of '62 and '63, the Army of Northern Virginia was encamped near and around Fredericksburg, and the writer was in command of a company of cavalry and attached to the headquarters of General Stonewall Jackson, then located near Hamilton's Crossing, about three miles below the town.

The battle of Fredericksburg, which took place the 13th of December, resulted in the defeat of Burnside, and his retreat across the river ended all active operations for the winter. So we settled down in quiet observation, awaiting with anxious expectation the advance of General Hooker, whose artillery crowned the heights of the other side of the river, where the white tents of the Federal army could be seen here dotting the same hills.

The spring was well advanced, the country all around us was covered with verdure, and the roads had become dry and hard, when we were awakened from our long holiday by the welcome announcement that the Federal commander's long-expected advance had at last commenced, and that a portion of his army had crossed the Rapidan at Gorman's Ford, and were marching upon Fredericksburg. General Lee at once put his whole army in motion, with Jackson's corps in the front, leaving one division, under General Early, to prevent the enemy from crossing at Fredericksburg and attacking his rear.

It will be remembered that two of the best divisions of Longstreet's corps had been detached and sent to Southeastern Virginia, leaving General Lee with scarcely fifty thousand infantry with which to meet that well-equipped and splendidly-appointed army of Hooker's, consisting of more than one hundred thousand men. After an arduous and exciting march, without rest, the army frequently advancing in line of battle, was expecting every moment to meet the enemy. The advance column, consisting of a portion of Hill's division, halted about sunset within less than a mile of the Chancellorsville house, in the vicinity of which the enemy was evidently concentrated, awaiting our attack. But the impenetrable nature of the thickets, which separated us, prevented any farther advance in that direction, and the whole army was forced to bivouac for the night. At this point a road, which was then known as the Bun road, intersected about at right angles the plank road, along which we had been moving, and here, with no other protection than the spreading arms of an immense oak, and without camp equippage of any kind, the two generals—Lee and Jackson—slept for the night, myself and a few of my troops lying within a few feet of them.

I was awakened next morning by a light touch on my shoulder, and on jumping up had the mortification to find that the sun had already risen and General Lee had gone. General Jackson, who was just mounting his horse, turned to me with a kindly word and smile, telling me to follow as soon as possible, and dashed off at a furious gallop down the Mine Run road, along which his troops had been rapidly marching since daylight. I did not succeed in overtaking the general again for several hours, and when at last I came up with him, he was far in advance of his columns, standing talking to General Fitzhugh Lee in the old turnpike road, at a point about five miles distant from Chancellorsville, having made a circuit of fifteen miles, thus putting the whole Federal army between himself and General Lee, and the two divisions of Longstreet's corps which were with him. As the several divisions of the corps came up they were formed in line of battle, and about 4 o'clock in the evening everything was in readiness for the attack.

While Fitzhugh was talking to the General a half-dozen troopers rode up, bringing with them a Yankee lieutenant, whom they had just captured. Lee turned to the officer and asked him smilingly what would Hooker think if old Stonewall were to suddenly fall upon his rear. "Ah," said the Federal officer, "Hooker has both Jackson and your great Lee in the hollow of his hand, and it is only a matter of a very short time when your whole army will be bagged." Jackson's lips closed in a grim smile, but he said nothing, and Lee and his troopers rode away, laughing, leaving us alone.

The General turned to me and asked how far behind was the advance of his army. I replied that the leading division ought to be up in an hour. We both dismounted. Jackson seating himself on a log by the road, studying a map, which he spread out before him. After tying our horses I took my seat not far from him, and, being somewhat fatigued from the long ride, I fell asleep. Waking with a start, I turned and saw the General kneeling, with his arms resting on the log, in earnest prayer. I was profoundly impressed, and a feeling of great security came over me. Surely this great soldier, who held such close and constant communion with his Maker, must certainly succeed in whatever he undertook!

Presently the General, who was still seated on the log, called me to his side, and ordered me to ride down the turnpike as far as possible in the direction of the enemy, and ascertain if any of his pickets were stationed in the direction facing our advance, and to gather any other information it was possible to obtain.

Taking one man with me, I mounted my horse and galloped rapidly down the road until I came within sight of the camp fires of the enemy. Dismounting, I tied my horse in a thicket near the road, advanced cautiously, expecting every moment to come in contact with some outlying picket, but met no enemy until I came to an opening in the woods, overlooking a large field, where I saw a sight most amazing and unexpected. No less than a vast force of Federals in every conceivable state of disorder, without any formation; several batteries of artillery unlimbered; hundreds gathered around the camp fires cooking, some lying sunning themselves in the bright May sunshine, as apparently unconscious of danger as if they had been encamped around the environs of Washington city—no sentinels, no pickets, no line of battle anywhere. My heart bounded with exultation, and I could have shouted for joy. "Verily," I said to myself, "the God of battles has this day delivered these people into our hands." But I had time only for a brief glance. Hurrying to where I had tied my horse, I mounted and rode with all possible speed back to where I had left the General. I made my report. Not a word escaped his lips. He raised his eyes to heaven, and his lips seemed to murmur a prayer, and then turning to General Hill said, "Order the whole line to advance, General Hill; but slowly, with great caution, and without noise."

And so the movement commenced slowly, silently, with no sound save the occasional cracking of a stick beneath the feet of the men; those long grey lines stretching far into the gloom of the forest, pressed on; twenty-five thousand veterans of many a hard fought field, who had never moved save in the path of victory; on and on in the gathering evening, the sinking sun casting long shadows behind them, the frightened birds twittering and chirping as they flew from tree to tree, and an occasional bark of a squirrel as he looked out, startled at the unwonted scene, were the only sounds that interrupted the stillness, solemn and oppressive; a strange calm preceding a storm, the light of which has rarely been chronicled in the annals of war.

When our line of battle debouched from the dense wood which effectually concealed the advance, it came immediately upon the Federal encampment and directly in the rear of their whole line. The first intimation the enemy had of our approach was the characteristic Confederate yell, which rolled along the line, and rung out clear and loud above the thunderous clash of musketry and re-echoed through the forest, which had until then been as silent as the grave. Never was surprise so complete, never was a victory more easily won. As our lines swept like an avalanche over the Federal camps, they were overwhelmed and outnumbered at every point, resistance was paralyzed, and the panic which ensued is indescribable. On the part of the enemy it was not a retreat, but the wildest flight—a race for life.

At one time during the evening a young officer, wild with enthusiasm, dashed up to the General, crying: "General, they are running too fast for us; we can't come up with them." "They never run too fast for me, sir," was the immediate response. And thus onward rushed pursuers and pursued down the road toward Chancellorsville. Now and then Jackson would press his horse to a gallop and dash to the front, and whenever he appeared the troops would break ranks and rush around him with the wildest cheers I ever heard from human throats. When night closed upon the scene the victory seemed to be complete. The infantry of the enemy had disappeared from our immediate front, falling back under cover of several batteries of artillery, which, halting upon every eminence, poured a furious fire of shot and shell down the road upon our advancing columns. In order to avoid this furious fire as much as possible, our men were formed in columns and made to march up the edges of the dense wood, and parallel with the road. This they were able to do by the aid of the moon, which shone very brightly, rendering all objects in our immediate vicinity clearly distinct. About this time General A.P. Hill rode up, and Jackson and himself had a conference of some length. I did not hear all that was said, but both were deeply absorbed, for shells from the battery of the enemy were bursting all around us and ploughing up the ground under our horses' feet without either of them taking the slightest notice of the little incident. As for myself, I cared but little either, as I was then impressed with the idea that the bullet had not been moulded which was to kill our General. The firing soon ceased and Hill rode away.

At this juncture the General had no officer with him, except Lieutenant Keith Boswell, an officer belonging to his signal corps, and myself, together with a dozen of my own men, who were riding behind. A Confederate brigade was marching slowly in column on the left of the road and close to the woods, Keith Boswell was riding on the right of the General, and myself on the left, between him and our lines. The General turned to me and asked: "Whose brigade is that?" "I don't know sir," I replied, "but will find out in a moment." I at once rode up to our line and asked the first officer I met whose brigade it was. He replied: "Lane's North Carolina." I rode back to Jackson, giving him the reply. "Go and tell the officer in command," he said, "to halt his brigade." I rode up to the same officer, gave the command, and told him that it came from General Jackson in person. The order was passed along the line, and the whole brigade halted at once, making a half-wheel to the right, facing the road, and rested upon their arms. We continued our movement in the same order, walking our horses very slowly towards the front of the brigade. Suddenly the General asked: "Captain, is there a road near our present position leading to the Rappahannock?" I replied that not far from where we stood there was a road which led into the woods in the direction of the Rappahannock river.

"This road must be found, then, at once," he said. He had hardly uttered these words when a few scattering random shots were heard in the woods to our right. The men in line on our left, excited apparently by this fire, commenced firing across the road into the woods beyond, not in regular volleys, but in a desultory way without order, here and there along the line.

General Jackson turned to me and said: "Order those men to stop that fire, and tell the officers not to allow another shot fired without orders."

I rode up and down the line and gave the order to both men and officers, telling them also that they were endangering the lives of General Jackson and his escort, but in vain. Those immediately in my front would cease as I gave the order, but the firing would break out above or below me, and instead of decreasing the shots increased in frequency, I rode back to Jackson and said: "General, it is impossible to stop these men. I think we had best pass through their line and get into the woods behind them." "Very well said," was the reply. So, making a half whirl to the left, thus presenting a front of, say sixty yards, our little company commenced the movement to pass through the line, and thus put ourselves beyond the range of the fire.

A few more seconds would have placed us in safety, for we were not over three yards from the line, but as we turned, looking up and down as far as my eye could reach, I saw that long line of shining bayonets rise and concentrate upon us. I felt what was coming, and driving spurs into my horse's flanks, a powerful animal and full of spirit, he rose high in the air, and as we passed over the line the thunder crash from hundreds of rifles burst in full in our very faces. I looked back as my horse made the leap, and everything had gone down like leaves before the blast of a hurricane. The only living thing besides myself that passed through that stream of fire was Boswell's black stallion, my attention being called to him by the rattle of a chain-halter that swung loose from his neck, as he passed out of sight in the darkness of the wood. But his saddle was empty. Boswell, too, an old comrade of many a perilous scout, had gone down with all the rest before that inexcusable and unwarranted fire. My own horse was wounded in several places, my clothes and saddle were perforated with bullets, yet I escaped without a wound, the only living man to tell the fearful story.

As soon as I could control my horse, rendered frantic by his wounds, I rode among our men, who were falling back into the woods, and from behind the trees were still continuing that reckless and insane fire, and urging them to form their line and come back to the road, telling them that they had fired not upon the enemy, but upon General Jackson and his escort.

Then sick at heart I dashed back to the road, and there the saddest tragedy of the war was revealed in its fullest horror.

I saw the General's horse, which I recognized at once, standing close to the edge of the road, with his head bent low, and a stream of blood running from a wound in his neck. Jumping from my horse I hastened to the spot and saw the General himself lying in the edge of the woods. He seemed to be dead, and I wished all the bullets had passed through my own body rather than such a happening as this. I threw myself on the ground by his side and raise his head and shoulders on my arm. He groaned heavily.

"Are you much hurt, General?" I asked, as soon as I could find voice and utterance.

"Wild fire, that sir; wild fire," he replied, in his usual rapid way. This was all he said. I found that his left arm was shattered by a bullet just below the elbow, and his right hand was lacerated by a minie ball that passed through the palm. Not a living soul was in sight then, but in a few moments A.P. Hill rode up, and then Lieutenant Smith, one of his aides. General Hill ordered me to mount my horse and bring an ambulance as quickly as possible. "But don't tell the men that it is General Jackson who is wounded," he said. I soon found two of the ambulance corps with a stretcher, and ordered them to the front, saying that a wounded officer needed their services. Then I rode further on to find an ambulance. Before coming up with one I met Sandy Pendleton, Jackson's adjutant-general, and told him what had occurred, and he ordered me to go and find General J.E.B. Stuart and tell him to come up at once.

"Where shall I find him?" I asked.

"Somewhere near the Rappahannock," he replied, "not more than four or five miles away."

I rode off through the woods in the direction of the river, and by a piece of good luck soon struck a well-defined road, which seemed to lead in the right direction. After riding along that road for a few miles I had the good fortune to meet General Stuart himself with a small escort of cavalry. I stated that General Jackson had been badly wounded, and that Pendleton had ordered me to tell him to come to the army at once. Without making any comment, he dashed off at full speed. I tried to follow, but by this time my horse was much weakened by the loss of blood, and began to stagger under me. I was obliged to dismount, and found that he was shot through both thighs, and slightly wounded in several other places, so I was forced to walk, leading the wounded animal slowly behind me.

This ended my connection with the tragic incident of this most memorable night. I did not reach headquarters until 2 o'clock that night. I saw Dr. McGuire, and, asking him about the General's condition, he told me that his arm had been amputated below the elbow, his wounded hand had been dressed, and that he was resting quietly. The wounds were serious and very painful, he said, but not necessarily fatal, and there seemed to be no reason why he should not recover.

If asked why and how such a fire could have occurred, I can only answer that it was then and is still a mystery, wholly unaccountable and without provocation or warrant. We had been for some time walking our horses along the road in close proximity to this very brigade from which the fire came. The moon, which was not far from full, poured a flood of light upon the wide, open turnpike. Jackson and his escort were plainly visible from every point of view, and the General himself must have been recognized by any one who had ever seen him before. There was no reason for mistaking us for an enemy, and when turning to pass through our line to avoid the scattering random fire which was sending bullets around and about us, I did not for a minute dream that there was a possibility of the guns of our men being directed upon us. An accident inexplicable, unlooked for, and impossible to foresee, deprived the army of its greatest general at a time when his services were indispensable. If Jackson had lived that night he would without doubt have marched his columns along the very road upon which I met Stuart, thus throwing his entire force in the rear of Hooker's army, his left resting upon the Rappahannock, cutting off the enemy's communications and forming around his flanks a net of steel from which he could never have extricated himself.

Broken, dispirited, panic-stricken, his right wing routed and doubled back upon his center, tangled in a wilderness without room to employ his immense force. His very numbers working to its disadvantage, hemmed in on every side, with Jackson's victorious corps in his rear and Lee in his front, strange as it may seem, Hooker's immense army of 100,000 men, would have been forced to surrender, and the war would have ended with a clap of thunder. The whole North would have been laid open, and Lee's victorious army, augmented by thousands of enthusiastic volunteers. Washington and Baltimore would have been occupied and all of Maryland aroused.

This young and virile Confederacy sprung all at once armed and equipped a very Cyclops from the brain of Minerva, would have taken its place high up among the family of nations.

That blast in the wilderness put an end to the almost assured result, and the hope of a great southern empire became only a dream.

Was it Providence, or fate? Who can tell?

FREDERICK L. HITCHCOCK

Misadventures in the Wilderness

A nine months regiment mustered into service in August 1862, the 132nd Pennsylvania fought its last battle at Chancellorsville. Serving with the Third Brigade of French's division in the II Corps, the 132nd was heavily engaged on the Federal center.

On April 28 our corps broke camp and joined the column northward. The winter's rest had brought some accessions to our ranks from the sick and wounded, though the severe picket duty and the excessively damp weather had given us a large sick list. We had, to start with, upward of three hundred and seventy-five men, to which was added some twenty-five or thirty from the sick list, who came up to us on the march. It is a curious fact that many men left sick in camp, unable to march with the regiment leave, will get themselves together after the former has been gone a few hours and pull out to overtake it. I saw men crying like children because the surgeon had forbidden them going with the regiment. The loneliness and homesickness, or whatever you please to call it, after the regiment has gone are too much for them. They simply cannot endure it, and so they strike out and follow. They will start by easy marches, and they generally improve in health from the moment they start. Courage and nerve are both summoned for the effort, and the result is that at the end of the second or third day they rejoin the regiment and report for duty. This does not mean that they were not really sick, but that will power and exercise have beaten the disease. I have heard many a sick man say he would rather die than be left behind.

We marched about six miles the first day, much of our route being through a wooded country, some of it so wet and spongy that corduroy roads had to be built for the wagons and artillery. The army can, as a rule, move as rapidly as it can move its artillery and supply trains, and no faster. Of course, for short distances and special expeditions, where circumstances require, both cavalry and infantry move very rapidly, ignoring the wagon trains and artillery; but on a general campaign this is impossible, and so where the ground is bad these must be helped along. In a wooded country the usual method is by corduroy road. Extra details are made to assist the pioneer corps, who cut down young saplings three to six inches in diameter and about six feet in length and lay them side by side on the ground, which is roughly leveled to receive them. They do not make a handsome road to speed over, but they bear up the artillery and army schooners, and that is all that is wanted of them.

The second day we crossed the Rappahannock at United States ford on a pontoon bridge. There had been a sharp skirmish here when the first troops crossed a couple of days before, and a battery of artillery was still in position guarding the crossing. We now began to experience once more the unmistakable symptoms of approaching battle,—sharp spurts of cannonading at irregular intervals some distance to the south and west of us, with the hurry of marching troops, ambulances and stretcher corps toward the front; more or less of army debris scattered about, and the nervous bustle everywhere apparent. We reached the famous Chancellorsville House shortly after midnight. This was an old-time hostelry, situated on what was called the Culpeper plank-road. It stood with two or three smaller houses in a cleared square space containing some twenty or thirty acres, in the midst of the densest forest of trees and undergrowth I ever saw. We had marched all day on plank and corduroy roads, through this wild tanglewood forest, most of the time in a drizzling rain, and we had been much delayed by the artillery trains, and it was after midnight when we reached our destination. The distance marched must have been twelve or more miles, and our men became greatly fatigued towards the last.

It was my first experience with the regiment on the march in the field in my new position as major. As adjutant my place had been with the colonel at the head of the column. Now my duties required me to march in the rear and keep up the stragglers. After nightfall it became intensely dark, and at each rest the men would drop down just where they were and would be instantly sound asleep. Whether they dropped down into mud or not made little difference to many of them, for they were soaking wet and were so exhausted that they did not care. My troubles began when the "forward" was sounded, to arouse these seeming logs and get them on their feet once more, and started. All who were practically exhausted had drifted to the rear and were on my hands. We had a provost guard in the rear, whose duty it was to bring up every man and permit no straggling, but they were in almost as bad a plight as the rest of the regiment. To arouse these sleeping men I had occasionally to resort to a smart blow with the flat of my sword and follow it up with the most energetic orders and entreaties. An appeal to their pluck and nerve was generally sufficient, and they would summon new courage and push manfully on. My own condition was scarcely better than that of the men. I rode that night considerable distances between our halts for rest, sitting bolt upright in my saddle fast asleep. I had all day alternated with some of the men in marching whilst they rode, and was not only thoroughly tired, but wet through. The march was much more trying to us because of our unseasoned condition owing to the long winter's exemption from this exercise. Furthermore, we had been marching towards the firing, and were under the nervous strain always incident to operations in the presence of the enemy. Nothing will quicker exhaust men than the nervous tension occasioned by the continued firing which indicates the imminence of a battle.

At daylight we were aroused and under arms again. We found we were at the head-quarters of the army. The Chancellorsville House, which had been vacated by its occupants, was used for office purposes, and much of the open space around it was occupied by the tents of General Hooker and staff and hospital tents. Of the latter there were three or four pitched so as to connect with each other, and over them was flying the yellow flag of our corps hospital. The First and Third Divisions of our Second Corps were massed in this Chancellorsville square, beside Pettit's battery. Our brigade now consisted of the Fourth New York, First Delaware, and our regiment. The first named was sent off on some guard duty, which left Colonel Albright, of our regiment, the senior officer in command of the brigade. The ominous rattle of musketry not far away became momentarily more pronounced, and ambulances and stretcher-carriers were passing back and forth to the hospitals, carrying wounded men. The dead body of a regular army captain was soon brought back from the front, where Sykes's division of regulars was sharply engaged. I do not know the name of this captain, but he was a fine-looking young officer. He had been killed by a minie-ball squarely through his forehead.

We were marching out the plank-road as they brought this body in. Passing out of the clearing, the woods and undergrowth each side the road was so dense that we could not see into it a half-dozen steps. We had gone possibly a quarter of a mile when we were overtaken by a staff-officer, who in whispers ordered us to turn back, regardless of orders from the front, and get back to the Chancellorsville House as rapidly as possible, and to do so absolutely noiselessly; that a heavy force of rebels were in the woods on both sides of us, and we were in great danger of being cut to pieces and captured. We obeyed, and he rapidly worked his way to the front of the brigade and succeeded very quickly in getting us all safely out. We formed line near the Chancellorsville House and were resting on our arms when I noticed another brigade going down that same road from which we had just been so hurriedly gotten out. The circumstance was so strange that I inquired what brigade it was, and learned that it was Colonel (afterwards Governor) James A. Beaver's brigade of Hancock's division of our corps. They had been gone but a short time when the rebels opened upon them from both sides of the road, and they were very roughly handled. Colonel Beaver was soon brought back, supposed mortally wounded. I saw him as he was brought to the rear. It was said he shot through the body. Afterwards, whilst he was governor, I mentioned the circumstance to him, and asked how he succeeded in fighting off the last enemy at that time. He said he then fully believed his wound was mortal. The bullet had struck him nearly midway of his body and appeared to have passed through and out of his back, and he was bleeding freely. He was brought to the hospital, where the corps surgeon—his own family physician at home—found him, and with an expression of countenance indicating the gravest fear proceeded to examine his wound. Suddenly, with a sign of relief, he exclaimed: "Colonel, you are all right; the ball has struck a rib and followed it around and out." It was one of the hundreds of remarkable freaks performed by those ugly minie-balls during the war. Why that brigade should have been allowed to march into the ambuscade, from which we had so narrowly escaped, I could not understand. It was one of the early *faux pas* of that unfortunate comedy, rather tragedy of errors,—battle.

In view of the events of the next two days, it will be interesting to recall the somewhat windy order published to the army by General Hooker on the morning of the 1st of May, the date of the first day's battle, on which the events narrated in the last chapter occurred. This is the order:

It is with heartfelt satisfaction the commanding general announces to the army that the operations of the last three days have determined that our enemy must either ingloriously fly or come out from behind his defenses and give us battle on our own ground, when certain destruction awaits him.

My recollection recalls a phrase in this order reading something like this: "We have got the enemy where God Almighty can't save him, and he must either ingloriously," etc. I have been surprised not to find it in the records, and my memory is not alone in this respect, for a lieutenant-colonel of Portland, Me., in his account of this battle alludes to Hooker's blasphemous order.

The purpose of this order was to encourage the men and inspire them with the enthusiasm of forthcoming victory. But when we consider that the portion of the army operating around Chancellorsville was at that very moment apparently as thoroughly caged up in a wilderness of almost impenetrable undergrowth, which made it impossible to move troops, and into which one could not see a dozen feet, as though they were actually behind iron bars, it will be seen how little ground there was for encouragement. I can think of no better comparison of the situation than to liken it to a fleet of ships enveloped in a dense fog endeavoring to operate against another having the advantage of the open.

It will be remembered that when this movement commenced the Army of the Potomac numbered from one hundred and twenty thousand to one hundred and thirty thousand men, about double the opposing rebel force. Hooker divided this army, taking with him four corps, numbering probably seventy thousand men, to operate from Chancellorsville towards Fredericksburg, and leaving three corps, about fifty thousand men, under Sedgwick, to move upon the latter place from below. The purpose was to get Lee's army between these two forces and crush him. All historians of this battle agree that up to a certain point Hooker's strategy was most admirable. General Pleasanton, who commanded our cavalry forces in that action, says that up to a certain point the movement on Chancellorsville was one of the most brilliant in the annals of war. He put that point at the close of Thursday, April 30. He had made a full reconnoissance of all that country and had informed General Hooker of the nature of the ground, that for a depth of from four to five miles it was all unbroken tanglewood of the densest undergrowth, in which it was impossible to manoeuvre an army or to know anything of the movements of the enemy; that beyond this wilderness the country was open and well adapted to military movements, and he had taken occasion to urge upon him the importance of moving forward at once, so as to meet the enemy in open ground, but his information and advice, he tells us, fell upon leaden ears.

Lee had, up to this time, no information of the movement upon Chancellorsville, having been wholly occupied with Sedgwick at Fredericksburg. The former was therefore a complete surprise to him. The "golden moment," according to Pleasanton, to move forward and carry the battle out into the open, where the army could have been handled and would have had a chance, was on that day, as instantly the movement was disclosed, the enemy, being familiar with every foot of the country, would detach a sufficient force to operate in the open, and along the edge of the wilderness could keep us practically bottled up there and beat us in detail; and that is precisely what seems to have been done. The inexplicable question is "Why did fighting Joe Hooker, with seventy thousand as good troops as ever fired a gun, sit down in the middle of that tanglewood forest and allow Lee to make a monkey of him while Sedgwick was doing such magnificent work below?" Two distinguished participants in all these events holding high commands, namely, General Alfred Pleasanton, quoted above, and General Doubleday, commanding First Division, First Army Corps, have written articles upon this battle, agreeing on the feasibility and brilliancy of the movement, but by inference and things unsaid have practically left the same question suspended in the air. It is possible the correct answer should not now be given.

To return to our own doings, on that Friday, 1st of May, our division was drawn up in line of battle in front of the Chancellorsville House, and we were permitted to rest on our arms. This meant that any moment we might be expected to move forward. The battle was now on in earnest. Heavy firing was heard some miles below us, which was Sedgwick's work at Fredericksburg. Nearer by there was cannonading and more or less severe musketry firing. Ambulances and stretcher-carriers were constantly coming back from the front with wounded soldiers, taking them to the field hospital, which was just in our rear, and we could see the growing piles of amputated legs and arms which were thrown outside with as little care as if they were so many pieces of wood. We were evidently waiting for something, nobody seemed to know what. Everything appeared to be "at heads." Our corps and division commanders, Couch, Hancock, and French, with their staffs, were in close proximity to the troops, and all seemed to be in a condition of nervous uncertainty. What might be progressing in those black woods in front, was the question. A nearer volley of musketry would start everybody up, and we would stand arms in hand, as if expecting the unseen enemy to burst through the woods upon us. Then the firing would slacken and we would drop down again for a time.

In the mean time shells were screeching over us continually, and an occasional bullet would whiz uncomfortably near. The nervous strain under such conditions may be imagined. This state of affairs continued all through Friday night and most of Saturday. Of course, sleep was out of the question for any of our officers. On Thursday and Friday nights the men got snatches of sleep, lying on their arms, between the times all were aroused against some fresh alarm.

On Saturday some beef cattle were driven up and slaughtered in the open square in front of our lines, and the details were progressing with the work of preparing the meat for issue when the storm of disaster of Saturday afternoon burst upon us and their work was rudely interrupted. We had anxious premonitions of this impending storm for some hours. Captain Pettit, who commanded the famous battery of that name, which was posted immediately in our rear, had spent much of his time in the forenoon of Saturday high up in a tall tree which stood just in front of the Chancellorsville House and close to our line, with his field glass reconnoitring. Several time he had come down with information that heavy bodies of the enemy were massing for a blow upon our front and where he believed they would strike. This information, we were told, he imparted to Hooker's chief of staff, and begged permission to open at long range with his rifled guns, but no attention was paid to him. I saw him up the tree and heard some of his ejaculating, which indicated that he was almost wild with apprehension of what was coming. Once on coming down he remarked to General Hancock that we would "catch h__l in less than an hour." The latter seemed to be thoroughly alive to the situation and exceedingly anxious, as were Couch and French, to do something to prepare for what was coming, yet nothing more was done until suddenly the firing, which had been growing in volume and intensity and gradually drawing nearer, developed in a storm of musketry of terrific fury immediately in our right front, apparently not more than three hundred yards away.

We could not see a thing. What there might be between us and it, or whether it was the onslaught of the enemy or the firing of our troops, we knew not. But we had not long to wait. Soon stragglers, few in numbers, began to appear, emerging form the woods into our clearing, and then more of them, these running, and then almost at once an avalanche of panic-stricken, flying men without arms, without knapsacks, many bareheaded, swearing, cursing, a wild, frenzied mob tearing to the rear. Instantly they began to appear, General Couch, commanding our corps, took in the situation and deployed two divisions to catch and hold the fugitives. Part of the Third Corps was also deployed on our left. We were ordered to charge bayonets and permit no man to pass through our ranks. We soon had a seething, howling mob of Dutchmen twenty to thirty feet in depth in front of our line, holding them back on the points of our bayonets, and still they came. Every officer of our division, with drawn sword and pistol, was required to use all possible endeavor to hold them, and threatening to shoot the first man who refused to stand as ordered. General French and staff were galloping up and down our division line assisting in this work.

In the mean time another line of battle was rapidly thrown in between these fugitives and the woods to stay the expected advance of the enemy. This was the famous break of the Eleventh Corps, starting with Blenker's division and finally extending through the whole corps, some fifteen thousand men. It seemed as though the whole army was being stampeded. We soon had a vast throng of these fugitives dammed up in our front, a terrible menace to the integrity of our own line as well as of all in our rear. We were powerless to do anything should the enemy break through, and were in great danger of being ourselves swept away and disintegrated by this frantic mob. All this time the air was filled with shrieking shells from our own batteries as well as those of the enemy, doing, however, little damage beyond adding to the terror of the situation. The noise was deafening. Pandemonium seemed to reign supreme in our front. Our line, as well as that of the Third Corps on our left, was holding firm as a rock. I noticed a general officer, I thought it was General Sickles, was very conspicuous in the vigor of his efforts to hold the line. A couple of fugitives had broken through his line and were rapidly going to the rear. I heard him order them to halt and turn back. One of them turned and cast a look at him, but paid no further attention to his order. He repeated the order in stentorian tones, this time with his pistol leveled, but it was not obeyed, and he fired, dropping the first man dead in his tracks. He again ordered the other man to halt, and it was sullenly obeyed. These men seemed to be almost stupid, deaf to orders or entreaty in their frenzy.

An incident in our own front will illustrate. I noticed some extra commotion near our colors and rushed to see the cause. I found an officer with drawn sword threatening to run the color-sergeant through if he was not allowed to pass. He was a colonel and evidently a German. My orders to him to desist were answered with a curse, and I had to thrust my pistol into his face, with an energetic threat to blow his head off if he made one more move, before he seemed to come to his senses. I then appealed to him to see what an example he as an officer was setting, and demanded that he should get to work and help to stem the fight of his men rather than assist in their demoralization. To his credit be it said, he at once regained his better self, and thenceforth did splendid work up and down amongst these German fugitives, and later on when they were moved to the rear, he rendered very material assistance. I did not learn who he was, but he was a splendid-looking officer and spoke both English and German fluently.

One may ask why those men would have lost their heads so completely. To answer the question intelligently, one needs to put oneself into their place. The facts as we were told at the time were: That the Eleventh Corps, which contained two divisions of German troops, under Schurz and Blenker (I think Steinwehr commanded the latter division of this action), was posted on the right of Hooker's line in the woods, some distance in front and to the right of the Chancellorsville House. That at the time Stonewall Jackson made his famous attack, above referred to, he caught one of those divisions "napping"—off their guard. They had stacked their guns and knapsacks, and were back some twenty yards, making their evening coffee when suddenly the rebel skirmishers burst through the brush upon them, followed immediately by the main line, and before they realized it were between these troops and their guns. Consternation reigned supreme in an instant and a helterskelter fight followed. Jackson followed up this advantage with his usual impetuosity, and although the other divisions of the Eleventh made an effort to hold their ground, this big hole in the line was fatal to them and all were quickly swept away. Of course, the division and brigade commanders were responsible for that unpardonable carelessness. No valid excuse can be made for such criminal want of watchfulness, especially for troops occupying a front line, and which had heard, or should have heard, as we a half mile farther in the rear had, all the premonitions of the coming storm. But it was an incident showing the utter folly of the attempt to maintain a line of battle in the midst of a dense undergrowth, through which nothing could be seen. It is exceedingly doubtful whether they could have held their line against Jackson's onset under those conditions had they been on the alert, for he would have been on and over them almost before they could have seen him. To resist such an onset needs time to deliver a steady volley and then be ready with the bayonet.

It was towards six o'clock in the evening when this flying mob struck our lines, and darkness had fallen before we were rid of them and something like order had been restored. In the mean time it certainly seemed as if everything was going to pieces. I got a little idea of what a panic-stricken army means. The fearful thing about it was, we knew it was terribly contagious, and that with all the uncertainties in that black wilderness from which this mob came and the pandemonium in progress all about us, it might seize our own troops and we be swept away to certain destruction in spite of all our efforts. It is said death rides on horseback with a fleeing army. Nothing can be more horrible. Hence a panic must be stopped, cost what it may. Night undoubtedly came to our rescue with this one.

One of the most heroic deeds I saw done to help stem the fleeing tide of men and restore courage was not the work of a battery nor a charge of cavalry, but the charge of a band of music! The band of the Fourteenth Connecticut went right out into that open space between our new line and the rebels, with shot and shell crashing all about them, and played "The Star-Spangled Banner," the "Red, White, and Blue," and "Yankee Doodle," and repeated them for fully twenty minutes. They never played better. Did that require nerve? It was undoubtedly the first and only band concert ever given under such conditions. Never was American grit more finely illustrated. Its effect upon the men was magical. Imagine the strains of our grand national hymn, "The Star-Spangled Banner" suddenly bursting upon your ears out of that horrible pandemonium of panic-born yells, mingled with the roaring of musketry and the crashing of artillery. To what may it be likened? The carol of birds in the midst of the blackest thunder-storm? No simile can be adequate. Its strains were clear and thrilling for a moment, then smothered by that fearful din, an instant later sounding bold and clear again, as if it would fearlessly emphasize the refrain, "Our flag is still there."

ROBERT P. DOUGLAS

Behind Confederate Lines

Robert Douglas was a private in Company E of the 155th Pennsylvania and suffered the misfortune of being captured by the enemy after he was left behind by his army to care for wounded soldiers that could not be removed from the field in the Federal retreat from Chancellorsville. Later paroled and exchanged, Douglas survived the war to embark on a fruitful career as manager of the Eliza Furnace Works in Pittsburgh. This article titled "In the Enemy's Lines After Chancellorsville" appeared in the history of his regiment, *Under the Maltese Cross*.

The writer's experience after the battle of Chancellorsville was a most unusual one. About the time the Fifth Corps crossed the Rappahannock at Kelly's Ford, Jacob Landsburger, of Company F, and the writer were detailed, by order of our Regimental Surgeon, Dr. Reed, acting surgeon in charge of the Second Division, Fifth Corps field hospital, for duty at that hospital. We were considered very fortunate in getting this detail, as we were relieved of our arms and the burden of our knapsacks, which were thrown into the ambulances and not seen again. Landsburger and the writer, after reporting, remained on duty with the Division hospital corps until the night of May 5th, when we were left, with other Union soldiers, to guard some of the wounded of both armies in an old saw-mill on the road from Chancellorsville to the United States Ford. The corps had been withdrawn across the Rappahannock, and we knew we were then outside our lines. In this field hospital, thus abandoned, there was a wounded Confederate Captain, two Lieutenants and twenty or more of their enlisted men, also wounded, and a few of our own wounded, unable to be moved. Orders came from headquarters of the Fifth Corps to allow none of the enemy's wounded to overhear, or to obtain any news from us of Hooker's retreat.

All that night we heard the retreating columns of our army marching back to the Rappahannock. We would have been only too glad to have gone along, but our strict orders were to remain at our posts, and as good soldiers we remained in obedience to those orders. The little squad of abandoned guards, thus left at the saw-mill, were in for developments, which soon came. At one o'clock in the morning of the 6th of May, Dr. Reed, surgeon in charge of the United States forces, sent an orderly to the guards and nurses just before the retreat, with orders to destroy all medical stores, to cut the leather medicine bags, and to break up all the medicine chests, to prevent them from falling into the enemy's hands. These stores would have been a great boon to them at any time, and especially at this time when they had thousands of their wounded requiring attention. We carried out our orders to the letter.

When our wounded were taken within our lines, after a delay of two weeks following the retreat of Hooker's army, a flag of truce arrangement was made by Generals Hooker and Lee, by which all the Union wounded, aggregating several thousand left within the Confederate lines, should be paroled and removed to Hooker's hospital on the north side of the Rappahannock near the United States Ford. The guards and nurses naturally expected to go back with them, but in this they were sorely disappointed. When the Fifth Corps ambulance trains under a flag of truce came out, Corporal John M. Lancaster, of Company E, was in charge of the detail. Dr. Reed, our Regimental Surgeon, a non-combatant, under orders, withdrew with this detail. Several trips were made by the ambulance trains of the Fifth corps from the north side of the Rappahannock, by way of the United States Ford. The distance was about five miles, and required time and care to transport so many sufferers back within the Union lines. There were about one hundred of our men originally detailed in all the squads besides ourselves; many from the Sixty-second Pennsylvania, the One Hundred and Fortieth New York, and some of the Sixty-third Pennsylvania, of the Third Corps, their duties being the same as Landsburger's and the writer's viz., to nurse and care for our wounded. These nurses were subsequently not permitted by the Confederates under the terms of the flag of truce to return to their regiments after the removal of our wounded, except those who were not fit to be removed. The Confederates had taken charge of their own wounded at the saw-mill hospital and elsewhere the day following Hooker's retreat. All the Union details of nurses and guards immediately after the retreat of our army were made prisoners of war.

The first knowledge of and introduction to the enemy occurred on the 6th of May, about eight o'clock in the morning. We saw some cavalry approaching wearing the Union uniform. The writer remarked to Comrade Landsburger, "We are all right yet. Here comes our cavalry." A cavalryman rode up to us and drawing a huge navy revolver, with great bravado and many foul oaths, boisterously threatened to shoot us. None of the Union soldiers in the details of guards and nurses was armed, so we, being in the same condition, could offer no resistance. We expostulated with our captor, showing him we were unarmed, being non-combatants on detail in charge of Confederate wounded as well as of our own, that had not been able to be removed under a flag of truce regularly agreed on by the commanders of both armies. It was a very exciting experience, and nerve-racking in the extreme to look into the chambers of a huge "Colt," which our blood-thirsty captor held so close to the writer's head that he could plainly see the bullets in the cylinder. When the remainder of the Confederate scouts came up, we were declared prisoners by the commanding officer, and at once marched to the rear of Lee's army, where the officer in whose charge we were given, immediately placed us in a Confederate hospital to take care of many wounded Union prisoners.

On our march from the saw-mill to the rear, we passed over the battlefield, and our little party saw many horrible scenes. Many of the dead of both armies lay unburied where they fell, with their clothing burned from their bodies by the fire which swept over the field after the battle on Sunday afternoon, May 3rd.

Around the trees where there were patches of grass, many wounded of both armies had crawled and died. The writer noticed that the trousers of many of these dead soldiers had been burned to the knees and that the woolen material had not burned further than where the bodies had been lying among the dried leaves. The fresh grass would not ignite, and the fire in the clothing had gone out. The dried leaves and brush had been set on fire by the explosive shells used by each army. All such wood fires spread rapidly and many wounded and dying had met a horrible end. These grewsome and terrible sights convey an apt illustration of General Sherman's celebrated epigram—'War is hell.'

The writer noticed particularly an oak tree that had been hit three times during the battle by cannonballs from the Union artillery, each shot cutting off a section of the tree, and it had been literally cut down at the stump by bullets. This stump was not far from where General Jackson was killed.

On this same march, as prisoners, we passed an old tobacco house where there were still many of our wounded mostly belonging to Howard's (Eleventh) Corps. There the writer gave away the last cracker he had to a wounded Union soldier, suffering the pangs of hunger and pain. The condition of all the wounded in this hospital was terrible in the extreme.

Outside of the tobacco shed lay five dead Union soldiers, stripped of every stitch of their clothing. These horrors were all observed on the Eleventh Corps' line. These five dead bodies were utterly neglected and unburied three days. The writer gave them a decent burial.

After a halt here by our little band of prisoners for ten days we were marched to a point near Gordonsville, Va., and were halted at a farm house in which there were about seventy-five Union wounded in the recent battle, who were, of course, prisoners. With a comrade of the Sixty-second Pennsylvania, the writer was left by the officer in charge of the prisoners, to care for these wounded. There was no lint and no medicines of any kind on hand and nothing from which we could make bandages. Many of these suffering ones were in even worse condition than those at the tobacco house we had just left. In a word, it was frightful. Many, thus neglected, died of blood poisoning. We cleaned the sores of those still alive by using plenty of cold water, going from one sufferer to another day and night. This was long before the day of antiseptic surgery, but it was there, the best and only treatment possible.

Jackson's old corps, now commanded by General J.E.B. Stuart, was encamped close by, and one day, while off duty, the writer took a stroll through their camps. While watching the Confederate bakers making bread, one of their soldiers said, "Yank, aren't you afraid to be here, sah, by yourself?" To which the writer replied, "No, sir, I am unarmed, and a prisoner in charge of our wounded." "Yes, sah," he replied, "but you might be taken for a spy." Realizing at once the risks being taken, the writer began to move off for the hospital when the same man said, "Yank, you see those boys over there? Those uns are North Carolina troops. They didn't want to fight for the South, sah, but we placed them in the front, sah, at Chancellorsville, and they had to fight."

A few days after this conversation, one of these same North Carolina soldiers came to the hospital of the Union prisoners and begged the guards to arrange for him to be sent through the Confederate lines with the Union wounded, which was expected to be ordered at any time. He declared he was tired fighting and had had enough of it. This man came every day to the hospital for nearly a week. One of the Union wounded—a Berdan sharpshooter—died. The North Carolina visitor was told that if he would help bury the body, we would let him have the deceased's uniform, and he could take his name and in that manner get through the lines with the convalescent Union wounded. He donned the Union uniform and worked with us in the hospital for another week before the Union wounded and their guards were to start for exchange and parole at Annapolis, Md. When the day came, the entire party was marched to United States Ford on the Rappahannock River, under escort of a squad of Confederate cavalry, where the North Carolina "Johnny" metamorphosed into a Berdan sharpshooter of the Union army, stood right at my left when the Union wounded crossed. Captain Kyd Douglass, Adjutant-General of Jackson's Corps, recorded the names of the party and gave out the paroles both to the returning guard and the nurses. The North Carolina deserter passed without detection, and crossed with the wounded, and we never saw him again.

My comrade of the Sixty-second Pennsylvania and myself were very glad when our North Carolina friend passed safely through into our lines. We greatly feared that he might prove traitor and inform the Confederate office in charge of our party of our connivance in his escape, in which event our lives would not have been greatly prolonged.

The wounded turned over to the Union army here were the last of the prisoners captured at Chancellorsville, all of whom were wounded, numbering about five thousand and upwards in that battle. The detachment of guards and nurses and prisoners were treated as a distinct body separate and aside from the wounded. The Confederates at the United States Ford, when the exchange was made, seemed to have doubts as to the military status of our party, and of our right to be treated as non-combatants under the flag of truce which the Confederates evidently construed as applying only to the wounded prisoners. We were much surprised and disappointed, therefore, after all the wounded were transferred with the Union lines, when we were informed that our little party were still prisoners of war. We were marched to Richmond and put in Libby prison, where we remained four days without rations. In the meantime, our status having been settled by the Confederates, we were, on the fourth day taken out of Libby and marched again to United States Ford, a distance, I suppose, of about fifty miles. This was close to where we had been made prisoners, and we had been able to see something of the country between there and the Confederate capital.

This time, to our very great joy, we were passed through the lines at the Ford without delay. We were not paroled prisoners and our next destination was Camp Parole, at Annapolis, where we were to remain until formally exchanged. This was another surprise to us. This was about the middle of June. Three of our party, all from Pittsburg, decided to take "French leave" and go home, and we were not long in starting.

The three of us remained at home for six weeks. The writer, weary of the monotony of this kind of military life, went on duty with the provost guard, being prevented from service with his company at the front until duly exchanged. Comrade Landsburger, the writer's fellow-nurse on this detail, on being exchanged some time afterward, returned to the Regiment, and remained on duty with his company until badly wounded in the first day's battle in the Wilderness.

Chapter VII

THE ROAD TO GETTYSBURG

Hooker's defeat at Chancellorsville opened the way for Lee to launch his second great invasion above the waters of the Potomac. Charged to meet this dire threat to the north was George Gordon Meade who was given command of the Army of the Potomac after Hooker's removal. On 1 July, detachments from both Union and Confederate forces met to the northwest of Gettysburg in a battle that continued to grow in intensity until two Federal and two Confederate corps were engaged in heavy fighting. By nightfall, the rest of the grand armies were gravitating towards that small Pennsylvania town to play out one of the greatest moments in American military history.

W.W. BLACKFORD

Riding with J.E.B Stuart

One of the most controversial performances of the Gettysburg Campaign was J.E.B. Stuart's handling or rather mishandling of the cavalry of the Army of Northern Virginia. After being roughed up by mounted Yankee troopers at Brandy Station, Stuart attempted to redeem himself by embarking on one of his famous rides entirely around the Federal army.

While it was a spectacular performance, Stuart's move failed to keep Lee informed about the movements of the enemy thus allowing the Confederates to blunder into a major engagement at Gettysburg. One of Stuart's commanders, W.W. Blackford gives this account of Brandy Station and Stuart's controversial ride in his *War Years with J.E.B. Stuart*.

A grand review was ordered for the 5th of June and all at headquarters were exerting themselves to the utmost to make it a success. Invitations were issued far and near, and as the time approached every train came loaded with visitors. I wrote to the University, and Mary Minor and a troop of Charlottesville girls attended. I was very sorry that my wife could not attend, but she was over three hundred miles away in Abingdon, and dreaded the journey.

When the day of review arrived the Secretary of War, General Randolph, came from Richmond to see it, and many infantry Generals and prominent men. The staff was resplendent in new uniforms, and horses were in splendid condition as we rode to the field on the level plains near Brandy Station. The ground was admirably adapted to the purpose, a hill in the centre affording a reviewing stand from which the twelve thousand men present could be seen to great advantage. It must be borne in mind that cavalry show much larger than infantry, and that these twelve thousand mounted men produced the effect of at least three times their number of infantry. General Stuart, accompanied by his brilliant staff, passed down the front and back by the rear at a gallop in the usual way, the general officers and their staff joining us as we passed, so that by the time we got back to the stand there were nearly a hundred horsemen, all officers, dashing through the field. Then the lines broke into column of squadrons and marched by at a walk, making the entire circuit; then they came by at a trot, taking the gallop a hundred yards before reaching the reviewing stand; and then the "charge" at full speed past the reviewing stand, yelling just as they do in a real charge, and brandishing their sabres over their heads. The effect was thrilling, even to us, while the ladies clasped their hands and sank into the arms, sometimes, of their escorts in a swoon, if the escorts were handy, but if not they did not. While the charging was going on, Beckham with the horse artillery was firing rapidly and this heightened the effect. It would make your hair stand on end to see them. How little did we then think that on this very ground a few days later just such charges would be made in reality in the greatest cavalry action of modern times.

That night we gave a ball at headquarters on the turf by moonlight, assisted by huge wood fires, firelight to dance by and moonlight for the strolls.

General Lee arrived rather unexpectedly and on the 7th we moved to "Fleetwood," an old plantation residence near Brandy Station. The next day we had another cavalry review for General Lee's benefit. This was a business affair, the spectators being all soldiers. Many men from Hood's division were present who enjoyed it immensely. During the charges past the reviewing stand the hats and caps of the charging column would sometimes blow off, and then, just as the charging squadron passed and before the owners could come back, Hood's men would have a race for them and bear them off in triumph. This was the last of our frolics for a long time, for on the morrow we were to begin the fighting which was kept up almost daily until two weeks after the battle of Gettysburg, and we were to begin it in a severe action.

Up to this time the cavalry of the enemy had not been able to stand before us, but during the past winter great attention had been bestowed upon that branch of their service and it had become much more formidable. We were to meet the next day in nearly equal numbers upon the plain around Fleetwood in the great cavalry action, Fleetwood Fight, June 9, '63.

General Stuart's headquarters, as I have before stated, were at Fleet-wood, an old homestead, situated on a hill half a mile from Brandy Station and four miles from the Rappahannock, and our cavalry was encamped for the most part along the river in front. Pleasanton then commanded the cavalry of the enemy and had been encamped twelve miles north of the river, but under pressing orders from Hooker to find out something of Lee's movements, he had the night before moved down to the river with the intention of crossing at daylight the next morning to attack Stuart at the Court House. Thus each commander was nearer the river than the other thought. Pleasanton moved in two columns, one under Buford to cross at Beverly's ford nearly in our front, and the other under Gregg at Kelly's ford six miles below. Both of these columns bivouacked about two miles north of the river.

At daylight our camp was aroused by a rattling fire proceeding from the bank of fog which hung over the valley. Stuart awaited impatiently the news, and presently a courier from General Jones, who was opposite Beverly's ford, reported that the enemy had charged through the ford, had driven in the picket there and had attacked the camp with great fury. Jones had met them with dismounted men and held them in check until his command could saddle up, had then struck his camp, packed his wagons and sent everything to the rear and was awaiting further developments. A sharp action followed without further advance on the part of the enemy. They were disconcerted at meeting such a force at that place, and awaited the movements of Gregg with the other wing six miles away.

Everything remaining quiet, Stuart accompanied by his staff rode down to the scene of action about the middle of the day, having previously sent Gen. Beverly Robertson with his brigade off to our right towards Kelly's ford to guard against an advance from that direction. This move was made on general principles of military strategy, he not having at that time knowledge of the movements of Gregg's column, and if General Robertson had done his duty we would have had ample notice of any advance on that flank. Major McClellan, our Adjutant General, had been left by Stuart on Fleetwood hill with some couriers to receive any communications arriving and to forward them to him. Time rolled on, and Stuart with his shrewdness suspected that some scheme was brewing and sent one of his aides, Lieutenant Goldsborough, off to Colonel Butler near Stevensburg to find out if he knew anything of the

enemy in his direction. Goldsborough was a fine, handso
young fellow but he had only joined the staff a few days b
as it turned out, inexperienced, and lacking in that hal
necessary for a staff officer in riding up to a body of
battlefield; he must be sure who they are before he joins tl
larly in dusty weather when blue and gray are covered alike with dust so
as not to be distinguishable. The roads were deep in dust and Goldsborough, poor fellow, had not gone far down the Kelly's ford road before he
dashed full tilt into the head of a column of the enemy and was captured.

I must now explain how this force came to be there close upon our
flank and we not to know of their approach. Gregg had crossed at Kelly's
ford without opposition and had then divided his force, bringing two
brigades under Sir Percy Wyndham, an Englishman, and Colonel Kilpatrick up to form a junction with Buford and sending Colonel Duffie with
the other part on towards Culpeper C.H. General Robertson, most
unaccountably, did not attack either of these forces but allowed Gregg
to go on towards our main army and Sir Percy Wyndham to pass him
and go on towards Stuart's exposed flank and rear, and it was this latter
column Goldsborough met. The first intimation any one had of this
attack in flank and rear was their appearance in sight of Fleetwood.
McClellan at once sent courier after courier to notify General Stuart, and
as good luck would have it he was enabled to make some show of
resistance by finding a piece of artillery accidentally passing the road
across the hill. With this he immediately opened fire, the boom of the
guns reaching us just as the courier brought the news to General Stuart,
and satisfied him that McClellan was not mistaken, which at first he
thought must be the case.

There now followed a passage of arms filled with romantic interest
and splendor to a degree unequaled by anything our war produced. The
waste of war had removed the obstacles to cavalry maneuvers usually met
with in our country—fences and forests; and the ground was open, level
and firm; conditions which led to the settlement of the affair with the
sabre alone. Fleetwood hill was the key to the position. Artillery upon
the commanding ground would render the surrounding plain untenable,
and for its possession the battle was fought over its surface and on the
levels beyond. There was here presented in a modern battle the striking
phenomenon of gunpowder being ignored almost entirely. Not a man
fought dismounted, and there was heard but an occasional pistol shot

and but little artillery, for soon after the opening of the fight the contest was so close and the dust so thick that it was impossible to use either without risk to friends.

General Stuart turned to me and ordered me to gallop along the line and order every commanding officer of a regiment to move on Fleetwood at a gallop. It was a thrilling sight to see these dashing horsemen draw their sabres and start for the hill a mile and a half in rear at a gallop. The enemy had gotten a battery almost to the top of the hill when they arrived. This was taken and retaken three times, we retaining it finally. The lines met on the hill. It was like what we read of in the days of chivalry, acres and acres of horsemen sparkling with sabres, and dotted with brilliant bits of color where their flags danced above them, hurled against each other at full speed and meeting with a shock that made the earth tremble. Sir Percy Wyndham after a gallant fight was repulsed before Buford, who was pushing Rooney Lee vigorously, could come to his assistance.

Col. M.C. Butler heard of Duffie's advance, and with great good judgment, without awaiting orders to that effect, threw his regiment in his front and arrested his advance, falling desperately wounded himself. The same cannonball which took off his leg killed Captain Farley of our staff who was riding by his side.

As soon as this repulse was completed, General Stuart told me to watch closely to see if the enemy showed any infantry support, for if they did I must at once inform General Lee or General Longstreet. It was not long before I found them with my powerful field glasses deployed as skirmishers and though they kept low in the grass I could see the color of their trimmings and their bayonet scabbards. Informing Stuart, he sent me to report the fact and after a hot ride of six miles I reached General Longstreet's quarters and reported the fact to him. General Lee then came down himself with some infantry but they were not brought into action. Gen. W.H.F. Lee charged and drove back Buford who was still advancing and then a final advance on our part pressed them back across the Rappahannock.

By all the tests recognized in war the victory was fairly ours. We captured three cannon and five hundred prisoners, and held the field.

Colonel Hampton of the 2nd South Carolina, and Col. Sol. Williams of the 2nd North Carolina were killed, while Gen. W.H.F. Lee, Col. M.C. Butler and many others were wounded. Our loss on the staff was Captain

Farley killed, Captain White wounded, and Lieutenant Goldsborough taken prisoner. Goldsborough's fate was a sad one. Taken prisoner in this his first battle, he remained in prison two years; he was then exchanged, and in the first battle after his return, during the retreat from Richmond, only a few days before the surrender at Appomattox, he was killed. During his short stay on the staff he made warm friends of all of us by his gallant bearing and unassuming, attractive manners. He was a son of Commodore Goldsborough of the navy, and one of the handsomest young fellows in the army.

During the action, in galloping from one part of the field to the other carrying orders, friend and foe were so mixed together and all so closely engaged that I had some capital pistol practice, and emptied every barrel of my revolver twice at close range. I could not tell with certainty what effect my shots had, for galloping by one cannot take a second glance, but at a target I seldom failed to hit a hat at that distance and in that manner. Pistol practice from the saddle at a gallop was our favorite amusement on the staff and it is surprising how accurately one can shoot in this way.

After the engagement Stuart ordered headquarters camp to be pitched on the same hill from which it had been moved in the morning, but when we reached the place it was covered so thickly with the dead horses and men, and the bluebottle flies were swarming so think over the blood-stains on the ground that there was not room enough to pitch the tents among them. So the General reluctantly consented to camping at another place. He regretted this, for as a matter of pride he was inclined to hold the field as he held it in the morning even in this particular. The next morning we rode over the field and most of the dead bore wounds from the sabre, either by cut or thrust. I mean the field around Fleetwood; in other places this was not the case to so great an extent.

General Lee now began his march towards Pennsylvania. His proposed route was to cross the Blue Ridge and follow the valley of Virginia with his main army, while Stuart was to move on the east side of the mountains to cover his flank at least as far as Middleburg. Winchester was occupied by a strong force of the enemy and Ewell was sent on ahead to clear the valley. This he did gloriously, capturing four or five thousand prisoners and some thirty pieces of artillery.

Stuart pushed on up into Fauquier where Mosby met us. Mosby by this time had become famous. I had not seen him for more than a year and the change in his appearance was striking. When he was a member of my company and afterwards when he became Adjutant of our regiment, the 1st Virginia Cavalry, he was careless about his dress and mount and presented anything but a soldierly appearance. As we were riding along the road at the head of the column one evening we saw a horseman, handsomely dressed, gallop across the field towards us and lift his horse lightly over the fence a short distance ahead, and approach us. I could scarcely believe my eyes when I recognized in this dashing looking officer my old friend and the now celebrated guerrilla chief, Mosby. He had been scouting, and was fully posted as to the movements of the enemy, whose cavalry was following us in a parallel line some miles to the east of Bull Run Mountain. During all this period Mosby and his men kept us thoroughly informed of all movements of the enemy in that country.

On the 18th of June we reached Middleburg and on the 19th their cavalry attacked us with great fury. The day before there had been several combats in which we had been in the main successful, capturing many prisoners. The fight at Upperville was a very hot one and at one time we were forced back. General Stuart with his staff around him was slowly leaving the field before the advance of a heavy line of dismounted skirmishers who were pouring their fire into us, the only group of horsemen they could see at that time. We were going up the side of a gently sloping hill and the bullets pattered around us on the hard, hoof-trodden ground like drops of rain. Just then I heard a thump very much like some one had struck a barrel a violent blow with a stick. I knew well enough what it meant, and I can never forget the agony of suspense with which I looked around to see which one of our group would fall. My first glance was towards General Stuart, but there he sat as firm as a rock in his saddle. I then saw von Borcke who was riding close by my side drop his bridle hand and become limp, his horse bounding forward as the rein was relaxed. I saw at once that his spur was going to hang in the blanket strapped behind his saddle, for he slowly slid sideways from his seat with both hands clutching the horse's mane. I spurred Magic up alongside instantly, and, leaning over, took his foot in both hands and threw it over, clear of the saddle. His feet fell to the ground and this jerked loose his hold on the mane, letting him down easily on his back. Frank Robertson and myself sprang to the ground while someone caught the horse and brought him back. Seeing that our poor comrade was shot in the back of the neck I had little hope for him but determined to get his body off the field if possible. Von Borcke had often expressed his horror of filling a nameless grave and he once asked me, if the occasion should ever arise, to mark the place so that his friends could find it. The horse, as I have said, was brought to us but he was in a state of great excitement from the constant hissing of the bullets, for the approaching skirmish line, seeing the party halted, were bestowing special attention on us. I was at my wits' end to know how we were to throw our friend's body, weighing two hundred and fifty pounds, across the rearing, plunging charger, and how we were to keep it there if we succeeded in doing so. I then recollected a thing von Borcke had once told me was taught in the Prussian Cavalry schools for this very emergency, and I made a courier twist the horse's ear severely and keep it twisted while he led the horse off the field with von Borcke on him, the horse becoming perfectly quiet immediately. How strange that von Borcke's mentioning this little trick on a long night march in a general conversation to while away the time should have saved the narrator from capture, and quite likely from death from neglect in prison.

When we first lifted him von Borcke was as limp as a rag, but to our great surprise and pleasure he then showed signs of returning consciousness and stiffened himself on his legs enough for us to lift one foot to the stirrup, and then with a mighty effort to hoist him to the saddle, where with assistance on both sides he kept his balance until we could get him to an ambulance.

Von Borcke's strong constitution enabled him to survive this wound, though it was a very severe one. The bullet passed through the collar of his jacket an inch or two from the spine and entered his throat, and for months he coughed up pieces of his clothing which had been carried in. He was never able, however, to enter active service again with us. A few months before the surrender he returned to his own country and in the war with Austria held a position on Prince Frederick Charles' staff, though obliged to ride mostly in a carriage. In 1884 he visited this country and I dined with him at the Maryland Club in Baltimore, an elegant entertainment given in his honor at which there were present some twenty-odd old comrades of his, including Generals Wade Hampton and M.C. Butler of South Carolina, Gen. W.H.F Lee of Virginia and Col. R. Snowden Andrews and Gen. Bradley T. Johnson of Baltimore. When I met him on this occasion he threw his arms around me and his eyes filled with tears. I spent a couple of days with him in Baltimore and we called to see the "New York rebel" who happened to be on a visit to the city at the time. She was still unmarried. This was the beautiful girl we met at Urbana, Maryland, during the Antietam Campaign in 1862, the one with whom I was dancing at our memorable ball when the wounded arrived. We had many pleasant memories to recall, but it was hard to realize that the middle-aged, matronly looking lady and the huge gentleman weighing between four and five hundred pounds were those who danced so gracefully then. Von Borcke told me he had not been able to reach his feet to tie his shoes for years on account of his corpulency. He was immense—his neck quite as large as his head, and all his manly beauty gone.

When he visited this country von Borcke had just lost his wife. He showed me her picture, and the picture of his two boys. She was a beautiful woman, judging by the photograph.

When Col. Chas. Venable visited Prussia, von Borcke invited him to his castle and ran up the Prussian flag on one tower and the Confederate flag on the other.

The improvement in the cavalry of the enemy became painfully apparent in the fights around Upperville. It was mainly in their use of dismounted men, and in their horse artillery, however, for they could not stand before us yet in a charge on horseback. Around Upperville the fields were much enclosed by stone fences which greatly favored dismounted troops, and greatly impeded the mounted men. They were much better provided with long-range carbines than our cavalry, which gave them an advantage dismounted. Their cavalry too had been largely recruited from the infantry and had seen service and been drilled as such, which of course was greatly to their advantage serving on foot, while our cavalry had served from the beginning in their branch of the service, and had been drilled mainly mounted.

In the series of combats from Aldie to Middleburg from the 17th to the 21st it must be borne in mind that we were following a *defensive* policy, Stuart's only object being to cover the gaps of the Blue Ridge. This of course places cavalry at a disadvantage as it is mainly an *offensive* arm of the service and our object was successfully obtained, for the enemy never even entered a gap of the mountain. From a captured dispatch Stuart found that a strong force of infantry was supporting their attack and he then called upon General Longstreet for a detachment. These reached us, or rather reached a point within supporting distance in

Ashby's Gap, but were not brought into action, nor even in sight of the enemy, as shown by General Pleasanton's report of the action.

We were not about to start on an expedition which for audacious boldness equaled if it did not exceed any of our dashing leader's exploits; but before entering upon the subject we must take a glance at the position of the contending forces: Lee occupied the valley from Winchester to the Potomac, and Meade awaited his movements in Loudoun and Fauquier, the two counties opposite, on the eastern side of the Blue Ridge. Stuart, as I have stated, guarded the passes of the mountain, and occupied the space between the Blue Ridge and the low range of hills parallel thereto called Bull Run Mountain, with headquarters at Rector's crossroads. General Lee being now ready to begin his march northwards, Early crossed the Potomac with his division as the advanced guard on June 22nd.

The question now arose as to how Stuart was to reach the head of Lee's advancing column, now entering Pennsylvania. It was impossible for him to move along the eastern slope of the Blue Ridge between the mountain and Meade's forces, and all the roads leading northward through the valley were densely filled with the trains of artillery, and quartermaster, commissary and ordnance wagons, to say nothing of the infantry columns. Two plans were presented by Stuart and submitted to General Lee's consideration: one, to take the route through the valley and the other, which Stuart was ardently in favor of, to sweep around the rear of Meade's army and dash northward past him, and between him and Washington; cutting his communications, breaking up the railroads, doing all the damage possible, and then to join Early in Pennsylvania. General Lee left the decision of the question to Stuart, and Stuart immediately prepared to carry it into execution.

It was clearly necessary to leave a strong force of cavalry to guard the passes until Meade had left his position, else their cavalry could pour through and fall upon Lee's rear. Stuart had with him about five thousand men. This force he divided, leaving Wm. E. Jones' and Robertson's brigades, three thousand men, under command of Robertson to hold the passes until their front was clear and then to operate with the main army as Gen. R.E. Lee might direct; and he took three brigades, Hampton's, Fitz Lee's and W.H.F. Lee's, the latter under the command of Colonel Chambliss, numbering about two thousand men.

These three brigades were ordered to rendezvous at Salem on the night of the 24th, and a little after midnight on the morning of the 25th of June we started. No one could ride along the lines of this splendid body of men and not be struck with the spirit which animated them. They knew they were starting on some bold enterprise, but their confidence in their leader was so unbounded that they were as gay and lively as it was possible for them to be, for up to that time no reverse had crossed their path and they believed themselves and their leader invincible. Often have I heard, when some danger threatened and Stuart galloped by to the front, the remark, "Ah boys! I feel all right now, there is General Stuart."

Mosby had reported the enemy still in their encampments the day before and Stuart expected to move eastward through Haymarket and thence direct to Fairfax C.H., but at Haymarket, early in the first day's march, he found Hancock's corps on the march occupying the road he wished to cross for many miles each way. After shelling them awhile and capturing some prisoners, he had to wait most of the morning for them to pass, and then by a detour he passed around their rear and by a more circuitous route pushed on, crossing the Occoquan at Wolf Run shoals, capturing a small force at Fairfax C.H., passing through Dranesville, and reaching Rowser's Ford of the Potomac on the night of the 27th. The ford was wide and deep and might well have daunted a less determined man than our indomitable General, for the water swept over the pommels of our saddles. To pass the artillery without wetting the ammunition in the chests was impossible, provided it was left in them, but Stuart had the cartridges distributed among the horsemen and it was thus taken over in safety. The guns and caissons went clean out of sight beneath the surface of the rapid torrent, but all came out without the loss of a piece or a man, though the night was dark, and by three o'clock on the morning of the 28th of June we all stood wet and dripping on the Maryland shore.

Oh, what a change! From the hoof-trodden, warwasted lands of old Virginia to a country fresh and plentiful. The march for three days had been through a country naturally poor at its best, but stripped by war of all the little it once had. Not a mouthful of grain had even I been able to beg, borrow, or steal for my horses; and where I could not find it there was apt to be none to find. Poor Magic looked as thin as a snake but cocked her ear as gayly as ever. Manassas had been wounded during our attack on Hancock's corps at Haymarket, but could still do duty, though much in want of food. The necessity for stopping to graze the horses on this march had delayed us a good deal, both in the time it took and the weakening of the animals from such light diet. I rode Manassas on the march and had Magic led, saving her for the big battle that we knew was brewing. It was absolutely necessary, though time was so precious, to allow the artillery horses some rest and a chance to eat the fine grass around us after their hard night's work; so it was nearly the middle of the day before we reached Rockville, a pretty village on the main road leading from Washington and nine or ten miles from that city. We had just arrived when a long wagon train of a hundred and fifty wagons appeared on the road slowly approaching from the direction of Washington, and a detail from Hampton's brigade was at once sent to capture it, which I accompanied. Galloping full tilt into the head of the train, we captured a small guard and a lot of gayly dressed quartermasters, and over half the wagons, before they could turn round; but then those beyond took the alarm, turned and fled as fast as their splendid mule teams could go. After them we flew, popping away with our pistols at such drivers as did not pull up, but the more we popped the faster those in front plied the whip; finally, coming to a sharp turn in the road, one upset and a dozen or two other piled up on top of it, until you could see nothing but the long ears and kicking legs of the mules striking above bags of oats emptied from the wagons upon them. All behind this blockade were effectually stopped, but half a dozen wagons had made the turn before this happened and after them two or three of us dashed. It was as exciting as a fox chase for several miles, until when the last was taken I found myself on a hill in full view of Washington. One hundred and twenty-five uninjured wagons were taken and safely brought into our lines, together with the animals of the others. Here was a godsend to our poor horses, for every wagon was loaded with oats intended for Meade's army and it did one's heart good to see the way the poor brutes got on the outside of those oats. After giving my horses all they could eat I slung half a bag, saddle-bag fashion, across my saddle for future use, and my horse seemed to know what this additional load was, for he occasionally turned an affectionate glance back towards it.

There was a large female academy in Rockville, and flocks of the pretty maidens congregated on the front to greet us, showing strong sympathy for our cause, and cutting off all the buttons they could get hold of from our uniforms as souvenirs. In passing along the street I saw a very duplicate of my little daughter Lizzie. Never have I seen so remarkable a likeness between two people. Frank Robertson was as much struck with it as I was. Twenty years after he met her there, a grown woman.

With the exception of a squadron of the enemy, encountered at Winchester, we met no opposition until Hanover was reached about noon on the 30th. It seems remarkable that the enemy should not have used more enterprise than this, for we were destroying his communications as we advanced. At Hanover, however, we met Kilpatrick's division of cavalry and had a hot affair with them. We were just opposite Gettysburg and if we could have made our way direct, the fifteen miles of distance to that place would have passed that day, and we would have effected a junction with General Lee the day before the battle began. It was here the wagon train began to interfere with our movements, and if General Stuart could only have known what we do now it would have been burned; but he knew nothing of the concentration which accidental circumstances were to bring about at Gettysburg in the next two days, and as he expected to meet Early at York very soon, he held on to them.

The 2nd North Carolina Regiment made the first charge through the town, driving the enemy out, but receiving strong reinforcements they rallied and drove the North Carolinians back in their turn in great confusion. As General Stuart saw them rushing out of the place, he started down the road to meet them, calling me to follow him. We tried to rally them, but the long charge *in* and the repulse *out* and the hot skirmish fire opened upon them from the windows on the street by citizens had thrown them into utter confusion, and in spite of all we could do they got by us, and before we were aware of it we found ourselves at the head of the enemy's charging column.

The road was lined on each side by an ill-kept hedge grown up high, but at some places, fortunately for us, there were gaps of lower growth. Stuart pulled up and waving his sabre with a merry laugh, shouted to me, "Rally them, Blackford!" and then lifted his mare, Virginia, over the hedge into the field. I knew that he only said what he did to let me know that he was off, so I followed him. I had only that morning, fortunately, mounted Magic, having had her led previously, and Stuart had done the same with Virginia, so they were fresh. As we alighted in the field, we found ourselves within ten paces of the front of a flanking party of twenty-five or thirty men which was accompanying the charging regiment, and they called to us to halt; but as we let our two thoroughbreds out, they followed in hot pursuit, firing as fast as they could cock their pistols. The field was in tall timothy grass and we did not see, nor did our horses until close to it, a huge gully fifteen feet wide and as many deep stretched across our path. There were only a couple of strides of distance for our horses to regulate their step, and Magic had to rise at least six feet from the brink. Stuart and myself were riding side by side and as soon as Magic rose I turned my head to see how Virginia had done it, and I shall never forget the glimpse I then saw of this beautiful animal away up in mid-air over the chasm and Stuart's fine figure sitting erect and firm in the saddle. Magic, seeing the size of the place and having received a very unusual sharp application of my spurs, had put out her strength to its full in this leap and she landed six or seven feet beyond the further bank, making a stride of certainly twenty-seven feet. The moment our horses rose, our pursuers saw that there was something there, and it was with difficulty they could pull up in time to avoid plunging headlong into it, and their firing was of course arrested. This time Magic's activity had saved me from capture, but ten minutes later her quickness saved my life.

General Stuart galloped on up towards the top of a hill to direct the fire of a battery on the pursuing regiment, while I, wishing to get Magic cooled down away from the excitement of other horses, took a path which would round the foot of the hill. I had just quieted her, so that she had put her head down and was walking with the reins on her neck, when I heard the clatter of a horse's hoofs behind me at full speed. Thinking it was someone who wished to join company, I did not turn to look until I found the horse was not going slower as it approached. I then looked back, and there, within a couple of horses' lengths, came dashing a Yankee sergeant bending low on his horse's neck with his sabre "encarte" ready to run me through. It was the work of a second to seize the slackened reins, pull them over to the right and plunge my left spur into her flank. As quick as lightning Magic bounded to the right, so quickly that my left arm was lifted a little from my side, and at the same instant there gleamed the bright blade of a sabre between my arm and body as my pursuer made his thrust; but by the time I could gather the reins and turn, the man was fifty yards away. Then I heard some cheering, and looking up the left, on a hill nearby saw a general officer and his staff, towards whom my man was making his way. It was evident that, seeing me alone, this man had made the pass as a little sword practice for the amusement of his comrades and his own glorification. I would have given anything if I could only have had half a minute's notice of his coming, for I don't think there would have been then anything for them to cheer. From where they stood it looked exactly as if he had succeeded in running me through, and he no doubt did not disabuse their minds as to the facts. I could only show my feelings upon the subject by shaking my fist at them as I moved slowly on to the battery on our hill.

It was night before we withdrew from Hanover, and Kilpatrick had been so roughly handled that he did not follow us on the first. On approaching York, Stuart found that Early had left there, moving westward, and he sent Maj. Andrew R. Venable of his staff on his trail to get orders from General Lee. Later in the day Capt. Henry Lee of Fitz Lee's staff was sent on a similar errand. During our night march the wagon train and nearly four hundred prisoners, who had been taken since the first batch of four hundred were paroled four days before, were a source of unmitigated annoyance. The mules in the captured wagon trains could neither be fed nor watered, and had not been for several days, while the prisoners fared nearly as badly. The consequence was great difficulty in moving them. Expecting to get rations in Carlisle, Stuart sent his commissary on ahead to make a requisition on the town, but since the withdrawal of Early the place had been occupied by the enemy. Stuart reached the place on the evening of July 1, and found it occupied by two brigades of militia under command of Gen. W.F. Smith. Of this officer he demanded a surrender, which was refused; whereupon Stuart opened his batteries and shelled the town and burned the barracks.

About midnight Venable and Lee returned with the first information we had received from our army and with orders from Gen. R.E. Lee for Stuart to march to Gettysburg at once. They also brought us intelligence of the successful combat of that day at Gettysburg.

We started from Carlisle about one o'clock A.M. on July 2, and effected a junction with our army at Gettysburg early in the day, Hampton becoming engaged in a sharp conflict with Kilpatrick's division before reaching there.

The brigades of Jones and Robertson, left at Upperville when Stuart started on his expedition, remained there long after the enemy left their front, and did not rejoin us until after the Battle of Gettysburg was fought and we were withdrawing towards the Potomac. Whose fault this was I cannot say but certainly not Stuart's. If Robertson had not been a West Pointer he would have been deprived of his command for his

324

inactivity in letting General Wyndham's command pass him as he did at Fleetwood Fight on the 9th of June, and the same qualities in the man which made him play such a part there may have been the cause of the delay on this occasion. General Robertson was an excellent man in camp to train troops, but in the field, in the presence of the enemy, he lost all self-possession, and was perfectly unreliable. But had he not sat upon the benches at West Point? Certainly he had, and he must consequently be made a general without ever having done one single thing in action to deserve that promotion. Our cause died of West Point as much as of any one thing. General Lee and General Stuart must have been convinced of his incapacity by this affair, for he was relieved of his command soon after and sent elsewhere.

It is easy enough to say that some other course would have been better than the one Stuart followed, looking back now with the knowledge of *what has since happened*; but is it fair to blame him for acting for the best with the *knowledge he then had?* If the Battle of Gettysburg had been won by us, as it very nearly was, this expedition would have been called a magnificent achievement. As it was the injury inflicted on the enemy by the diversion of troops was alone enough to justify it. Maj. H.B. McClellan gives a very able defense of Stuart on this point in his book, *The Campaigns of Stuart's Cavalry*, and shows clearly that the effect of Stuart's movement accomplished as much, if not more, diversion and neutralization of the forces of the enemy as any plan he could have pursued.

SIR ARTHUR FREMANTLE

On to Gettysburg

One of the more lively accounts of the battle of Gettysburg belongs to Sir Arthur Fremantle, a colonel of the Coldstream Guards serving as a British observer with the Army of Northern Virginia at the time. His diary during his term of service in this position was published in 1863 and entitled *Three Months in the Southern States*. In it the colonel presumptuously predicts a Southern victory in the Civil War. Here he describes Lee's path to Gettysburg.

This morning, before marching from Chambersburg, General Long-street introduced me to the Commander-in-Chief. General Lee is, almost without exception, the handsomest man of his age I ever saw. He is fifty-six years old, tall, broad-shouldered, very well made, well set up—a thorough soldier in appearance; and his manners are most courteous and full of dignity. He is a perfect gentleman in every respect. I imagine no man has so few enemies, or is so universally esteemed. Throughout the South, all agree in pronouncing him to be as near perfection as a man can be. He has none of the small vices, such as smoking, drinking, chewing, or swearing, and his bitterest enemy never accused him of any of the greater ones. He generally wears a well-worn long grey jacket, a high black felt hat, and blue trousers bucked into his Wellington boots. I never saw him carry arms; and the only mark of his military rank are the three stars on his collar. He rides a handsome horse, which is extremely well-groomed. He himself is very neat in his dress and person, and in the most arduous marches he always looks smart and clean.

In the old army he was always considered one of its best officers; and at the outbreak of these troubles, he was Lieutenant-Colonel of the 2d cavalry. He was a rich man, but his fine estate was one of the first to fall into the enemy's hands. I believe he has never slept in a house since he has commanded the Virginian army, and he invariably declines all offers of hospitality, for fear the person offering it may afterwards get into trouble for having sheltered the Rebel General. The relations between him and Longstreet are quite touching—they are almost always together. Longstreet's corps complain of this sometimes, as they say that they seldom get a chance of detached service, which falls to the lot of Ewell. It is impossible to please Longstreet more than by praising Lee. I believe these two Generals to be as little ambitious and as thoroughly unselfish as any men in the world. Both long for a successful termination of the war, in order that they may retire into obscurity.

Soon after starting we got into a pass in the South mountain, a continuation, I believe, of the Blue Ridge range, which is broken by the Potomac at Harper's Ferry. The scenery through the pass is very fine. The first troops, alongside of whom we rode, belonged to Johnson's division of Ewell's corps. Among them I saw, for the first time, the celebrated "Stonewall" Brigade, formerly commanded by Jackson. In appearance the men differ little from other Confederate soldiers, except, perhaps, that the brigade contains more elderly men and fewer boys. All (except, I think, one regiment) are Virginians. As they have nearly always been on detached duty, few of them knew General Longstreet, except by reputation. Numbers of them asked me whether the General in front was Longstreet; and when I answered in the affirmative, many would run on a hundred yards in order to take a good look at him. This I take to be an immense compliment from any soldier on a long march.

At 2 P.M. firing became distinctly audible in our front, but although it increased as we progressed, it did not seem to be very heavy. A spy who was with us insisted upon there being "a pretty tidy bunch of *blue-bellies* in or near Gettysburg," and he declared that he was in their society three days ago.

After passing Johnson's division, we came up to a Florida Brigade, which is now in Hill's corps; but as it had formerly served under Longstreet, the men knew him well. Some of them (after the General had passed) called out to their comrades, "Look out for work now, boys, for here's the old bull-dog again."

At 3 P.M. we began to meet wounded men coming to the rear, and the number of these soon increased most rapidly, some hobbling alone, others on stretchers carried by the ambulance corps, and others in the ambulance wagons; many of the latter were stripped nearly naked, and displayed very bad wounds. This spectacle, so revolting to a person unaccustomed to such sights, produced no impression whatever upon the advancing troops, who certainly go under fire with the most perfect nonchalance: they show no enthusiasm or excitement, but the most complete indifference. This is the effect of two years' almost uninterrupted fighting.

We now began to meet Yankee prisoners coming to the rear in considerable numbers: many of them were wounded, but they seemed already to be on excellent terms with their captors, with whom they had commenced swapping canteens, tobacco, &c. Among them was a Pennsylvanian colonel, a miserable object from a wound in his face. In answer to a question, I heard one of them remark, with a laugh, "We're pretty nigh whipped already." We next came to a Confederate soldier carrying a Yankee colour, belonging, I think, to a Pennsylvanian regiment, which he told us he had just captured.

At 4:30 P.M. we came in sight of Gettysburg and joined General Lee and General Hill, who were on the top of one of the ridges which form the peculiar feature of the country round Gettysburg. We could see the enemy retreating up one of the opposite ridges, pursued by the Confederates with loud yells. The position into which the enemy had been driven was evidently a strong one. His right appeared to rest on a cemetery, on the top of a high ridge to the right of Gettysburg, as we looked at it.

General Hill now came up and told me he had been very unwell all day, and in fact he looks very delicate. He said he had had two of his divisions engaged, and had driven the enemy four miles into his present position, capturing a great many prisoners, some cannon, and some colours; he said, however, that the Yankees had fought with a determination unusual to them. He pointed out a railway cutting, in which they had made a good stand; also, a field in the centre of which he had seen a man plant the regimental colour, round which the regiment had fought for some time with much obstinacy, and when at last it was obliged to retreat, the colour-bearer retired last of all, turning round every now and then to shake his fist at the advancing rebels. General Hill said he felt quite sorry when he saw this gallant Yankee meet his doom.

General Ewell had come up at 3:30, on the enemy's right (with part of his corps), and completed his discomfiture. General Reynolds, one of the best Yankee generals, was reported killed. Whilst we were talking, a message arrived from General Ewell, requesting Hill to press the enemy in the front, whilst he performed the same operation on his right. The pressure was accordingly applied in a mild degree, but the enemy were too strongly posted, and it was too late in the evening for a regular attack. The town of Gettysburg was now occupied by Ewell, and was full of Yankee dead and wounded. I climbed up a tree in the most commanding place I could find, and could form a pretty good general idea of the enemy's position, although, the tops of the ridges being covered with pine-woods, it was very difficult to see anything of the troops concealed in them. The firing ceased about dark, at which time I rode back with General Longstreet and his Staff to his headquarters at Cashtown, a little village eight miles from Gettysburg. At that time troops were pouring along the road, and were being marched towards the position they are to occupy to-morrow. In the fight to-day nearly 6000 prisoners had been taken, and 10 guns. About 20,000 men must have been on the field on the Confederate side. The enemy had two *corps d'armée* engaged. All the prisoners belong, I think, to the 1st and 11th corps. This day's work is called a "brisk little scurry," and all anticipate a "big battle" to-morrow.

I observed that the artillerymen in charge of the horses dig themselves little holes like graves, throwing up the earth at the upper end. They ensconce themselves in these holes when under fire.

At supper this evening, General Longstreet spoke of the enemy's position as being "very formidable." He also said that they would doubtless intrench themselves strongly during the night. The Staff officers spoke of the battle as a certainty, and the universal feeling in the army was one of profound contempt for an enemy whom they have beaten so constantly, and under so many disadvantages.

RUFUS R. DAWES

The Iron Brigade's Great Battle

Perhaps the most famous unit in the Army of the Potomac was a brigade of hard fighting Westerners from Wisconsin, Michigan and Indiana, called the Iron Brigade for their fierce tenacity in combat. In a term of glorious service which began at the battle of Groveton just preceding Second Bull Run, the Iron Brigade's greatest fight was on McPherson Ridge on the first day of the Battle of Gettysburg on 1 July. This selection was taken from *The Sixth Wisconsin Volunteers* by Colonel Rufus R. Dawes, skipper of the 6th Wisconsin.

When General James S. Wadsworth's division of the first army corps marched toward Gettysburg on the morning of July first, 1863, the sixth Wisconsin was the last regiment in the order of march for the day. The brigade guard, two officers and one hundred men, marched immediately behind us, which accounts for their assignment to the regiment for duty when we became involved in battle. The column moved on the Emmitsburg Road. Three hundred and forty officers and enlisted men marched in the ranks of the regiment. All were in the highest spirits. To make a show in the streets of Gettysburg, I brought our drum corps to the front and had the colors unfurled. The drum major, R.N. Smith, had begun to play "The Campbells are Coming," and the regiment had closed its ranks and swung into the step, when we first heard the cannon of the enemy, firing on the cavalry of General Buford. The troops ahead turned across the fields to the left of Gettysburg, toward the Seminary Ridge. We stopped our music, which had at least done something to arouse the martial spirit of old John Burns, and turned to engage in the sterner duties involved in war. When the head of the regimental column reached the crest of Seminary Ridge, an aide of General Meredith, Lieutenant Gilbert M. Woodward, came on a gallop with the order, "Colonel, form your line, and prepare for action." I turned my horse and gave the necessary orders. The evolution of the line was performed on the double quick, the men loading their muskets as they ran. Hastening forward on a run to get to our position on the left flank of the "Iron Brigade," which, regiment after regiment, *en echelon*, was dashing into the McPherson woods, another aide, Lieutenant Marten, came galloping up and said, "Colonel, General Doubleday is now in command of the first corps, and he directs that you halt your regiment." General John F. Reynolds had been killed, but the fact was not disclosed to us by Lieutenant Marten. I halted the men and directed them to lie down on the ground. The brigade guard now reported to me for duty in the impending battle, and I divided them into two companies of fifty men each, and placed them upon the right and left flanks of the regiment.

The brigade guard comprised twenty men from each of the five regiments of the "Iron Brigade." The two officers, Lieutenant Lloyd G. Harris, sixth Wisconsin, were capable men and excellent leaders. Eighty-one men of the other regiments of the brigade were thus, by the emergency of sudden and unexpected battle, brought into the ranks of our regiment.

The situation on the field of battle of all the troops now engaged, will be made clear by a diagram. Two brigades of each army confronted each other. Archer's brigade opposed the "Iron Brigade," and Joseph R. Davis's brigade opposed Cutler's brigade of Wadsworth's division. Hall's battery was with Cutler's brigade.

Excepting the sixth Wisconsin, the whole of Wadsworth's division was hotly engaged in battle with the enemy. Lieutenant Meredith Jones came with orders from General Doubleday. He said, "General Doubleday directs that you move your regiment at once to the right." I immediately gave the order to move in that direction at a double quick. Captain J.D. Wood came and rode beside me, repeating the order from General Meredith and saying the rebels were "driving Cutler's men." The guns of Hall's battery could be seen driving to the rear, and Cutler's men were manifestly in full retreat.

Across our track we passed some officers carrying the body of our corps commander, General John F. Reynolds. We did not then know that he had been shot.

Suddenly my horse reared and plunged. It did not occur to me that she had been shot. I drew a tight rein and spurred her when she fell heavily on her haunches. I scrambled from the ground, where I had been thrown sprawling, in front of the regiment, and the men gave a hearty cheer. The gallant old mare also struggled to her feet and hobbled toward the rear on three legs. She had been struck in the breast by a minnie ball, which penetrated seventeen inches. For years she carried the bullet, which could be felt under the skin behind the left shoulder blade—but woe to the man who felt it, as her temper had been spoiled. For the rest of the battle I was on foot. The regiment halted at the fence along the Cashtown Turnpike, a long line of yelling Confederates could be seen running forward and firing, and our troops of Cutler's brigade were running back in disorder. The fire of our carefully aimed muskets, resting on the fence rails, striking their flank, soon checked the rebels in their headlong pursuit. The rebel line swayed and bent, and suddenly stopped firing and the men ran into the railroad cut, parallel to the Cashtown Turnpike. I ordered my men to climb over the turnpike fences and advance. I was not aware of the existence of the railroad cut, and at first mistook the maneuver of the enemy for retreat, but was undeceived by the heavy fire which they began at once to pour upon us from their cover in the cut. Captain John Ticknor, always a dashing leader, fell dead while climbing the second fence, and many were struck on the fences, but the line pushed on. When over the fences and in the field, and subjected to an infernal fire, I first saw the ninety-fifth New York regiment coming gallantly into line upon our left. I did not then know or care where they came from, but was rejoiced to see them. Farther to the left was the fourteenth Brooklyn regiment, but I was then ignorant of the fact. Major Edward Pye appeared to be in command of the ninety-fifth New York. Running to the major, I said, "We must charge." The gallant major replied, "Charge it is." "Forward, charge!" was the order I gave, and Major Pye gave the same command. We were receiving a fearfully destructive fire from the hidden enemy. Men who had been shot were leaving the ranks in crowds. With the colors at the advance point, the regiment firmly and hurriedly moved forward, while the whole field behind streamed with men who had been shot, and who were struggling to the rear or sinking in death upon the ground. The only commands I gave, as we advanced, were, "Align on the colors! Close up on the colors! Close up on the colors!" The regiment was being so broken up that this order alone could hold the body together. Meanwhile the colors fell upon the ground several times but were raised again by the heroes of the color guard. Four hundred and twenty men started in the regiment from the turnpike fence, of whom about two hundred and forty reached the railroad cut. Years afterward I found the distance passed over to be one hundred and seventy-five paces. Every officer proved brave, true, and heroic in encouraging the men to breast the deadly storm, but the real impetus was the eager and determined valor of our men who carried muskets in the ranks. I noticed the motions of our "Tall Sycamore," Captain J.H. Marston, who commanded company "E." His long arms were stretched out as if to gather his men together and push them forward. At a crisis he rose to his full height, and he was the tallest man in the regiment, excepting Levi Steadman of company "I," who was killed on this charge. How the rebels happened to miss Captain Marston I cannot comprehend. Second Lieutenant O.B. Chapman, commanding company "C," fell dead while on the charge. The commission of Lieutenant Thomas Kerr as captain of company "D," bears the proud date of July first, 1863—in recognition of his conduct. The rebel color was seen waving defiantly above the edge of the railroad cut. A heroic ambition to capture it took possession of several of our men. Corporal Eggleston, of company "H," sprang forward to seize it, and was shot and mortally wounded. Private Anderson of his company, furious at the killing of his brave young comrade, recked little for the rebel color, but he swung aloft his musket and with a terrific blow split the skull of the rebel who had shot young Eggleston. This soldier was well known in the regiment as "Rocky Mountain Anderson." Lieutenant William N. Remington was shot and severely wounded in the shoulder, while rushing for the color. Into this deadly melee came Corporal Francis A. Waller, who seized and held the rebel battle flag. His name will forever remain upon the historic record, as he received from Congress a medal for this deed.

My notice that we were upon the enemy, was a general cry from our men of: "Throw down your muskets! Down with your muskets!" Running forward through our line of men, I found myself face to face with hundreds of rebels, whom I looked down upon in the railroad cut, which was, where I stood, four feet deep. Adjutant Brooks, equal to the emergency, quickly placed about twenty men across the cut in position to fire through it. I have always congratulated myself upon getting the first word. I shouted: "Where is the colonel of this regiment?" An officer in gray, with stars on his collar, who stood among the men in the cut, said: "Who are you?" I said: "I command this regiment. Surrender, or I will fire." The officer replied not a word, but promptly handed me his sword, and his men, who still held them, threw down their muskets. The coolness, self-possession, and discipline which held back our men from pouring in a general volley saved a hundred lives of the enemy, and as my mind goes back to the fearful excitement of the moment, I marvel at it. The fighting around the rebel colors had not ceased when this surrender took place. I took the sword. It would have been the handsome thing to say, "Keep your sword, sir," but I was new to such occasions, and when six other officers came up and handed me their swords, I took them also. I held this awkward bundle in my arms until relieved by Adjutant Brooks. I directed the officer in command, Major John A. Blair, of the second Mississippi regiment, to have his men fall in without arms. He gave the command, and his men, (seven officers and two hundred and twenty-five enlisted men) obeyed: To Major John F. Hauser I assigned the duty of marching this body to the provost-guard. Lieutenant William Goltermann of Company "F," volunteered to command a line of volunteer skirmishers, which I called for as soon as Major Hauser moved his prisoners away. This line of men took possession of the ridge toward the enemy and guarded against a surprise by a return of the enemy to attack. One gun of Hall's second Maine battery stood upon the field before the railroad cut and between the hostile lines. After the surrender, Captain Rollin P. Converse took men enough for the purpose and pulled this gun to the turnpike, where Captain Hall took it again in charge.

Corporal Frank Asbury Waller brought me the captured battle flag. It was the flag of the second Mississippi Volunteers, one of the oldest and most distinguished regiments in the Confederate army. It belonged to the brigade commanded by Joseph R. Davis, the nephew of Jefferson Davis. It is a rule in battle not to allow sound men to leave the ranks. Sergeant William Evans of company "H," a brave and true man, had been severely wounded in the thighs. He was obliged to use two muskets as crutches. To him I intrusted the battle-flag, and I took it from the staff and wrapped it around his body.

Adjutant E.P. Brooks buckled on one of the captured swords, and he still retains it, but the other six were given to a wounded man and delivered to our chief surgeon, A.W. Preston. The enemy, when they took the town, captured the hospital and the swords. No discredit to the doctor is implied, as his hands were full of work with wounded men.

After this capture of prisoners in the railroad cut there was a lull in the battle. Our comrades of the "Iron Brigade," who had charged so brilliantly into the McPherson woods, had been completely victorious. They had routed Archer's brigade, capturing its commander and many of its men, and then they had changed front to move to the relief of Cutler's brigade, but our charge upon the railroad cut, and its success, obviated that necessity. By this charge Joseph R. Davis' brigade was scattered or captured. We had fairly defeated, upon an open field, a superior force of the veterans of the army of General Lee. It was a short, sharp, and desperate fight, but the honors were easily with the boys in blue.

While the regiment is being reorganized, let us follow Sergeant William Evans. Weak and faint from loss of blood, he painfully hobbled to Gettysburg, and became exhausted in the street. Brave and faithful friends came to his relief. Two young women assisted this wounded soldier into their home, and placed him upon a bed. The Union troops soon began to retreat in confusion through the town, and the cheers of the victorious enemy could be plainly heard. Evans begged of his friends to hide the rebel flag. They cut a hole in the bed-tick beneath him, thrust in the flag, and sewed up the rent. The flag was thus safely concealed until the enemy retreated from Gettysburg, and on the morning of July 4th Evans brought his precious trophy to Culp's Hill and gave it to me there.

In his official report General Doubleday says that when Cutler's regiments were overpowered and driven back, "the moment was a critical one, involving the defeat, perhaps the utter rout of our forces." Later in the day we marched through the railroad cut, and about one thousand muskets lay in the bottom of it. Only one regiment suffered as an organization, and that was the second Mississippi Volunteers. The ninety-fifth New York took prisoners, as did also the fourteenth Brooklyn. All the troops in the railroad cut threw down their muskets, and the men either surrendered themselves, or ran away out of the other end of the cut.

We next advanced, by order of General Wadsworth, to the ridge west of the Seminary Ridge. Here we encountered a heavy line of rebel skirmishers, upon whom we opened fire, and drove them into Willoughby Run. But the enemy turned upon us the fire of six pieces of artillery in position just south of the Cashtown Turnpike beyond Willoughby Run, and beyond the houses in the picture. The shell flew over us and burst around us so thickly that I was obliged to order the men to lie upon the ground under the brow of the ridge. The "Iron Brigade" was in the McPherson Woods, half a mile to our left. The space between us and that brigade was occupied by Colonel Roy Stone's Pennsylvania Bucktails. General Lysander Cutler's brigade was now upon our right. This was our position when the general attack was made by the rebel army corps of Hill and Ewell combined, at half past one o'clock in the afternoon. The first brunt of it struck the gallant brigade of Bucktails. They were fighting on Pennsylvania soil. Their conduct was more than heroic, it was glorious. I can not describe the charges and counter-charges which took place, but we all saw the banner of the one hundred and forty-ninth Pennsylvania planted in the ground and waving between the hostile lines of battle, while the desperate fight went on. This color was taken by the enemy.

Under pressure of the battle, the whole line of Union troops fell back to the Seminary Ridge. I could plainly see the entire movement. I saw Captain Hollon Richardson who acted as an aide to Colonel W.W. Robinson, now in command of the "Iron Brigade," carrying on his horse and waving aloft, the colors of the seventh Wisconsin, as the proud brigade slowly drew back from the McPherson Woods to the Seminary Ridge. We received no orders. Being a detached regiment it is likely that we were overlooked. The enemy (Ewell's corps) advanced so that the low ground between us and the Seminary Ridge in our rear was swept by their fire. It would cost many lives to march in line of battle through this fire. I adopted the tactics of the rebels earlier in the day, and ordered my men to run into the railroad cut. Then instructing the men to follow in single file, I led the way, as fast as I could run, from this cut to the cut in the Seminary Ridge. About a cart load of dirt was ploughed over us by the rebel shell, but otherwise not a man was struck. The ranks were promptly reformed, and we marched into the woods on the Seminary Ridge to the same position from which we had advanced. The whole first army corps was now in line of battle on the Seminary Ridge, and here that grand body of veteran soldiers made a heroic effort to stay the overwhelming tide that swept against them.

Battery "B," fourth U.S. artillery, under command of Lieutenant James Stewart, came up, and General Wadsworth directed me to support it with my regiment. James Stewart was as brave and efficient a man as ever fought upon a battle field. His battery was manned by men detailed from the volunteers, many of them from our brigade. And now came the grand advance of the enemy. During this time the attack was progressing, I stood among the guns of battery "B." Along the Seminary Ridge, flat upon their bellies, lay mixed up together in one line of battle, the "Iron Brigade" and Roy Stone's "Bucktails." For a mile up and down the open fields in front, the splendid lines of the veterans of the army of Northern Virginia swept down upon us. Their bearing was magnificent. They maintained their alignments with great precision. In many cases the colors of regiments were advanced several paces in front of the line. Stewart fired shell until they appeared on the ridge east of Willoughby Run; when on this ridge they came forward with a rush. The musketry burst from the Seminary Ridge, every shot fired with care, and Stewart's men, with the regularity of a machine, worked their guns upon the enemy. The rebels came half way down the opposite slope, wavered, began to fire, then to scatter and then to run, and how our men did yell, "Come on, Johnny! come on!" Falling back over the ridge they came on again more cautiously, and pouring upon us from the start a steady fire of deadly musketry. This killed Stewart's men and horses in great numbers, but did not seem to check his fire.

Lieutenant Clayton E. Rogers, aide on General Wadsworth's staff, came riding rapidly to me. Leaning over from his horse, he said very quietly: "The orders, colonel, are to retreat beyond the town. Hold your men together." I was astonished. The cheers of defiance along the line of the first corps, on Seminary Ridge, had scarcely died away. But a glance over the field to our right and rear was sufficient. There the troops of the eleventh corps appeared in full retreat, and long lines of Confederates, with fluttering banners and shining steel, were sweeping forward in pursuit of them without let or hindrance. It was a close race which could reach Gettysburg first, ourselves, or the rebel troops of Ewell's corps, who pursued our eleventh corps. Facing the regiment to the rear, I marched in line of battle over the open fields toward the town. We were north of the railroad, and our direction separated us from other regiments of our corps. If we had desired to attack Ewell's twenty thousand men with our two hundred, we could not have moved more directly toward them. We knew nothing about a Cemetery Hill. We could see only that the oncoming lines of the enemy were encircling us in a horseshoe. But with the flag of the Union and of Wisconsin held aloft, the little regiment marched firmly and steadily. As we approached the town, the buildings of the Pennsylvania College screened us from the view of the enemy. We could now see that our troops were retreating in a direction at right angles to our line of march. We reached a street extending through Gettysburg from the college to Cemetery Hill, and crossed it. We were now faced by the enemy, and I turned the course toward the Cemetery Hill, although then unconscious of the fact. The first cross street was swept by the musketry fire of the enemy. There was a close board fence, inclosing a barn-yard, on the opposite side of the street. A board or two off from the fence made what the men called a "hog-hole." Instructing the regiment to follow in single file on the run, I took a color, ran across the street, and jumped through this opening in the fence. Officers and men followed rapidly. Taking position at the fence, when any man obstructed the passage-way through it, I jerked him away without ceremony or apology, the object being to keep the track clear for those yet to come. Two men were shot in this street crossing. The regiment was reformed in the barn-yard, and I marched back again to the street leading from the Pennsylvania College to the Cemetery Hill. To understand why the street was crossed in the manner described, it should be remembered that men running at full speed, scattered in single file, were safer from the fire of the enemy than if marching in a compact body. By going into the inclosure, the regiment came together, to be at once formed into compact order. It was in compliance with the order, to keep my men together. The weather was sultry. The sweat steamed from the faces of the men. There was not a drop of water in the canteens, and there had been none for hours. The streets were jammed with crowds of retreating soldiers, and with ambulances, artillery, and wagons. The cellars were crowded with men, sound in body, but craven in spirit, who had gone there to surrender. I saw no men wearing badges of the first army corps in this disgraceful company. In one case, these miscreants, mistaking us for the rebels, cried out from the cellar, "Don't fire, Johnny, we'll surrender." These surroundings were depressing to my hot and thirsty men. Finding the street blocked, I formed my men in two lines across it. The rebels began to fire on us from houses and cross-lots. Here came to us a friend in need. It was an old citizen with two buckets of fresh water. The inestimable value of this cup of cold water to those true, unyielding soldiers, I would that our old friend could know.

After this drink, in response to my call, the men gave three cheers for the good and glorious cause for which we stood in battle. The enemy fired on us sharply, and the men returned their fire, shooting wherever the enemy appeared. This firing had a good effect. It cleared the street of stragglers in short order. The way being open I marched again toward the Cemetery Hill. The enemy did not pursue; they had found it dangerous business. We hurried along, not knowing certainly that we might not be marching into the clutches of the enemy. But the colors of the Union, floating over a well ordered line of men in blue, who were arrayed along the slope of Cemetery Hill, became visible. This was the seventy-third Ohio, of Steinwehr's division of the eleventh army corps. With swifter steps we now pressed on up the hill, and, passing in through the ranks open to receive us, officers and men threw themselves in a state of almost perfect exhaustion on the green grass and the graves of the cemetery. The condition of affairs on Cemetery Hill at this time has been a subject of discussion. If fresh troops had attacked us then, we unquestionably would have fared badly. The troops were scattered over the hill in much disorder, while a stream of stragglers and wounded men pushed along the Baltimore Turnpike toward the rear. But this perilous condition of affairs was of short duration. There was no appearance of panic on the Cemetery Hill. After a short breathing spell my men again promptly responded to the order to "fall in." Lieutenant Rogers brought us orders from General Wadsworth, to join our own brigade, which had been sent to occupy Culp's Hill. As we marched toward the hill our regimental wagon joined us. In the wagon were a dozen spades and shovels. Taking our place on the right of the line of the brigade, I ordered the regiment to intrench. The men worked with great energy. A man would dig with all his strength till out of breath, when another would seize the spade and push on the work. There were no orders to construct these breastworks, but the situation plainly dictated their necessity. The men now lay down to rest after the arduous labors of this great and terrible day.

Sad and solemn reflections possessed, at least, the writer of these papers. Our dead lay unburied and beyond our sight or reach. Our wounded were in the hands of the enemy. Our bravest and best were numbered with them. Of eighteen hundred men who marched with the splendid brigade in the morning, but seven hundred were here. More than one thousand men had been shot. There was to us a terrible reality in the figures which represent our loss. We had been driven, also, by the enemy, and the shadow of defeat seemed to be hanging over us. But that afternoon, under the burning sun and through the stifling clouds of dust, the Army of the Potomac had marched to the sound of our cannon. We had lost the ground on which we had fought, we had lost our commander and our comrades, but our fight had held the Cemetery Hill and forced the decision for history that the crowning battle of the war should be at Gettysburg.

It is a troubled and dreamy sleep at best that comes to the soldier on a battle field. About one o'clock at night we had a great alarm. A man in the seventh Indiana regiment, next on right, cried so loudly in his sleep that he aroused all the troops in the vicinity. Springing up, half bewildered, I ordered my regiment to "fall in," and a heavy fire of musketry broke out from along the whole line of men. At three o'clock in the morning, according to orders, the men were aroused. The morning of the second day found us lying quietly in our breastworks near the summit of Culp's Hill. We were in the shade of some fine oak trees, and enjoyed an excellent view of nearly the whole battle field. Our situation would have been delightful, and our rest in the cool shade would have been refreshing, if it had not been for the crack, crack, of the deadly sharp-shooters on the rebel skirmish line. Owing, probably, to the crooked line of our army, the shots came from all directions, and the peculiarly mournful wail of the spent bullet was constantly heard.

Chapter VIII

THE SECOND DAY OF SLAUGHTER

On 1 July, Confederates had managed to drive the Federals into a fishhook like formation on and around Cemetery Ridge. Though outnumbered and facing an enemy holding a strong position, Lee elected to launch a brutal attack on Meade's left the next day. His forces badly mangled the enemy, but the Confederate general found to his irritation that the Army of the Potomac refused to budge and almost patiently awaited his next move.

JAMES LONGSTREET

Gettysburg—The Second Day

Another controversial aspect of the Battle of Gettysburg was General James Longstreet's handling of his forces during the massive conflict. Because he was against the idea of engaging the Army of the Potomac at Gettysburg, Longstreet disagreed with his commander over the viability of making an assault against the overpowering numbers of entrenched Federals. Lee's lieutenant, who was charged to assail the unsteady Federal left, has often been harshly criticized for his delays in getting his troops into position and for launching a tardy attack on the enemy. Longstreet's view of the second day of the battle is taken from his epic memoirs of the war, *From Manassas to Appomattox.*

The stars were shining brightly on the morning of the 2d when I reported at General Lee's head-quarters and asked for orders. After a time Generals McLaws and Hood, with their staffs, rode up, and at sunrise their commands filed off the road to the right and rested. The Washington Artillery was with them, and about nine o'clock, after an all-night march, Alexander's batteries were up as far as Willoughby's Run, where he parked and fed, and rode to head-quarters to report.

As indicated by these movements, General Lee was not ready with his plans. He had not heard from his cavalry, nor of the movements of the enemy further than the information from a despatch captured during the night, that the Fifth Corps was in camp about five miles from Gettysburg, and the Twelfth Corps was reported near Culp's Hill. As soon as it was light enough to see, however, the enemy was found in position on his formidable heights awaiting us.

The result of efforts during the night and early morning to secure Culp's Hill had not been reported, and General Lee sent Colonel Venable of his staff to confer with the commander of the Second Corps as to opportunity to make the battle by his left. He was still in doubt whether it would be better to move to his far-off right. About nine o'clock he rode to his left to be assured of the position there, and of the general temper of affairs in that quarter. After viewing the field, he held conference with the corps and division commanders. They preferred to accept his judgment and orders, except General Early, who claimed to have learned of the topographical features of the country during his march towards York, and recommended the right of the line as the point at which strong battle should be made. About ten o'clock General Lee returned to his headquarters, but his engineer who had been sent to reconnoitre on his right had not come back. To be at hand for orders, I remained with the troops at his head-quarters. The infantry had arms stacked; the artillery was at rest.

The enemy occupied the commanding heights of the city cemetery, from which point, in irregular grade, the ridge slopes southward two miles and a half to a bold outcropping height of three hundred feet called Little Round Top, and farther south half a mile ends in the greater elevation called Round Top. The former is covered from base to top by formidable boulders. From the cemetery to Little Round Top was the long main front of General Meade's position. At the cemetery his line turned to the northeast and east and southeast in an elliptical curve, with his right on Culp's Hill.

At an early hour of the 2d the Union army was posted: the Twelfth Corps at Culp's Hill, extending its left to Wadsworth's division of the First; on Wadsworth's left the Eleventh Corps; on the left of the Eleventh the other troops of the First; on their left the Second, and left of that to Little Round Top the Third Corps; the Fifth Corps stood in reserve across the bend from the right of the Twelfth to the left of the Second Corps. Thus there was formed a field of tremendous power upon a convex curve, which gave the benefit of rapid concentration at any point or points. The natural defenses had been improved during the night and early morning. The Sixth Corps was marching from Manchester, twenty-two miles from Gettysburg. Its first order, received near Manchester before night of the 1st, was to march for Taneytown, but after passing the Baltimore pike the orders were changed, directing a prompt march to Gettysburg. The march has been variously estimated from thirty to thirty-five miles, but the distance from Manchester *via* Taneytown to Gettysburg is only twenty-nine miles, and as the ground for which the corps marched was three miles east of Gettysburg, the march would have been only twenty-six miles *via* Taneytown; as the corps marched back and took the Baltimore pike, some distance must have been saved. It was on the field at three o'clock of the afternoon,—the Union cavalry under General Pleasonton in reach.

The Confederate left was covering the north and east curve of the enemy's line, Johnson's division near Culp's Hill, Early's and Rodes's extending the line to the right through Gettysburg; Pender's division on the right of Rodes's; the other divisions of the Third Corps resting on Seminary Ridge, with McLaws's division and Hood's three brigades near general headquarters; Pickett's brigades and Law's of Hood's division at Chambersburg and New Guilford, twenty-two and twenty-four miles away. Law had received orders to join his division, and was on the march. The cavalry was not yet heard from. The line so extended and twisted about the rough ground that concentration at any point was not possible.

It was some little time after General Lee's return from his ride to the left before he received the reports of the reconnoissance ordered from his centre to his right. His mind, previously settled to the purpose to fight where the enemy stood, now accepted the explicit plan of making the opening on his right, and to have the engagement general. He ordered the commander of the Third Corps to extend the centre by Anderson's division, McLaws's and Hood's divisions to extend the deployment to his right. Heth's division of the Third was drawn nearer the front, and notice of his plans was sent the commander of the Second Corps.

At the intimation that the battle would be opened on the right by part of the First Corps, Colonel Alexander was asked to act as director of artillery, and sent to view the field in time to assign the batteries as they were up. It was eleven o'clock when General Lee's order was issued, but he had ordered Law's brigade to its division, and a wait of thirty minutes was necessary for it to get up. Law had received his orders at three in the morning, and had marched twenty-three miles. The battle-ground was still five miles off by the route of march, but Law completed his march of twenty-eight miles in eleven hours,—the best marching done in either army to reach the field of Gettysburg.

The battle was to be opened on the right by two divisions of the First Corps, supported on their left by four of the brigades of Anderson's division; the opening to be promptly followed on Lee's left by the Second Corps, and continued to real attack if the opportunity occurred; the Third (centre) Corps to move to severe threatening and take advantage of opportunity to attack; the movements of the Second and Third Corps to be prompt, and in close, severe cooperation, so as to prevent concentration against the battle of the right. The little cavalry that was with the army was kept on the extreme left. Not so much as one trooper was sent us.

General Lee ordered his reconnoitring officer to lead the troops of the First Corps and conduct them by a route concealed from view of the enemy. As I was relieved for the time from the march, I rode near the middle of the line. General Lee rode with me a mile or more. General Anderson marched by a route nearer the enemy's line, and was discovered by General Sickles, who commanded the Third Corps, the left of the Union line. A little uncomfortable at his retired position, and seeing that the battle was forming against him, General Sickles thought to put the Third Maine Regiment and the Berdan Sharpshooters on outpost in a bold woodland cover, to develop somewhat of the approaching battle, and presently threw his corps forward as far as the Peach Orchard, half a mile forward of the position assigned to it in the general line. The Tenth Alabama Regiment was sent against the outpost guard, and, reinforced by the Eleventh Regiment, drove it back, and Anderson's division found its place in proper line.

General Birney's account of the affair at the outpost puts it at twelve o'clock, and the signal accounts, the only papers dated on the field, reported, "The enemy's skirmishers advancing from the west one mile from here—11.45." And presently, "The rebels are in force; our skirmishers give way—12.55." There is no room for doubt of the accuracy of these reports, which go to show that it was one o'clock in the afternoon when the Third Corps, upon which the First Corps was to form, was in position.

Under the conduct of the reconnoitring officer, our march seemed slow—there were some halts and countermarches. To save time, I ordered the rear division to double on the front, and we were near the affair of Anderson's regiments with the outpost guard of Sickles. Anderson's division deployed,—Wilcox's, Perry's, Wright's, Posey's, and Mahone's brigades from right to left.

General Hood was ordered to send his select scouts in advance, to go through the woodlands and act as vedettes, in the absence of cavalry, and give information of the enemy, if there. The double line marched up the slope and deployed,—McLaws on the right of Anderson, Hood's division on his right, McLaws near the crest of the plateau in front of the Peach Orchard, Hood spreading and enveloping Sickles's left. The former was readily adjusted to ground from which to advance or defend. Hood's front was very rugged, with no field for artillery, and very rough for advance of infantry. As soon as he passed the Emmitsburg road, he sent to report of the great advantage of moving on by his right around to the enemy's rear. His scouting parties had reported that there was nothing between them and the enemy's trains. He was told that the move to the right had been proposed the day before and rejected; that General Lee's orders were to guide my left by the Emmitsburg road.

In our immediate front were the divisions of the Third Corps under Generals Humphreys and Birney, from right to left, with orders for supports of the flanks by divisions of the Second and Fifth Corps. The ground on the left of Birney's division was so broken and obstructed by boulders that his left was dropped off to the rear, forming a broken line. In rear of the enemy, and between his lines and Little Round Top, was a very rough elevation of eighty feet formed by upheavals that left open passage deep down Devil's Den. Smith's battery was on Birney's left, Winslow's between the right and next brigade. Other batteries in position were Clark's, Ames's, Randolph's, Seeley's, and Turnbull's.

As McLaws's division came up on line, Barksdale's brigade was in front of a battery about six hundred yards off. He appealed for permission to charge and capture it, but was told to wait. On his right was Kershaw's brigade, the brigades of Semmes and Wofford on the second line. Hood's division was in two lines,—Law's and Robertson's brigades in front, G.T. Anderson's and Benning's in the second line. The batteries were with the divisions,—four to the division. One of G.T. Anderson's regiments was put on picket down the Emmitsburg road.

General Hood appealed again and again for the move to the right, but, to give more confidence to his attack, he was reminded that the move to the right had been carefully considered by our chief and rejected in favor of his present orders.

The opportunity for our right was in the air. General Halleck saw it from Washington. General Meade saw and was apprehensive of it. Even General Pendleton refers to it in favorable mention in his official report. Failing to adopt it, General Lee should have gone with us to his right. He had seen and carefully examined the left of his line, and only gave us a guide to show the way to the right, leaving the battle to be adjusted to formidable and difficult grounds without his assistance. If he had been with us, General Hood's messengers could have been referred to general headquarters, but to delay and send messengers five miles in favor of a move that he had rejected would have been contumacious. The opportunity was with the Confederates from the assembling on Cemetery Hill. It was inviting of their preconceived plans. It was the object of and excuse for the invasion as a substitute for more direct efforts for the relief of Vicksburg. Confederate writers and talkers claim that General Meade could have escaped without making aggressive battle, but that is equivalent to confession of the inertia that failed to grasp the opportunity.

Beaten in the battle of the 1st, dislodged of position, and outgeneralled, the Union army would have felt the want of spirit and confidence important to aggressive battle; but the call was in the hands of the Confederates, and these circumstances would have made their work more facile, while the Union commander would have felt the call to save his capital most imperative. Even as events passed it was thought helpful to the Union side to give out the report that General McClellan was at hand and would command the army.

Four of the brigades of Anderson's division were ordered to advance in echelon in support of my left.

At three o'clock the artillery was ordered to open practice. General Meade was then with General Sickles discussing the feasibility of withdrawing his corps to the position to which it was originally assigned, but the opening admonished him that it was too late. He had just sent a cipher telegram to inform General Halleck, commander-in-chief, that in the event of his having no opportunity to attack, and should he find the Confederates moving to interpose between him and Washington, he would fall back on his supplies at Westminster. But my right division was then nearer to Westminster, and our scouting parties of infantry were within rifle range of the road leading to that point and to Washington. So it would have been convenient, after holding our threatening attitude till night, to march across his line at dark, in time to draw other troops to close connection before the next morning.

Prompt to the order the combat opened, followed by artillery of the other corps, and our artillerists measured up to the better metal of the enemy by vigilant work. Hood's lines were not yet ready. After a little practice by the artillery, he was properly adjusted and ordered to bear down upon the enemy's left, but he was not prompt, and the order was repeated before he would strike down.

In his usual gallant style he led his troops through the rocky vastnesses against the strong lines of his earnest adversary, and encountered battle that called for all of his power and skill. The enemy was tenacious of his strong ground; his skillfully-handled batteries swept through the passes between the rocks; the more deadly fire of infantry concentrated as our men bore upon the angle of the enemy's line and stemmed the fiercest onset, until it became necessary to shorten their work by a desperate charge. This pressing struggle and the cross-fire of our batteries broke in the salient angle, but the thickening fire, as the angle was pressed back, hurt Hood's left and held him in steady fight. His right brigade was drawn towards Round Top by the heavy fire pouring from that quarter, Benning's brigade was pressed to the thickening line at the angle, and G.T. Anderson's was put in support of the battle growing against Hood's right.

I rode to McLaws, found him ready for his opportunity, and Barksdale chafing in his wait for the order to seize the battery in his front. Kershaw's brigade of his right first advanced and struck near the angle of the enemy's line where his forces were gathering strength. After additional caution to hold his ranks closed, McLaws ordered Barksdale in. With glorious bearing he sprang to his work, overriding obstacles and dangers. Without a pause to deliver a shot, he had the battery. Kershaw, joined by Semmes's brigade, responded, and Hood's men, feeling the impulsion of relief, resumed their bold fight, and presently the enemy's line was broken through its length. But his well-seasoned troops knew how to utilize the advantage of their grounds and put back their dreadful fires from rocks, depressions, and stone fences, as they went for shelter about Little Round Top.

That point had not been occupied by the enemy, nor marked as an important feature of the field. The broken ranks sought shelter under its rocks and defiles as birds fly to cover. General Hood fell seriously hurt, and General Law succeeded to command of the division, but the well-seasoned troops were not in need of a close guiding hand. The battle was on, and they knew how to press its hottest contention.

General Warren, chief engineer of the Federal army, was sent at the critical moment to Little Round Top, and found that it was the citadel of the field. He called for troops to occupy it. The Fifth Corps (Sykes's) was hurried to him, and General Hancock sent him Caldwell's division of the Second Corps. At the Brick House, away from his right, General Sickles had a detachment that had been reinforced by General Hancock. This fire drew Anderson's brigade of direction (Wilcox) a little off from support of Barksdale's left. General Humphreys, seeing the opportunity, rallied such of his troops as he could, and, reinforced by Hays's division (Willard's brigade) of Hancock's corps, came against Barksdale's flank, but the latter moved bravely on, the guiding spirit of the battle. Wright's Georgia and Perry's Florida brigades were drawn in behind Wilcox and thrown against Humphreys, pushing him off and breaking him up.

The fighting had by this time become tremendous, and brave men and officers were stricken by hundreds. Posey and Wilcox dislodged the forces about the Brick House.

General Sickles was desperately wounded!

General Willard was dead!

General Semmes, of McLaws's division, was mortally wounded!

Our left relieved, the brigades of Anderson's division moved on with Barksdale's, passed the swale, and moved up the slope. Caldwell's division, and presently those of Ayres and Barnes of the Fifth Corps, met and held our strongest battle. While thus engaged, General Sykes succeeded in putting Vincent's and Weed's brigades and Hazlett's battery on the summit of Little Round Top, but presently we overreached Caldwell's division, broke it off, and pushed it from the field. Of his brigade commanders, Zook was killed, and Brooke and Cross were wounded, the latter mortally. General Hancock reported sixty percent of his men lost. On our side, Barksdale was down dying, and G.T. Anderson wounded.

We had carried Devil's Den, were at the Round Tops and the Wheat-Field, but Ayres's division of regulars and Barnes's division were holding us in equal battle. The struggle throughout the field seemed at its tension. The brigades of R.H. Anderson's division could hold off other troops of Hancock's, but were not strong enough to step to the enemy's lines. When Caldwell's division was pushed away Ayres's flank and the gorge at Little Round Top were only covered by a sharp line of picket men behind the boulders. If we could drive in the sharp-shooters and strike Ayres's flank to advantage, we could dislodge his and Barnes's divisions, occupy the gorge behind Sykes's brigades on Round Top, force them to retreat, and lift our desperate fighters to the summit. I had one brigade—Wofford's—that had not been engaged in the hottest battle. To urge the troops to their reserve power in the precious moments, I rode with Wofford. The rugged field, the rough plunge of artillery fire, and the piercing musket-shots delayed somewhat the march, but Alexander dashed up with his batteries and gave new spirit to the worn infantry ranks. By a fortunate strike upon Ayres's flank we broke his line and pushed him and Barnes so closely that they were obliged to use most strenuous efforts to get away without losing in prisoners as well as their killed and wounded. We gained the Wheat-Field, and were so close upon the gorge that our artillery could no longer venture their fire into it. We were on Little Round Top grappling for the crowning point. The brigade commanders there, Vincent and Weed, were killed, also the battery commander, Hazlett, and others, but their troops were holding to their work as firmly as the mighty boulders that helped them. General Meade thought that the Confederate army was working on my part of the field. He led some regiments of the Twelfth Corps and posted them against us, called a division of Newton's corps (First) from beyond Hancock's, and sent Crawford's division, the last of the Fifth Corps, splitting through the gorge, forming solid lines, in places behind stone fences, and making steady battle, as veterans fresh in action know so well how to make. While Meade's lines were growing my men were dropping; we had no others to call to their aid, and the weight against us was too heavy to carry. The extreme left of our lines was only about a mile from us across the enemy's concentric position, which brought us within hearing of that battle, if engaged, and near enough to feel its swell, but nothing was heard or felt but the clear ring of the enemy's fresh metal as he came against us. No other part of our army had engaged! My seventeen thousand against the Army of the Potomac! The sun was down, and with it went down the severe battle. I ordered recall of the troops to the line of Plum Run andDevil's Den, leaving picket lines near the foot of the Round Tops. My loss was about six thousand, Meade's between twelve and fourteen thousand; but his loss in general and field officers was frightful. When General Humphreys, who succeeded to Barksdale's brigade, was called back to the new line, he thought there was some mistake in the orders, and only withdrew as far as a captured battery, and when the order was repeated, retired under protest.

General Stuart came down from Carlisle with his column of cavalry late in the afternoon of the 2d. As he approached he met a cavalry force of the enemy moving towards the Confederate left rear, and was successful in arresting it. He was posted with Jenkins' three thousand cavalry on the Confederate left.

Notwithstanding the supreme order of the day for general battle, and the reinforcement of the cavalry on our left, the Second and Third Corps remained idle during all of the severe battle of the Confederate right, except the artillery, and the part of that on the extreme left was only in practice long enough to feel the superior metal of the enemy, when it retired, leaving a battery of four guns in position. General Early failed to even form his division in battle order, leaving a brigade in position remote from the line, and sending, later, another to be near Stuart's cavalry. The latter returned, however, before night.

At eight o'clock in the evening the division on our extreme left, E. Johnson's, advanced. The brigades were J.M. Jones's, Nicholls's, Steuart's, and Walker's. Walker's was detached, as they moved, to look for a detachment of the enemy reported threatening the far away left. When the three brigades crossed Rock Creek it was night. The enemy's line to be assaulted was occupied by Greene's brigade of the Twelfth Corps. It was reinforced by three regiments of Wadsworth's division and three from the Eleventh Corps. After brave attack and defense, part of the line was carried, when the fight, after a severe fusillade between the infantry lines, quieted, and Walker's brigade returned to the division. Part of the enemy's trenches, east of the point attacked (across a swale), vacated when the corps moved over to the left, General Johnson failed to occupy.

Before this, General Rodes discovered that the enemy, in front of his division, was drawing off his artillery and infantry to my battle of the right, and suggested to General Early that the moment had come for the divisions to attack, and drew his forces from entanglements about the streets to be ready. After E. Johnson's fight on our extreme left, General Early ordered two brigades under General Harry T. Hays to attack. Hays had with his Louisiana brigade Hoke's North Carolina brigade under Colonel Avery. He made as gallant a fight as was ever made. Mounting to the top of the hill, he captured a battery, and pushed on in brave order, taking some prisoners and colors, until he discovered that his two brigades were advancing in a night affair against a grand army, when he found that he was fortunate in having night to cover his weakness, and withdrew. The gallant Colonel Avery, mortally wounded and dying, wrote on a slip of paper, *"Tell father that I died with my face to the enemy."* When Rodes was prepared, Hays had retired, and the former did not see that it was part of the order for general engagement to put his division in night attack that could not be supported.

Thus the general engagement of the day was dwarfed into the battle of the right at three o'clock, that on the left at eight by a single division, and that nearer the centre at nine o'clock by two brigades.

There was a man on the left of the line who did not care to make the battle win. He knew where it was, had viewed it from its earliest formation, had orders for his part in it, but so withheld part of his command from it as to make co-operative concert of action impracticable. He had a pruriency for the honors of the field of Mars, was eloquent, before the fires of the bivouac and his chief, of the glory of war's gory shield; but when its envied laurels were dipping to the grasp, when the heavy field called for bloody work, he found the placid horizon, far and away beyond the cavalry, more lovely and inviting. He wanted command of the Second Corps, and, succeeding to it, held the honored position until General Lee found, at last, that he must dismiss him from field service.

General Lee ordered Johnson's division of his left, occupying part of the enemy's trenches about Culp's Hill, to be reinforced during the night of the 2d by two brigades of Rodes's division and one of Early's division. Why the other brigades of those divisions were not sent does not appear, but it does appear that there was a place for them on Johnson's left, in the trenches that were vacated by the Federal Twelfth Corps when called over to reinforce the battle of Meade's left. Culp's Hill bore the same relations to the enemy's right as Little Round Top did to his left. General Fitzhugh Lee quotes evidence from General Meade that had Culp's Hill been occupied, in force, by Confederates, it would have compelled the withdrawal of the Federal troops.

General Meade, after the battle of his left, ordered the divisions of his Twelfth Corps back to their trenches, to recover the parts occupied by the Confederate left. It was night when the First Division approached. General Ruger, commanding, thought to feel his way through the dark by a line of skirmishers. He found the east end of his trenches, across the swale, unoccupied, and took possession. Pressing his adventure, he found the main line of his works occupied by the Confederates in force, and disposed his command to wait for daylight. The Second Division came during the night, when General Williams, commanding the corps, posted it on the left of the First, and the division commanders ordered batteries in proper positions.

During the night, General Meade held a council, which decided to fight it out. So it began to look as if the vicissitudes of the day had so worked as to call General Meade from defensive to aggressive battle for Culp's Hill. But the Confederates failed to see the opportunity and force the issue as it was presented.

In General Meade's evidence before the Committee on the Conduct of the War, he puts his losses of the first and second days at twenty thousand and assigns two-thirds of these to the battle of the 2d. As the fighting against the three brigades of our left after night, and two brigades, later in the night, from our centre, could not have been very severe, I claim that his loss in the battle of his left was from twelve to fourteen thousand.

As events of the battle of the 2d passed, it seems fair to claim that with Pickett's brigades present at the moment of Wofford's advance for the gorge at Little Round Top, we could have had it before Crawford was there.

Under ordinary circumstances this account of the second day, made from the records, would be complete and conclusive; but the battle of Gettysburg, which may be called the epitome of the war, has been the subject of many contentions of words. Knights of the quill have consumed many of their peaceful hours in publishing, through books, periodicals, and newspapers, their plans for the battle, endeavoring to forestall the records and to find a scapegoat, and their representations may be given, though they do not deserve it, a word of reply.

General W. N. Pendleton led off when making a lecturing tour through the South for a memorial church for General Lee. He claims that he made a reconnoissance on the afternoon of the 1st of July, and that upon his reporting it, General Lee ordered General Longstreet to attack at sunrise the next day. He did not venture to charge that the Second and Third Corps, that were on the field and had had a good night's rest, were part of the command ordered for the early battle, for the commanders, both Virginians, and not under the political ban, could have brought confusing evidence against him; nor did he intend to put General Lee in the anomalous position, inferentially, of ordering part of the First Corps— that should march through the night and all night—to make the battle alone. The point of battle was east of the Emmitsburg road; to find it, it was necessary to cross that road, but General Sickles was moving part of his corps over the road during that afternoon, and rested there the latter part of the day and during the night. So, to make the reconnoissance, General Pendleton passed the Union troops in Confederate uniform—he was military in his dress—and found the point of battle. Giving him credit, for the moment, for this delicate work and the mythical order, let us find the end to which it would lead.

The only troops that could come under the order were McLaws's division, part of Hood's, and the artillery—about ten thousand men. These, after a hurried all-night's march, reached General Lee's head-quarters about sunrise of the 2d, and by continued forced march could have reached the point of battle, about five miles away, by seven o'clock, where they would have encountered a division of the Third Corps (Birney's); presently the Second and Fifth Corps under Hancock and Sykes; then the First, Eleventh, and Twelfth under Newton, Howard, and Slocum; then the balance of the Third coming in on our rear along the Emmitsburg road,—making sixty thousand men and more. There was reason to be proud of the prowess of the troops of the First Corps, but to credit a part of it with success under the circumstances was not reasonable.

That the Confederate Second Corps did not have orders for the alleged sunrise battle is evidenced by the report of its commander, who, accounting for his work about Culp's Hill during the night of the 1st and morning of the 2d, reported of the morning, "It was now daylight, and too late," meaning that it was too late for him to attack and carry that hill, as General Lee had authorized and expected him to do during the night before. If he had been ordered to take part in the sunrise battle, he would have been in the nick of time. That the Third Corps was not to be in it is evidenced by the position of the greater part of it on Seminary Ridge until near noon of the 2d. So General Lee must have ordered a position carried, at sunrise, by ten thousand men, after it had gathered strength all night—a position that he would not assault on the afternoon of the 1st with forty thousand men, lest they should encounter "overwhelming numbers."

As the other corps, after receiving their orders for the afternoon battle of the 2d, failed to engage until after nightfall, it is not probable that they would have found the sunrise battle without orders.

General Pendleton's official report is in conflict with his memorial lecture. In the former he makes no reference to the sunrise-battle order, but mentions a route by which the left of the enemy could be turned.

Letters from the active members of General Lee's staff and from his military secretary, General A.L. Long, show that the sunrise battle was not ordered, and a letter from Colonel Fairfax shows that the claim that it was so ordered was set up after General Lee's death.

Colonel Taylor claims that the attack by the Confederate right should have been sooner, and should have met the enemy back on his first or original line, and before Little Round Top was occupied. But Little Round Top was not occupied in force until after my battle opened, and General Sickles's advance to his forward lines was made in consequence of the Confederate threatening, and would have been sooner or later according as that threatening was made. He calls the message of General Lee to General Ewell on the afternoon of the 1st an order. General Lee says,

> The strong position which the enemy had assumed could not be attacked without danger of exposing the four divisions present, exhausted by a long and bloody struggle, to overwhelming numbers of fresh troops. General Ewell was thereupon instructed to carry the hill occupied by the enemy if he found it practicable.

It is the custom of military service to accept instructions of a commander as orders, but when they are coupled with conditions that transfer the responsibility of battle and defeat to the subordinate, they are not orders, and General Ewell was justifiable in not making attack that his commander would not order, and the censure of his failure is unjust and *very ungenerous*.

The Virginia writers have been so eager in their search for a flaw in the conduct of the battle of the First Corps that they overlook the only point into which they could have thrust their pens.

At the opening of the fight, General Meade was, with General Sickles, discussing the feasibility of moving the Third Corps back to the line originally assigned for it, but the discussion was cut short by the opening of the Confederate battle. If that opening had been delayed thirty or forty minutes the corps would have been drawn back to the general line, and my first deployment would have enveloped Little Round Top and carried it before it could have been strongly manned, and General Meade would have drawn off to his line selected behind Pipe Creek. The point should have been that the battle was opened too soon.

Another point from which they seek comfort is that Sedgwick's corps (Sixth) was not up until a late hour of the 2d, and would not have been on the field for an earlier battle. But Sedgwick was not engaged in the late battle, and could have been back at Manchester, so far as the afternoon battle was concerned. And they harp a little on the delay of thirty minutes for Law's brigade to join its division. But General Lee called for the two divisions, and had called for Law's brigade to join his division. It was therefore his order for the division that delayed the march. To have gone without it would have justified censure. As we were not strong enough for the work with that brigade, it is not probable that we could have accomplished more without it.

Colonel Taylor says that General Lee urged that the march of my troops should be hastened, and was chafed at their non-appearance. Not one word did he utter to me of their march until he gave his orders at eleven o'clock for the move to his right. Orders for the troops to hasten their march of the 1st were sent without even a suggestion from him, but upon his announcement that he intended to fight the next day, if the enemy was there. That he was excited and off his balance was evident on the afternoon of the 1st, and he labored under that oppression until enough blood was shed to appease him.

THEODORE GARRISH

The Stand of the 20th Maine

The anchor for the Federal line at Gettysburg was a steep prominence studded with rocky outcroppings, a hill known as Little Round Top. Had the Confederates ever managed to take it, Meade's position would have become untenable and he would be forced to retreat in ignominious defeat. Instrumental in the defense of this position was the gallant stand of the 20th Maine led by a former professor at Bowdoin College, Colonel Joshua Chamberlain. Despite being hard pressed, outnumbered, and low on ammunition, the soldiers from the Pine Tree State held their position and fiercely drove back the enemy. The story of this episode is related in this selection penned by a private of the 20th Maine, Theodore Garrish, in his work *Army Life: A Private's Reminiscences of the Civil War.*

On the 28th of June, General Hooker, at his own request, was relieved of his command, and it was given to General Meade. The latter had been in command of our corps. We knew him to be a brave and gallant officer, but feared a mistake had been made in changing commanders just as a battle was to be fought. Many rumors came back to us from the front, and from these we learned that Lee's troops numbered at least one hundred thousand, that he was concentrating his forces near Gettysburgh, and that a desperate battle would probably be fought near that place. We knew that the army of the Potomac did not number over eighty thousand men, that the authorities of the states of Pennsylvania and New York were moving so slowly in raising troops that but little aid would be received from them, and that unaided we must cope with our old foe.

On the first day of July we crossed the state line of Pennsylvania, and noted the event by loud cheering and much enthusiasm. And here, on the border of the state, we learned that our cavalry under General Buford, and our old First corps, under General Reynolds, had on that day encountered the rebels at Gettysburgh, and that on the morrow the great battle would be fought. Night came on, but we halted not. We knew that our comrades on the distant battle-field needed our aid, and we hastened on. It was a beautiful evening. The moon shone from a cloudless sky, and flooded our way with its glorious light. The people rushed from their homes and stood by the roadside to welcome us, men, women, and children all gazing on the strange spectacle. Bands played, the soldiers and the people cheered, banners waved, and white handkerchiefs fluttered from doors and windows, as the blue, dusty column surged on. That moonlight march will always be remembered by its survivors. A staff officer sat on his horse by the roadside. In a low voice he spoke to our colonel as he passed. "What did he say?" anxiously inquired the men. "McClellan is to command us on the morrow,"—McClellan, our first commander, who had been removed, criticised, and we thought he was forgotten; but our old love for him broke out afresh. He had never seemed one-half so dear to us before. Men waved their hats and cheered until they were hoarse and wild with excitement. It is strange what a hold little Mac had on the hearts of his soldiers. At midnight we halted, having marched more than thirty miles on that eventful day. The men threw themselves upon the ground to get a little rest and sleep. Sleep on, brave fellows, for the morrow's struggle will call for both strength and courage! While they are sleeping, we will step across the country for a few miles and view Gettysburgh in the moonlight, that we may better understand the battle-ground of to-morrow. It has been a bloody day around this little country village. Early in the morning the cavalry under General Buford had met the enemy advancing in great force, and bravely contested the ground with him. General Reynolds, hearing the heavy firing, had pushed the First corps forward to Buford's support, and formed his line of battle upon an eminence west of Seminary Ridge. The conflict soon became general. The gallant Reynolds was killed at the first volley, as he was riding to the front to ascertain the position of the enemy. General Doubleday assumed command of the corps. It was a fearful struggle. Hill's corps of the rebel army on the one side, and the First corps, much the inferior in numbers, upon the other.

General Howard arrives with the Eleventh corps. The rebels also receive reinforcements. Back and forth the contending lines press each other until late in the afternoon, when the Union troops are overpowered, and are hurled, bleeding and mangled, through the streets of

Gettysburgh, and up the slopes of Cemetery Ridge. General Hancock arrives at this moment from the headquarters of General Meade, and assumes the command, and in concert with General Howard, selected the line of battle. The village is filled with the highly elated rebels, who loudly boast that they can easily whip the Yankees on the morrow.

Things look a little desperate on Cemetery Hill. Reynolds and thousands of his gallant men have fallen, but their courage saved the position for the Union army, and on that hill our line of battle is being formed under the supervision of our brave generals,—Howard, the one-armed hero, Hancock the brilliant leader, Dan Sickles the irresistible commander of the Third corps, and brave Slocum of the Twelfth. Sykes and Sedgwick with their respective corps will put in an appearance on the morrow. At midnight General Meade arrives and assumes command of the entire line. It is evident at a glance that the old army of the Potomac is "on deck," and that if General Lee expects to win Gettysburgh by fighting a few brigades of raw militia, he is very much mistaken. The ridge on which our line of battle is being formed somewhat resembles a horseshoe in shape. Cemetery Hill, facing the northwest, is the point nearest Gettysburgh and Lee's headquarters, and that point we will call the toe calk of the horseshoe. To the left and rear is Round Top, which represents one heel calk, while Wolf's Hill to the right and rear represents the other. Howard, with the Eleventh corps, is stationed at Cemetery Hill. The First and Twelfth corps, under Generals Slocum and Wadsworth, formed our right, reaching from Howard to our extreme right at Wolf's Hill. At the left of Howard is Hancock and the Second corps, and at his left Sickles with the Third, in a somewhat advanced position, reaching unto our extreme left, near Little Round Top. It has been decided that General Sykes and Sedgwick shall be held in reserve to reinforce any part of our line upon which Lee may mass his troops. And thus through the hours of that night our preparations for the battle were being made.

If General Lee had pushed on his forces, and followed up his advantage gained in the afternoon, he would have been master of the situation, but this delay was fatal to him. The Union line is formed, the artillery is in position. The rebels outnumber us both in men and guns, but we have the ridge, and are on the defensive. The tired men sink upon the ground to catch a few moments' sleep before the battle opens. All is still in Gettysburgh save the groans of the wounded and dying. It is an anxious night throughout the great loyal North. Telegrams have been flashing all over the country, bearing the sad tidings of the death of Reynolds and the repulse of his troops. Every one knows that this battle is to decide, to a large extent, the fortunes of war. There is no sleep for the people. Strong men are pale with excitement and anxiety, as through the hours of night they talk of the coming conflict; Christians gather in their sanctuaries to pray that success may be ours on the morrow; mothers, wives and sisters, with pale, upturned faces, pray to God to protect their loved ones in the dangers of the battle. It is the most anxious night through which America ever passed. God grant that we shall never pass through another like it!

At daylight, on the morning of July 2d, we resumed our march, and in a few hours halted within supporting distance of the left flank of our army, about a mile to the right of Little Round Top. The long forenoon passed away, and to our surprise the enemy made no attack. This was very fortunate for our army, as it enabled our men to strengthen our lines of fortifications, and also to obtain a little rest, of which they were in great need. The rebels were also engaged in throwing up rude lines of defenses, hurrying up reinforcements, and in discussing the line of action they should pursue, for, to use General Lee's own words in his report of the battle, they "unexpectedly found themselves confronted by the Federal army."

The hour of noon passed, and the sun had measured nearly one-half the distance across the western sky, before the assault was made. Then, as suddenly as a bolt of fire flies from the storm cloud, a hundred pieces of rebel artillery open upon our left flank, and under the thick canopy of screaming, hissing, bursting shells, Longstreet's corps was hurled upon the troops of General Sickles. Instantly our commanders discerned the intention of General Lee. It was to turn and crush our left flank, as he had crushed our right at Chancellorsville. It was a terrible onslaught. The brave sons of the South never displayed more gallant courage than on that fatal afternoon of July 2d. But brave Dan Sickles and the old Third corps were equal to the emergency, and stood as immovable against the surging tides as blocks of granite. But a new and appalling danger suddenly threatened the Union army. Little Round Top was the key to the entire position. Rebel batteries planted on that rocky bluff could shell any portion of our line at their pleasure. For some reason Sickles had not placed any infantry upon this important position. A few batteries were scattered along its ragged side, but they had no infantry support. Lee saw at a glance that Little Round Top was the prize for which the two armies were contending, and with skillful audacity he determined to wrest it from his opponent. While the terrible charge was being made upon the line of General Sickles, Longstreet threw out a whole division, by extending his line to his right, for the purpose of seizing the coveted prize. The danger was at once seen by our officers, and our brigade was ordered forward, to hold the hill against the assault of the enemy. In a moment all was excitement. Every soldier seemed to understand the situation, and to be inspired by its danger. "Fall in! Fall in! By the right flank! Double-quick! March!" and away we went, under the terrible artillery fire. It was a moment of thrilling interest. Shells were exploding on every side. Sickles' corps was enveloped in sheets of flame, and looked like a vast windrow of fire. But so intense was the excitement that we hardly noticed these surroundings. Up the steep hillside we ran, and reached the crest. "On the right by file into line," was the command, and our regiment had assumed the position to which it had been assigned. We were on the left of our brigade, and consequently on the extreme left of all our line of battle. The ground sloped to our front and left, and was sparsely covered with a growth of oak trees, which were too small to afford us any protection. Shells were crashing through the air above our heads, making so much noise that we could hardly hear the commands of our officers; the air was filled with fragments of exploding shells and splinters torn from mangled trees; but our men appeared to be as cool and deliberate in their movements as if they had been forming a line upon the parade ground in camp. Our regiment mustered about three hundred and fifty men. Company B, from Piscataquis county commanded by the gallant Captain Morrill, was ordered to deploy in our front as skirmishers. They boldly advanced down the slope and disappeared from our view. Ten minutes have passed since we formed the line; the skirmishers must have advanced some thirty or forty rods through the rocks and trees, but we have seen no indications of the enemy; "But look!" "Look!" "Look!" exclaimed half a hundred men in our regiment at the same moment; and no wonder, for right in our front, between us and our skirmishers, whom they have probably captured, we see the lines of the enemy. They have paid no attention to the rest of the brigade stationed on our right, but they are rushing on, determined to turn and crush the left of our line. Colonel Chamberlain with rare sagacity understood the movement they were making, and bent back the left flank of our regiment until the line formed almost a right angle with the colors at the point, all these movements requiring a much less space of time than it requires for me to write of them.

How can I describe the scenes that followed? Imagine, if you can, nine small companies of infantry, numbering perhaps three hundred men, in the form of a right angle, on the extreme flank of an army of eighty thousand men, put there to hold the key of the entire position against a force at least ten times their number, and who are desperately determined to succeed in the mission upon which they came. Stand firm, ye boys from Maine, for not once in a century are men permitted to bear such responsibilities for freedom and justice, for God and humanity, as are now placed upon you.

The conflict opens. I know not who gave the first fire, or which line received the first lead. I only know that the carnage began. Our regiment was mantled in fire and smoke. I wish that I could picture with my pen the awful details of that hour,—how rapidly the cartridges were torn from the boxes and stuffed in the smoking muzzles of the guns; how the steel rammers clashed and clanged in the heated barrels; how the men's hands and faces grew grim and black with burning powder; how our little line, baptized with fire, reeled to and fro as it advanced or was pressed back; how our officers bravely encouraged the men to hold on and recklessly exposed themselves to the enemy's fire—a terrible medley of cries, shouts, cheers, groans, prayers, curses, bursting shells, whizzing rifle bullets and clanging steel. And if that was all, my heart would not be so sad and heavy as I write. But the enemy was pouring a terrible fire upon us, his superior forces giving him a great advantage. Ten to one are fearful odds where men are contending for so great a prize. The air seemed to be alive with lead. The lines at times were so near each other that the hostile gun barrels almost touched. As the contest continued, the rebels grew desperate that so insignificant a force should so long hold them in check. At one time there was a brief lull in the carnage, and our shattered line was closed up, but soon the contest raged again with renewed fierceness. The rebels had been reinforced, and were now determined to sweep our regiment from the crest of Little Round Top.

Many of our companies have suffered fearfully. Look at Company H for a moment. Charley, my old tent-mate, with a fatal wound in his breast, staggered up to brave Captain Land. "My God, Sergeant Steele!"

ejaculated the agonized captain as he saw the fate of his beloved sergeant. "I am going, Captain," cried the noble fellow, and fell dead, weltering in his blood. Sergeant Lathrop, with his brave heart and gigantic frame, fell dying with a frightful wound. Sergeant Buck, reduced to the ranks at Stoneman's Switch, lay down to die, and was promoted as his life blood ebbed away. Adams, Ireland, and Lamson, all heroes, are lying dead at the feet of their comrades. Libby, French, Clifford, Hilt, Ham, Chesly Morrison, West, and Walker are all severely wounded, and nearly all disabled. But there is no relief, and the carnage goes on. Our line is pressed back so far that our dead are within the lines of the enemy. The pressure made by the superior weight of the enemy's line is severely felt. Our ammunition is nearly all gone, and we are using the cartridges from the boxes of our wounded comrades. A critical moment has arrived, and we can remain as we are no longer; we must advance or retreat. It must not be the latter, but how can it be the former? Colonel Chamberlain understands how it can be done. The order is given "Fix bayonets!" and the steel shanks of the bayonets rattle upon the rifle barrels. "Charge bayonets, charge!" Every man understood in a moment that the movement was our only salvation, but there is a limit to human endurance, and I do not dishonor those brave men when I write that for a brief moment the order was not obeyed, and the little line seemed to quail under the fearful fire that was being poured upon it. O for some man reckless of life, and all else save his country's honor and safety, who would rush far out to the front, lead the way, and inspire the hearts of his exhausted comrades! In that moment of supreme need the want was supplied. Lieut. H.S. Melcher, an officer who had worked his way up from the ranks, and was then in command of Co. F, at that time the color company, saw the situation, and did not hesitate, and for his gallant act deserves as much as any other man the honor of the victory on Round Top. With a cheer, and a flash of his sword, that sent an inspiration along the line, full ten paces to the front he sprang—ten paces—more than half the distance between the hostile lines. "Come on! Come on! Come on, boys!" he shouts. The color sergeant and the brave color guard follow, and with one wild yell of anguish wrung from its tortured heart, the regiment charged.

The rebels were confounded at the movement. We struck them with a fearful shock. They recoil, stagger, break and run, and like avenging demons our men pursue. The rebels rush toward a stone wall, but, to our mutual surprise, two scores of rifle barrels gleam over the rocks, and a murderous volley was poured in upon them at close quarters. A band of men leap over the wall and capture at least a hundred prisoners. Piscataquis has been heard from, and as usual it was a good report. This unlooked-for reinforcement was Company B, whom we supposed were all captured.

Our Colonel's commands were simply to hold the hill, and we did not follow the retreating rebels but a short distance. After dark an order came to advance and capture a hill in our front. Through the trees, among the rocks, up the steep hillside, we made our way, captured the position, and also a number of prisoners.

JAMES O. BRADFIELD

"Until God stopped them..."

The division belonging to Kentuckian John Bell Hood was charged with
assaulting Little Round Top. Among Bell's ranks was Hood's old brigade
composed of an ornery group of Texans and Arkansians, informally
known as the Texas Brigade. James O. Bradfield, a private in Company
E of the First Texas Regiment, describes the attack of his unit on the
Yankee line in a selection from comrade J.B. Polley's *Hood's Texas
Brigade.*

Hood's division held the right flank of our army.... We began forming
our line of battle on a wide plateau leading back to the rear, while in
front about 200 yards distant was a skirt of timber on the brow of a hill
which led down to the valley below. In this timber, our batteries were
posted, and as the Texas Brigade was forming immediately in the rear,
we were in direct range of the enemy's guns on the mountain beyond. As
our artillery began feeling for their batteries, the answering shells struck
our lines with cruel effect. The Fourth Texas suffered most severely. As
they were passing this zone of fire, one shell killed and wounded fifteen
men. It certainly tries a man's nerve to have to stand still and receive such
a fire without being able to return it.

Just here occurred one of the little incidents that, happening at times
like this, are never forgotten. In our company was a tall, robust young
fellow named Dick Childers, who was noted for the energy and talent
he displayed in procuring rations. On this occasion Dick's haversack was
well stocked with nice biscuits which a kind Dutch lady had given him.
As we were marching by the right flank, our left sides were turned towards
the enemy. A shell from the mountain in front struck the ground near
our batteries, and came bouncing along across the field, and as Dick
happened to be just in the line of fire, it struck him, or rather, his
haversack, fairly, and scattered biscuits all over that end of Pennsylvania.

But the strange part of it is, that it did not knock the man down, but so paralyzed him that he fell, after it had passed, and lay there unable to move a muscle. The litter bearers picked him up and laid him on a stretcher, as if he had been a log. The boys all contended, however, that it was the destruction of Dick's rations, and not any shock the shell gave, that paralyzed him.

We marched onward by the right flank, about a quarter of a mile, moving parallel with the enemy's lines, and halting, left-faced and formed for work. We were on the brow of a hill which here sloped quite abruptly down into the narrow valley. We could see the enemy's lines of battle—the first on the level space below us, behind a heavy rock fence; the second, at the top of a ridge a hundred or two yards further on, while still further, and entirely out of our reach, at the summit of the higher range, their batteries were posted so as to sweep the whole space over which we were to advance. Their battle flags floated proudly in the breeze, above the almost perfect natural breastworks formed by the fence and the large rocks that crowned the low ridge upon which they stood. There were but two small cannon on the lower ridge, and these were captured and pulled off the hill by the First Texas regiment.

About 2 o'clock in the afternoon, the order was given to advance all along the line. We moved quietly forward down the steep decline, gaining impetus as we reached the more level ground below. The enemy had already opened fire on us, but we did not stop to return it. 'Forward—double quick,' rang out, and then Texas turned loose. Across the valley and over the little stream that ran through it, they swept, every man for himself. The first man down was my right file man, William Langley, a noble, brave boy, with a minie-ball straight through the brain. I caught him as he fell against me, and laid him down, dead. As I straightened up to move on, that same familiar 'spat' which always means something, sounded near, and looking around, I saw Bose Perry double over and catch on his gun. He did not fall, however, but came on, dragging his wounded leg, and firing as he advanced. But it was getting too hot now to pay attention to details.

The enemy stood their ground bravely, until we were close on them, but did not await the bayonet. They broke away from the rock fence as we closed in with a rush and a wild rebel yell, and fell back to the top of the ridge, where they halted and formed on their second line. Having passed the rock fence, and as we were moving on up the hill, an order came to halt. No one seemed to know whence it came, nor from whom. It cost us dearly, for as we lay in close range of their now double lines, the enemy poured a hail of bullets on us, and in a few minutes a number of our men were killed or wounded. We saw that this would never do, and so, without awaiting orders, every man became his own commander and sprang forward toward the top of the hill at full speed.

By this time, Benning's brigade, which had been held in reserve, joined us and together we swept on to where the Blue Coats stood behind the sheltering rocks to receive us. Just here, and to our right, in a little cove called the "Devil's Den," which was covered by the Fourth and Fifth Texas, Law's Alabama and Anderson's Georgia brigades, occurred one of the wildest, fiercest struggles of the war—a struggle such as it is given to few men to pass through and live.

The opposing lines stood with only the sheltering rocks between them—breast to breast, and so close that the clothing of many of the enemy was set on fire by the blaze from the Confederate rifles. This continued for some time, but finally, our fire grew so hot that brave as they were, the Federals could no longer endure it, but gave way and fled down the slope, leaving us in possession of the field. The Lone Star flag crowned the hill, and Texas was there to stay. Not alone, however, for just to our right stood Benning—'Old Rock'—that peerless old hero than whom no braver man ever lived. Striding back and forth in front of his line, he was calling to his gallant Georgians: 'Give them h__ll, boys—give them h__ll,' and the 'boys' were giving it to them according to instructions.

On the right of Benning stood Anderson and Law, and the Fourth and Fifth Texas, as firm as the rocks which sheltered them. I cannot hope to describe the deeds of daring and heroism that were enacted. Beyond the valley in our front, on the summit of the practically impregnable ridge that stretched north toward Gettysburg, stood the enemy's batteries, 200 guns. Of these, about forty were playing in close range upon the position we occupied. Their fire and that of our own batteries, and the constant roar and rattle of thousands of muskets, made the earth tremble beneath our feet, while the fierce, angry shriek of shells, the strident swirl of grape and canister as they tore hurtling through the air and broke like a wave from the ocean of death upon that devoted spot, the hissing bullets, and their 'spat' as they struck rock, tree or human flesh—all this, with the shouts and imprecations, the leaping to and fro and from boulder to boulder of powder-begrimed men, seemingly gone wild with rage and excitement, created a scene of such indescribable, awe-inspiring confusion that an on-looker might well believe that a storm from the Infernal regions was spending its fury in and around a spot so fitly named, 'The Devil's Den.' Had it not been for the protection afforded us by the large rocks and boulders which lay scattered over the hill-top, no living thing could have remained on its summit.

The fearful artillery fire of the enemy was intended to cover the massing of their infantry, who were now to make one more grand effort to regain the ground they had lost. Our boys prepared for this by gathering up all abandoned muskets within reach, and loading them. Some of us had as many as five or six lying by us, as we awaited the attack.

We had not long to wait, for soon the long blue line came in view, moving in gallant style up the valley. The Federals were led by splendid officers, and made a noble charge: but when they met the murderous fire from behind the rocks where we crouched, they faltered. Only for a moment, though, and on they came right up to the rocks. Again they faltered, for now, most of their officers were down. Again it was but for a second, and cheered on by some of the bravest men I have ever seen, they rallied in the very face of death, and charged right up to the muzzles of our guns.

There was one officer, a major, who won our admiration by his courage and gallantry. He was a very handsome man, and rode a beautiful, high-spirited gray horse. The animal seemed to partake of the spirit of the rider, and as he came on with a free, graceful stride into that hell of death and carnage, head erect and ears pointed, horse and man offered a picture such as is seldom seen. The two seemed the very impersonation of heroic courage. As the withering, scathing volleys from behind the rocks cut into the ranks of the regiment the major led, and his gallant men went down like grain before a scythe, he followed close at their heels, and when, time and again, they stopped and would have fled the merciless fire, each time he rallied them as if his puissant arm alone could stay the storm. But his efforts were, in the end, unavailing; the pluck of himself and his men only made the carnage the more dreadful, for the Lone Star banner and the flag of Georgia continued floating from the hill, showing who stood, defiant and unyielding, beneath their folds.

In the last and most determined charge they made on us, the gallant officer made his supreme effort. Riding into our very midst, seeming to bear a charmed life, he sat proudly on the noble gray, and still cheered on his men. 'Don't shoot at him—don't kill him' our boys shouted to each other; 'he is too brave a man to die—shoot his horse and capture the man.' But it could not be. In a second or two, horse and rider went down together, pierced by a dozen balls. Thus died a hero—one of the most gallant men that ever gave up his life on the red field of carnage. Though it was that of an enemy, we honored the dead body as if it had been that of one of our own men. Such courage belongs not to any one army or country, but to mankind.

It was about this time that a spectacular display of reckless courage was made by a young Texan, Will Barbee, of the First Texas. Under twenty years old, he was ordinarily a jolly, whole-souled lad, not at all given to extraordinary performances. But when a fight was going on, he went wild, seemed to have no sense of fear whatever, and was a reckless dare-devil. Although a courier for General Hood, he never failed to join his regiment, if possible, and go into battle with it. On the present occasion, when General Hood was wounded, Barbee hunted us up. In the hottest of the fight, I heard some one say 'Here comes Barbee' and looking down from the rock on which I was lying I saw him coming as fast as his little sorrel horse could run, and waving his hat as he came. Just before reaching us, the sorrel fell, but Barbee did not stop to see what had happened to the brute. He hit the ground running, and snatching up a gun as he came, was soon in line.

About five paces to my left was a large, high rock behind which several of our wounded were sheltering themselves. To the top of that, where the very air was alive with missiles of death, Barbee sprang, and standing there, erect and fearless, began firing—the wounded men below him passing up loaded guns as fast as he emptied them. But no living being could stay unhurt long in such a fire. In a few minutes, Barbee was knocked off the rock by a ball that struck him in the right leg. Climbing instantly back, he again commenced shooting. In less than two minutes, he was tumbled off the rock by a ball in the other leg. Still unsatisfied, he crawled back a second time, but was not there more than a minute before, being wounded in the body, he again fell, this time dropping on his back between the rock that had been his perch, and that which was my shelter. Too seriously wounded this time to extricate himself from the narrow passageway, he called for help, and the last time I saw him that day, he was lying there, crying and cursing because the boys would not come to his relief and help him back on to the rock.

There were many in the regiment as brave as Barbee, but none so reckless. The best blood of Texas was there, and in the Fourth and Fifth Texas, and General Lee could safely place the confidence he did in Hood's Texas Brigade. But God must have ordained our defeat. As was said by one of the speakers at a reunion of 'the Mountain Remnant Brigade': 'At the first roll of the war drum, Texas sent forth her noblest and best. She gave the Army of Northern Virginia Hood's matchless brigade—a band of heroes who bore their country's flag to victory on every field, until God stopped them at Little Round Top.'

VAL C. GILES

"Both sides were whipped . . ."

Another member of the Texas Brigade to view the combat was private Val C. Giles who, in a selection also taken from Polley's *Hood's Texas Brigade*, presents a lighter side to Little Round Top.

It was near 5 o'clock when we began the assault against an enemy strongly fortified behind logs and stones on the crest of a mountain, in many places perpendicular. It was more than half a mile from our starting point to the edge of the timber at the base of the ridge, comparatively open ground all the way. We started off at quick time, the officers keeping the column in pretty good line until we passed through the peach orchard and reached the level ground beyond. We were now about four hundred yards from the timber and the fire from the enemy, both artillery and musketry, was fearful. In making that long charge our brigade got 'jammed.' Regiments overlapped each other and when we reached the woods and climbed the mountains as far as we could go, we were a badly mixed crowd.

Confusion reigned supreme everywhere. Nearly all our field officers were gone. Hood, our major general, had been shot from his horse. Robertson, our brigadier, had been carried from the field. Colonel Powell of the Fifth Texas was riddled with bullets. Colonel Van Manning of the Third Arkansas was disabled and Colonel Carter of my regiment lay dying at the foot of the mountain.

The sides of the mountain were heavily timbered and covered with great boulders, that had tumbled from the cliffs above years before, which afforded great protection to the men.

Every tree, rock and stump that gave any protection from the rain of minie-balls, that was poured down upon us from the crest above us, were soon appropriated. John Griffith and myself pre-empted behind a moss-covered old boulder about the size of a 500-pound cotton bale.

By this time order and discipline were gone. Every fellow was his own general. Private soldiers gave commands as loud as the officers—nobody paying any attention to either. To add to this confusion, our artillery on the hill in our rear was cutting its fuse too short. The shells were bursting behind us, in the treetops, over our heads, and all around us.

Nothing demoralizes troops quicker than to be fired into by their friends. I saw it occur twice during the war. The first time we ran, but at Gettysburg we couldn't.

This mistake was soon corrected and the shells burst high on a mountain or went over it.

Major Rogers, then in command of the Fifth Texas regiment, mounted an old log near my boulder and began a Fourth of July speech. He was a little ahead of time, for that was about 6:30 o'clock on the evening of the 2d. Of course, nobody was paying any attention to the oration as he appealed to the men to stand fast. He and Captain Cussons of the Fourth Alabama were the only two men I saw standing. The balance of us had settled down behind rocks, logs and trees. While the speech was going on, John Haggerty, one of Hood's couriers, then acting for General Law, dashed up the side of the mountains, saluted the major and said: 'General Law presents his compliments and says hold the place at all hazards.' The major checked up, glared down at Haggerty from his perch and shouted: 'Compliments, hell! Who wants compliments in such a damned place as this? Go back and ask General Law if he expects me to hold the world in check with the Fifth Texas regiment.'

The major evidently thought he had his regiment with him, while, in fact, these men were from every regiment in the Texas Brigade all around him.

But I must back to my boulder at Gettysburg. It was a ragged line of battle, strung out along the side of Cemetery Ridge and in front of Little Round Top. Night began settling around us, but the carnage went on. It is of that night that I started out to speak.

There seemed to be a viciousness in the very air we breathed. Things had gone wrong all the day and now pandemonium came with the darkness.

Alexander Dumas says the devil gets in a man seven times a day, and if the average is not over seven times he is almost a saint.

At Gettysburg that night it was about seven devils to each man. Officers were cross to the men, and the men were equally cross to the officers. It was the same way with the enemy. We could hear the Yankee officer on the crest of the ridge in front of us cursing the men by platoons, and the men telling them to go to a country not very far from them just at that time. If that old satanic dragon has ever been on earth since he offered our Saviour the world if He would serve him, he was at Gettysburg that night.

Every characteristic of the human race was presented there, the cruelty of the Turk, the courage of the Greek (old style), the endurance of the Arab, the dash of the Cossack, the fearlessness of the Bashibazouk, the ignorance of the Zulu, the cunning of the Comanche, the recklessness of the American volunteers and the wickedness of the devil thrown in to make the thing complete.

The advance lines of the two armies in many places were not more than fifty yards apart. Everything was on the shoot; no favors asked, and none offered.

My gun was so dirty that the ramrod hung in the barrel, and I could neither get it down nor out. I slammed the rod against a rock a few times and drove home ramrod, cartridge and all, laid the gun on a boulder, elevated the muzzle, ducked my head, halloed 'Look out!' and pulled the trigger. She roared like a young cannon and flew over my shoulder, the barrel striking John Griffith a smart whack on the left ear. John roared, too, and abused me like a pickpocket for my carelessness. It was no trouble to get another gun there. The mountain side was covered with them.

Just to our left was a little fellow from the Third Arkansas regiment. He was comfortably located behind a big stump, loading and firing as fast as he could, and between biting cartridges and taking aim, he was singing at the top of his voice:

'Now let the wide world wag as it will, I'll be gay and happy still.'

The world was wagging all right—no mistake about that, but I failed to see where the 'gay and happy' part came in.

That was a fearful night. There was no sweet music to soothe the savage beast. The 'tooters' had left the shooters to fight it out, and taken 'Home, Sweet Home' and 'The Girl I Left Behind Me' off with them.

Our spiritual advisers, chaplains of regiments, were in the rear, caring for the wounded and dying soldiers. With seven devils to each man, it was no place for a preacher, anyhow.

A little red paint and a few eagle feathers were all that was necessary to make that crowd on both sides the most veritable savages on earth. 'White-winged Peace' didn't roost at Little Round Top that night. There was not a man there who cared a snap for the Golden Rule or that could have remembered one line of the Lord's Prayer. Both sides were whipped and all were mad about it.

D. AUGUST DICKERT

On the Attack against Sickles

Kershaw's brigade was charged with attacking elements of Sickles' corps
that held the Peach Orchard. After pummeling through Union lines,
they were hit in the flank. Brigadier General Paul J. Semmes called for
more reinforcements as his brigade joined the fray with assistance from
Barkesdale's and Wofford's brigades. While they almost drove a gap in
the Union line, the Federals were able to throw some forces to push back
the enemy threat. Once again, D. Augustus Dickert relates the action
in *History of Kershaw's Brigade.*

When the troops were aroused from their slumbers on that beautiful clear
morning of the 2d of July, the sun had long since shot its rays over the
quaint old, now historic, town of Gettysburg, sleeping down among the
hills and spurs of the Blue Ridge. After an all night's march, and a hard
day's work before them, the troops were allowed all the rest and repose
possible. I will here state that Longstreet had with him only two divisions
of his corps, with four regiments to a division. Pickett was left near
Chambersburg to protect the numerous supply trains. Jenkins' South
Carolina brigade of his division had been left in Virginia to guard the
mountain passes against a possible cavalry raid, and thus had not the
opportunity of sharing with the other South Carolinians in the glories
that will forever cluster around Gettysburg. They would, too, had they
been present, have enjoyed and deserved the halo that will for all time
surround the "charge of Pickett," a charge that will go down in history
with Balaclava and Hohenlinden.

A.P. Hill, aided by part of Ewell's corps, had fought a winning fight
the day before, and had driven the enemy from the field through the
streets of the sleepy old town of Gettysburg to the high ground on the
east. But this was only the advance guard of General Meade, thrown
forward to gain time in order to bring up his main army. He was now

375

concentrating it with all haste, and forming in rear of the rugged ridge running south of Gettysburg and culminating in the promontories at the Round Top. Behind this ridge was soon to assemble an army, if not the largest, yet the grandest, best disciplined, best equipped of all time, with an incentive to do successful battle as seldom falls to the lot of an army, and on its success or defeat depended the fate of two nations.

There was a kind of intuition, an apparent settled fact, among the soldiers of Longstreet's corps, that after all the other troops had made their long marches, tugged at the flanks of the enemy, threatened his rear, and all the display of strategy and generalship had been exhausted in the dislodgement of the foe, and all these failed, then when the hard, stubborn, decisive blow was to be struck, the troops of the First corps were called upon to strike it. Longstreet had informed Lee at the outset, "My corps is as solid as a rock—a great rock. I will strike the blow, and win, if the other troops gather the fruits of victory."

How confident the old "War Horse," as General Lee called him, was in the solidity and courage of his troops. Little did he know when he made the assertion that so soon his seventeen thousand men were to be pitted against the whole army of the Potomac. Still, no battle was ever considered decisive until Longstreet, with his cool, steady head, his heart of steel and troops who acknowledged no superior, or scarcely equal, in ancient or modern times, in endurance and courage, had measured strength with the enemy. This I give, not as a personal view, but as the feelings, the confidence and pardonable pride of the troops of the 1st corps.

As A.P. Hill and Ewell had had their bout the day before, it was a foregone conclusion that Longstreet's time to measure strength was near at hand, and the men braced themselves accordingly for the ordeal.

A ridge running parallel with that behind which the enemy stood, but not near so precipitous or rugged, and about a mile distant, with a gentle decline towards the base of the opposite ridge, was to be the base of the battle ground of the day. This plain or gentle slope between the two armies, a mile in extent, was mostly open fields covered with grain or other crops, with here and there a farm house, orchard and garden. It seems from reports since made that Lee had not matured his plan of battle until late in the forenoon. He called a council of war of his principal Lieutenant to discuss plans and feasibilities. It was a long time undecided whether Ewell should lead the battle on the right, or allow

Longstreet to throw his whole corps on the Round Top and break away these strongholds, the very citadel to Meade's whole line. The latter was agreed upon, much against the judgment of General Longstreet but Lee's orders were imperative, and obeyed with alacrity. At ten o'clock the movement began for the formation of the columns of assault. Along and in rear of the ridge we marched at a slow and halting gait. The Washington artillery had preceded us, and soon afterwards Alexander's battery passed to select positions. We marched and countermarched, first to the right, then to the left. As we thus marched we had little opportunity as yet to view the strongholds of the enemy on the opposite ridge, nor the incline between, which was soon to be strewn with the dead and dying. Occasionally a General would ride to the crest and take a survey of the surroundings. No cannon had yet been fired on either side, and everything was quiet and still save the tread of the thousands in motion, as if preparing for a great review.

Longstreet passed us once or twice, but he had his eyes cast to the ground, as if in a deep study, his mind disturbed, and had more the look of gloom than I had ever noticed before. Well might the great chieftain look cast down with the weight of this great responsibility resting upon him. There seemed to be an air of heaviness hanging around all. The soldiers trod with a firm but seeming heavy tread. Not that there was any want of confidence or doubt of ultimate success, but each felt within himself that this was to be the decisive battle of the war, and as a consequence it would be stubborn and bloody. Soldiers looked in the faces of their fellow-soldiers with a silent sympathy that spoke more eloquently than words an exhibition of brotherly love never before witnessed in the 1st corps. They felt a sympathy for those whom they knew before the setting of the sun, would feel the touch of the elbow for the last time, and who must fall upon this distant field and in an enemy's country.

About now we were moved over the crest and halted behind a stone wall that ran parallel to a county road, our center being near a gateway in the wall. As soon as the halt was made the soldiers fell down, and soon the most of them were fast asleep. While here, it was necessary for some troops of Hill's to pass over, up and through the gate. The head of the column was lead by a doughty General clad in a brilliant new uniform, a crimson sash encircling his waist, its deep, heavy hanging down to his sword scabbard, while great golden curls hung in maiden ringlets to his very shoulders. His movement was superb and he sat his horse in true knightly manner. On the whole, such a turn-out was a sight seldom witnessed by the staid soldiers of the 1st Corps. As he was passing a man in Company D, 3d South Carolina, roused up from his broken sleep, saw for the first time the soldier wonder with the long curls. He called out to him, not knowing he was an officer of such rank, "Say Mister, come right down out of that hair," a foolish and unnecessary expression that was common throughout the army when anything unusual hove in sight.

This hail roused all the ire in the flashy General, he became as "mad as a March hare," and wheeling his horse, dashed up to where the challenge appeared to have come from and demanded in an angry tone, "Who was that spoke? Who commands this company?" And as no reply was given he turned away, saying," D____d if I only knew who it was that insulted me, I would put a ball in him." But as he rode off the soldier gave him a Parthian shot by calling after him, "Say Mister, don't get so mad about it, I thought you were some d__n wagon master."

Slowly again our column began moving to the right. The center of the division was halted in front of little Round Top. Kershaw was then on the right, Barksdale with his Mississippians on his left, Wofford and Sumner with their Georgians in rear as support. Everything was quiet in our front, as if the enemy had put his horse in order and awaited our coming. Kershaw took position behind a tumbled down wall to await Hood's movements on our right, and who was to open the battle by the assault on Round Top. The country on our right, through which Hood had to manœuvre, was very much broken and thickly studded with trees and mountain undergrowth, which delayed that General in getting in battle line. Anderson's Georgians, with Hood's old Texas Brigade under Robertson, was on McLaws' immediate right, next to Kershaw. Law's Alabama Brigade was on the extreme right, and made the first advance. On McLaws' left was Wilcox, of General "Tige" Anderson's Division of the 3d Corps, with Posey and other troops to his left, these to act more as a brace to Longstreet as he advanced to the assault; however, most of them were drawn into the vortex of battle before the close of the day. In Kershaw's Brigade, the 2d under Colonel John D. Kennedy and Lieutenant Colonel Frank Gilliard, the 15th under Colonel W.D. Dessausure and Major Wm. Gist, the 3d under Colonel James D. Nance and Major R.C. Maffett, the 7th under Colonel D. Wyatt Aiken and Lieutenant

Colonel Elbert Bland, the 3d Battallion under Lieutenant Colonel W.G. Rice, the 8th under Colonel John W. Henegan, Lieutenant Colonel Hood and Major McLeod, went into battle in the order named, as far as I remember Major Wm. Wallace of the 2d commanded the brigade skirmish line or sharpshooters, now some distance in our front. A battery of ten guns was immediately in our rear, in a grove of oaks, and drew on us a heavy fire when the artillery duel began. All troops in line, the batteries in position, nothing was wanting but the signal gun to put these mighty forces in motion. Ewell had been engaged during the morning in a desultory battle far to our left and beyond the town, but had now quieted down. A blue puff of smoke, a deafening report from one of the guns of the Washington Artillery of New Orleans, followed in quick succession by others, gave the signal to both armies—the battle was now on.

It was the plan of action for Hood to move forward first and engage the enemy, and when once the combat was well under way on the right, McLaws to press his columns to the front. Law, with his Alabamians, was closing around the southern base of greater Round Top, while Robertson, with his three Texas regiments and one Arkansas, and Anderson with his Georgians, were pushing their way through thickets and over boulders to the front base of the Round Tops and the gorges between the two. We could easily determine their progress by the "rebel yell" as it rang out in triumph along the mountain sides.

The battery in our rear was drawing a fearful fire upon us, as we lay behind the stone fence, and all were but too anxious to be ordered forward. Barksdale, on our left, moved out first, just in front of the famous Peach Orchard. A heavy battery was posted there, supported by McCandless' and Willard's Divisions, and began raking Barksdale from the start. The brave old Mississippian, who was so soon to lose his life, asked permission to charge and take the battery, but was refused. Kershaw next gave the command, "forward," and the men sprang to their work with a will and determination and spread their steps to the right and left as they advanced. Kershaw was on foot, prepared to follow the line of battle immediately in rear, looking cool, composed and grand, his steel-gray eyes flashing the fire he felt in his soul.

The shelling from the enemy on the ridge in front had, up to this time, been mostly confined to replying to our batteries, but as soon as this long array of bristling bayonets moved over the crest and burst out suddenly in the open, in full view of the cannon-crowned battlements, all guns were turned upon us. The shelling from Round Top was terrific enough to make the stoutest hearts quake, while the battery down at the base of the ridge, in the orchard, was raking Barksdale and Kershaw right and left with grape and shrapnell. Semms' Georgians soon moved up on our right and between Kershaw and Hood's left, but its brave commander fell mortally wounded at the very commencement of the attack. Kershaw advanced directly against little Round Top, the strongest point in the enemy's line, and defended by Ayer's Regulars, the best disciplined and most stubborn fighters in the Federal army. The battery in the orchard began graping Kershaw's left as soon as it came in range, the right being protected by a depression in the ground over which they marched. Not a gun was allowed to be fired either at sharpshooters that were firing on our front from behind boulders and trees in a grove we were nearing, or at the commoners who were raking our flank on the left. Men fell here and there from the deadly minnie-balls, while great gaps or swaths were swept away in our ranks by shells from the batteries on the hills, or by the destructive grape and canister from the orchard. On marched the determined men across this open expanse, closing together as their comrades fell out. Barksdale had fallen, but his troops were still moving to the front and over the battery that was making such havoc in their ranks. Semms, too, had fallen, but his Georgians never wavered nor faltered, but moved like a huge machine in the face of these myriads of death-dealing missiles. Just as we entered the woods the infantry opened upon us a withering fire, especially from up the gorge that ran in the direction of Round Top. Firing now became general along the whole line on both sides. The Fifteenth Regiment met a heavy obstruction, a mock-orange hedge, and it was just after passing this obstacle that Colonel Dessausure fell. The center of the Third Regiment and some parts of the other regiments, were practically protected by boulders and large trees, but the greater part fought in the open field or in sparsely timbered groves of small trees. The fight now waged fast and furious.

Captain Malloy writes thus of the 8th: "We occupied the extreme left of the brigade, just fronting the celebrated 'Peach Orchard.' The order was given. We began the fatal charge, and soon had driven the enemy from their guns in the orchard, when a command was given to 'move to the right,' which fatal order was obeyed under a terrible fire, this leaving the 'Peach Orchard' partly uncovered. The enemy soon rallied to their guns and turned them on the flank of our brigade. Amid a storm of shot and shell from flank and front, our gallant old brigade pushed towards the Round Top, driving all before them, till night put an end to the awful slaughter. The regiment went in action with 215 in ranks, and lost more than half its number. We lost many gallant officers, among whom were Major McLeod, Captain Thomas E. Powe, Captain John McIver, and others." The move to the right was to let Wofford in between Barksdale and Kershaw.

Barksdale was pressing up the gorge that lay between little Round Top and the ridge, was making successful battle and in all likelihood would have succeeded had it not been for General Warren. General Meade's Chief Engineer being on the ground and seeing the danger, grasped the situation at once, called up all the available force and lined the stone walls that led along the gorge with infantry. Brigade after brigade of Federal infantry was now rushed to this citadel, while the crown of little Round Top was literally covered with artillery. Ayer's Regulars were found to be a stubborn set by Kershaw's troops. The Federal volunteers on our right and left gave way to Southern valor, but the regulars stood firm, protected as they were by the great boulders along their lines. Barksdale had passed beyond us as the enemy's line bent backward at this point, and was receiving the whole shock of battle in his front, while a terrific fire was coming from down the gorge and from behind hedges on the hill-side. But the Mississippians held on like grim death till Wofford, with his Georgians, who was moving in majestic style across the open field in the rear, came to his support.

General Wofford was a splendid officer, and equally as hard a fighter. He advanced his brigade through the deadly hail of bullets and took position on Barksdale's right and Kershaw's left, and soon the roar of his guns were mingling with those of their comrades. The whole division was now in action. The enemy began to give way and scamper up the hill-side. But Meade, by this time, had the bulk of his army around and in rear of the Round Top, and fresh troops were continually being rushed in to take the places of or reinforce those already in action. Hood's whole force was now also engaged, as well as a part of A.P. Hill's on our left. The smoke became so dense, the noise of small arms and the tumult raised by the "Rebel Yell," so great that the voices of officers attempting to give commands were hushed in the pandemonium. Along to the right of the 3d, especially up the little ravine, the fire was concentrated on those who held this position and was terrific beyond description, forcing a part of the line back to the stone house. This fearful shock of battle was kept up along the whole line without intermission till night threw her sable curtains over the scene of carnage and bloodshed and put an end to the strife. Wofford and Barksdale had none to reinforce them at the gorge, and had to fight it out single-handed and alone, while the Regulars, with their backs to the base of little Round Top, protected by natural formations, were too strong to be dislodged by Kershaw. As soon as the firing ceased the troops were withdrawn to near our position of the forenoon.

The work of gathering up the wounded lasted till late at night. Our loss in regimental and line officers was very great. Scarcely a regiment but what had lost one of its staff, nor a company some of its officers. Dr. Salmond, the Brigade Surgeon, came early upon the field and directed in person the movements of his assistants in their work of gathering up the wounded. "The dead were left to take care of the dead" until next day.

When the brigade was near the woodland in its advance, a most deadly fire was directed towards the center of the 3d both by the battery to our left, and sharpshooting in the front. It was thought by some that it was our flag that was drawing the fire, four color guards having gone down, some one called out "Lower the colors, down with the flag." Sergeant Lamb, color bearer, waved the flag aloft, and moving to the front where all could see, called out in loud tones, "This flag never goes down until I am down."

Then the word went up and down the line "Shoot that officer, down him, shoot him," but still he continued to give those commands, "Ready aim, fire," and the grape shot would come plunging into our very faces. The sharpshooters, who had joined our ranks, as we advanced, now commenced to blaze away, and the cannoneers scattered to cover in the rear. This officer finding himself deserted by his men, waved his sword defiantly over his head and walked away as deliberately as on dress parade, while the sharpshooters were plowing up the dirt all around him, but all failed to bring him down. We bivouaced during the night just in rear of the battle ground.

HENRY F. WEAVER

<hr>

Under Fire

To maintain his control of Little Round Top and bolster his increasingly beleaguered left, Meade was forced to rely on reinforcements tapped from his right which had remained unengaged for most of the day. The 155th Pennsylvania went into action at Little Round Top and fought elements of the Texas Brigade. Corporal Henry F. Weaver of Company B of the 155th Pennsylvania suffered a wound that day and lost his foot. He went on to serve as a notary public, auditor, and secretary of financial institutions in Pittsburgh. This short work originally entitled, *At Gettysburg—Under Front and Rear Fire* was taken from *Under the Maltese Cross.*

Weed's Brigade, Sykes' Division, Fifth Corps, and the One Hundred and Fifty-fifth Regiment Pennsylvania Volunteers, arrived on the field at Gettysburg early on the morning of July 2nd, somewhere near Culp's Hill, on the right of the Union line. Except to shift from one position to another, we did nothing for several hours. The order announcing that General George G. Meade had taken charge of the Army of the Potomac was read to the troops while in line of battle in the woods, with skirmishers thrown out. While I do not think that any more impressive or patriotic order could be read to any troops on the eve of battle and the assumption of command by a new General, I confess that I was disappointed when the order was signed George G. Meade and not George B. McClellan, but Providence directed otherwise.

We remained in this position for some time, the men making coffee—many of them bathing in the creek. So the hours passed pleasantly away. The command had rested and taken short naps at halts. It was ominously quiet along our front, the quietness being broken only by some desultory infantry and artillery firing, doubtless both armies being occupied in getting ready to renew the contest.

About 4 P.M., the report of a solitary cannon was heard away over to the left. It was from Sickles, and the battle of the 2nd of July had commenced. This single cannon firing was followed by more and then *one, two*, somewhat broken. Then came the final crash and roar of musketry and booming of artillery together.

Sykes' Fifth Corps was then ordered to Little Round Top, following no roadway. Tearing down fences, the men double-quicked out past Little Round Top, near where two brigades of Regulars of Ayres' Division were already engaged. Weed's Brigade halted behind a battery actively engaged. The One Hundred and Fifty-fifth men loaded muskets and then by orders countermarched, left in front, and took position on Little Round Top. The One Hundred and Fifty-fifth, of Weed's Brigade, was on the right of the line and Company B on the right of the Regiment. A good view of that portion of the field, when not obscured by the smoke of battle, was afforded. The two small brigades of United States Regulars of Ayres' Division had advanced beyond the position of the One Hundred and Fifty-fifth on Little Round Top, toward the Wheatfield, this movement being made by the United States Regulars to support General Sickles. The Regulars fought with determined skill and bravery for nearly an hour, and then reluctantly fell back as if on drill, but sharply and bravely contesting every foot of the ground. These things I saw, and I am glad, as a volunteer, to bear tribute to the United States Regulars.

The remaining portion of the Third Corps and Regulars were overwhelmed, and fell back to Little Round Top. There were two batteries of artillery, one of steel and the other of brass pieces, one in front and one over to the right of the Regiment, which kept up their fire until the very last, two of the steel guns being captured, and one of them recaptured later from the enemy. In the meantime the Regulars reformed in line of battle a little below the position of the One Hundred and Fifty-fifth on the crest of Little Round Top, and the fire in our immediate front slackened temporarily. The enemy appeared and advanced from the Devil's Den and to the left of it, and owing to the formation of the ground, struck the left of the line of Weed's Brigade at its extended concave portion, and the fight became terrific.

Just then Robertson's Brigade of Texans swung across the foot of the hill and advanced to attack the positions occupied by the One Hundred and Fortieth and One Hundred and Forty-sixth New York, and the Ninety-first and One Hundred and Fifty-fifth Pennsylvania Volunteers. I wondered why our battery immediately above us did not open fire. Five minutes pass away. What is the matter? Then the battery opened, and over our head went a screaming, whistling shell followed by another and another and so on. Still the enemy kept on advancing on the positions of the four regiments mentioned which formed Weed's Brigade. Impatiently waiting as we were, it was hard to repress our fire. At last the order came to us, "Steady—Ready—Aim—Fire!" We arose and delivered our fire at close buck-and-ball range of our muskets, and reloaded and fired again, but still the Confederates kept advancing, halting to fire volleys as they advanced.

The Confederates were brave, resolute, and determined men. At this time I was wounded in the ball of the right ankle joint. I felt a stinging sensation extending to the thigh, but no pain. The enemy's bullets kept coming as numerous apparently as the drops of rain in a heavy storm. As I lay there wounded I expected to get a bullet in my head at any moment, but fortunately did not. Looking in front of my position, I saw Corporal David M. Smith, of our company, lying mortally wounded behind a shelving rock about five yards from my position. Being hit in the left groin, the ball must have severed the femoral artery. He turned to me and said, "Oh! I am shot." The stretcher-bearers carried him back a short time after, but he died just as they reached the foot of the hill. While I was trying all in my power to encourage Corporal Smith, a bullet struck Comrade William Douglass, of my company, fairly in the center of the forehead, and with a terrible shriek, he fell back dead. I shall never forget the sight.

In the light of "after discovered evidence," a charge, which Major A.L. Pearson sought permission to make at that time and was refused, would have been wrong. Weed's Brigade having been assigned and ordered to hold that portion of Little Round Top only. General Meade wisely provided other troops for that purpose, and ordered them to do the charging.

Lieutenant Luke J. Dooling, of Company I, seeing that I was wounded and unable to stand, the pain having become excruciating, ran up to me exclaiming, "Poor boy! are you hurt—are you wounded?" I threw my arms around his and Comrade Pat Lyon's necks, and was thus taken back some distance, until we met some stretcher-bearers from the Sixth Corps, who carried me a short distance to the rear, at the foot of Little Round Top, passing what was evidently a brigade of the Sixth Corps being formed in line of battle one behind the other in perfect formation, which did me good to see, as the musketry fire at the front occupied by Weed's Brigade was still severe, and the battle by no means decided. General

Meade's provision for the reserve line of battle was perfect. Shells and balls from the enemy were coming through the trees and knocking off the branches here and there, during the passage of the wounded to the rear. We also passed two members of our company bearing the body of Corporal Smith, who had just died from his wounds.

I was next placed in an ambulance, which, after receiving other wounded soldiers, not of our regiment, started back along the Taneytown road and we were deposited on the ground near Meade's headquarters, on the left center of the Union lines, where we lay all night.

Some time later the Union batteries on the ridge in front of where the wounded were placed opened on the enemy. I never could understand this, as our yellow hospital flags were flying and plainly visible from the small buildings. Why our artillerists at that time should draw the enemy's fire at a point where their answering missiles would fall among the already wounded men seemed incomprehensible. The enemy at once responded, and their fire became so warm as to compel the removal of the wounded, who were taken in ambulances to our right and laid under trees and woods. Escaping from the fire of the enemy in this position, the wounded were not so fortunate otherwise, as during the night one terrific thunderstorm after another broke out over our heads, followed by vivid flashes of lightning, continuing through the night. I pulled my gum blanket over my head and wrapped it around my body the best I could, and was thus afforded some protection from the rain. Early in the morning I was carried and laid on the ground a short distance from the field-hospital operating table. The rain still continuing, I made a pillow of my haversack, and again pulling my gum blanket over my face, lay there as patiently as I could, waiting my turn to be operated on. During a lull in the battle, Pat Lyon and Isaac Craig, of our Company, hunted me up, and Pat, taking his blanket from his shoulder, threw it over me, as I, being well-drenched, was shivering with cold.

A period of several hours followed, during which we heard but little firing at the front. Suddenly the artillery fire from a hundred guns opened and the din was terrific, evidently being the initial attack on our side to repel Pickett's charge. During all this noise and confusion, I was removed and placed on the operating table, and had my foot amputated by Doctor Reed, Regimental Surgeon of the One Hundred and Fifty-fifth, assisted by the surgeon of the Ninety-first Pennsylvania Volunteers. As they were about to administer the chloroform to me, I heard Dr. Billings, a Regular army surgeon, say "Let us be as quick as we can, as some of us may be killed during the operation." The shells and stray balls from the Confederates at that time were whistling through the location of the field hospital and the limbs of the trees were falling in every direction. There did not seem to be safety at any place in this trying period of the battle.

After the operation had been performed in this exposed field hospital in the immediate rear of Little Round Top, and the shelling and noise had subsided at the front, and I was lifted from the operating table still in a semiconscious state, I was again laid on the ground which had been covered with straw taken by "eminent domain" from neighboring barns. Soon after small tents were erected, and all the wounded were placed in them as fast as they were put up, so as to guard against drenching rains.

Color-Corporals Thomas J. Tomer, of Company E, and John H. Mackin, of Company F, who also had been wounded while with the colors, about the same time I was wounded, secured quarters in one of these tents. Privates Charles F. McKenna, of Company E, and Samuel W Hill, of Company F, as soon as the firing in front ceased, were allowed to leave the ranks to visit Corporals Tomer, Mackin, myself and other companions in a field hospital in rear of Little Round Top and their visit cheered us very much.

From the tents the wounded could see most grewsome sights. Amputations of arms and legs by the army surgeons, to save the lives of the wounded, ran up into thousands; and for want of assistance these dissevered members, the first few days, were suffered to accumulate in piles several feet in height. The bodies of the poor comrades not surviving these operations, and the hundreds of dead from wounds or blood poisoning were placed in the dead-house close by, to await burial. These harrowing environments were not conducive towards cheering or comforting the suffering wounded.

Night, letting her sable mantle down, shut from view the terrible scenes of human wrath. Everything quieted down, and we slept fitfully until the next morning, the Fourth of July. Late in the day, the surgeon in charge came in and greeting the wounded, said, "Well, while you are all in pretty bad shape, you seem to be in good spirits, and I have good news for you. This battle is won, the rebels are retreating—Vicksburg has also fallen, and so this is a good and glorious Fourth of July after all. Don't you think so?"

It is needless to say we answered him with an affirmative shout.

Chapter IX

HIGHWATER MARK OF THE CONFEDERACY

Unhappy with his inability to crack Meade's line on 2 July, Lee planned a daring attack on the Federal center composed of 15,000 men of Pickett's and two of A.P. Hill's divisions. After a massive bombardment from 130 Confederate cannon, the mammoth force left the protective cover near Seminary Ridge and set off on a long and desperate march over half a mile of clear ground to attack the enemy lines on Cemetery Ridge. In a battle lasting only one hour, the Confederates were forced to fall back after losing roughly 6,500 men. The high water mark of the Confederacy had been reached, Lee had met defeat, and there was nothing left for the Army of Northern Virginia to do but fall back across the Potomac and wait for the next major Federal offensive.

RAWLEY W. MARTIN

In Pickett's Ranks

On 3 July, after a tremendous bombardment around 1500, the doomed
assault forever known as Pickett's Charge was launched on its impossible
mission. As the picturesque lines of butternut and gray advanced against
the enemy, their ranks were torn apart by the increasing swell of
thundering cannon and eruptions of deadly musketry. Though some
Southerners were able to break through the Yankee defenses, these gains
were quickly lost and the survivors retreated to the safety of their own
lines. Rawly Martin, member of the 53rd Virginia, wrote of his recollections of the fatal offensive in the *Southern Society Historical Papers*.

In the effort to comply with your request to describe Pickett's charge at
Gettysburg, I may unavoidably repeat what has often been told before,
as the position of troops, the cannonade, the advance, and the final
disaster are familiar to all who have the interest or the curiosity to read.
My story will be short, for I shall only attempt to describe what fell under
my own observation.

You ask for a description of the "feelings of the brave Virginians who
passed through that hell of fire in their heroic charge on Cemetery
Ridge." The *esprit du corps* could not have been better; the men were in
good physical condition, self reliant and determined. They felt the
gravity of the situation, for they knew well the metal of the foe in their
front; they were serious and resolute, but not disheartened. None of the
usual jokes, common on the eve of battle, were indulged in, for every
man felt his individual responsibility, and realized that he had the most
stupendous work of his life before him; officers and men knew at what
cost and at what risk the advance was to be made, but they had
deliberately made up their minds to attempt it. I believe the general
sentiment of the division was that they would succeed in driving the
Federal line from what was their objective point; they knew that many,

very many, would go down under the storm of shot and shell which would greet them when their gray ranks were spread out to view, but it never occurred to them that disaster would come after they once placed their tattered banners upon the crest of Seminary Ridge.

I believe if those men had been told: "This day your lives will pay the penalty of your attack upon the Federal lines," they would have made the charge just as it was made. There was no straggling, no feigned sickness, no pretense of being overcome by the intense heat; every man felt that it was his duty to make that fight; that he was his own commander, and they would have made the charge without an officer of any description; they only needed to be told what they were expected to do. This is as near the feeling of the men of Pickett's Division on the morning of the battle as I can give, and with this feeling they went to their work. Many of them were veteran soldiers, who had followed the little cross of stars from Big Bethel to Gettysburg; they knew their own power, and they knew the temper of their adversary; they had often met before, and they knew the meeting before them would be desperate and deadly.

Pickett's three little Virginia brigades were drawn up in two lines, Kemper on the right (1st, 3d, 7th, 11th and 24), Garnett on the left (8th, 18th, 19th, 28th and 56th), and Armistead in the rear and center (9th, 14th, 38th, 53d and 57th) Virginia Regiments, covering the space between Kemper's left and Garnett's right flanks. This position was assigned Armistead, I suppose, that he might at the critical moment rush to the assistance of the two leading brigades, and if possible, put the capstone upon their work. We will see presently how he succeeded. The Confederate artillery was on the crest of Seminary Ridge, nearly in front of Pickett; only a part of the division had the friendly shelter of the woods; the rest endured the scorching rays of the July sun until the opening of the cannonade, when the dangers from the Federal batteries were added to their discomfort. About 1 o'clock two signal guns were fired by the Washington Artillery, and instantly a terrific cannonade was commenced, which lasted for more than an hour, when suddenly everything was silent. Every man knew what that silence portended. The grim blue battle line on Seminary Ridge began at once to prepare for the advance of its antagonists; both sides felt that the tug of war was about to come, and that Greek must meet Greek as they had never met before.

From this point, I shall confine my description to events connected with Armistead's brigade, with which I served. Soon after the cannonade ceased, a courier dashed up to General Armistead, who was pacing up and down in front of the 53d Virginia Regiment, his battalion of direction (which I commanded in the charge and at the head of which Armistead marched), and gave him the order from General Pickett to prepare for the advance. At once the command "Attention, battalion!" rang out clear and distinct. Instantly every man was on his feet and in his place; the alignment was made with as much coolness and precision as if preparing for dress parade. Then Armistead went up to the color sergeant of the 53d Virginia Regiment and said: "Sergeant, are you going to put those colors on the enemy's works to-day?" The gallant fellow replied: "I will try sir, and if mortal man can do it, it shall be done." It was done, but not until this brave man, and many others like him, had fallen with their faces to the foe; but never once did that banner trail in the dust, for some brave fellow invariably caught it as it was going down, and again bore it aloft, until Armistead saw its tattered folds unfurled on the very crest of Seminary Ridge.

After this exchange of confidence between the general and the color-bearer, Armistead commanded: "Right shoulder, shift arms. Forward, march." They stepped out at quick time, in perfect order and alignment—tramp, tramp, up to the Emmittsburg road; then the advancing Confederates saw the long line of blue, nearly a mile distant, ready and awaiting their coming. The scene was grand and terrible, and well calculated to demoralize the stoutest heart; but not a step faltered, not an elbow lost the touch of its neighbor, not a face blanched, for these men had determined to do their whole duty and reckoned not the cost. On they go; at about 1,100 yards the Federal batteries opened fire; the advancing Confederates encounter and sweep before them the Federal skirmish line. Still forward they go; hissing, screaming shells break in their front, rear, on their flanks, all about them, but the devoted band, with the blue line in their front as their objective point, press forward, keeping step to the music of the battle. The distance between the opposing forces grows less and less, until suddenly the infantry behind the rock fence poured volley after volley into the advancing ranks. The men fell like stalks of grain before the reaper, but still they closed the gaps and pressed forward through that pitiless storm. The two advance brigades have thus far done the fighting. Armistead has endured the terrible ordeal without firing a gun; his brave followers have not changed their guns from the right shoulder. Great gaps have been torn in their ranks; their field and company officers have fallen; color-bearer after color-bearer has been shot down, but still they never faltered.

At the critical moment, in response to a request from Kemper, Armistead, bracing himself to the desperate blow, rushed forward to Kemper's and Garnett's line, delivered his fire, and with one supreme effort planted his colors on the famous rock fence. Armistead himself, with his hat on the point of his sword, that his men might see it through the smoke of battle, rushed forward, scaled the wall, and cried: "Boys, give them the cold steel!" By this time, the Federal hosts lapped around both flanks and made a counter advance in their front, and the remnant of those three little brigades melted away. Armistead himself had fallen, mortally wounded, under the guns he had captured, while the few who followed him over the fence were either dead or wounded. The charge was over, the sacrifice had been made, but, in the words of a Federal officer: "Banks of heroes they were; they fled not, but amidst that still continuous and terrible fire they slowly, sullenly recrossed the plain—all that was left of them—but few of the five thousand."

When the advance commenced General Pickett rode up and down in rear of Kemper and Garnett, and in this position he continued as long as there was opportunity of observing him. When the assault became so fierce that he had to superintend the whole line, I am sure he was in his proper place. A few years ago Pickett's staff held a meeting in the city of Richmond, Va., and after comparing recollections, they published a statement to the effect that he was with the division throughout the charge; that he made an effort to secure reinforcements when he saw his flanks were being turned, and one of General Garnett's couriers testified that he carried orders from him almost to the rock fence. From my knowledge of General Pickett I am sure he was where his duty called him throughout the engagement. He was too fine a soldier, and had fought too many battles not to be where he was most needed on that supreme occasion of his military life.

The ground over which the charge was made was an open terrene, with slight depressions and elevations, but insufficient to be serviceable to the advancing column. At the Emmettsburg road, where the parallel fences impeded the onward march, large numbers were shot down on account of the crowding at the openings where the fences had been thrown down, and on account of the halt in order to climb the fences. After passing these obstacles, the advancing column deliberately rearranged its lines and moved forward. Great gaps were made in their ranks as they moved on, but they were closed up as deliberately and promptly as if on the parade ground; the touch of elbows was always to the centre, the men keeping constantly in view the little emblem which was their beacon light to guide them to glory and to death.

I will mention a few instances of individual coolness and bravery exhibited in the charge. In the 53d Virginia Regiment, I saw every man of Company F (Captain Henry Edmunds, now a distinguished member of the Virginia bar) thrown flat to the earth by the explosion of a shell from Round Top, but every man who was not killed or desperately wounded sprang to his feet, collected himself and moved forward to close the gap made in the regimental front. A soldier from the same regiment was shot on the shin; he stopped in the midst of that terrific fire, rolled up his trousers leg, examined his wound, and went forward even to the rock fence. He escaped further injury, and was one of the few who returned to his friends, but so bad was his wound that it was nearly a year before he was fit for duty. When Kemper was riding off, after asking Armistead to move up to his support, Armistead called him, and, pointing to his brigade, said: "Did you ever see a more perfect line than that on dress parade?" It was, indeed, a lance head of steel, whose metal had been tempered in the furnace of conflict. As they were about to enter upon their work, Armistead, as was invariably his custom on going into battle, said: "Men, remember your wives, your mothers, your sisters and your sweethearts." Such an appeal would have made those men assault the ramparts of the infernal regions.

You asked me to tell how the field looked after the charge, and how the men went back. This I am unable to do, as I was disabled at Armistead's side a moment after he had fallen, and left on the Federal side of the stone fence. I was picked up by the Union forces after their lines were reformed, and I take this occasion to express my grateful recollection of the attention I received on the field, particularly from Colonel Hess, of the 72d Pennsylvania (I think). If he still lives, I hope yet to have the pleasure of grasping his hand and expressing to him my gratitude for his kindness to me. Only the brave know how to treat a fallen foe.

I cannot close this letter without reference to the Confederate chief, General R.E. Lee. Somebody blundered at Gettysburg but not Lee. He was too great a master of the art of war to have hurled a handful of men against an army. It has been abundantly shown that the fault lay not with him, but with others, who failed to execute his orders.

SIR ARTHUR FREMANTLE

"All this has been my fault..."

With the Confederate commanders during the great attack, Sir Arthur
Fremantle played witness to the reactions of Lee and Longstreet as the
final drama of Pickett's Charge was played out. Despite suffering a
disappointing and destructive defeat, the leaders and men of the Army
of Northern Virginia remained calm even though the tide of battle as
well as the entire war had turned against them.

At 6 A.M. I rode to the field with Colonel Manning, and went over that
portion of the ground which, after a fierce contest, had been won from
the enemy yesterday evening. The dead were being buried, but great
numbers were still lying about; also many mortally wounded, for whom
nothing could be done. Amongst the latter were a number of Yankees
dressed in bad imitations of the Zouave costume. They opened their
glazed eyes as I rode past in a painfully imploring manner.

We joined Generals Lee and Longstreet's Staff: they were reconnoitring and making preparations for renewing the attack. As we formed
a pretty large party, we often drew upon ourselves the attention of the
hostile sharpshooters, and were two or three times favoured with a shell.
One of these shells set a brick building on fire which was situated between
the lines. This building was filled with wounded, principally Yankees,
who, I am afraid, must have perished miserably in the flames. Colonel
Sorrel had been slightly wounded yesterday, but still did duty. Major
Walton's horse was killed, but there were no other casualties amongst my
particular friends.

The plan of yesterday's attack seems to have been very simple—first
a heavy cannonade all along the line, followed by an advance of Longstreet's two divisions and part of Hill's corps. In consequence of the
enemy's having been driven back some distance, Longstreet's corps (part
of it) was in a much more forward situation than yesterday. But the range

of heights to be gained was still most formidable, and evidently strongly intrenched.

The distance between the Confederate guns and the Yankee position—*i.e.*, between the woods crowning the opposite ridges—was at least a mile,—quite open, gently undulating, and exposed to artillery the whole distance. This was the ground which had to be crossed in to-day's attack. Pickett's division, which had just come up, was to bear the brunt in Longstreet's attack, together with Heth and Pettigrew in Hill's corps. Pickett's division was a weak one (under 5000), owing to the absence of two brigades.

At noon all Longstreet's dispositions were made; his troops for attack were deployed into line, and lying down in the woods; his batteries were ready to open. The General then dismounted and went to sleep for a short time. The Austrian officer and I now rode off to get, if possible, into some commanding position from whence we could see the whole thing without being exposed to the tremendous fire which was about to commence. After riding about for half an hour without being able to discover so desirable a situation, we determined to make for the cupola, near Gettysburg, Ewell's headquarters. Just before we reached the entrance to the town, the cannonade opened with a fury which surpassed even that of yesterday.

Soon after passing through the toll-gate at the entrance of Gettysburg, we found that we had got into a heavy cross-fire; shells both Federal and Confederate passing over our heads with great frequency. At length two shrapnel shells burst quite close to us, and a ball from one of them hit the officer who was conducting us. We then turned round and changed our views with regard to the cupola—the fire of one side being bad enough, but preferable to that of both sides. A small boy of twelve years was riding with us at the time: this urchin took a diabolical interest in the bursting of the shells, and screamed with delight when he saw them take effect. I never saw this boy again, or found out who he was. The road at Gettysburg was lined with Yankee dead, and as they had been killed on the lst, the poor fellows had already begun to be very offensive. We then returned to the hill I was on yesterday. But finding that, to see the actual fighting, it was absolutely necessary to go into the thick of the thing, I determined to make my way to General Longstreet. It was then about 2.30. After passing General Lee and his Staff, I rode on through the woods in the direction in which I had left Longstreet. I soon began to meet many wounded men returning from the front; many of them asked in piteous tones the way to a doctor or an ambulance. The further I got, the greater became the number of the wounded. At last I came to a perfect stream of them flocking through the woods in numbers as great as the crowd in Oxford Street in the middle of the day. Some were walking alone on crutches composed of two rifles, others were supported by men less badly wounded than themselves, and others were carried on stretchers by the ambulance corps; but in no case did I see a sound man helping the wounded to the rear, unless he carried the red badge of the ambulance corps. They were still under a heavy fire; the shells were continually bringing down great limbs of trees, and carrying further destruction amongst this melancholy procession. I saw all this in much less time than it takes to write it, and although astonished to meet such vast numbers of wounded, I had not seen *enough* to give me any idea of the real extent of the mischief.

When I got close up to General Longstreet, I saw one of his regiments advancing through the woods in good order; so, thinking I was just in time to see the attack, I remarked to the General that *"I wouldn't have missed this for anything."* Longstreet was seated at the top of a snake fence at the edge of the wood, and looking perfectly calm and imperturbed. He replied, laughing, *"The devil you wouldn't! I would like to have missed it very much; we've attacked and been repulsed: look there!"*

For the first time I then had a view of the open space between the two positions, and saw it covered with Confederates slowly and sulkily returning towards us in small broken parties, under a heavy fire of artillery. But the fire where we were was not so bad as further to the rear; for although the air seemed alive with shell, yet the greater number burst behind us.

The General told me that Pickett's division had succeeded in carrying the enemy's position and capturing his guns, but after remaining there twenty minutes, it had been forced to retire, on the retreat of Heth and Pettigrew on its left. No person could have been more calm or self-possessed than General Longstreet under these trying circumstances, aggravated as they now were by the movements of the enemy, who began to show a strong disposition to advance. I could now thoroughly appreciate the term bulldog, which I had heard applied to him by the soldiers. Difficulties seem to make no other impression upon him than to make him a little more savage.

Major Walton was the only officer with him when I came up—all the rest had been put into the charge. In a few minutes Major Latrobe arrived on foot, carrying his saddle, having just had his horse killed. Colonel Sorrel was also in the same predicament, and Captain Goree's horse was wounded in the mouth.

The General was making the best arrangements in his power to resist the threatened advance, by advancing some artillery, rallying the stragglers, &c. I remember seeing a General (Pettigrew, I think it was) come up to him, and report that "he was unable to bring his men up again." Longstreet turned upon him and replied with some sarcasm, *"Very well; never mind, then, General; just let them remain where they are: the enemy's going to advance, and will spare you the trouble."*

He asked for something to drink: I gave him some rum out of my silver flask, which I begged he would keep in remembrance of the occasion; he smiled, and, to my great satisfaction, accepted the memorial. He then went off to give some orders to McLaws' division. Soon afterwards I joined General Lee, who had in the meanwhile come to that part of the field on becoming aware of the disaster. If Longstreet's conduct was admirable, that of General Lee was perfectly sublime. He was engaged in rallying and in encouraging the broken troops, and was riding about a little in front of the wood, quite alone—the whole of his Staff being engaged in a similar manner further to the rear. His face, which is always placid and cheerful, did not show signs of the slightest disappointment, care, or annoyance; and he was addressing to every soldier he met a few words of encouragement, such as, "All this will come right in the end: we'll talk it over afterwards; but, in the mean time, all good men must rally. We want all good and true men just now," &c. He spoke to all the wounded men that passed him, and the slightly wounded he exhorted "to bind up their hurts and take up a musket" in this emergency. Very few failed to answer his appeal, and I saw many badly wounded men take off their hats and cheer him. He said to me, "This has been a sad day for us, Colonel—a sad day; but we can't expect always to gain victories." He was also kind enough to advise me to get into some more sheltered position, as the shells were bursting round us with considerable frequency.

Notwithstanding the misfortune which had so suddenly befallen him, General Lee seemed to observe everything, however trivial. When a mounted officer began licking his horse for shying at the bursting of a shell, he called out, "Don't whip him, Captain; don't whip him. I've got just such another foolish horse myself, and whipping does no good."

I happened to see a man lying flat on his face in a small ditch, and I remarked that I didn't think he seemed dead; this drew General Lee's attention to the man, who commenced groaning dismally. Finding appeals to his patriotism of no avail, General Lee had him ignominiously set on his legs by some neighbouring gunners.

I saw General Wilcox (an officer who wears a short round jacket and a battered straw hat) come up to him, and explain, almost crying, the state of his brigade. General Lee immediately shook hands with him and said, cheerfully "Never mind, General, *all this has been MY fault*—it is *I* that have lost this fight, and you must help me out of it in the best way you can." In this manner I saw General Lee encourage and reanimate his somewhat dispirited troops, and magnanimously take upon his own shoulders the whole weight of the repulse. It was impossible to look at him or to listen to him without feeling the strongest admiration, and I never saw any man fail him except the man in the ditch.

It is difficult to exaggerate the critical state of affairs as they appeared about this time. If the enemy or their general had shown any enterprise, there is no saying what might have happened. General Lee and his officers were evidently fully impressed with a sense of the situation; yet there was much less noise, fuss, or confusion of orders than at an ordinary field-day: the men, as they were rallied in the wood, were brought up in detachments, and lay down quietly and coolly in the positions assigned to them.

We heard that Generals Garnett and Armistead were killed, and General Kemper mortally wounded; also, that Pickett's division had only one field officer unhurt. Nearly all this slaughter took place in an open space about one mile square, and within one hour.

At 6 P.M. we heard a long and continuous Yankee cheer, which we at first imagined was an indication of an advance; but it turned out to be their reception of a general officer, whom we saw riding down the line, followed by about thirty horsemen. Soon afterwards I rode to the extreme front, where there were four pieces of rifled cannon almost without any infantry support. To the non-withdrawal of these guns is to be attributed the otherwise surprising inactivity of the enemy. I was immediately surrounded by a sergeant and about half-a-dozen gunners, who seemed in excellent spirits and full of confidence, in spite of their exposed situation. The sergeant expressed his ardent hope that the Yankees might have spirit enough to advance and receive the dose he had in readiness for them. They spoke in admiration of the advance of Pickett's division, and of the manner in which Pickett himself had led it. When they observed General Lee they said, "We've not lost confidence in the old man: this day's work won't do him no harm. 'Uncle Robert' will get us into Washington yet; you bet he will!" &c. Whilst we were talking, the enemy's skirmishers began to advance slowly, and several ominous sounds in quick succession told us that we were attracting their attention, and that it was necessary to break up the conclave. I therefore turned round and took leave of these cheery and plucky gunners.

At 7 P.M., General Lee received a report that Johnson's division of Ewell's corps had been successful on the left, and had gained important advantages there. Firing entirely ceased in our front about this time; but we now heard some brisk musketry on our right, which I afterwards learned proceeded from Hood's Texans, who had managed to surround some enterprising Yankee cavalry, and were slaughtering them with great satisfaction. Only eighteen out of four hundred are said to have escaped.

At 7.30, all idea of a Yankee attack being over, I rode back to Moses's tent, and found that worthy commissary in very low spirits, all sorts of exaggerated rumours having reached him. On my way I met a great many wounded men, most anxious to inquire after Longstreet, who was reported killed; when I assured them he was quite well, they seemed to forget their own pain in the evident pleasure they felt in the safety of their chief. No words that I can use will adequately express the extraordinary patience and fortitude with which the wounded Confederates bore their sufferings.

I got something to eat with the doctors at 10 P.M., the first for fifteen hours.

I gave up my horse to-day to his owner, as from death and exhaustion the Staff are almost without horses.

JOHN D. IMBODEN

Retreat from Gettysburg

On the 4th of July, 1863, Robert E. Lee put his battered Army of Northern Virginia on the roads that led back to Virginia and safety. Guarding the wagon trains and ambulances during the retreat was Brigadier General John D. Imboden's cavalry command. A resourceful Virginian, Imboden rose from the ranks after winning a captain's rank in the artillery. His reminiscences are taken from *Battles and Leaders of the Civil War.*

During the Gettysburg campaign, my command—an independent brigade of cavalry—was engaged, by General Lee's confidential orders, in raids on the left flank of his advancing army, destroying railroad bridges and cutting the canal below Cumberland wherever I could—so that I did not reach the field till noon of the last day's battle. I reported direct to General Lee for orders, and was assigned a position to aid in repelling any cavalry demonstration on his rear. None of a serious character being made, my little force took no part in the battle, but were merely spectators of the scene, which transcended in grandeur any that I beheld in any other battle of the war.

When night closed the struggle, Lee's army was repulsed. We all knew that the day had gone against us, but the full extent of the disaster was only known in high quarters. The carnage of the day was generally understood to have been frightful, yet our army was not in retreat, and it was surmised in camp that with to-morrow's dawn would come a renewal of the struggle. All felt and appreciated the momentous consequences to the cause of Southern independence of final defeat or victory on that great field.

It was a warm summer's night; there were few camp-fires, and the weary soldiers were lying in groups on the luxuriant grass of the beautiful meadows, discussing the events of the day, speculating on the morrow, or watching that our horses did not straggle off while browsing. About 11 o'clock a horseman came to summon me to General Lee. I promptly mounted and, accompanied by Lieutenant George W. McPhail, an aide on my staff, and guided by the courier who brought the message, rode about two miles toward Gettysburg to where half a dozen small tents were pointed out, a little way from the roadside to our left, as General Lee's headquarters for the night. On inquiry I found that he was not there, but had gone to the headquarters of General A.P. Hill, about half a mile nearer to Gettysburg. When we reached the place indicated, a single flickering candle, visible from the road through the open front of a common wall-tent, exposed to view Generals Lee and Hill seated on camp-stools with a map spread upon their knees. Dismounting, I approached on foot. After exchanging the ordinary salutations General Lee directed me to go back to his headquarters and wait for him. I did so, but he did not make his appearance until about 1 o'clock, when he came riding alone, at a slow walk, and evidently wrapped in profound thought.

When he arrived there was not even a sentinel on duty at his tent, and no one of his staff was awake. The moon was high in the clear sky and the silent scene was unusually vivid. As he approached and saw us lying on the grass under a tree, he spoke, reined in his jaded horse, and essayed to dismount. The effort to do so betrayed so much physical exhaustion that I hurriedly rose and stepped forward to assist him, but before I reached his side he had succeeded in alighting, and threw his arm across the saddle to rest, and fixing his eyes upon the ground leaned in silence and almost motionless upon his equally weary horse,—the two forming a striking and never-to-be-forgotten group. The moon shone full upon his massive features and revealed an expression of sadness that I had never before seen upon his face. Awed by his appearance I waited for him to speak until the silence became embarrassing, when, to break it and change the silent current of his thoughts, I ventured to remark, in a sympathetic tone, and in allusion to his great fatigue:

"General, this has been a hard day on you."

He looked up, and replied mournfully:

"Yes, it has been a sad, sad day to us," and immediately relapsed into his thoughtful mood and attitude. Being unwilling again to intrude upon his reflections, I said no more. After perhaps a minute or two, he suddenly straightened up to his full height, and turning to me with more animation and excitement of manner than I had ever seen in him before, for he was a man of wonderful equanimity, he said in a voice tremulous with emotion:

"I never saw troops behave more magnificently than Pickett's division of Virginians did to-day in that grand charge upon the enemy. And if they had been supported as they were to have been,—but, for some reason not yet fully explained to me, were not,—we would have held the position and the day would have been ours." After a moment's pause he added in a loud voice, in a tone almost of agony, "Too bad! *Too bad!* Oh! Too bad!"

I shall never forget his language, his manner, and his appearance of mental suffering. In a few moments all emotion was suppressed, and he spoke feelingly of several of his fallen and trusted officers; among others of Brigadier-Generals Armistead, Garnett, and Kemper of Pickett's division. He invited me into his tent, and as soon as we were seated he remarked:

"We must now return to Virginia. As many of our poor wounded as possible must be taken home. I have sent for you, because your men and horses are fresh and in good condition, to guard and conduct our train back to Virginia. The duty will be arduous, responsible, and dangerous, for I am afraid you will be harassed by the enemy's cavalry. How many men have you?"

"About 2100 effective present, and all well mounted, including McClanahan's six-gun battery of horse artillery."

"I can spare you as much artillery as you require," he said, "but no other troops, as I shall need all I have to return safely by a different and shorter route than yours. The batteries are generally short of ammunition, but you will probably meet a supply I have ordered from Winchester to Williamsport. Nearly all the transportation and the care of all the wounded will be intrusted to you. You will recross the mountain by the Chambersburg road, and then proceed to Williamsport by any route you deem best, and without a halt till you reach the river. Rest there long enough to feed your animals; then ford the river, and do not halt again till you reach Winchester, where I will again communicate with you."

After a good deal of conversation about roads, and the best disposition of my forces to cover and protect the vast train, he directed that the chiefs of his staff departments should be waked up to receive, in my presence, his orders to collect as early next day as possible all the wagons and ambulances which I was to convoy, and have them in readiness for me to take command of them. His medical director [Dr. Lafayette Guild] was charged to see that all the wounded who could bear the rough journey should be placed in the empty wagons and ambulances. He then remarked to me that his general instructions would be sent to me in writing the following morning. As I was about leaving to return to my camp, as late, I think, as 2 A.M., he came out of his tent to where I was about to mount, and said in an undertone: "I will place in your hands by a staff-officer, to-morrow morning, a sealed package for President Davis, which you will retain in your possession till you are across the Potomac, when you will detail a reliable commissioned officer to take it to Richmond with all possible dispatch and deliver it into the President's own hands. And I impress it on you that, whatever happens, this package must not fall into the hands of the enemy. If unfortunately you should be captured, destroy it at the first opportunity."

On the morning of July 4th my written instructions, and a large official envelope addressed to President Davis, were handed to me by a staff-officer.

It was apparent by 9 o'clock that the wagons, ambulances, and wounded could not be collected and made ready to move till late in the afternoon. General Lee sent to me eight Napoleon guns of the famous Washington Artillery of New Orleans, under the immediate command of Major Eshleman, one of the best artillery officers in the army, a four-gun battery under Captain Tanner, and a Whitworth under Lieutenant Pegram. Hampton's cavalry brigade, then under command of Colonel P.M.B. Young, with Captain James F. Hart's four-gun battery of horse artillery, was ordered to cover the rear of all trains moving under my convoy on the Chambersburg road. These 17 guns and McClanahan's 6 guns gave us 23 pieces in all for the defense of the trains.

Shortly after noon of the 4th the very windows of heaven seemed to have opened. The rain fell in blinding sheets; the meadows were soon overflowed, and fences gave way before the raging streams. During the storm, wagons, ambulances, and artillery carriages by hundreds—nay, by thousands, were assembling in the fields along the road from Gettysburg to Cashtown, in one confused and apparently inextricable mass. As the afternoon wore on there was no abatement in the storm. Canvas was no protection against its fury, and the wounded men lying upon the naked boards of the wagon-bodies were drenched. Horses and mules were blinded and maddened by the wind and water, and became almost unmanageable. The deafening roar of the mingled sounds of heaven and earth all around us made it almost impossible to communicate orders, and equally difficult to execute them.

About 4 P.M. the head of the column was put in motion near Cashtown, and began the ascent of the mountain in the direction of Chambersburg. I remained at Cashtown giving directions and putting in detachments of guns and troops at what I estimated to be intervals of a quarter or a third of a mile. It was found from the position of the head of the column west of the mountain at dawn of the 5th—the hour at which Young's cavalry and Hart's battery began the ascent of the mountain near Cashtown—that the entire column was seventeen miles long when drawn out on the road and put in motion. As an advance-guard I had placed the 18th Virginia Cavalry, Colonel George W. Imboden, in front with a section of McClanahan's battery. Next to them, by request, was placed an ambulance carrying, stretched side by side, two of North Carolina's most distinguished soldiers, Generals Pender and Scales, both badly wounded, but resolved to bear the tortures of the journey rather than become prisoners. I shared a little bread and meat with them at noon, and they waited patiently for hours for the head of the column to move. The trip cost poor Pender his life. General Scales appeared to be worse hurt, but stopped at Winchester, recovered, and fought through the war.

After dark I set out from Cashtown to gain the head of the column during the night. My orders had been peremptory that there should be no halt for any cause whatever. If an accident should happen to any vehicle, it was immediately to be put out of the road and abandoned. The column moved rapidly, considering the rough roads and the darkness, and from almost every wagon for many miles issued heart-rending wails of agony. For four hours I hurried forward on my way to the front, and in all that time I was never out of hearing of the groans and cries of the wounded and dying. Scarcely one in a hundred had received adequate surgical aid, owing to the demands on the hardworking surgeons from still worse cases that had to be left behind. Many of the wounded in the wagons had been without food for thirty-six hours. Their torn and bloody clothing, matted and hardened, was rasping the tender, inflamed, and still oozing wounds. Very few of the wagons had even a layer of straw in them, and all were without springs. The road was rough and rocky from the heavy washings of the preceding day. The jolting was enough to have killed strong men, if long exposed to it. From nearly every wagon as the teams trotted on, urged by whip and shout, came such cries and shrieks as these:

"O God! why can't I die?"

"My God! will no one have mercy and kill me?"

"Stop! Oh! for God's sake, stop just for one minute; take me out and leave me to die on the roadside."

"I am dying! I am dying! My poor wife, my dear children, what will become of you?"

Some were simply moaning; some were praying, and others uttering the most fearful oaths and execrations that despair and agony could wring from them; while a majority, with a stoicism sustained by sublime devotion to the cause they fought for, endured without complaint unspeakable tortures, and even spoke words of cheer and comfort to their unhappy comrades of less will or more acute nerves. Occasionally a wagon would be passed from which only low, deep moans could be heard. No help could be rendered to any of the sufferers. No heed could be given to any of their appeals. Mercy and duty to the many forbade the loss of a moment in the vain effort then and there to comply with the prayers of the few. On! On! we *must* move on. The storm continued, and the darkness was appalling. There was no time even to fill a canteen with water for a dying man; for, except the drivers and the guards, all were wounded and utterly helpless in that vast procession of misery. During this one night I realized more of the horrors of war than I had in all the two preceding years.

And yet in the darkness was our safety, for no enemy would dare attack where he could not distinguish friend from foe. We knew that when day broke upon us we should be harassed by bands of cavalry hanging on our flanks. Therefore our aim was to go as far as possible under cover of the night. Instead of going through Chambersburg, I decided to leave the main road near Fairfield after crossing the mountains, and take "a near cut" across the country to Greencastle, where daybreak on the morning of the 5th of July found the head of our column. We were now twelve or fifteen miles from the Potomac at Williamsport, our point of crossing into Virginia.

Here our apprehended troubles began. After the advance—the 18th Virginia Cavalry—had passed perhaps a mile beyond the town, the citizens to the number of thirty or forty attacked the train with axes, cutting the spokes out of ten or a dozen wheels and dropping the wagons in the streets. The moment I heard of it I sent back a detachment of cavalry to capture every citizen who had been engaged in this work, and treat them as prisoners of war. This stopped the trouble there, but the Union cavalry began to swarm down upon us from the fields and cross-roads, making their attacks in small bodies, and striking the column where there were few or no guards, and thus creating great confusion. I had a narrow escape from capture by one of these parties—of perhaps fifty men that I tried to drive off with canister from two of McClanahan's guns that were close at hand. They would perhaps have been too much for me, had not Colonel Imboden, hearing the firing turned back with his regiment at a gallop, and by the suddenness of his movement surrounded and caught the entire party

To add to our perplexities still further, a report reached me a little after sunrise, that the Federals in large force held Williamsport. I did not fully credit this, and decided to push on. Fortunately the report was untrue. After a great deal of desultory fighting and harassments along the road during the day, nearly the whole of the immense train reached Williamsport on the afternoon of the 5th. A part of it, with Hart's battery, came in next day, General Young having halted and turned his attention to guarding the road from the west with his cavalry. We took possession of the town to convert it into a great hospital for the thousands of wounded we had brought from Gettysburg. I required all the families in the place to go to cooking for the sick and wounded, on pain of having their kitchens occupied for that purpose by my men. They readily complied. A large number of surgeons had accompanied the train, and these at once pulled off their coats and went to work, and soon a vast amount of suffering was mitigated. The bodies of a few who had died on the march were buried. All this became necessary because the tremendous rains had raised the river more than ten feet above the fording stage of water, and we could not possibly cross them. There were two small ferry-boats or "flats" there, which I immediately put into requisition to carry across those of the wounded, who, after being fed and having their wounds dressed, thought they could walk to Winchester. Quite a large number were able to do this, so that the "flats" were kept running all the time.

Our situation was frightful. We had probably ten thousand animals and nearly all the wagons of General Lee's army under our charge, and all the wounded, to the number of several thousand, that could be brought from Gettysburg. Our supply of provisions consisted of a few wagon-loads of flour in my own brigade train, a small lot of fine fat cattle which I had collected in Pennsylvania on my way to Gettysburg, and some sugar and coffee procured in the same way at Mercersburg.

The town of Williamsport is located in the lower angle formed by the Potomac with Conococheague Creek. These streams inclose the town on two sides, and back of it about one mile there is a low range of hills that is crossed by four roads converging at the town. The first is the Greencastle road leading down the creek valley; next the Hagerstown road; then the Boonsboro' road; and lastly the River road.

Early on the morning of the 6th I received intelligence of the approach from Frederick of a large body of cavalry with three full batteries of six rifled guns. These were the divisions of Generals Buford and Kilpatrick, and Huey's brigade of Gregg's division, consisting, as I afterward learned, of 23 regiments of cavalry, and 18 guns, a total force of about 7000 men.

I immediately posted my guns on the hills that concealed the town, and dismounted my own command to support them—and ordered as many of the wagoners to be formed as could be armed with the guns of the wounded that we had brought from Gettysburg. In this I was greatly aided by Colonel J.L. Black of South Carolina, Captain J.F. Hart commanding a battery from the same State, Colonel William R. Aylett of Virginia, and other wounded officers. By noon about 700 wagoners were organized into companies of 100 each and officered by wounded line-officers and commissaries and quartermasters,—about 250 of these were given to Colonel Aylett on the right next the river,—about as many under Colonel Black on the left, and the residue were used as skirmishers. My own command proper was held well in hand in the center.

The enemy appeared in our front about half-past one o'clock on both the Hagerstown and Boonsboro' roads, and the fight began. Every man under my command understood that if we did not repulse the enemy we should all be captured and General Lee's army be ruined by the loss of its transportation, which at that period could not have been replaced in the Confederacy. The fight began with artillery on both sides. The firing from our side was very rapid, and seemed to make the enemy hesitate about advancing. In a half hour J.D. Moore's battery ran out of ammunition, but as an ordnance train had arrived from Winchester, two wagon-loads of ammunition were ferried across the river and run upon the field behind the guns, and the boxes tumbled out, to be broken open with axes. With this fresh supply our guns were all soon in full play again. As the enemy could not see the supports of our batteries from the hill-tops, I moved the whole line forward to his full view, in single ranks, to show a long front on the Hagerstown approach. My line passed our guns fifty or one hundred yards, where they were halted awhile, and then were withdrawn behind the hill-top again, slowly and steadily.

Leaving Black's wagoners and the Marylanders on the left to support Hart's and Moore's batteries, Captain Hart having been put in command by Colonel Black when he was obliged to be elsewhere, I moved the 18th Virginia Cavalry and 62d Virginia Mounted Infantry rapidly to the right, to meet and repel five advancing regiments (dismounted) of the enemy. My three regiments, with Captain John H. McNeill's Partisan Rangers and Aylett's wagoners, had to sustain a very severe contest. Hart, seeing how hard we were pressed on the right, charged the enemy's right with his little command, and at the same time Eshleman with his eight Napoleons advanced four hundred yards to the front, and got an enfilading position, from which, with the aid of McClanahan's battery, he poured a furious fire into the enemy's line. The 62d and Aylett, supported by the 18th Cavalry, and McNeill, charged the enemy who fell back sullenly to their horses.

Night was now rapidly approaching, when a messenger from Fitzhugh Lee arrived to urge me to "hold my own," as he would be up in a half hour with three thousand fresh men. The news was sent along our whole line, and was received with a wild and exultant yell. We knew then that the field was won, and slowly pressed forward. Almost at the same moment we heard distant guns on the enemy's rear and right on the Hagerstown road. They were Stuart's, who was approaching on that road, while Fitzhugh Lee was coming on the Greencastle road. That settled the contest. The enemy broke to the left and fled by the Boonsboro' road. It was too dark to follow. When General Fitzhugh Lee joined me with his staff on the field, one of parted from the general that morning. He had left with his staff to ride toward Hagerstown, where a heavy artillery fire indicated an attack by the enemy in considerable force. When I overtook him he said that he understood I was familiar with the fords of the Potomac from Williamsport to Cumberland, and with the roads to them. I replied that I was. He then called up one of his staff, either General Long or General Alexander, I think, and directed him to write down my answers to his questions, and required me to name and describe ford after ford all the way up to Cumberland, and to describe minutely their character, and the roads and surrounding country on both sides of the river, and directed me, after I had given him all the information I could, to send to him my brother and his regiment, the 18th Virginia Cavalry, to act as an advance and guide if he should require it. He did not say so, but I felt that his situation was precarious in the extreme. When about to dismiss me, referring to the freshet in the river he laughingly said: "You know this country well enough to tell me whether it ever quits raining about here? If so, I should like to see a clear day soon." I did not see him again till he left the Shenandoah Valley for the east side of the Blue Ridge.

SAMUEL LOVER

"The Girl I Left Behind"

A tearful song lamenting the pains of leaving a lover to face possible death on the fields of battle, "The Girl I Left Behind Me" enjoyed a great deal of popularity among Union troops. Yankee bands played the song as Hooker led the Army of the Potomac out of the encampment at Falmouth to move on Chancellorsville and the Iron Brigade went into the fight at Gettysburg to the same tune.

The hour was sad I left the maid, a lingering
    farewell taking,
Her sighs and tears my steps delay'd, I thought
    her heart was breaking;
In hurried words her name I bless'd, I breathed
    the vows that bind me,
And to my heart in anguish press'd the girl I left
    behind me.
Then to the East we bore away, to win a name
    in story,
And there where dawns the sun of day, there
    dawns our sun of glory;
Both blazed in noon on Alma's height, where in
    the post assign'd me,
I shar'd the glory of that fight, Sweet Girl I left
    Behind Me.

CHARLES C. SAWYER

―――――――――

"When This Cruel War Is Over"

One of the greatest "hits" of the Civil War was Charles Sawyer's "When This Cruel War Is Over." It eventually sold over a million copies. Soldiers on both sides played the tune and sang the word "gray" or "blue" depending on their allegiance. The lyrics were so sentimental that troops were often moved to tears.

> *Dearest love, do you remember,*
>   *When we last did meet,*
> *How you told me that you loved me,*
>   *kneeling at my feet?*
> *Oh, how proud you stood before me,*
>   *In your suit of blue,*
> *When you vowed to me and country*
>   *Ever to be true.*
>
> *Chorus—*
> *Weeping, sad and lonely*
>   *Hopes and fears how vain!*
> *Yet praying, when this cruel war is over,*
>   *Praying that we meet again!*

Sources

Alexander, Edward P., *Military Memoirs of a Confederate*
Barron, S.P., *The Lone Star Defenders*
Bedford, H.L., *Southern Society Historical Papers*
Blackford, W.W., *War Years with J.E.B. Stuart*
Bradfield, James O., *Hood's Texas Brigade*, J.B. Polley
Bryner, Lloyd, *Bugle Echoes*
Couch, Darius N., *Battles and Leaders of the Civil War*
Dawes, Rufus R., *The Sixth Wisconsin Volunteers*
Dickert, D. Augustus, *History of Kershaw's Brigade*
Douglas, Robert P., *Under the Maltese Cross*
Foster, Stephen, "My Old Kentucky Home" (song)
Fremantle, Arthur, *Three Months in the Southern States*
Garrish, Theodore, *A Private's Reminiscences of the Civil War*
Giles, Val C., *Hood's Texas Brigade*, J.B. Polley
Gilmore, Patrick S., "When Johnny Comes Marchin' Home" (song)
Grant, Ulysses S., *Personal Memories of U.S. Grant*
Hays, Will S., "Drummer Boy of Shiloh" (song)
Hitchcock, Frederick L., *War from the Inside*
Jenny, William L.B., *Personal Recollections of Vicksburg*
Imboden, John B., *Battles and Leaders of the Civil War*
Johnson, M.D., Charles B., *Muskets and Medicine*
Longstreet, James, *From Manassas to Appomattox*
Lover, Samuel, "The Girl I Left Behind" (song)
Marshall, Albert O., *Army Life: From a Soldier's Journal*
Martin, Rawley W., *Southern Society Historical Papers*
Maury, Dabney H., *Southern Society Historical Papers*
Randolph, W.F., *Southern Society Historical Papers*
Sawyer, Charles C., "When this Cruel War is Over" (song)
Steele, B.P., "Charge of the First Tennessee at Perryville" (poem)
Stevenson, William G., *Thirteen Months in the Rebel Army*
Stillwell, Leander, *The Story of a Common Soldier*
Wallace, Lew, *Battles and Leaders of the Civil War*
Walke, Henry, *Battles and Leaders of the Civil War*
Weaver, Henry F., *Under the Maltese Cross*
Wheeler, Joseph, *Battles and Leaders of the Civil War*